Fractured Loyalties

Masculinity, Class and Politics in Britain, 1900–30

To the Memory of
W.G. Forrest
and
C.E. Stevens
Historians, Mentors

FRACTURED LOYALTIES

Masculinity, Class and Politics in Britain, 1900–30

T.G. ASHPLANT

Rivers Oram Press
London, Chicago, Sydney

Published in 2007
by Rivers Oram Press, an imprint of Rivers Oram Publishers Ltd
144 Hemingford Road, London, N1 1DE

Distributed in the USA by
Independent Publishers Group, Franklin Street, Chicago, IL 60610
Distributed in Australia and New Zealand by
UNIReps, University of New South Wales, Sydney, NSW 2052

Set in MT Baskerville by NJ Design
and printed in Great Britain by T.J. International Ltd, Padstow

British Library Cataloguing in Publication Data
A CIP catalogue record for this publication is available from the British Library
ISBN 978 185 489 168 6 (pb)
ISBN 978 185 489 167 9 (hb)

Contents

Acknowledgments

This book has been many years in the making, and in that time I have received support, encouragement and intellectual stimulation from a wide range of colleagues and friends. It is a pleasure to have this opportunity to thank them.

At Liverpool John Moores University, Elspeth Graham, as Head of Department, created an environment in which interdisciplinary research could flourish. My colleagues at the Research Centre for Literature and Cultural History awarded me two periods of sabbatical leave, and covered some of my administrative duties during my absence; I am very grateful to them. I have benefited, too, from the interdisciplinary teaching and research in which we have engaged since the late 1980s, and from many individual conversations over these years. The Arts and Humanities Research Council (AHRC) awarded me a term's leave under their Research Leave Scheme, which proved crucial in bringing the book to completion.

Scholarship depends on the co-operative support and assistance of many institutions and individuals. Much of my research was conducted at the Bodleian Library, University of Oxford. I am grateful to staff in many divisions of the library, and especially the Old Library Upper Reserve, for their unstinting helpfulness and their good-natured and efficient problem solving. I wish to thank Maureen Watry, Katy Hooper and their colleagues in Special Collections and Archives, Sydney Jones Library, University of Liverpool, for facilitating my access to the letters and related papers of Scott Macfie in the Gypsy Lore Society Archive, and the Scott Macfie Gypsy Collection; and for granting permission to quote from this material. I am grateful to Pamela Pehkonen for permission to quote from Scott Macfie's wartime letters to his family, and related papers, in the Department of Documents, Imperial War Museum, London, whose staff I also wish to thank. I have also been helped by the staffs of the Taylor Institution Library, English Faculty Library and Social Science Library, University of Oxford; and the British Library. Kenneth Blackwell, Russell Archivist, McMaster University, Hamilton, Ontario, valuably drew my attention to the writings of Graeme West. My former student, Brenda Giblin, has kindly allowed me to quote from her unpublished research; supervising her Master's dissertation impelled me to reconsider my approach to the Great War. Throughout my research, I have received substantial and generous-spirited administrative and technical support from Amanda Greening, Irene Haworth, Cathy Pepp, Pryce Roberts and Ric Tyson. Maria Manifava carried out research-assistant tasks with speed and efficiency.

I first began thinking about the relationships between gender, identity and politics in the framework of the Psychoanalysis and History group, which met in London in the mid 1980s. I learned much from their formal seminars and informal meetings; I am grateful to all those who participated, including John Forrester, Cora Kaplan, Barry Richards, Ann Scott and Barbara Taylor. Since then, among colleagues and friends, Sally Alexander, Carolyn Steedman and John Tosh have offered continuing support and encouragement throughout the development of this research. At different stages Fatima Fernandes, Ursula Howard, Glenda Norquay and Joanna Price discussed and commented on drafts. Working intensively with Graham Dawson and Michael Roper while editing a book on war memory stimulated my thinking about the relationship between individuals and public discourses. Sandro Portelli's seminars as Visiting Professor at the Research Centre for Literature and Cultural History demonstrated methodologically rigorous and ethically sensitive approaches to the interpretation of violent human conflicts.

Paul Thompson introduced me to the European Social Science History Conferences, whose international scholarly networks have proved very fruitful. Challenging conversations there with Ela Hornung about our respective research projects sustained my sense of the value of such enquiry, while encouraging me to articulate key ideas more boldly. The editorial collective of *L'Homme: Zeitschrift für Feministische Geschichtswissenschaft* invited me to participate in their seminar 'Maleness, Whiteness'...'Die Kategorien in der feministischen Geschichtswissenshaft' (Free University, Berlin, 2005); revising my contribution for publication led me to think about the fracturing of identities.

In addition, I have some more personal debts to acknowledge. Since 1999, I have benefited from research collaboration and exchanges with a group of colleagues in Bulgaria. Besides several invitations to present aspects of this research at lectures, seminars and conferences (at 'St Kliment Ohridski' University, and the Centre for Advanced Studies, in Sofia; and at South-Western University 'Neofit Rilski', and the International University Seminar for Balkan Studies and Specialization, in Blagoevgrad), the academic commitment, intellectual stimulus and personal warmth which they have offered (while working in conditions substantially more difficult than British academics face) have afforded me a sustaining sense of the value of scholarly work. Daniela Koleva first invited me to contribute to a conference in Bulgaria. Kristina Popova and Petar Vodenicharov extended a further invitation for the following year, as did Diana Mishkova and Alexander Kiossev subsequently. Through these initiatives, I came to know Krassimira Daskalova, Stefan Detchev, Snezhana Dimitrova, Ivan Elenkov, Vanya Elenkova, Miroslava Georgieva, Todorka Kamenova, Anelia Kasabova, Tanya Kotzeva, Ilya Nedin, Alexey Pamporov, Anastasija Pashova, Tsvetelin Stepanov and Nikolai Vukov. To all these colleagues, from whose writings, conversation and friendship I have greatly profited, I offer my gratitude and thanks.

Adrian Wilson first suggested that I should develop some tentative thoughts about the relationship between gender formation and political identity into a research project. I owe a great deal to discussions with him over many years about this research, and about questions of historical methodology. Elspeth Graham, amid myriad other demands on her time and energy, was a constant source of encouragement and intellectual exploration. Daphne Briggs responded positively to an early draft, and generously shared with me her professional knowledge of psychoanalytic theory. Stephen Yeo has provided sustained support throughout, and been an engaged reader and discussant of various drafts. Ursula Tarkowski has been the best of neighbours, offering tea, coffee and stimulating conversation as remedies for brain fatigue.

Finally, the dedication of this book expresses my debt to my Ancient History tutors of long ago. George Forrest insisted, vehemently but with good humour, on the relevance of historical enquiry for the contemporary world; while 'Tom Brown' Stevens combined rigorous analysis of sources with a sceptical eye for the self-serving rhetoric of the powerful. I learned much from them, and remember them (as do their many pupils) with great affection.

T.G. Ashplant
2007

Research for this book was supported by

Abbreviations of Organisations

ASU	Arts and Science Union (Ruhleben)
GLS	Gypsy Lore Society
OTC	Officers' Training Corps
QMS	Quarter Master Sergeant
RAMC	Royal Army Medical Corps
RWF	Royal Welch Fusiliers

Abbreviations of Main Works Cited

Ackerley	Frederick George Ackerley, 'Friend of all the world: a Memoir of Robert Andrew Scott Macfie', *Journal of the Gypsy Lore Society* (3rd series) 14 [Special number] (1935), 5–43
Graves, *BISGO*	Robert Graves, *But It Still Goes On* (Jonathan Cape, 1930)
Graves, *Letters*	Paul O'Prey, (ed.), *In Broken Images: Selected Letters of Robert Graves, 1914–46* (Hutchinson, 1982)
Graves, *GTAT*	Robert Graves, *Goodbye To All That: an Autobiography* (Jonathan Cape, 1929)
Graves, *GTAT* 1957	Robert Graves, *Goodbye To All That* (rev. edn, 1957; Harmondsworth: Penguin, 1960)
Macfie, GLS	Scott Macfie Letters and Papers, Gypsy Lore Society Archive, and Scott Macfie Gypsy Collection, Special Collections and Archives, Sydney Jones Library, University of Liverpool

Macfie, IWM	Scott Macfie Papers, Department of Documents, Imperial War Museum, London
Macfie, *WGB*	R.A. Scott Macfie, *With Gypsies in Bulgaria, by Andreas ('Mui Shuko')* (Liverpool: Henry Young & Sons, 1916)
'Memories'	'Memories of R.A. Scott Macfie', by his friends, *Journal of the Gypsy Lore Society* (3rd series) 14 [Special number] (1935), 47–110
RPG (1)	R.P. Graves, *Robert Graves: the Assault Heroic, 1895–1926* (Weidenfeld & Nicolson, 1986)
RPG (2)	R.P. Graves, *Robert Graves: the Years with Laura, 1926–40* (Weidenfeld & Nicolson, 1990)
RPG (3)	R.P. Graves, *Robert Graves and the White Goddess, 1940–1985* (Weidenfeld & Nicolson, 1995)
RPG 1995	Robert Graves, *Goodbye to All That: an Autobiography,* ed. R.P. Graves (Oxford: Berghahn, 1995)

Introduction

The Roots of Individual Political Identities

> . . .not for everything in the world would I like to live through those days of inner struggle again! [On the one hand] this driving, burning desire to throw oneself into the powerful current of the general, national tide, and, on the other, the terrible spiritual fear of following that desire fully, of surrendering oneself to the mood which roared about one, and which, if one looked deep into one's heart, had long since taken possession of the soul. This fear: will you not also betray yourself and your cause? Can you not feel as your heart feels? [Thus it was] until suddenly—I shall never forget the day and the hour—the terrible tension was resolved; until one dared to be what one was; until—despite all principles and wooden theories—one could, for the first time in almost a quarter of a century, join with a full heart, a clean conscience and without a sense of treason in the sweeping, stormy song: 'Deutschland, Deutschland, über alles'.

These words about the outbreak of war in August 1914, spoken by Konrad Haenisch, a former left radical within the German Social Democratic Party, close Carl Schorske's *German Social Democracy 1905–17: the Development of the Great Schism.*[1] They form a vivid ending to Schorske's narrative of the separation that had existed between the mass German working-class socialist movement and the political elite of Wilhelmine Germany, as well as a stark reminder of the collapse of the anti-war aspirations and plans of almost all the parties affiliated to the Second International.

Samuel Hynes opens his study of the Western Front, in *The Soldier's Tale: Bearing Witness to Modern War*, with an account of the Grenfell cousins, two pairs of brothers who were all killed during the first year of the war.[2] In depicting Julian, the poet and a regular Army officer since 1910, he paints a vivid sketch of a man who experienced war as a sport, an arena for his immense yet controlled physical energy. In his letters home, 'Julian sounds much like his cousin Francis. We hear the Grenfell voice, the voice of a class and a profession—excited, interested, elated by war, pleased with the way the men have performed, enjoying a soldier's work.'[3] This picture was starkly underlined, for visitors such as myself to the Imperial War Museum's 2002–3 exhibition *Anthem for Doomed Youth: Twelve Soldier Poets of the First World War*, by the display of Grenfell's game book. Successive entries from early October 1915, in the column headed 'Bag', read: 105 partridges (while at home on leave), '1 Pomeranian' (16 November), '2 Pomeranians' (17 November).[4] Hynes writes, of Julian's diary record of these events:

> Grenfell feels satisfaction in the skills he is using—a hunter's satisfaction, such as he might have felt at home when he bagged a brace of pheasants...There is no feeling for the men he kills. Nor are there any of the inflating terms of romantic war—'glory' and 'courage' and 'heroism' and all that. For Grenfell, war was a field sport, and like other such sports, it gave pleasure when you did it well.[5]

When I saw the game book, it made Grenfell, hitherto for me a barely recognised name, into a vivid and troubling figure. It led me, in the museum's bookshop, to pick up, browse through and then buy Nicholas Mosley's recently reprinted biography of Grenfell. Mosley's narrative substantially complicates the picture of Grenfell the happy warrior exulting in his strength and competence. He retrieves a hidden history of rebellion, in which, while at Oxford in 1909, Grenfell had composed a philosophical work heavily critical of the assumptions of the world in which he grew up. He was "laughed" out of this rebellion by his mother, to whom he was strongly attached, and by his family and friends; and subsequently joined the army, turning himself into a competent and enthusiastic officer.[6]

Taken together, these two vignettes from the opening phase of the First World War pose questions about the nature of individual *political* affiliations which this book will explore. How do individuals come to form political affiliations? What are the origins of the bonds of attachment and loyalty which develop between individuals, political parties and movements, and the nation state? What fosters and strengthens these bonds, and how can they be ruptured? I approach these and related questions first by examining how individuals are socialised into class and gender roles in ways that invite and foster powerful affiliations with social institutions and ideologies; and then by considering how both individual disruptions of that process of socialisation, and a profound historical rupture such as the outbreak of the First World War, could challenge, call into question, and sometimes dramatically realign, those affiliations.

Aims and Approaches

The central concern of this book is with the processes of formation and transformation of individual men's social and political identities; and the interaction of gender, sexuality, class and nation in those processes. It explores the ways in which an individual's political and social identity is shaped by the conflictual processes through which that individual, in reaction to their socialisation into gender and class roles, comes to form a personal identity which is itself both gendered and class specific. The term identity is understood in both a psychoanalytic and a social-historical sense. That is, I employ a psychoanalytically influenced model of the formation of an adult gendered identity, and of the vicissitudes of that process of formation; while embedding that process in a specific class (and hence also national) context, where children grew to adulthood within historically particular familial and institutional forms. Gender is taken as a central component in the formation of a class-specific identity, and so disruptions in the formation of gendered identity have implications also for the formation and stability of class identity. This in turn has implications for the nature of those identifications (such as with class, with nation, with political institutions, loyalties and values) central to political action. The book will examine the processes by which individuals, endowed with the characters and aptitudes with which they were born, were both shaped by and struggled against a variety of social institutions and situations, in coming to form their adult identity. It will consider their experiences with significant figures in their family and household of origin (parents, relatives, servants), and then through the succession of institutions (preparatory and public schools, university, armed forces) designed to prepare them for the social identity of an upper-middle-class adult male ready to pursue a career and form a family within the British nation.

Through analysis of their life histories, this book traces the experiences of several upper-middle-class British men who at key stages in their lives became "dissident" to the extent that they negotiated, resisted or rejected their expected roles.[7] Both the nature and the outcomes of this dissidence can, I believe, only be understood if it is viewed also in terms of what it dissents from. The very rejection of available identities of gender, class and nation led to a new political identity still marked and shaped by what was rejected. While such disruption of identity could occur in different social and political contexts, this book focusses particularly on the impact of the First World War, which put the existing values of that class under severe strain. It examines the ways in which, both during and after the war, these men sought to negotiate the conflicts of identity, attachment and values which the war provoked.

In working through these themes, I have two further aims. The first is, through these case studies, to cast light on more general processes of the formation of identities. Tracking the origins and form of one particular political trajectory—upper-middle-class dissidence—may also illuminate more general processes of the formation of *individual* personal and political identity; while exploring the nature and limitations of the oppositional stances adopted by these individuals may indicate something about the roots and structures of other *collective* political identities. The second aim is to contribute to the deployment of psychoanalytic concepts in historical writing. I have argued elsewhere that such endeavours have had difficulty in linking analyses of individual character and behaviour with accounts of the social processes in which those individuals take part.[8] This study will seek to clarify this problem by its specific points of focus. In exploring the formation of personal identity, and its links with habitation of and adherence to social collectivities, I will not be offering *individual* psycho-biographies of the men concerned. Rather, I shall be exploring significant (shared or divergent) *patterns* of identity formation through the comparative analysis of key relationships and developmental moments from childhood to early adulthood in these lives. Nor will I be concerned with emotional processes within the *group* identity of particular social collectivities as a whole; I will not be offering psychoanalytic readings of the institutions of British imperialism or the Communist Party. Rather I will examine the emotional linkages formed between individuals and the collectivities they inhabited; and the role in those attachments of the psychosocial legacies which individuals brought from childhood and adolescence.[9] Through this focus, I hope to demonstrate one specific way in which psychoanalytic concepts can illuminate the understanding of political identity.

The Shaping of Identity

This book seeks to trace the *trajectories of socialisation* through which individuals passed during childhood and adolescence to prepare them for their roles as adult men of the next generation; the *identifications with institutions and ideologies* which that socialisation encouraged; the *patterns of attachment* to those institutions and ideologies which their trajectories laid the emotional groundwork for; and the *potentials for rupture* with expected loyalties and identifications which their life histories had created.

In exploring these themes, I have used a range of theoretical writings, sometimes overlapping in their approach, which deal with the formation of individual gendered subjectivity, patterns of masculinity, the nation as an arena of belonging, and potential spaces for the renegotiation of identity. For thinking about the formation of subjectivity, I have used the work of several psychoanalytic theorists, including Freud, the British object-relations school, and Erik Erikson.[10] Understanding the interaction between the biological and the psychological, their duality, in human behaviour and development poses considerable difficulties. Dana Breen has argued that Freud deliberately worked in the overlap between these two levels; and that much subsequent psychoanalytic work has tended to collapse to one or other level.[11] The pressure to privilege explanations at either the biological or the psychological level has been a constant theme within the evolution of psychoanalytic thought (as Breen shows in her mapping of the divergent psychoanalytical approaches in Britain, America and France).[12] Even more difficult to accommodate has been a third level—that of the social. The fierce controversy which raged in the 1980s around Freud's supposed abandonment of the 'seduction theory' was concerned precisely with the conflict between explanations of hysteria in terms of either intrapsychic developmental conflict, or response to external abuse. Feminist re-readings of this and other aspects both of Freud's work and that of later psychoanalysts have repeatedly argued that they display an underestimation (or at times a complete neglect) of the impact of the external world.[13] More recently, as critical writing on the history of psychoanalysis has flourished, and exchanges between psychoanalytic and other traditions in psychology and sociology have increased, there has come a recognition that different traditions within psychoanalysis have given different degrees of weight to the external world, even while retaining their focus on intrapsychic responses.[14]

Psychoanalysis begins from the premise that human beings, as mammals, are shaped to a significant (but debatable) degree by their biology. All humans die, and that dying is always a biological death (however it may be mediated by human action, for example by being the outcome of a deliberate killing). Apart from mortality, two other aspects of human biology are of particular interest to psychoanalysis: infantile helplessness or weakness, and the shaping of gender identity and sexuality. Already in the immediate familial setting the handling of different aspects of an infant's helplessness—such as its hunger, need for touch, fear of disintegration—combines the infant's own 'constitutional' qualities (and those of its parents) with the impact of social forces mediated through parents and other caretakers (such as patterns of child care, or attitudes towards the child's development and destiny). The consolidation of gender identity and maturing of sexuality are still more powerfully shaped by extra-familial institutions and discourses.

What I take from psychoanalysis is firstly the idea that the progression from infancy through childhood to (gendered and sexually mature) adulthood is necessarily a conflictual one. The maturing human has to cope with the psychological consequences of their own initial helplessness, the long process of learning to engage epistemologically and emotionally with the world around them, the structuring of self/other differentiation, the consolidation of gender identity and of sexual orientation, and the development of the capacity for sexual relating. The inevitable conflicts (between love and hate, dependence and independence, envy and gratitude, etc.) which this process entails are handled by the child's family within a specific historical setting, including institutions and ideologies which shape both the methods and goals of child rearing. It is here that the psychological and the social are intertwined. Second, I take the concepts of identification and transference as key mechanisms through which people engage with their surroundings. In particular, I focus on the individual's identifications with social institutions, and the transference to those institutions of patterns of attachment formed earlier in life; and on the ways in which societies encourage such identifications. Third, I take the ideas of psychic depth, and internalised conflict, figured in the notion of the unconscious. I try to show how ideologies, and the contradictions within and struggles between them, are internalised emotionally; that is, that they operate not simply as cognitive frames through which the world is perceived, but as emotional frames through which the world is embraced.[15]

In thinking about gender, and specifically masculinity, I have found most valuable the work of David Gilmore and R. W. Connell. Gilmore offers a cross-cultural perspective, informed by psychoanalysis, on what he terms the 'making of manhood'. Drawing on a range of anthropological materials, he identifies social tasks which boys are trained to undertake in adulthood, for the defence, preservation and perpetuation of their society. This training is required precisely because it involves the subordination of individual to group needs, and the overcoming of 'regressive' psychodynamic tendencies towards self-preservation and the protected world of boyhood.[16] Connell too strives to give appropriate weight to the respective importance of the social, the psychological and the biological.[17] He defines masculinity as a relational concept, one dimension of a gender order itself in turn structured by relations of power, production and cathexis (emotional attachment). In *Masculinities* he reviews the range of theoretical and empirical work which has sought to understand masculinity. He sees Freud's work as containing the germs of a theory of masculinity as constructed; but regards it as radically incomplete, having lost touch with issues of social power and the clash between the social order and desire following the splits with Alfred Adler and Karen Horney in the 1910s and 1920s.[18] He recognises other work influenced by psychoanalysis as having contributed depth-psychological elements to a theory of masculinity, including that of Wilhelm Reich (on patriarchy), and the Frankfurt School (Erich Fromm, Max Horkheimer, Theodor Adorno) on the diversity of psychosexual masculinities both across time and contemporaneously.[19] While acknowledging the value of Lacanian and semiotic work in theorising masculinity as the occupancy of the (unmarked) position in symbolic and social gender relations, he rejects this as a comprehensive account, insisting on the importance of the body as more than a neutral surface on which social symbolism is imprinted.[20] His own preferred emphasis tends to be Sartrean, stressing gender as a project with which people actively engage.[21] While I draw heavily on Connell's conceptualisation of gender, my own approach lays more emphasis on depth psychology. I believe that he tends to understate the adhesiveness (or conservatism) of cathexes, patterns of emotional attachment formed earlier in life, and the difficulty with which these are modified.

Connell also draws on sex role theory, arguing that the idea of masculinity as an internalised male sex role seems (unlike, in his perception, psychoanalysis) to allow for historical change; conflict could arise from contradictory or unmanageable social expectations rather than repression.[22] I too draw on the idea of conflicting social expectations within sex roles, but would argue that this is not incompatible with psychoanalysis. In my perspective, the internal structures and conflicts with which psychoanalysis is concerned provide some of the binding energy from which attachments to sex roles derive. Consequently, conflicts within sex roles arise not only from incompatible demands placed upon men by the masculine roles which they occupy or into which they have been socialised, but also by the nature of the attachments to their roles which men form. To take an example which will be central to this book. Junior officers on the western front were confronted with demands which some of them found intolerable: between the instinct to preserve their own life, and the requirement to continue to serve in situations of acute danger; and between the wish to help and protect their men, and the order to lead them over the top. The conflict which arose was not just between instinct and social expectation, between wish and order, but lay also within the attachments which they had to those instincts, expectations, wishes and orders—how they cathected them.

Individuals are brought up to identify successively with parents and family, and then school and other intermediate institutions between themselves and the overarching collectivity to which they belong—in the modern world, usually the nation state. In understanding the ties which bind individuals to collectivities, I have drawn on Benedict Anderson's concept of 'imagined communities', and its extension by Ross Poole to incorporate gender.[23] Their work foregrounds key modalities through which the modern nation state offers its citizens a potential identity narrative that can afford meaning and permanence to individual life experience; and suggests reasons for its power and success. I examine some of the intermediate institutions through which the rhetorical and narrative appeal of national identity is transmitted to the growing individual; while also identifying other mechanisms through which the nation state mobilises support. In Chapter 8, I suggest a further extension to the concept of imagined community, to accommodate the fact that in the twentieth century there were other collectivities, which offered themselves as potential (and at times actual) alternative 'imagined communities' to the nation state—seeking to attract the affiliation of individuals through similar mechanisms and a similar appeal.

Finally, I use the work of the anthropologist Victor Turner and the psychoanalyst Erik Erikson to delineate those times and spaces which may facilitate the modification or transformation of current identities. Turner extended Arnold van Gennep's conceptualisation of liminality as a stage within a fixed ritual of transition in order to analyse liminal times, places and roles within complex contemporary societies. These interstitial locations are potential arenas for the defamiliarisation of taken-for-granted social values and practices, and the creative reworking of existing and new elements into altered configurations of value and practice.[24] Erikson's account of late adolescence, and especially his concept of moratorium, can be aligned with Turner's work, as indicating a liminal stage within the life cycle at which identity formation is still labile, and individuals may seek to resist identity patterns proffered by family or society.[25] I use the concepts of liminality and moratorium to explore particular situations and moments within the life experiences of the key figures in this book, suggesting ways in which they created, or took advantage of, disruption of conventional norms to seek different objects of identification and loyalty, different patterns of belonging.

The approach I have adopted seeks to accommodate two countervailing perspectives. In emphasising the historical *construction* of class and gendered identities in the trajectory from childhood to adulthood, and the potentials for rupture which they contain, I seek to show how it is possible for individuals to break with the patterns proffered to them of affiliation to and identification with the institutions and ideologies of their society or imagined community. By also emphasising the power and adhesiveness of the bonds established during those trajectories, I seek to capture the difficulties such ruptures involve. So when using the term identity, I do not intend to refer to stable, pre-given sense of self which unfolds, or towards which the individual strives in a search for authenticity. Rather,

I refer to a *relatively enduring constellation* or sense of self, open certainly to change but often at considerable cost.

It follows from this that I understand a political or ideological position held (adopted, occupied) by an individual at any given moment not as singular and seamless, but as existing in a matrix or field of force constituted by elements both 'external' and 'internal' to that individual, elements themselves constructed both diachronically and synchronically.[26] The diachronic 'external' elements are constructed over the preceding life course. They comprise stances towards the world created within the institutions of socialisation from the family onwards. These provide a range of possible political and ideological positions which the individual is both prepared and invited (by the process of offering recognition in return for affiliation) to occupy. These initially proffered positions may be modified by a range of extra-familial and extra-school influences and experiences (including mentors and moratoria). The synchronic 'external' elements comprise the pressures bearing on, and the possibilities open to, the individual at a given historical conjuncture. In particular, in situations of crisis new political and ideological positions may emerge which challenge and compete with established positions. The 'internal' elements include the characteristic patterns of attachment created during the individual's transit through the institutions of socialisation. These patterns of attachment help to shape the ways in which individuals negotiate between dominant and emergent political/ideological stances. In particular they help to determine the emotional adhesiveness or lability with which individuals cleave to, exchange, or move between competing political and ideological options. Consequently, it is not possible simply to interpret an individual's political/ideological stance at a given moment at face value, as singular or unconflicted. Rather, it is necessary to understand it as a constellation, a temporary (if perhaps relatively enduring) configuration whose fuller meaning can only be grasped by analysing its constitutive forces. To uncover those forces requires an understanding of the interplay of the various elements in the matrix.[27]

'History from below', as it has been practised and theorised over the past forty years and more, has been concerned to recover and make audible the voices of those who, excluded from centres of power and cultural authority, had hitherto figured little if at all in dominant historical narratives.[28] By analogy, one of the aims of this book is to direct attention to 'voices within'. That is, I want to attend to the inner conflicts, the contradictory voices, at work within individuals—whether they lead to a rupture with dominant values and proffered trajectories (as when Gerald Brenan flees England to walk to the Pamirs), or a silencing of inner doubt (as when W.H.R. Rivers closes his bedroom door), or an embracing of the hitherto rejected (as when Haenisch sings 'Deutschland über alles').[29] I am concerned to illuminate the interaction of the forces—individual and social; psychological, cultural and material—which give rise to these conflicts; and to stress the dynamics at work as well as the outcomes resulting. The case studies which follow aim to explore this approach in concrete detail.

Life Histories and Families

This book explores the interrelationships between masculinity, class and politics through three in-depth biographical case studies. I have selected these case studies in order to develop a comparative mode of interpretation which will illuminate issues of personal and social identity within their lives. The validity of this mode of interpretation rests on the value of the connections it reveals and the analyses of them which I offer. If these prove fruitful, then the approaches adopted here could be used to explore other configurations of identity, differing in gender, class, and political stance. In this section I first sketch my approach to the use of life-history analysis as a resource for social history. Then I locate the families of these men in their social milieus, and trace out similarities and differences between their individual situations and trajectories in early life.

The core of this book comprises a comparative study of the life histories of three men from upper-middle-class families: Robert Graves (1895–1985), Robert Andrew Scott Macfie (1868–1935) and Alick West (1895–1972). My concern with processes of psychosocial and psychosexual development has led me to focus on family environment, childhood, adolescence, and early adulthood up to the establishing of a work identity, a pattern of sexual relating, and an engagement with the public sphere. Hence I have structured the narratives of their lives so as to allow where possible comparisons of their experiences at each of these life stages. But I have also sought to locate the individuals firmly in their historical context. Since these men are separated in age by nearly thirty years, attention has also to be paid to the specific context in which each encountered a particular life transition.[30] The most important historical variable was undoubtedly the First World War.[31] For Graves and West, who were nineteen in 1914, the outbreak of war was their entry into adulthood; their late adolescent reconfiguration and consolidation of identity occurred under uniquely stressful circumstances.[32] Macfie, by contrast, was forty-six; the war offered an opportunity for a further realignment of a dissident identity which he had forged with difficulty in his twenties.

This book uses the comparative study of individual lives to support a range of more general arguments. Accordingly, Part I sets out: a general model of the making of masculinity (Chapter 1); the particular structures and life stages through which the British upper-middle class reproduced itself in the late nineteenth century—family, school, leaving home, entering adulthood and the public sphere, defining sexual identity (Chapter 2); and the experience of the First World War (Chapter 3). Part II offers three detailed case studies structured according to the themes set out in Part I: Robert Graves (Chapter 4), Scott Macfie (Chapter 5), and Alick West (Chapter 6). The historical arguments in Chapters 2 and 3 are cross referenced where appropriate to the case studies which follow in Part II. In addition, the three case studies are supported by less detailed reference to life histories of contemporaries from similar social backgrounds: W.H.R. Rivers (1864–1922), Leonard Woolf (1880–1969), Noel Chavasse (1884–1917), Siegfried Sassoon (1886–1967), Julian Grenfell (1888–1915), Graeme West (brother of Alick; 1891–1917), Gerald Brenan (1894–1987) and Charles Sorley (1895–1915).[33] These serve both to make concrete the more general or abstract points being made in Chapters 2 and 3, and to offer points of similarity and difference with the three full case studies. In the case studies, I have tried to recount aspects of these men's lives in sufficient depth, and in their own words, so that a coherent picture of each individual emerges, so that contrasts as well as comparisons between them are possible, and so that the reader has sufficient materials to appraise and interrogate my interpretations.[34] Part III locates these men's responses to the First World War in a wider context of the re-making of identities. Chapter 7 revisits the encounter between Siegfried Sassoon and W.H.R. Rivers at Craiglockhart Hospital in 1917. Through a reconsideration of the impact of the two men on each other, I seek to demonstrate both how the nation state policed its citizens during wartime, and what was at stake in their respective struggles to free or to police themselves. Chapter 8 reviews the experiences of the case studies in Part II in the light of the theoretical perspectives of Part I. I suggest that situating these men within the broad spectrum of British responses to the war highlights contradictions in the ideology of the liberal nation state exposed by the war, leading to a questioning of notions of self-sacrifice sanctioned by religious and national ideologies. The resulting fractures opened spaces for alternative imaginings of the relations between self, nation, and politics. Chapter 9 concludes by tracing the experiences of Macfie, Graves and Alick West in the 1920s. The latter two, entering the post-war world in their mid-twenties, struggled to find new patterns of living and sources of values to replace those which the war, for them, had discredited or destroyed.

The case studies, and the other life-history vignettes, were selected for their pertinence to my theme, and the availability of significant amounts of source material, including especially life writing, about each.[35] It does not follow from this that any patterns traceable in their lives must be regarded as merely idiosyncratic. In the next section, I locate each of these individuals and their families of origin in the British upper and upper-middle classes. Chapters 2 and 3 contextualise their particular experiences—of family, schools, universities, career choices, patterns of sexual relating, and the war—against the wider patterns to be found among their contemporaries.[36]

The three case studies are of men who came from upper-middle-class professional families. Graves's father was an educationalist and writer, from a long-established Irish family which included both literary and religious men. After being widowed, he married Graves's mother, the daughter of a distinguished German family. Graves attended Charterhouse, and was destined for Oxford.[37] Macfie was born into an Anglo-Scottish family which for a century had owned and run sugar refineries; they were Liberal in politics and Scottish Presbyterian in religion. Macfie himself was educated at Oundle, and then at the Universities of Cambridge, Göttingen and Edinburgh, before joining the family firm.[38] West's father, the son of a Nonconformist clergyman, gave up his engineering career for a period to work as a missionary. Having returned to England and engineering, he married the daughter of a Baptist minister. He later acquired private means, which enabled him to relinquish his profession, and combine a life of gentlemanly leisure with charity work. In both religion and trade the elder West represented a class fraction still in the process of being absorbed into the traditional upper-middle-class, a transition figured by his second marriage into an Anglo-Irish military/professional family who belonged to the Church of Ireland. West himself attended Highgate School and was also destined for Oxford.[39]

In their geographical origins and ties (Scottish and Irish-ascendancy families, of each of which a branch had settled in England; and English provinces) and religious affiliations (Scottish Presbyterian, conventional Anglican, devout Nonconformist), their families represented the range of diversity of the upper-middle-class; while their (actual or intended) educations (prep and public school, then Oxbridge) were also typical of their class. All the families had close personal connections with the Empire. Macfie's family business was built on colonial sugar. Graves had elder brothers in the colonial service in the Middle East, and sisters married to such men. West's father had trained as a missionary in New Zealand and served in India; while his step-mother's family had educational and army ties to Egypt and India.

Their contemporaries whose life histories I have also drawn upon for comparative purposes came from similar backgrounds. Their families ranged from the fringes of the aristocracy through middle-class professional, business or artistic backgrounds. All but one were brought up in the Church of England; most attended public schools (as boarders or day boys), and went to or were destined for Oxbridge. They themselves entered professional jobs or the army.

Two came from landed backgrounds. Julian Grenfell came from the most socially elevated of these families. He was the eldest son of parents from families with strong links to the aristocracy and the political elite. His father was first a Liberal then a Conservative MP (he switched parties over Home Rule in 1893), who was elevated to the Lords as Baron Desborough in 1905, and held many public offices. Grenfell himself was educated at Eton and Oxford, and then entered the army.[40] Both Brenan's parents came from well-established Irish landed and military families with industrial connections. His father was a subaltern in an Irish regiment, who after active service in South Africa, Ceylon and India was invalided home from the Boer War in 1900. Soon after, he had received a substantial inheritance, and settled down to the life of a country gentleman in the Cotswolds. Brenan himself was educated at Radley, and intended by his father to go directly into the army.[41]

Three were from more or less well-established professional families. W. H. R. Rivers came from a solidly middle-class Kentish family, with navy and Church of England associations. His father was a clergyman who married into a farming family whose younger sons also went into the navy or the church. Rivers went to prep school and then Tonbridge as a day-boy. Prevented by illness from taking scholarship examinations for Cambridge, he studied medicine at the University of London before becoming a successful academic researcher.[42] Noel Chavasse's father, from a middle-class family with medical, clergy, army and legal ties, was an evangelical clergyman, who later became Bishop of Liverpool. Educated at grammar schools and then Oxford, Chavasse himself trained as a doctor and practised medicine in Liverpool.[43] Charles Sorley was born into a Lowland Scottish family which had become somewhat impoverished on the early death of his paternal grandfather, a founder of the Scottish Free Church. His father, who also had strong theological interests, married a woman from a family which included ministers and educationalists; he became Professor of Moral Philosophy successively at the Universities of Aberdeen and Cambridge. Sorley, brought up as an Anglican, attended Marlborough and was due to go to Oxford in 1914.[44]

Two came from more complex backgrounds, both socially and religiously. Siegfried Sassoon's grandfather came from a wealthy Sephardic Jewish family of Persian background, and had settled in England in the 1850s. His father, a financier and sculptor with a substantial private income, had married a fellow artist who came from a (Gentile) Cheshire farming family with engineering and artistic interests. The marriage, which led to his being disowned by his family, broke up when his son was seven; and he died two years later. Sassoon himself then attended prep school, Marlborough, and Cambridge. He left without taking his degree, and adopted the life of a country gentleman and amateur *littérateur*.[45] Leonard Woolf's family was Jewish on both sides. His father's father was a tailor who had prospered in mid-Victorian London, and 'educated his sons out of their class'. His mother's father was a Dutch Jewish diamond merchant, who moved to London in her childhood; her generation, however, had used up most of the family's prosperity. Woolf's father (a non-practising Jew) was a barrister who became a highly paid QC. Though individually a highly successful professional, his Jewish origins, one generation removed from West End tailoring, and lack of secure family capital made him the most marginal and insecure of these members of the English upper-middle-class. He died when his son was eleven. Woolf went to St Paul's and then Cambridge. Not having done well enough in the Civil Service examinations for a home posting, he chose to join the Ceylon Civil Service where he served for six years from 1904–11. On returning to England on sabbatical, he resigned his post and set out to make his living as a writer.[46]

Part 1
Theoretical and Historical Perspectives

1

Theoretical Perspectives: Identity, Masculinity, Nation, Class, Liminality

This chapter has three main interconnecting themes. First, it conceptualises the process of the formation of *personal identity* as simultaneously psychic and social.[1] Within psychoanalysis, following Freud, adult gendered identity has been seen as the outcome of a complex staged process of the transformation of identity, a process liable to many vicissitudes. Later work in the Freudian tradition (especially that of Erik Erikson) has extended this approach by attempting to link psychoanalytic concepts with those of developmental psychology, and of the sociology of life stages. Within a different domain, social history, much work in the last thirty years has been devoted to examining the ways in which social identities (such as those of class, religion or ethnicity) are not the automatic reflex of a given socio-economic position, but are continually constructed and transformed through processes of ideological and cultural work—processes in which a great range of social groups, institutions and ideologies play a part. In this study, the concepts of identity and masculinity (further developed in the first two sections below) will be used to bring these two perspectives together, to explore ways in which psychic and social processes of identity formation are intertwined so that the acquisition of an adult identity is simultaneously gender-, class- and nation-specific.[2] Individual identity is seen to be formed not simply in early childhood in relation to parents and other family/household members, but also throughout adolescence into early adult life within a range of institutional matrixes. These institutions engage with and help to shape growing individuals through emotional as well as cognitive processes. So Chapter 2 situates the early development of these men historically within the immediate context of their family and household, and examines the means by which their schooling trained them as adolescents for their future class/national destinations.

Second, *social collectivities* are understood as engaging with the adults who inhabit them through intersecting, and sometimes contradictory, dynamics: of coercion, provision, and recognition.[3] Coercion and provision are relatively straightforward: a nation state levies taxes, supplies education; a political party demands support for policies, wins benefits for its constituency. By recognition, I mean the process whereby a social collectivity invites its inhabitants to identify themselves with it, offering them in return recognition both as individuals and as sharers of an identity that extends beyond the individual through time and space.[4] It is through the combined effects of these three dynamics that a social collectivity may be said to 'mobilise' its inhabitants for actions it requires of them.[5] The mechanisms of engagement, the nature of the hold of institution over individual, are not uniform across the range of social collectivities. They may be positioned along a spectrum: from the purely voluntary (such as a political party for its members), through the inherited but rejectable (a class or nation for those born into it), to the compulsory (an army for its soldiers).[6] The structuring and relative weight of the dynamics of coercion, provision, and recognition will vary accordingly. Nevertheless, such varied collectivities as a social class, a nation state and a political party might each exercise authority over, provide benefits for, and generate a sense of purpose in individuals who inhabited them. In the final two sections below I develop this point more fully in relation to nation and class.

Third, such collectivities, through their dynamics of coercion, provision and recognition, can tap into *patterns of loyalty and identification*, and the emotions which they 'bind', formed in those earlier familial and institutional matrixes.[7] In so doing, they can activate identifications for their own ends, shaping and transforming them in the process. They can, however, also come into conflict with such identifications, especially where normative patterns of development have been broken or cut across, thereby interrupting common transferences of loyalty. So the case-studies in Chapters 4–6 examine the impact of various collectivities which these individuals inhabited as they moved both through their individual life cycles, and through the public world of their time with the First World War as its centrepiece.

The remainder of this chapter first sets out the models of identity formation, and of the construction of masculinity, which structure the subsequent analysis of the life histories; and then employs the concept of 'imagined community' to link the collectivities of nation and class. It is in five parts. In the first section, I sketch a model of the personal and social formation of identity which is both psychoanalytically informed and historically specific. In the second section, I examine the interaction between psychic and social dynamics underlying the construction of masculinity in general, and then consider the structures of hegemonic and subordinate masculinities and the modes of their reproduction within industrial capitalist societies. In the third section, I explore the ways in which the nation as 'imagined community' attracts the loyalty and capacity for self-sacrifice of its citizens by offering them an arena for the formation and confirmation of identity. In the fourth section, the threads of the previous three sections are drawn together in a discussion—with specific reference to upper-middle-class men in late-nineteenth-century Britain—of the process whereby a social class reproduces itself by bringing up the children of the next generation, within the family and other formal and informal social institutions, to occupy a social role which is gender-, class- and nation-specific. The final section suggests that the concepts of liminal times and spaces, or moments in the life cycle (moratoria), can be used to explore the ways in which individuals responded to, or initiated, disruptions of their proffered or expected life trajectory.

Identity: Psychic and Social

Central to the process of individual development is the acquisition of a gendered identity. In this and the following section, I look first at general issues of the formation of identity, and then specifically at masculinity. In thinking about identity and masculinity, I have found psychoanalytic concepts helpful because of their historicity. One of Freud's central emphases was that the formation of an adult personality is not the unfolding of a biological or natural given, an innate essence there from the start, but the outcome of a historical development in which both psychic (initially internal) and social (initially external) forces, both unconscious and conscious processes, combine to create the adult identity. However, there are some important issues to be considered regarding the use of psychoanalytic concepts in this context. First, psychoanalytic models of the development of gendered identity must be understood as precisely that—models. They sketch a set of psycho-social tasks facing the developing human individual, a standard pattern for their accomplishment, and common forms of disturbance to development.[8] They thereby provide an interpretative frame for an analyst to orientate themself in relation to the analysand's developing narrative. But in fact any individual life course will be more complex and multi-dimensional in its development than can be captured within the terms of a standard model.[9] Second, even if a given psychoanalytic model of development be accepted, and its limitations in capturing the complexity of any individual registered, further problems are encountered either in relating such a model to a particular individual in the past, or in using it to illuminate the reproduction and transformation of specific gendered identities on a collective scale.[10] With regard to these two issues, I have treated such psychoanalytic models as indicating a series of transitions and potential conflicts in the process of human growth from infancy to adulthood, and identifying patterns of response to those conflicts. These models thereby provide a hermeneutic tool for exploring the significance of specific elements within particular familial experiences, and wider social patterns, of child rearing.

Finally, and perhaps most importantly, psychoanalytic theory has often severely circumscribed its own recognition of historicity. Much writing by psychoanalysts, taking its lead from Freud, has focussed on the interaction of parents and children within the confines of the immediate family unit, and privileged the (relatively timeless and apparently ahistorical) psychic level as that which explains the (epiphenomenal and transient) social. A contrasting and more valuable perspective is one which sees the psychic and the social as more closely interconnected. Thus Erikson, struggling to tackle this problem in 1968, wrote as follows.

> The traditional psychoanalytic method...cannot quite grasp identity because it has not developed terms to conceptualise the environment. Certain habits of psychoanalytic theorising, habits of designating the environment as 'outer world' or 'object world', cannot take account of the environment as a pervasive actuality. The German ethologists introduced the word 'Umwelt' to denote not merely an environment which surrounds you, but which is also in you. And indeed, from the point of view of development, 'former' environments are forever in us...One methodological precondition, then, for grasping identity would be a psychoanalysis sophisticated enough to include the environment; the

> other would be a social psychology which is psychoanalytically sophisticated; together they would obviously institute a new field which would have to create its own historical sophistication.[11]

Subsequently, work has been published in both history and psychoanalysis which takes seriously this notion of an environment which 'not merely surrounds you but is also in you'. Such work has begun to show in detail how the patterns of childhood relating and conflict which contribute to the formation of identity derive from relatively constant components of human developmental growth (such as separation of infant from the mother, acquisition of language, inter- and intra-generational relations with parents and siblings) which yet are always lived out within historically specific social structures (of family, culture, religion, etc.) which shape the way in which those human constants are managed. To put it another way, in any given social context there will be pressures towards resolving general human developmental tasks in a way which meets the particular requirements of that social group.

How does the surrounding and permeating environment make its impact on the development of the infant and young child? The growing child, in forming their personality, has as potential objects of identification family and household members, and close friends, whose own identities are shaped by the social structures of a particular historical moment.[12] Wider themes drawn from their shared culture also enter the child's world as possible focusses of identification through such collective media as story and song.[13] Erikson comments: 'historical processes have already entered the individual's core in childhood. Past history survives in the ideal and evil prototypes which guide the parental imagery and which color fairy tale and family lore, superstition and gossip, and the simple lessons of early verbal training.'[14] The formation of identity, then, is shaped both by actual others with whom the child comes into contact, and by imaginary others encountered through a variety of cultural forms.[15]

This book focusses on the way in which the identities formed in childhood and adolescence feed into, and help to shape, the identity adopted in adult life, in its socio-political as much as in its psycho-sexual dimensions. There is a developmental sequence whereby the infant-becoming-child-becoming-adolescent-becoming-adult shifts or transfers the focus of their emotional loyalties and identifications from their parents, from other significant household members, and from other early objects of identification, to more remote individuals and to social institutions. Together with the transfer of *focus* goes a transfer of the *structure* of this pattern of loyalties and identifications, including the conflicts within it.[16] Although this sequence is a continuous one, certain nodal moments—moments of sharper change or choice requiring a renegotiation of identifications and loyalties—may be defined for heuristic purposes. These nodal moments include: separation from the mother; the oedipal relation with the father; entering the extra-familial world of school; the sexual awakening of puberty; consolidation of sexual orientation and object choice; choice of career or profession; choice of sexual partner; identification with a national, ethnic or religious group. To talk of a series of moments, successively encountered, does not imply that these transitions are, once experienced, left behind for good. On the contrary, they remain as emotional focuses which can be reawakened by later events.[17]

Three features of those patterns of identification need to be stressed: their intensity, their stability or conservatism, and their potentially conflicted nature. The *intensity* of emotional attachment which the child initially displays towards their parents is subsequently displayed in muted but still powerful form towards those institutions and beliefs (and people) which form part of the adult's identity. The force of such attachment is far in excess of any simple rational calculation of self-interest. Such attachment can be profoundly *conservative*, maintained in the face of intense difficulties, given up only with great reluctance.[18] Nor is such conservatism without point. Not to have such identifications and attachments means to stand alone. On the one hand, to have to be one's own source of meaning and purpose, without the continual support and encouragement (or constant compulsion) which comes from membership of a social group; and on the other hand, to have to support oneself alone in a competitive society.[19] Attachments can also be riven by, even constructed around, *conflict*. Freud emphasised contradiction within the personality, and stressed the way in which the achieved adult identity necessarily involves the repression and repudiation of some of the individual's desires and identifications. This is true even of the most well-integrated member of a social group or class. It is these repressed wishes and desires, which cannot normally be given direct, public, social and conscious expression, which afford the raw material for the formation of altered or different identities in periods of crisis and change, whether individual (as in conversion, breakdown, or therapy), or social (as in social movements, religious revivals or political revolutions). It is necessary, then, to be alive to the existence of contradictory elements within the personality, within the achieved and relatively stable unity to be found in most socially-functioning people; and yet, to give full weight to the tenacity with which this achieved identity is clung to, and the great difficulty with which it is modified.[20]

The men on whom this book focusses went through a class-, gender-, nation-, and period-specific version of the general developmental sequence just outlined. Many of them experienced one or more of the nodal moments referred to above as a crisis which they were unable to resolve in the way expected of them. As a result they were often forced to create a more idiosyncratic identity for themselves. To use an imperfect metaphor, disruptions had occurred in the series of psychic mappings between the individual, his immediate family, and wider social institutions and ideologies. These disruptions opened up spaces for new mappings, new juxtapositions, new identifications. On the one hand, this new identity was marked by its oppositional character. On the other hand, there were important continuities imposed by emotional conservatism. Such a process of rejection of the available and proffered identities and roles of class and gender, of saying 'goodbye to all that' and carving out 'a life of one's own', did not in fact lead to a complete shedding of the initial identifications and loyalties.[21] The resulting identity was also marked and shaped by what was rejected, if only by the adoption of its mirror opposite. And the formation of that new identity demanded another focus to which loyalty and identification could be transferred—whether that new focus be an individual, an institution, a vocation or whatever. The following section will consider the social pressures shaping the construction of masculine identities within a complex, internally-divided society.

Masculinity: Dynamics, Structures and Reproduction

The term masculinity has been used variously to refer to: male personality structures; male social roles; and the social expectations (prescribed and/or internalised) concerning those personality structures and social roles. Here, I shall use it to refer either to the general notion of such an ensemble ('the reproduction of masculinity'), or to historically specific ensembles of such personalities/roles/expectations ('upper-middle-class masculinity'). I shall begin by examining the psycho-social dynamics of masculinity in terms of the general demand that men work, reproduce themselves, and defend their society. Masculinity is, however, an abstraction which (like class) can be useful for analytic purposes, but can never in practice be understood in isolation.[22] It is always defined by contrast with its opposite—femininity; and the gender structure which they together comprise is always imbricated with other structures—such as those of class, nation, race, or religion. So I shall go on to consider the structures and reproduction of masculinity with more specific reference to industrial and class-divided societies.

Masculinity is built upon a biological basis: all societies distinguish between male and female.[23] Nevertheless, it is a social, not a biological nor simply a psychological category.[24] By the psycho-social dynamics of masculinity, I mean the arena of mediation between the biological, psychological and social dimensions of becoming masculine. That mediation always takes place in historically specific social contexts, but at the same time deals with some relatively enduring dimensions of human experience which arise from biology, including childhood weakness and sexual difference, and are experienced psychologically. Psychoanalysis is concerned with this very arena, exploring ways in which psychic structures are formed that mediate between biologically-based needs and drives, and social demands and prohibitions.[25]

My initial concern is with how societies structure notions of masculinity which fit and impel men to serve contemporary social needs. David Gilmore's cross-cultural anthropological survey (mainly of pre-industrial, and internally less differentiated, societies), *Manhood in the Making*, takes this as its central theme.[26] His account, though its portrayal of the shaping of masculinity is ultimately somewhat consensual and functionalist, is valuable precisely for its considerable attention to the intersection of psychic and social.[27] Gilmore argues that most societies establish preferred male and female roles, gendered identities designed to fit men and women to carry out tasks required of them by their society and/or groupings within it.[28] His analysis indicates a widespread, though not universal, pattern of what he terms 'stressed' or 'pressured' masculinity; and it suggests that this pattern is designed to produce adult men willing to meet societal demands. He argues that masculinity (or manhood, in his preferred term) is in these societies culturally constructed or reinforced; there is no natural process of growth by which boys become men.[29] Masculinity is held to be an achievement, the result of a painful and risky struggle, achieved with difficulty and always held precariously. Consequently, men are constantly having to prove their insecure masculinity to themselves and others.[30] The dynamics behind this process of construction can be uncovered by examining both the social expectations of masculine behaviour, and the processes by which boys were helped to become men.

In these societies, to be recognised as fully masculine demanded of an individual man the performance of a male role, which involved begetting children, providing for them, and protecting family and other dependents, thereby contributing to the wealth of kin and society.[31] This performance must be carried out in a way that could be publicly validated or tested both by other men and by women.[32] The male role had to be publicly structured, and emphatically enforced and reinforced by society, for reasons both external and internal to the individual. Externally, Gilmore focusses on the demands posed by the need to provision and defend. Men were required to wrest food and other forms of wealth from nature and from other men (e.g. by hunting, rustling, or trading); and to defend their community against threats both from nature (natural disasters, wild animals) and from other men.[33] Such endeavours required men, at the limit, to risk their lives for the sake of the community; to regard themselves as individually expendable in the struggle to defend or extend it. Since most men are frightened of war, Gilmore argues, a great effort is needed to render them willing to fight and if necessary die.[34]

Internally, he focusses on society's need to guard against the threat posed to the performance of the male role by the psychodynamic pull of regression. Masculinity was difficult because it required a constant battle against the temptation to regress, back to the world of boyhood when one's needs were provided for by one's mother.[35] Hence the great stress on masculine activity, and the corresponding fear of passivity.[36] Myths of masculinity similarly stressed the danger of regression, and the need for a man to make his way successfully in the wider world.[37] Those who failed to do so, to compete successfully as men in the public realm, were scorned by men and women alike.[38] Some pre-industrial societies dealt with this potential threat by means of complex rituals or series of rituals, extending in some cases over more than ten years, whereby boys made the transition from childhood to manliness.[39] Such rituals, designed to prepare them for the demands of their role as adult men, formed a classic *rite de passage*, involving the stages of separation, transition and reincorporation as the boy graduated to manhood. The founding moment of this process was forcible and publicly marked separation from the female/maternal world, a separation constantly reinforced in adulthood; while its culmination was access to adult male status, an access accorded recognition by women as well as other men.[40] Even where no formal ritual existed, Gilmore argues that such a process of separation and induction into the adult male role can be traced in many other pre-industrial societies.[41] In contrast, he does find a few societies where no great social difference is prescribed between male and female roles, and where masculinity is not an identity which men feel themselves impelled to live up to. These societies, he suggests, are characterised by relative economic plenty, and either lack of enemies, or the possibility of fleeing from enemies.[42]

Gilmore's analysis valuably brings into focus key elements for a cross-cultural understanding of the dynamics of masculinity: in particular, his materialist account of the demands on men to be providers for and defenders of their community in situations of relative economic scarcity; his psychodynamic depiction of the interplay between regressive drives and social demands; and his delineation of the social mechanisms designed to contain the threat posed by the latter to the former. These analytic methods and themes can help to illuminate the construction of masculinity in late nineteenth-century Britain.[43] There are, however, important elements missing from Gilmore's analysis. In particular, he pays little attention to intra-community power differentials and conflicts, and the possibility that they might give rise to differing patterns of masculinity; and he largely ignores the issue of male exploitation of women.[44] Both of these are equally crucial elements in an adequate account of the overall structures of masculinity.

Whereas Gilmore's account of the social construction of masculinity sees it as fairly unproblematically aimed at producing men able to provision, reproduce and defend their community, in a society divided by class and gender (and perhaps race) the processes of constructing masculinity have to serve more complex ends. While most men must work and reproduce themselves, among the ruling elites men must also be able defend their multiple privileges of power, gender and race; while among subordinate groups, men must be able to sustain whatever partial advantages their gendered or racial identity may offer. In addition, all men may be called upon to defend their nation, despite whatever may divide them. The work of R.W. Connell offers a complex structural account of masculinity in contemporary, class-divided industrial societies, two aspects of which are of particular value here. First, he shows that masculinities are in a double sense hierarchical: he distinguishes different masculinities—hegemonic, subordinate, complicit—in conflict within a single society; all of which nevertheless rest on (varying) positions of power over and exploitation of women.[45] John Tosh has suggested the need to modify and extend this aspect of Connell's argument, suggesting that masculinities are sustained and defended not simply to secure men's continuing power over women, but also to maintain other forms of power such as those of a class or race. Moreover, he suggests, Connell's emphasis on the patriarchal dimension of masculinities oversimplifies the homosocial dynamic, underplaying the 'dialectic of comradeship and competition' whereby men compete and combine in a range of activities to assert superiority/dominance over other men and thereby gain peer-group status, material success and social prestige.[46] Second, Connell defines three interrelated social structures which order gender relations: labour (especially the gender division of the public labour force, and the separation between public and domestic labour); power (especially that of the state and other social institutions); and cathexis (the structures of desire and aggression). Each of these contributes some part to the structure of a particular masculinity, and that masculinity can be understood only in terms of the ensemble as a whole; while various masculinities (and femininities) contribute to the overall structures of power, labour and cathexis in a particular society.[47]

In a multiply divided society, there is a variety of masculinities, organised in subordinate relations to a hegemonic masculinity. That hegemonic masculinity is primarily an ideological construction, which may be variously appropriated by and influential among different social groups.[48] It is not necessarily identical with the actual lived masculinity of male elites who propagate it.[49] Maintenance of this hegemonic masculinity, and management of challenges to it, is a task for the state.[50] Many men do not share all or many of the qualities demanded by that hegemonic masculinity, nor partake of many of the benefits of masculine elites. Yet they may be motivated to defend it, partly because to do so may reduce anxiety or gratify fantasy related to their sense of their own masculinity, but perhaps especially because it is a cultural expression of power over women from which most men benefit.[51] Subordinate masculinities may exist in various forms: they may be those of a subordinate class, race or national minority; they may be those of a specific professional or work group; they may be temporary phases of a life cycle (e.g. apprenticeship); they may comprise a stable and relatively enduring, or a proscribed and hence partly hidden, identity based on a common sexuality (such as, respectively, contemporary gay identity, or the emergent homosexual identity *c.*1900); or they may remain the identity of individuals or small groups which do not receive wider social recognition.[52] Connell stresses that all such masculinities, hegemonic or subordinate, are always in the process of being reproduced or newly constructed, and are riven by internal contradictions.[53]

Much of the critical writing on masculinity, whether by feminist women, or gay or anti-sexist men, has presented it as both fraught and fragile; painful in the limitations and costs it imposes on men, and maintained as an identity only by unremitting struggle.[54] As Connell suggests, this can only be a partial picture; it omits the material benefits (in both power and wealth) which accrue to men, and also the real satisfactions which derive both from the content of the role and from its successful performance. If there were no such benefits, it is hard to see how such masculinities could continue.[55] Nevertheless, both desire for the benefits to be obtained, and anguish at the price exacted, by living out a prescribed masculine role lead to conflicts between hegemonic and subordinate masculinities, and to the enforcement of definitions of femininity on women.[56] Michael Kaufman and David Gilmore have both argued that central to masculinity is the capacity to be active (or, to hold the status of agent, subject); it is something which must be defended at all costs, generating in men a phobic fear of passivity.[57] Hence the status around which conflicting masculinities contend is that of being a 'real man'. Failure to achieve or retain this status leaves one branded a 'fag' or 'sissy', a homosexual or effeminate man; that is, someone onto whom passivity (and its accompanying fear) has been projected. Further, all these masculinities also define themselves by differentiation from or opposition to femininity. 'Woman', as Simone de Beauvoir argued, becomes the universal Other onto whom men's (fear of) passivity and objectification can be projected.[58] Consequently, men must distance themselves from women as from effeminate men.[59]

Masculinity is reproduced in a double sense: it is constantly re-produced among the men of a particular generation, and it is constructed over again as that generation reproduces itself through its children. In the former sense, masculinity is re-produced not solely through explicit ideological messages, but also, perhaps even more importantly, through men's living and re-enacting their roles within the arenas of power, labour and cathexis—roles which are in part defined by notions of masculinity. Generational reproduction of masculinity, the particular concern of this book, is a complex process extended through time, conducted initially within the family and then through wider social institutions.[60] Reproduction of masculinity occurs at both conscious and unconscious levels; a growing boy internalises not only his father's and mother's explicit instructions about how to be a boy/man, but also the emotional patterns of relating which they bring to the family interactions.[61] Furthermore, since the building of masculinity is a process which extends from birth to entry into the world of work, unconscious processes are built up and come into play not only during infancy but throughout this period, perhaps especially at moments of crisis. Hence the influences of other significant figures, such as siblings, other relatives, friends, teachers and mentors, work in the growing boy's experience in unconscious as well as conscious ways.

As emphasised in the previous section, the development of identity is necessarily conflicted. Though the family undoubtedly constitutes a major matrix within which powerful models of masculinity are offered, and a boy's developing personality is strongly shaped, it would be wrong to treat the boy simply as passive recipient of these pressures. To view the process as *reproduction* of masculinity is to see it solely from the perspective of parents or society; from the boy's perspective, it may better be termed *achieving* masculinity. Difficulties in negotiating the available class-gender developmental process may provoke a crisis; and the boy may then rework the psychic and ideological materials available to him in the light of his experiences of the world outside his immediate family, particularly school and community.[62] Such disruptions may be located within each of the structures of power, labour or cathexis. For instance, studies have shown that specific masculinities are first built up and reinforced, only to be later undermined, by the dynamic of the changing labour process within capitalism.[63] In certain situations, such crises have served to problematise a particular masculinity and inflect it in a politically dissident direction.[64] In the case of the men discussed in this book, however, it seems primarily to have been issues of power and cathexis which produced this outcome. So subsequent chapters will be concerned mainly with the reproduction of masculinity in those arenas; and the intersection between that process, and the formation of a political identity. The discussion in this section—focussed on some general dynamics of masculinity, and on broad structures of masculinity in complex, industrialised, class-divided societies—has necessarily been rather abstract. But lived gender identities are always particular, requiring historically specific analysis.[65] After discussion in the next section of the nation as arena for the formation of identity, the following section will explore the common inherited masculinity of these men, that of upper-middle-class Britain in the late-nineteenth century, and its modes of reproduction.

Nation as Imagined Community

This section will be concerned with those wider communities of power within which these men constructed their lives. I will begin by examining Benedict Anderson's concept of 'imagined community', expanded to embrace a gender dimension by Ross Poole; and suggest how it may be further extended and modified. The next section will then sketch the changing nature of British nationalism in the later nineteenth century, and its imbrication with structures of class and gender. As will be seen below (Chapters 4–8), the apparatuses of power and ideology of the nation state had a direct and powerful impact on these men's lives.

Recent studies of nationalism as a central phenomenon of nineteenth- and twentieth-century history have articulated its role, cultural as much as economic, in making possible the transition to a modern, market-based, industrial society.[66] Ernest Gellner emphasised its rational dimension in organising a common culture of universal literacy, one which can educate a flexibly trained workforce for a highly mobile society with a 'division of labour...which is complex and persistently, cumulatively changing'.[67] Tom Nairn by contrast pointed to the psychic and emotional aspects of nationalism, what he termed its darker Janus face, which by an appeal to an imaginary past permits the massive summoning of energy required for the emergence into modernity.[68] Powerfully developing Nairn's insight, Benedict Anderson used the term 'imagined communities' to define the general character, and in particular the mobilising power, of the nation states which, during the last two-hundred years, have become the overwhelmingly dominant mode of sovereign political organisation. Anderson has elegantly traced the various routes by which creole, new European, official, and postcolonial nationalists in the nineteenth and twentieth centuries set about state building or state redefining, stressing how each nation was both 'imaginary' and capable of seizing the imagination.[69]

Two aspects of Anderson's account of the nation may be stressed here. First, he defines the nation as: 'an imagined political community...It is imagined because the members of even the smallest nation will never know most of their fellow members, meet them, or even hear of them, yet in the minds of each lives the image of their communion.' In doing so, he links the nation with many other forms of community identity, as necessarily involving an imaginative projection of links between the self and others now and perhaps forever unknown.[70] Second, Anderson explores those aspects of the nation which—even though it is imagined—nevertheless constitute it as something to which people feel profoundly attached, and for which they are willing to die.[71] He notes the way in which the imagining of the nation overrides awareness of certain deep forms of internal conflict:

> it is imagined as a *community*, because, regardless of the actual inequality and exploitation that may prevail in each, the nation is always conceived as a deep, horizontal comradeship. Ultimately it is this fraternity that makes it possible, over the past two centuries, for so many millions of people, not so much to kill, as willingly to die for such limited imaginings.[72]

He also argues that nationalist imagining has much in common with religious imagining. The great religious traditions were concerned with man's place in the cosmos, and with the contingency of human life. Their survival 'attests to their imaginative response to the overwhelming burden of human suffering'.[73] Religious thought also, he suggests, offers intimations of immortality, transforming individual fatality into collective continuity; hence it is concerned with links between the dead and the yet unborn. Nationalism arose in the late eighteenth century at a time when religious thought was beginning to lose its universal sway in Europe and the Americas. It served to offer a secular way of transforming fatality into continuity, contingency into meaning, chance into destiny.[74]

This depiction of the quasi-transcendent dimension of the nation was strikingly developed, and linked to gendered identity, by Ross Poole.[75] Starting from Gellner's and Nairn's recognition that the hegemony of the nation state developed in tandem with the spread of capitalism, Poole argues that the market both requires and produces an *abstract* individuality, independent of ties to particular work or personal relations. Both these latter have to be changeable at need or will. Such market structures have not only (at least until recently) been predominantly staffed by men, but have helped to form what is a central dimension of both hegemonic and many subordinate masculinities—impersonality and devotion to instrumental reason. Consequently, enduring commitments to particular self-identities and to relationships with specific others, a hindrance within the realm of the market, are largely dispersed into two other realms.[76] They are found in the sphere of the family, where they are needed for the bringing up of children, and are made central to many forms of femininity.[77] But they are also required by the nation, Poole argues, precisely in order to protect the market. Just as the market's successful daily internal workings necessitate some sacrifice of self-interest on the part of individuals (policed by the state through law), so its protection against external threat demands that at the limit the state can call on its citizens to sacrifice their lives for its defence. 'The content of the obligations involved goes beyond anything that might voluntarily be assumed...by a market individual. The state embodies the power of death; and death is, from the perspective of that individual, both the ultimate sacrifice of self-interest and the ultimate irrationality.'[78]

How is this to be achieved? Both Anderson and Poole locate the source of the nation's capacity to evoke sacrifice in the character of the community it presents itself as: natural, relational, equal, enduring. One's nation, Anderson notes, is traditionally figured in the language of kinship or home, both of which 'denote something to which one is naturally tied'; that is to say, just as they are unchosen, so one cannot help one's national identity. He comments: 'And in these 'natural ties' one senses what one might call 'the beauty of *gemeinschaft*'. To put it another way, precisely because such ties are not chosen, they have about them a halo of disinterestedness.'[79]

Anderson draws a parallel here with the family, likewise natural because unchosen, and able to call forth powerful feelings of love and commitment.[80] Poole concurs: the nation must present itself as representing a deeper community which subsumes that of the market. National identity, like the family and unlike the market, involves relatively enduring and emotionally cathected relationships: the nation is one's source, one's fellow citizens one's kin. It offers to the individual a self whose identity derives from a fellowship with others who share it, thereby making patriotic deeds both expressive of one's identity and necessary to sustain it. In this way the nation is offered as a framework for meaning after death which is more collective than the egocentric ends of the market, and more extensive than the parochial realm of the family. Commemoration of war, he suggests, is central to the rituals of nationalism. It highlights patriotic willingness to lay down life; while celebrating men's capacity for the values of mutual caring and selfless sacrifice usually located in women.[81] To sum up: for Anderson, the nation can evoke love and self-sacrifice because it offers itself as an enduring community whose continuity can give meaning to the contingent, suffering and mortal nature of an individual life; for Poole, because it offers (to men especially) validation of the capacity for continuing commitment and self-sacrifice, and participation in a collective and transcendent identity, both negated within the workings of the market.

Thus far, what is being offered is an *analogy* between the nation and the family. This needs to be strengthened by exploring specific links between them. Poole comments that Anderson's concept of imagination does not help us to understand 'the extent to which we find ourselves subject to an object we have ourselves created'; why do people respond to the call to sacrifice themselves?[82] His suggested answer is the form of recognition which the nation offers.

> The family is the source of one's physical existence; but it is equally the source of a certain kind of social identity. So too is one's country. Just to the extent that this mode of social existence enters into one's conception of what one is, then to that extent the nation is one's parent—one's father *and* mother—and one's fellow nationals constitute one's kin.[83]

In other words, both family and nation provide for, and at the same time offer recognition to, the individual. The psychic investment already made by the individual in the family is extended and relocated into a wider network of relationships. The nation then offers to the individual citizen reciprocal recognition of their identity. People do not imagine the nation simply as something outside which exists over against them; rather, they also form a conception of themselves as existing in relation to it. As the members of a nation recognise each other, they also recognise themselves; hence the nation both exists as an imagined community, and offers a form of identity within whose images and structures the individual can actively find/form themself. It is this which explains why the appeal of the nation meets a response.[84]

The image which these studies have delineated, of the nation as an imagined community, mobilising its population to secure and defend the transition to statehood and industrialisation, is a powerful and revealing one. I want both to modify and to extend it. I want to modify it by relating it to the dynamics of engagement between social collectivities and their inhabitants—coercion, provision, recognition—which I posited earlier.[85] Anderson's text, and much of the subsequent work which it helped to inspire, has laid particular stress on the ideological (or recognition conferring) dimensions of nationalism and nation building, what has been termed 'narrating the nation'.[86] While this emphasis has been valuable, I would reframe it in three ways. First, I want to reinsert the coercive or repressive as well as the hegemonic or ideological aspects of the nation. Just as what may be termed the prototypical nations of eighteenth-century Europe, paradigmatically Britain and France, commanded state forces with which to impose their authority on their populations (and on any sections of them which might wish to secede), so too the nation builders of the Americas at the century's end, of central and eastern Europe through the nineteenth century, and of the former colonial territories of Africa and Asia in the twentieth, did not simply imagine the new nation, but (where possible) organised armed force to create it, in the process compelling some populations to adhere, others to flee.[87] The same applies once a nation has been constituted as a sovereign state. Anderson's vision of people willingly dying for their country captures one part of the truth; but his formulation tends to occlude two others—the coercion of conscription, with the firing squad for deserters; and the imperative to kill the Other who stands in the way of the nationalist project.[88] Second, I want to draw attention also to those dimensions of the nation which are neither simply coercive nor simply ideological, but derive from the role of the state as defender of and provider for its population. Men were willing to fight, and if necessary die, for their country not simply because they were conscripted, or inspired with patriotic sentiment, but also because the nation, actually or potentially, provided an institutional framework which offered them material benefits, to hold onto or to obtain. It is from the intersection of all three of these dynamics that the nation acquires its mobilising power.[89] Third, I want to indicate a development of the links identified by Anderson and Poole between the family and the ideological power of the nation. In Chapter 2, I will suggest that there is not simply a linguistic or an analytic *parallel* between family and nation (both natural and unchosen, both arenas of commitment and sacrifice), but a structural *continuity*, since the family forms an initial template in which the values of, and ways of identifying oneself with, the nation are laid down.

Gender and Class: Structures and Individuals

Specific masculinities are constructed and lived within complex fields of force, comprising national (and even transnational) as well as more local class and other imperatives.[90] Two dimensions are of particular importance to the argument of this book: nation and class. I will begin this section by considering the construction of hegemonic masculinity, before examining in more detail the interrelation of national and class elements in the model masculinity of the upper-(middle) class.

Late-nineteenth-century Britain contained a range of different masculinities, defined in part both by their respective relationships to 'hegemonic masculinity', and by their sharp differentiation both from femininity and from other (especially homosexual) masculinities.[91] Connell stresses the central organising role of hegemonic masculinity within the gender order of a given society.[92] It will seek to define what constitutes appropriate masculine behaviour for that society, and to differentiate itself from various Others—the feminine, the effeminate, the homosexual, the foreign. Its centrality derives from its symbolic importance, rather than from its being universally—or even widely—lived out.[93] Connell also points out that 'the winning of hegemony often involves the creation of models of masculinity which are quite specifically fantasy figures'.[94] Such models could equally well be fictional, or based on historical or contemporary personalities.[95] An example of such a masculine fantasy figure from this period in Britain is Lawrence of Arabia. Graham Dawson has offered an elegant analysis of the myth of this 'blond Bedouin' at the moment of its construction in 1920. This first portrait of Lawrence offered a picture which, in historically specific ways, restated certain dominant characteristics of English-British masculinity potentially damaged by the recently ended world war.[96] The mythical figure thereby created could circulate as a potent image of masculinity within both high and popular culture, appealing as a national hero to boys and men of all classes.[97] Such hegemonic images of masculinity could command the support of many men whose actual lives took very different forms: they provided opportunities for fantasy fulfilment and for displacement of aggression, but above all they helped express the subordination of other masculinities and of women.[98]

Gender identity, both masculine and feminine, is in modern societies integrally linked to class. To ensure that their children could maintain or even improve their social status, parents had to induct them into acceptable patterns of gender identity.[99] Consequently, although the power of hegemonic masculinity was felt throughout society, and some aspects of lived masculinity (and femininity) might cross class boundaries, for the most part particular lived masculinities were class specific.[100] Such patterns of masculinity were also linked to national identity: to be an Englishman (that fused term) was, in part, to be differentiated from men of other nations and races. Building on Connell's concept, I would suggest that one can identify, in addition to a hegemonic masculinity within the gender order of society as a whole, related, but more specific, 'leading masculinities' within particular gender regimes such as those of classes, or religious and occupational groups. These more limited leading masculinities, which derived part of their power from their consonance with the overall hegemonic masculinity, could exercise considerable symbolic power within groups whose way of life they were more immediately related to. This book explores the role of public schools in constructing a form of leading masculinity that included both national and class elements (Chapter 2); and the role of such a masculinity in motivating men to fight during the First World War (Chapter 3). In the shadow of these leading masculinities existed a variety of subordinated masculinities, some acceptable but carrying less prestige either symbolically or practically, others marginalised or repressed.[101]

Masculinity and class are so tightly bound together in part because of the role of gender in the process of class reproduction at the level of the individual.[102] In abstract theory, it would be possible to imagine a capitalist society in which the various class roles were played by individuals recruited regardless of their class of origin.[103] In practice, however, capitalist societies do not operate in that way. One's class position of origin is a major determinant of one's own class position, because the initial conditions of privilege or disadvantage powerfully shape the life possibilities open to any individual. Britain in the late-nineteenth century was not even in theory a meritocratic society, and powerful barriers operated to prevent the marketisation of many areas of life. Privileged social classes were reproduced in significant part by recruitment from the children of their own members; and so individual families adopted or developed strategies for enabling their own children to succeed to, or improve upon, the parents' class position both as successful class members in their own lifetime and as parents of a subsequent generation.[104] Such social reproduction of classes by internal recruitment from the new generation involves biological reproduction, requiring the construction of individuals as males or females ready to carry out that reproductive role. Hence a class identity is always also gendered; children are brought up to be not simply upper-middle-class, but upper-middle-class men or women.[105]

Later nineteenth-century Britain was a society in which socially constructed gender roles, particularly among the middle and upper classes, were highly differentiated; although some challenges to the rigidity of that differentiation began to emerge in the last decades of the century.[106] Accordingly the pattern of recruitment, and the associated institutions, even the very definition of life cycle stages, were different for boys and girls, young men and young women. This study is concerned with men, and that has determined the particular stages of the life cycle and the specific extra-familial institutions in terms of which I have chosen to interpret these life histories.[107] Parents bringing up a new generation in this way were helped by the existence of a large number of institutions—formal and informal—embodying strategies of class-gender reproduction at different stages of the life cycle. For the purposes of this book, the most important of these are the household (consisting of nuclear family and live-in servants), the school system (especially the secondary level public schools and their feeder preparatory schools), the universities (especially Oxford and Cambridge), the various professional career structures, and the social events which helped to structure the marriage market.[108]

Most British boys within the upper-middle class in the nineteenth and twentieth centuries were both born into and reared within nuclear families. As infants, they formed strong and intense ties of emotional attachment first to their mothers, and later to other significant figures within the household. These included most obviously the father and siblings, but also other relatives such as uncles, aunts, or grandparents (if resident), and servants (especially nannies and nurses).[109] A growing boy had first to give up his close contact and identification with his mother, and transfer that identification to his father, to whose place—in the family and in society—he would eventually succeed. This transfer involved, in particular, a relative repression of the emotional and feeling side of the boy's personality—since attending to people's emotional needs was a predominantly female task. Instead, the boy had to orient himself primarily to the impersonal world of social institutions, and find a way of relating his individual personality to that world. Here, the school was the crucial institution, the place where boys were trained for their future role as public men. From school, the boy was introduced to the various institutions of the upper-middle-class adult world—university, the army, a business or profession. The intense attachment, the identification and modelling, which had at first been concentrated entirely on his parents and other family (and household) members, were gradually diversified and diffused across a range of social institutions—school, profession, religion, nation, and so on. Finally, the young adult man was expected to choose as his sexual partner a woman from his own social circle who, as his wife and the mother of his children, would enable him to succeed his own father in the role of husband and father, *pater familias*. Consequently, imperatives of class and nation entered not only into the work and power dimensions of masculinity, but also its patterns of cathexis and in particular sexual attraction. As Connell comments: 'The social patterning of desire is most obvious as a set of prohibitions.... Yet the prohibitions would be pointless without injunctions to love and marry the right kind of person, to find such-and-such a kind of masculinity or femininity desirable.'[110]

What has been sketched here is a general model of the transition from boyhood to manhood among the upper-middle classes of late-nineteenth-century Britain. Two notes of caution about the use of such a model must be entered. First, the social practices from which this model has been drawn were neither uniform nor unchanging. As will be seen below

(Chapter 2), even within this single social milieu, there were dominant, emergent, and residual patterns of masculinity overlapping within one historical moment. Consequently, there could co-exist within institutions individuals and groups pursuing divergent and at times contradictory goals in support of particular definitions of masculinity.[111] Second, as Connell has indicated, any such gender structure is always the outcome of a continuing process of construction: 'It is a unity—always imperfect and under construction—of historical composition.'[112] That process could fail, could be resisted by those individuals who were its objects. Boys could be unable or unwilling to become the sort of men their families wanted them to be; could negotiate or resist as well as adopt the roles for which they were brought up. Connell comments: '"Agencies of socialization" cannot produce mechanical effects in a growing person. What they do is invite the child to participate in social practice on given terms. The invitation may be, and often is, coercive—accompanied by heavy pressure to accept and no mention of an alternative.' As he goes on to argue, both force (by the socialising agencies) and choice (on the part of the growing boy) contribute to the eventual outcome. A satisfactory account of gender formation has to explain the emergence of those who reject, as well as those who accept, the roles held out to them.[113]

The role of institutions in attracting loyalties and identifications during the formation of masculinity has a further implication. As will be seen in the case of schools (Chapter 2), institutions were not social machines working impersonally, but were held together by and gave rise to strong and contradictory dynamics of power and emotion. Consequently, it became possible for the institution itself to become cathected—whether positively, negatively or ambivalently—in its own right, and not simply as a transference object of emotional patterns created within the family.[114] This laid the ground for the cathecting of other institutions later in life, whether they be university, regiment, career or political party.[115] Andrew Tolson expresses very well one of the consequences of such emotional investments.

> In our society…masculinity is 'institutionalized'…beyond the mere routine of everyday life, 'institutionalization' also implies a certain social *regulation*, even an *exploitation* of gender identity. What is specific about our society is the way in which particular masculine ambivalences are system-

atically *reinforced*. In their explicit emphasis on 'masculine' qualities the major social institutions penetrate to the core of a man's personality. In so far as they highlight his frailties or insecurities they touch a powerful source of energy. By playing on personal weaknesses, social institutions are able to enlist the emotional commitment of men themselves.[116]

Liminal Times and Places

This book is particularly concerned with the potentialities for disruption of expected life trajectories. In this respect, I have found valuable the work of Victor Turner on liminal times/places, and of Erik Erikson on late adolescent moratoria. Turner developed Arnold van Gennep's concept of a *rite de passage*. He focussed on the characteristics of the middle (transitional or liminal phase), which he termed 'betwixt and between', in an established ritual. The liminal group of neophytes:

> ...are withdrawn from their structural positions and consequently from the values, norms, sentiments, and techniques associated with those positions. They are also divested of their previous habits of thought, feeling, and action. During the liminal period, neophytes are alternately forced and encouraged to think about their society, their cosmos, and the powers than generate and sustain them. Liminality may partly be described as a stage of reflection. In it those ideas, sentiments, and facts that had been hitherto for the neophytes bound up in configurations and accepted unthinkingly are, as it were, resolved into their constituents.

As a consequence, liminality may be thought of as 'a realm of pure possibility whence novel configurations of ideas and relations may arise'.[117] In his later work, he extended the concept to cover aspects of more complex contemporary societies where formal rituals play a much less significant role. In contrast to social structure, with its relative fixity, he defined experiences of anti-structure as instances of 'communitas', the other major mode of human relating. Communitas could be situated at different locations in relation to social structure: in the interstices (liminality), on the edges (marginality), or beneath/outside (inferiority/outsiderhood). Communitas could be experienced as a temporary phase within social structure; but in contemporary societies it could also offer a permanent vocation (for example, as an artist or religious).[118] Occasions of communitas then afford opportunities for creative cultural improvisation and challenges to the norm-governed, institutionalised social structure.[119] Turner thus comes to see liminality (and other forms of communitas) as one aspect of social experience, no longer confined to (though sometimes taking the form of) ritual.

Erikson's attempt to define and characterise one aspect of adolescence—as a period of transition within the life cycle—clearly links to the themes which Turner explored. Erikson developed the concept of a 'moratorium' while working with adolescents in America in the 1950s, and went on to employ it historically in his famous study of Martin Luther.[120] For Erikson, the life cycle is simultaneously both psychosexual and psychosocial; the potential for development, viewed psychosexually, of an individual person is always actualised within a specific social context which shapes through its structures and values those tasks and roles which that individual is expected or permitted to undertake. He writes of adolescence:

> The adolescent process...is conclusively complete only when the individual has subordinated his childhood identifications to a new kind of identification, achieved in absorbing sociability and in competitive apprenticeship with and among his age mates. These new identifications...with dire urgency...force the young individual into choices and decisions which will, with increasing immediacy, lead to commitments 'for life'.[121]

On an analogy with the psychoanalytic concept of a 'latency period' preceding puberty, which he sees as allowing the child to learn 'the technical and social rudiments of a work situation', he defines a similar period after puberty of prolonged adolescence, which he terms 'a psychosexual moratorium during which the young adult through free role experimentation may find a niche in some section of his society'. This period allows the adolescent to develop an identity which is accepted by society and yet also acceptable to him.[122] He generalises the social availability of such a moratorium. 'Each society and each culture institutionalises a certain moratorium for the majority of its young people. For the most part, these moratoria coincide with apprenticeships and adventures that are in line with the society's values.' Finally, he notes that a moratorium does not have to be consciously experienced as such.

> On the contrary, the young individual may feel deeply committed and may learn only much later that what he took so seriously was only a period of transition…any experimentation with identity images means also to play with the inner fire of emotions and drives and to risk the outer danger of ending up in a social 'pocket' from which there is no return.[123]

Erikson notes the wider implications of choice of career as a task of the late-adolescent stage: 'the choice of an occupation assumes a significance beyond the question of remuneration and status. It is for this reason that some adolescents prefer not to work at all for a while rather than be forced into an otherwise promising career which would offer success without the satisfaction of functioning with unique excellence.'[124] In his study of *Young Man Luther*, he used William James's work on sick souls and the divided self, noting that the late teens and early twenties were the most common age for the conversion experiences which James identified.[125] He pointed to the search for an ideology, in the form of a movement or at least a way of life. Searching for and embracing such an ideology demanded both devotion and rejection; it involved the discarding of the 'old'—a previous way of life including parental perspectives, a part of the self which is suppressed, or the world view of other groups of people (who then became expendable).[126] Moratorium, then, could be seen as a socially sanctioned liminal time, or period of communitas, in which the late adolescent is allowed to delay an immediate commitment to a specific aspect of social structure. Erikson's concept bears hallmarks of the place and period of its forging, in particular its putative universality of application, and its tendency to ascribe an almost benign intentionality to an organic society.[127] Nevertheless, used with caution it can be a valuable heuristic device for understanding aspects of the transition from adolescence to adulthood.

In this book, I shall use the concepts of liminality and moratorium to explore various facets of these men's experiences. Moratorium can perhaps be most fruitfully considered as a *way of looking at* the *use made of* experiences, situations or opportunities by late adolescents and young adults. I will stretch Turner's concept of liminality even further from its original source in ritual, using it to refer not to discrete locations or moments of social experience in their entirety, but to aspects of them. I will suggest that, viewed objectively, these locations/moments displayed at least some of the elements of communitas; while, viewed subjectively, these men responded to certain situations or experiences as though they were liminal.

2

From Boys to Men: Upper-Middle-Class Masculinity in Late-Nineteenth-Century Britain

Class and Nation in Imperial Britain

For those born into the upper and middle classes in Britain, a long-established nation-state, identification with class was closely imbricated with, indeed at times barely separable from, that with nation. But as the British state faced new challenges in the later nineteenth century, so too its elite classes were compelled to adapt to changing circumstances. The emergence of an expanding international system of nation states necessarily affected and re-oriented the identity even of such a long unified (and already industrialised) nation as Britain.[1]

If of the eighteenth century it might be said that Britain had acquired an empire piecemeal, in the new world order which was emerging in the nineteenth century this was no longer possible. From mid-century onwards, in the context of growing inter-imperialist conflict, Britain too adopted some of the practices of what Benedict Anderson has termed 'official nationalism'.[2] A newly self-conscious and more explicitly imperial British nationalism was forged. Abroad, the bonds of empire had to be formalised and strengthened.[3] At home, ensuring the human resources for defence of empire, and the capacity to mobilise them, became a central concern, one which was matched in other industrialised countries. With the gradual extension of the franchise in the later nineteenth-century, the growing democratisation of politics in much of western Europe made the citizen voter's attitude to the state crucial. In part, Hobsbawm argues, this was because of the heavier impact of the state on the mass of the population, its greater involvement in the regulation of their everyday lives.[4] But the state simultaneously demanded a greater commitment from its population: 'states required a civic religion ("patriotism") all the more because they increasingly required more than passivity from their citizens.'[5] This need was most pressing when it came to military preparedness. The model of the mass citizen army, dominant since the French Revolution, meant that the willingness and ability of ordinary citizens to serve the state as soldiers was essential as never before.[6]

Democratising and modernising states, as they sought to strengthen their power to mobilise, resorted to what Eric Hobsbawm and Terence Ranger have termed 'the invention of tradition'.[7] In Britain, this redefinition of national identity involved the reworking of a repertoire of patriotic tropes, deriving from the anti-French Revolutionary wars and earlier, to fit the new world of imperialist rivalry.[8] On the symbolic level, the period from the late 1870s to 1914 saw the role of the British monarchy, its rituals, and the settings in which they were performed, significantly enhanced, and an imperial dimension added. Great royal events, from the Golden Jubilee of 1887 onwards, both expressed and sublimated international rivalry.[9] Such initiatives could also emerge from civil society, as with the founding of Empire Day, first celebrated in 1904.[10] On the practical level, the military setbacks and prolonged course of the Boer War (1899–1902) provoked considerable alarm about the readiness and capacity of the mass of the population to defend the empire. In the face of deep-rooted hostility to conscription (widely adopted elsewhere in Europe), serious efforts were made to overhaul the mechanisms for producing trained volunteers ready for mobilisation in the event of war.[11]

During the same period the expanding upper-middle and middle classes were redefining their class identities, both by strengthening the institutional links within civil society which held them together nationally and locally, and by marking themselves off in new ways from those below them in the social hierarchy.[12] The upper-middle class could to a degree adapt the model of the existing ruling elite, through emulation of their lifestyle. But more significantly, both they and the wider middle class forged common bonds of identity and inclusion through a variety of formal and informal means. Two in particular may be singled out here. One crucial pre-requisite was a shared form of education. The public school system was extensively developed as both the provider of a common culture for their children, and the source of valuable networks of contacts for later life.[13] Another was a mechanism for enabling members of the middle classes to mix socially (and—especially for the young—to meet potential marriage partners), while excluding those of lower social status. Here, sport played an important role. It provided both a means of extending elements of a shared elite lifestyle to the expanding middle class, and a way of bringing together people of diverse occupations and backgrounds but similar status.[14] In the last three decades of the century many competitive sports were codified (or newly invented) and institutionalised for the first time.[15] The organisation of sport helped to define boundaries of exclusion and inclusion both between classes (with the code of 'amateurism' separating gentlemen from players) and within classes (agreements to share fixtures marking a crucial recognition of comparable status between public schools).[16]

These redefinitions of nation and class intersected. To be educated into the upper-middle or middle classes was to be invested with an identity that was simultaneously national and class. Imperial destiny, Christian service and the games ethic were preached in the public schools as forming warp and woof of the same cloth from which the pattern of the English gentleman was cut. The nineteenth century, notes John Tosh, saw the entrenching of 'an entrepreneurial, individualistic masculinity, organised around a punishing work ethic, [and] a compensating validation of home'.[17] Sexuality too was shaped to meet these pressures. Nation building in nineteenth-century Germany, as George Mosse has shown, involved a redefinition of masculinity, and of the appropriate expression of male sexuality, which simultaneously served national and middle-class needs.[18] Later nineteenth-century British nationalism too redefined the acceptable forms of male sexual expression, especially in the imperial context, with a new emphasis on respectability and racial purity.[19]

Consequently, those born into the upper and middle classes in the later nineteenth century experienced an upbringing which was inextricably both class and national. For middle-class men in Britain around 1900, public school and university acted as transitional institutions through which patterns of belonging and loyalty formed within the family were extended and strengthened, making possible their transfer both to the adult career which formed the basis of class identity, and more broadly to the nation. However, this transition was neither inevitable nor fixed in form. Though Anderson rightly stresses that family and nation (and national tongue) shared the characteristics of being unchosen, enduring and disinterested, and that this 'naturalness' strengthened their attractive power, nevertheless they were capable of being displaced. For the individual, the transfer from family to broader focusses of belonging and loyalty involved transitions in institutional location and status, and realignments of psychic fantasy. When for some reason the pattern of transitions was disrupted, this could open up spaces in which adherence to alternative imagined communities might be explored or adopted.[20] Such imagined communities might at specific moments challenge the dominant identity-conferring power of the nation, though in general they remained subordinate to it.[21]

Social classes are not politically monolithic; at a given time, each supports a range of contending political stances. In later nineteenth-century Britain, these were largely contained within the framework of the broad alliances which constituted the two major parliamentary parties, Conservatives and Liberals. The former was the dominant party of the upper and upper-middle classes, the latter of the lower-middle and working classes; but each also drew significant support from outside its core constituency.[22] However, the half-century from 1880 to 1930 saw a profound change in the structure of the British party system. The Liberals, dominant since 1850, began to fragment from the late 1880s, losing many of their remaining upper and upper-middle class supporters to the Conservatives over imperial issues, while the newly formed Labour Party was beginning to erode their working-class support over social issues.[23] Further, the nascent socialist movement from the 1880s offered a challenge to the dominant political and economic order which extended beyond the current terrain of parliamentary politics; while that challenge was to be greatly reinforced after the catastrophe of the First World War by the emergence of the Communist movement which sought to operate across the boundaries of the nation state.[24] Thus the whole terrain of party politics was being slowly transformed, traditional patterns of party/class allegiance challenged, and new locuses of political affiliation emerging.

Parents and Household

In the upbringing of a boy as a member of the next generation, his father obviously played a central role. At its simplest, the growing boy might imitate and internalise central features of his father's character and habits.

Graves adapted from his father's life an intensive work ethic centred around writing, and West admired and sought to find analogies in his own life for his father's practical skills, just as Julian Grenfell acquired the countryman's skills of stalking and hunting.[25]

But fathers, in addition to their individual personal qualities, were representatives of authority in the external world. They were the crucial mediating figures between the patterns of loyalty and identification formed within the family, and the institutions of the wider social world to which the growing boy had gradually to transfer his allegiance. What emerges in the lives of these men is the considerable tension generated in childhood by the need to negotiate between on the one hand an individual person, whose qualities might be variously adopted, adapted or rejected, and on the other the representative of social values and imperatives; and the difficulties posed in adolescence and early adulthood when the mode of relating which came out of that negotiation was carried into wider social institutions beyond the family. The form and intensity of any resulting conflict was shaped both by the strength and nature of the characters of father and son, and by the role of the mother within the particular family constellation.

In both West's and Macfie's life histories, their fathers appear as dominating figures against whom their sons have to wage a classically oedipal struggle to establish an independent identity.[26] Another stark example is offered by Gerald Brenan. He spent much of his early life in conflict with his father, but the account he gives of him is much less coloured by ambivalence, much more simply negative, than West's of his. In Brenan's early life, his mother was the dominant figure, the more so because of the separations imposed when his father was away on active service.[27] Though in early childhood, Brenan saw little of him, and was not frightened of him ('When I thought of him, it was less, I imagine, as a person than as the head of that very sacred and unique thing—our family'), this began to change at the age of five, when his father decided to teach him arithmetic ('for he was a great believer in the disciplinary effect of mathematics and thought that for this reason they ought to be imparted by a man').[28] Once his father had come into his inheritance, left the army and settled in England, when Brenan was seven, he became a more important figure in his son's life. He is presented as a typical soldier—sharp, definite and unimaginative. From early on, he represented the self-reliant, solitary, independent side of Brenan's life, which was to be at times an important resource for him.[29] But Brenan also saw him as a hard, neurotic, unsociable man, largely out of sympathy with the circumstances of his own life. His most marked characteristics were his need to exercise power over the members of his family, which he did by the force of his 'moods' and his occasional outbursts of violent anger; and his insistence on duty, discipline and correct behaviour. He and his son had almost nothing in common. Except for a brief period in his early teens, when his father enjoyed teaching him riding, shooting and other practical skills, Brenan never drew close to him.[30] His father's main concern was to see his son (whom he regarded as a slacker) securely established in a career which would prevent his ever being a financial liability. Brenan's adolescence and early adulthood was largely devoted to his efforts to evade his father's career plans for him, and carve out his own life.[31]

None of these men's mothers went out to work after their marriages; all, typically for their class and period, acted as companion and hostess for their husband while bringing up their children with the help of the servants. While all accepted the notion of a wife's place as helpmate to her husband, their own strength of character, and sometimes tensions within the marriage, meant that they could have as powerful an effect on their sons as the fathers. Hence each of them proved an important source of values. Sometimes, as with Graves, this was a reinforcement of shared familial values, so powerful that conflict with the mother became the prime site of the struggle for identity.[32] Another striking example of such an intense and conflicted mother-son relationship was that of Julian Grenfell. While he clearly took some qualities from his rather distant father, as Nicholas Mosley's biography shows the dominant parent throughout his life was his mother.[33] She resembled Graves's mother in two ways: in encouraging in the growing boy a striving for success (at prep school and Eton) which came to seem the necessary price of her love, and in insisting that he accept her values (though these were more the conventional social values of her generation among the aristocracy than the socially minded Christian ethos espoused by Amy Graves).[34] Grenfell's late adolescence and early adulthood was marked by his battle (which he described as a matter of life or death for him) to free himself from these values, while retaining his mother's love.[35] As it developed, he struggled to understand the double bind in which she placed him: urging him to be open with her, but eliciting guilt by expressing her pain when he disagreed with her and ceased to be the perfectly loving child. This battle was conducted first through their face-to-face arguments, and the (usually) guilt-stricken letters which he subsequently wrote her.[36] The social rules which limited attempts at any emotional or sexual intimacy with women of their own age both intensified young men's need to repress desire and to place these women on a pedestal, and reinforced their mothers' position as chief source of emotional comfort and understanding, to whom they owed everything.[37] Hence in part the intensity of the mother-son bond, and Grenfell's assertion that his struggle to separate from her was his 'fight for life'.[38]

Sometimes by contrast, as with Macfie, the mother was seen as offering values different from, or even antithetical to, those of the father, and hence a resource of the growing boy to draw upon in struggling to define his identity in the face of paternal demands.[39] Another example of this is offered by Brenan's mother. They were alone together for much of his early childhood when his father was serving abroad. In addition, Brenan saw himself as having become the alternative target of her ambitions and energy. 'From the moment that I was old enough to understand, she set herself to pour into me all those impulses towards a deeper and fuller life that she had felt as a girl…No child was ever so charged as I was.'[40] Through this intimate contact and influence in his early childhood, she became the key source of some of the values most central to his adult life, especially his passion for literature, and for foreign countries. She encouraged his reading and love of adventure stories; and intensified the significance for him of his childhood times abroad, building up a 'personal legend' in which Brenan was 'a remarkable child, not for what I was in myself, but because of the impressions that remote countries had made on me. Geography, in the semblance of a God, had selected me, marked me, sealed me.'[41] With their return to her family in Ireland from India when Brenan was six, and then his father's retirement from the army the following year, her central importance in his life gradually diminished.[42]

All these men were brought up in households which included living-in servants. These servants, the great majority of whom were women, fell broadly into two categories—upper servants such as nurses and governesses who dealt directly with the oversight, bodily needs, health and education of the children; and lower servants, accorded fewer privileges, who dealt with more impersonal matters affecting the whole family—such as cooking, cleaning and gardening.[43] Being brought up in such a household had certain effects on the development of male children. The system of child rearing in an upper-middle-class servant-keeping household enforced in the daily life of the infant and child a separation between a distant mother who cared for emotional, moral and religious instruction; and a working-class servant woman who attended to physical needs and functions. Graves's family clearly exemplified this pattern.[44]

Female servants, who were often close to these boys emotionally and played a major part in attending to their physical needs, could come to represent the bodily as both exciting and potentially shameful. Burgeoning sexual curiosity and desire could be directed towards these women who were simultaneously intimate and outside the taboo circle of female purity represented by the mother.[45] As well as providing a focus for emotional intimacy or sexual curiosity, servants could also be a source of knowledge.[46] Their company could offer an escape from the stiff etiquette of an upper-middle-class upbringing. Within the home, much of children's time was spent—often in play—with the servants, who could form a haven for more relaxed behaviour; while they also connected home life with other less rigid alternatives outside.[47] Servants might provide the first encounter with the wider class structure of society in which they were lowly figures. It was often they who first took the child into the extra-familial world outside the house; and in any case, they offered a different window on the world, a source of contact with quite different parts of society from those among whom the parents moved.[48] The servants formed an important element in Graves's growing awareness of class.[49]

Within the household, children occupied an ambiguous position vis-à-vis the servants. Like the servants, they were subject to the authority of the parents. West's account of his father's role exactly fits this pattern: his father, under the overarching authority of the throne, enforced his instructions on children and servants alike, while West himself as a child still had to share the side entrance to the house with the servants. Eventually, though, the children would be expected to succeed to the authority and superior class position of the parents (West would now go in the front door), an authority and position to which the servants would always be subject and subordinate; and so their ties with the servants should fall away.[50] They as the locus of power and civilisation should be clearly differentiated from the powerless and uncivilised.

However, there were other ways in which the ambiguous situation of the growing upper-middle-class child, and the ambivalent identifications it encouraged, might shape the structure of adult identity. Fractures sometimes occurred in the transition to that proffered superior and segregated position. While the children's closest ties ought to have been with their parents and the course they mapped out, emotional intimacy, sexual curiosity and a desire for freedom might build instead a considerable attachment to the world of the servants. Thus a pattern seems sometimes to have developed whereby servants, and later by extension other outside groups which they either belonged to or could represent—such as the working classes and foreigners, came to be seen as a source of both values and opportunities which were denied or excluded in the dominant culture represented and transmitted through the parents.

Growing Up: Schooling, Sexuality and Religion

By the last decades of the nineteenth century, a public-school education was seen by many upper-middle-class families as an essential step in preparing their sons to take their adult place in the world.[51] From the perspective of a particular family, the purpose of sending boys to such a school was both to prepare them for entry into, and success within, the competitive hierarchies of the upper-middle-class career world; and also to confirm or advance the family's status in the next generation through the kudos attached to public-school education.[52] Such education was therefore an investment, a means to the end of occupational and economic status.[53]

Such a schooling offered a induction into the mores and conventions of upper-middle-class life, through its rules and codes and its practice of sport, at least as important as any intellectual training it provided. It also formed an important step in the acquisition of an informal curriculum vitae, as a marker of parental status or (for scholarship boys) personal achievement, as a channel towards further education or career openings, and as a source of contacts and friendships which for many lasted throughout adult life. In addition, it served to inculcate in each new generation of the upper-middle class the political and social attitudes which would fit them to take on a role in public life. Within this overall framework there were many distinctions between schools—of status and specific orientation (religious ethos, career specialisms)—which demanded the exercise of parental choice. For the sons of the upper-middle class, school was the major institutional link between childhood within the family and the demands of adult life. They were separated from parents and family while boarding for at least four years in their mid to late teens. It also became common for boys destined for such schools to attend prep schools first, as preparation both for the entrance exams, and for the way of life they were to encounter.[54] These men all came from families which patronised such prep and then public schools. Graves boarded at prep schools and then Charterhouse, and Macfie at Oundle, while West attended a day school—Highgate.[55]

From the perspective of the wider society, such schools served to prepare pupils for their future roles as workers (especially leaders and functionaries of the existing political, economic and ideological bureaucracies), fathers and citizens.[56] The last two decades of the nineteenth century saw important shifts and developments in the structures of the public school system as they both responded and contributed to shifts in the pattern of hegemonic masculinity. Dominant approaches to such central questions as the propriety of close friendships between masters and boys and between boys of different ages, the forms of emotional expression appropriate to masculinity, the best way to deal with adolescent boys' developing sexuality, and the proper role of games, all underwent substantial changes. Within the school, a more emotionally constrained model of masculinity became dominant, alongside growing fears about the implications of close friendships between boys. Participation in organised games became compulsory, and the arranging of sporting fixtures played an important part in helping to demarcate an elite of schools which recognised one another's claim to public school status.[57]

Like its precursor the family, and its successor communities of career and nation, the school operated through the dynamics of coercion, provision and recognition. Though its coercive powers included corporal punishment and the ultimate sanction of expulsion, the public school system prided itself above all on instilling self-discipline into its pupils, and on reinforcing this with the boys' mutual self-policing in service of house and school. The rewards of recognition lay in the many formal and informal marks of distinction which the different stages of a school career could offer. The public school operated as a form of total institution, achieving its aims in shaping and toughening its boys at least as much through its control of every aspect of daily life as through its formal educational curriculum. It could function as such a total institution because it boarded its pupils for a large part of the year; it was for this reason that it was preferred by the parents who chose it.[58] Cut off from the outside world, which they could only imitate through debating societies or cadet corps, its pupils were increasingly confined to the narrow cohort of their own immediate age-mates.[59] The detailed organisation of time, space, dress and relationships, and the symbolic meanings they carried, were important in socialising boys into the meanings and values the school wished to transmit, and in marking them off from rest of the (extra-school) world. A boy had to learn the (often unwritten) rules governing such organisation in order to negotiate his way successfully through them.[60]

The school itself constituted an elaborate and complex hierarchy.[61] Seen under one aspect, this hierarchy was competitive.[62] There were two main arenas for this competition—academic and sporting success. Until 1914, classics still dominated the curriculum, their position at least as strong as a century earlier, and elaborately defended as a form of mental training, source of values, and essential element in the notion of a gentleman. Increasingly towards the end of the century schools introduced a Modern (or Army) side for those planning a military or colonial career; but these pupils remained a minority. Teaching of maths, science, modern languages and other subjects had less prestige and received fewer resources.[63] Success in school examinations, as a training for university and career entrance exams, was highly regarded by both heads and parents.[64]

The nineteenth century had also seen a massive elaboration of the supposed educative (in the broad sense) and moral role of participation in competitive team sports. In tandem with, and often contributing to, the codification of such sports as rugby and football in society at large, the public schools introduced organised games into their timetable, as a way of controlling boys' time and energies, affording new arenas of co-operation between masters and boys, and fostering collective loyalties.[65] The system of houses within the school introduced a further element of competitive hierarchy. A boy's first loyalty was to his house (whether as academic or especially as sporting unit), his rivals members of other houses.[66] But then the whole school reunited in rivalry with other schools, a rivalry whose symbolic elaborations reinforced identification with its central consensual values.[67] The organising of regular fixtures in the key sports was one of the means by which schools recognised one another as members of the public school system.[68] The leading sportsmen of the school, especially in rugby and cricket, readily became heroes for younger boys who sought to emulate them.[69]

Another aspect of the hierarchy was non-competitive—the strictly delimited age-categories with their carefully graded and gradually more extensive privileges, reinforced symbolically by elaborate codes of dress, stance and freedom of movement.[70] Here, mere survival—not leaving or being expelled—guaranteed progression up the hierarchy whereby a boy could rise from service as a fag to power as a sixth former or prefect. These two aspects reinforced one another: all could achieve a measure of success by surviving and honouring the code; many could compete for different forms of individual success, each carrying varying esteem. The system prepared boys for lives as men in similarly competitive hierarchies: politics, the home and imperial civil services, the armed services or the professions.[71]

Public schools were sustained by, and in turn transmitted, complex webs of interacting and sometimes conflicting ideologies. One strand was provided by the religious impulse which was central to the Arnoldian revolution of the 1840s, and was then transmuted into the ideal of muscular Christianity in the 1850s and 1860s. Though the latter remained a widely proclaimed ideology, J.A. Mangan has suggested that by the 1870s many schools practised something closer to a code of social Darwinism to prepare their pupils for the harsh world they would encounter.[72] The new emphasis on conflict and struggle was accompanied from the 1880s by an increasingly explicit imperialist ideology, which stressed the right and duty of the Englishman to rule and civilise the empire, and put before the boys images of worthwhile sacrifice drawn from both religious and national discourses. Expansion of the cadet corps, and increasing pressure on boys to join, provided the practical link between imperial ideology and the competitive structures of the school routine.[73] The structures of power within the school, especially the rigid hierarchies and the emphasis on loyalty and conformity to the group ethic, prepared the pupils for future leadership.[74] Sport was explicitly valued as a preparation for imperial and military service, and as a source of wider moral values.[75] Such preaching and practice addressed material as well as ideal interests; well into the inter-war years, a public school education and sporting prowess could secure a post in branches of the colonial service.[76]

Entry into first prep and then public school involved the rupturing of ties of dependency which had previously existed between the boy and his family, especially his mother. Mothers' major direct influence on their sons came in infancy and early childhood; after the age of five it was increasingly limited, and boarding was a crucial step in severing links with that mother-dominated domestic world of childhood.[77] Thenceforth, a mother's role was to be confined largely to offering emotional support for her son, and dealing with the school over questions of his welfare.[78] He was now to be cut off from that source of dependence, and compelled to suppress his emotional needs. School replaced parents, for most of the year, as source of authority, provision and recognition.

Success in the competitive hierarchies of the public school was held to demand a process of toughening, of developing ways of coping unflinchingly with emotional pain and stress, which was characteristic of the dominant model of masculinity in the late nineteenth century. 'Learning to endure misery and fear silently without expression was a fundamental aspect of growing up from a boy into a man…If emotions could not be suppressed or "contained"…then they had to be hidden.'[79] The costs which this imposed are powerfully depicted by Leonard Woolf. After his father's death when he was eleven, he was first sent away to prep school for two years and then attended St Paul's as a day boy.[80] Woolf's autobiography describes what he terms the hardening process whereby a boy becomes a man. He links the 'withdrawal' inwards of his self in reaction to his father's death, with that which took place during his adolescent years at the school. He laid particular stress on the construction of a front behind which to shelter his individuality.[81] 'It was the fear of ridicule or disapproval if one revealed one's real thoughts or feelings, and sometimes the fear of revealing one's fears, that prompted one to invent that kind of second-hand version of oneself which might provide for one's original self the safety of a permanent alibi.'[82] Summing up his school days, Woolf wrote:

> This passage from boyhood to manhood is in many respects the most difficult and painful period psychologically of one's life…First, one experiences the iron, ruthless impact of society upon the eager, naked

> tender ego…it was this vulnerable inhabitant of our bodies over which the irresistible steam roller of society pounded in whatever private or public school to which our parents happened to have sent us, flattening us all out in the image of manliness or gentlemanliness which our parents or lords and masters considered appropriate.[83]

In the era of compulsory games, sporting values were held supreme and encouraged a general anti-intellectualism. One common pattern was for boys to be divided between those committed to sporting success, who made heroes of the successful sportsmen and sustained the values of the 'bloods' or 'hearties'; and those (often a minority) whose commitment was to intellectual and aesthetic interests and associated values.[84] Questions of gender identity were centrally implicated in this division. Sporting ability, with its emphasis on physical activity, became for many adolescent boys a touchstone of their developing (robust) masculinity; while the intellectual was often suspect or derided as effeminate.[85] Though Woolf claims that he 'was never bullied and, unlike many of my future friends, was never actively miserable at school'—though a 'swot', his sporting interests and abilities were sufficient to protect him from direct attack—nevertheless he was isolated by, and suffered considerably from, the hostile attitude of his school mates. It was only in his final two years at the school that he met, first a teacher and then some fellow and former pupils, who shared his intellectual interests.[86]

J. de S. Honey discusses the toughening Woolf referred to as a form of initiation process, undergone in two stages—first at prep and then at public school. The growing boy twice entered as a novice, forced to suppress his feelings, and find his way through a bewildering new maze of formal and informal rules, customs and forms of language, before beginning his climb up the hierarchy. 'Fighting his way up through the double cycle of this system, learning to endure pain and to know his place, the boy was tested and re-tested in a process of prolonged and constantly renewed attrition by which a new type of social personality was formed.'[87] Parents were prepared to accept the harsher aspects of the public school regime, in return for their sons developing 'character'—toughness, independence and social self-confidence.[88]

In boys cut off from their families and childhood friends, the hierarchical structure of the school, with its interacting competitive and non-competitive aspects, could give rise to powerful loyalties: to formal elements such as house and school, but also to informal elements such as clusters of boys with a shared stance to school life (bloods, aesthetes) and more intimate groups of friends. This hierarchical structure extended in several dimensions beyond the group of boys in the school in a given year. Within the bounds of the school itself, the head and his masters stood outside the boys' hierarchy, defining, regulating and administering it, separated by age and training. Yet they also offered one representation of what a boy could aspire to become in manhood—many public school boys returned to their own or other schools to teach.[89] The school itself could readily become, and might remain after a boy had left it, what Honey terms an 'object of worship', in some cases despite the hatred which the boy might have felt for it while a pupil there.[90] If a boy's father had been at the same (or a similar) school, then the hierarchy and its loyalties extended back into the past. When a boy left, he might extend them into the future by becoming an Old Boy of his school, thereby maintaining his connection with his co-evals and linking himself with generations who had left and those yet to come.[91] Honey suggests that in this period public schools came to take over, for some, functions previously performed within the upper-middle-class family or its local community.[92] Beyond the confines of a single school, lay the wider public-school system, the extent of whose boundaries was constantly being questioned and re-defined.[93] Like the family, the school was a face-to-face and intimate community towards which loyalties could be generated; but it also provided a primary template for the mechanisms by which such immediate loyalties could be extended towards a variety of imagined communities—the 'Old School' in its trans-generational sense, the public-school community, one's class and nation.[94]

To achieve the toughening into a man which Woolf and others described, a complete separation of the growing boy from the world of women—the company of mother, sisters (if any), and female servants—was believed to be required. Mothers were made into anti-models, with boys 'taught to eschew anything babyish, cissy or womanish'.[95] A boarder inhabited an almost entirely male world. The only female company might be the matron, or the female domestics who took care of the junior boys; otherwise, very few women or girls had access to the school.[96] Moreover, the whole public school system was predicated on the superiority of men over women; Heward refers to the school as 'emphasising the authority of older men and subordination of women', and believing that 'women's influence could endanger men's true purpose'.[97] It was not just women themselves, but what were taken to be 'feminine' values, that were excluded.[98] Such an overwhelmingly homosocial environment encouraged a form of exclusively masculine identity, with regard to both internal and external objects of attachment. Both dependent and burgeoning erotic feelings were split off from women as potential objects, and either directed exclusively towards males, or suppressed; while potential female identifications in the adolescent boy himself were also repressed.[99]

Consequently, public-school boys spent a large part of the year, throughout their adolescent sexual maturing (and even earlier if they attended prep school too), almost exclusively in the company of other males. This affected the development of their sexuality, and the ways they learned to deal with their own emotions, and to relate both to women and to men.[100] As R.W. Connell suggests, the resulting conflicts were structural.

> The patriarchal order prohibits forms of emotion, attachment and pleasure that patriarchal society itself produces. Tensions develop… around the prohibition on homosexual affection (given that patriarchy constantly produces homo-social institutions) and around the threat to social order symbolised by sexual freedoms.[101]

Within this hierarchical, highly regimented and disciplined world, cut off from family and female support in dealing with issues of attachment, boys had either to suppress feelings of dependency, or turn towards other boys, teachers, or more abstractly the institution itself, for affection, sympathy or confirmation of worth. It was not uncommon for a pupil to look to other boys for emotional support; 'pals'—whatever close and sympathetic friends he could make—might play a crucial role in enabling a boy to survive emotionally, and find a way through the pressures imposed both by the school authorities and by his fellow pupils.[102] Masters too, who as figures of authority and as role models formed potential father figures in place of the absent father, could become objects of attachment. The normative model of masculinity demanded that romantic and sexual feelings between boys, and between boys and masters, should be sublimated into friendships, and into loyalty to the institution of the school and its ideals.[103] Sport, above all, was treated as the appropriate vehicle for construction of a manly identity, robustly physical but with any sexual element wholly sublimated.[104]

As well as offering emotional support, fellow pupils could also become partners in sexual explorations; while masters were on occasion sources of sexual exploitation. Anxiety about the control of sexuality in public schools seems to have intensified, and taken new forms, during the later nineteenth century. Honey has shown that official attacks on 'immorality' or 'vice' among the boys, which in the 1840s frequently referred to indiscipline or drunkenness, changed in character so that by the 1860s these terms had taken on increasingly explicit sexual connotations, which by the 1880s had become somewhat obsessive. Masturbation was a particular target for guilt-inducing sermons; and religious exhortation, often linked to preparation for confirmation, was seen as the chief way of preventing it.[105] But concern about 'unsuitable friendships' within schools, meaning those—whether with other boys or with masters—into which a potential or overtly homosexual element entered, seems to have developed rather later. From the 1880s, in the atmosphere of moral panic following the Criminal Law Amendment Act (1885) and the Oscar Wilde case (1895), there was a proliferation of rules and informal codes designed to discourage unsuitable friendships among boys, especially between those of different ages; and these could interfere with them forming attachments which made survival easier.[106] It is not clear how far this anxiety about sexual relations between boys was realistic. Heward summarises recent writers as arguing that 'schools and periods vary widely and that moral and sexual norms in schools could change dramatically'.[107]

In addition to the pressure towards conformity, the treatment of their sexuality is the most pervasive issue in these men's accounts of their school days; though each offers a different narrative emphasis, in accordance with their overall thematic aims. For Graves, Woolf and Brenan, their experience was a combination of overt moral preaching reinforced by religious sanction against sexual expression, coexisting with a covert 'hothouse' homoerotic atmosphere among many of the boys, sometimes involving a master too. They all present themselves as sexually ignorant and prudish, their 'innocence' making them easy targets for the aggressive sexual teasing common among adolescent boys.[108]

In this period, the Christian religion still formed a major component of the ethos and ideologies dominant among the upper-middle class, and a source of real intellectual, moral and religious commitment for many individuals. Furthermore, it was central to the values of the public schools, and inextricably entwined with their ideals of masculinity: imperial rule, public service, chaste sexuality, sporting demeanour, were knitted together in the figure of the Christian gentleman. All these men (except Woolf whose family were non-practising Jews) were brought up as Christians, within families in which religion was taken seriously; and attended schools in which the Christian faith was part of the official system of belief and instruction. Graves and Macfie before the war, and West during it, all came to question and then reject orthodox religion during their late adolescence or early adulthood. So too did Sassoon, Grenfell, Brenan and Sorley before the war; while for Graeme West it seems to have been the war itself which provoked this questioning. The terms of this rejection implied a questioning of authority (they were usually in opposition to a strongly religious parent), and sometimes also an assertion of their burgeoning sexuality.[109]

Some of these men managed their time at public school successfully. Sorley found things to enjoy, both in the curriculum and in the countryside around Marlborough. He was, however, critical of much of the wider public-school ethos, especially the emphasis on competition, the exaggerated importance given to school achievements, and the dangers implicit in the vaunted system of self-policing by senior boys. He expressed these criticisms in letters he wrote explaining his decision to leave Marlborough early.[110] Others, however, reacted much more negatively. Graves, Woolf and Brenan all experienced these schools and their code in very similar ways: determined to enforce conformity through an elaborate network of formal rules and informal conventions; hostile to them and their individuality (especially their intellect); anti-sex while covertly homosexual; and morally bullying. Their response to this was a struggle to develop a public persona which would enable them to survive their schooldays, while preserving some freedom to pursue their own interests. Their time there was made bearable, if no more, by forging close friendships with a few fellow pupils who taught them the ropes, shared a minority or oppositional interest, and by an occasional sympathetic master.[111]

Viewed as a rite of passage into adult masculinity, the years at (preparatory and) public school paralleled the stages of separation, transition and reincorporation, training adolescents to become men able to provision, defend and reproduce their society. In this segregated environment, boys were made into men; their masculine identities were forged in an environment where women were excluded and their sexuality was policed. They were imbued with the avowedly Christian ethos of the public school system, with its intertwined class, national and gender elements which together would shape them into English gentlemen. This ethos fitted them (at this period largely through a generalist cultural formation, rather than specific technical training) to take up their future economic role, enabling them later to found and support a family; and prepared them if necessary to become defenders of empire (both through ideological indoctrination, and increasingly through rudimentary technical preparation in military cadet corps). The resultant masculinity was one in which the elements of labour, power and to a considerable extent desire were closely linked. The work for which public-school boys were ideally fitted was the exercise of authority within a competitive hierarchy where they were strongly bonded both to their fellows and to the institution itself. On leaving school, they would move towards reincorporation by proceeding to university or professional training, or step directly into adult roles as employees.

Leaving Home: University, Career, Moratorium

The period between the end of secondary schooling and the beginning of a career was crucial to the formation of an adult identity, in the spheres of both work and sexuality. It was also a time of potential conflict between the expectations and demands of parents and family, and the developing aspirations of the maturing adolescent. Formal and informal social mechanisms helped to shape the transition from dependent to independent status. Formally, attending university was becoming the norm for this generation of upper-middle-class young men. Informally, they themselves often created groupings of friends bound together by shared ideals and tastes, which helped them to define a self-chosen identity, and formed a bridge between the narrower sphere of family and school, and the wider world beyond. University could be the setting for such a grouping.

After leaving school, the upper-middle-class young man was expected (unless he enjoyed sufficient private wealth, as did Sassoon) to select, and establish himself in, an appropriate career and to secure economic independence, before embarking on marriage. The father's influence and the family's traditions powerfully shaped this development, from the choice and financing of preparatory and public school to the provision of a range of contacts in the proposed career. To achieve success in these careers required not only the academic ability and training to pass examinations, but also the drive and ambition, the 'character', to rise through the hierarchy.[112] For this reason, many upper-middle-class parents preferred public schools, with their emphasis on building character, to grammar schools or mere crammers which concentrated entirely on success in examinations.[113]

Steering sons through this transition from family via schooling to career and independent manhood was a long-term process, and one open to conflict between the intentions and plans of parents, especially fathers, and the gradually clarifying wishes and aspirations of sons. For parents, schooling was both a financial and a social investment, designed to achieve concrete goals. Heward has analysed the intentions of parents who sent their boys to Ellesmere:

> Bringing up their sons was about social class and gender and their interrelationship. In order to maintain or possibly improve their family's social position they had to ensure their sons were, above all, capable providers, prepared for occupations and careers, 'able to earn a good living'...Manliness was first and foremost about being a good breadwinner, having a high, secure income from a respected occupation, preferably professional.[114]

This desirable outcome was seen, Heward argues, as requiring careful strategy. 'For all these parents men were made not born. The parents' task was to decide on their goal and to bring up their sons and educate them in a way that would ensure they achieved that model. Bringing up sons was an important family enterprise to which a significant part of the family's energies and resources was devoted.'[115]

These strategies were executed along gendered lines. Fathers were the directors of the process: authority figures, in determining the educational course to be taken; career models, often literally so if they expected or demanded that their sons follow them; and economic providers—'a role essential to their own and their sons' understanding of their masculinity.'[116] The role of mothers (unless they became widowed) was to be their husbands' supportive partners.[117] Father-son relations could be distant and ambivalent.[118] Sons could hope to follow their fathers, while also striving to outdo them. 'The domination of sons by fathers...presaged their own future position, enabling them to accept the more problematic aspects of their relations with their fathers.'[119] However, where a father's wishes were forced upon a son unwilling to follow the path intended for him, severe conflict could follow, as can be seen in the cases of West and Brenan.[120]

Before 1914, career patterns were less rigidly defined than later, so that for instance the number of professions for which a university degree was a prerequisite was much smaller. But it was becoming increasingly common for those who had passed through public schools to go on to university, especially if they aspired to a position in politics or administration without a substantial family position or patronage behind them. Graves, Alick West and Macfie all attended university, as did Rivers, Woolf, Chavasse, Sassoon, Grenfell and Graeme West. Sorley was due to do so; Brenan's mother had hoped he could follow the university route to an army commission, but his father rejected this as unnecessary.[121]

These early adult years, the time of leaving the supervised existence of home and boarding school for the more independent world of university and early career steps, can be seen as forming a crucible in which elements of the developing individual fused together to form a relatively enduring adult personality. At the same time, precisely because for the first time the individual was free from the supervision of childhood and adolescence and capable economically of making his own way in the world, it was a moment when a realistic challenge could be offered to the goals and plans laid down for him by his family, and the values they enshrined. At times, this search for an independent identity led these men to a direct challenge to parental and social norms, involving a repudiation of inherited values, a flight from the direction planned for them, and a search for a source of alternative values. Erik Erikson's concept of a late adolescent moratorium—understood here to refer to the uses these men made of opportunities they created or encountered (rather than a space offered to them by their society)—is valuable in understanding these experiences.[122]

Early adult life, then, offered opportunities both for the development and consolidation of, and a challenge to and reworking of, the pattern of expectations laid down for the growing boy by his family and wider social institutions. In addition, the particular historical conjuncture when adulthood was reached was also important in determining the opportunities open to these men, and the decisions they made. Various combinations of consolidation and challenge can be found in their early adult lives. Of those who entered adulthood before the war, some made or attempted their first rupture with their upbringing at university and in the sphere of values—Macfie at Cambridge in the late 1880s and Grenfell at Oxford in the late 1900s. Macfie's successful rejection of the Christianity in which he had been brought up was followed by dramatic but temporary attempts to flee the career in the family firm on which he had embarked after university; eventually, he developed a way of occupying that role while making space for his own passions.[123]

During his third year at Oxford, in spring 1909, Grenfell generalised his insights into the pressure to conform, exercised on the emerging adult by his family and society, in a manuscript book of essays. In this he critiqued what he termed conventionalism, whose central tenet was that every man should think and do as others did. In particular, he singled out the demands for both competitiveness and self-sacrifice, which he argued were contradictory save insofar as, together, they were weapons to make men conform. Competitiveness for social position fostered adaptation to conventional rules; while the call for self-sacrifice and duty was a plea for social convention against individual reason.[124] This was Grenfell's major effort to separate himself from the values in which he was brought up ('conventionality envelops [the future man] like a pall, thrown over him by his parents and his relations'), and to assert instead the need for individual self-realisation.[125] The members of his family and his friends responded with mockery, humorous 'chaffing' and (between themselves) hostility.[126] Grenfell's text had already anticipated this response, noting that only a few escape convention, who 'spend their lives in one long battle for their own independence, through misery often and through pain. Everybody thinks that they are mad, and they are of course conscious of this, and it drives them to further extremes.'[127]

This hostility helped pitch Grenfell, some months later, into a depression with suicidal undertones.[128] Thereafter, he seems to have abandoned his all-out struggle for an independent life. He wrote to a young woman to whom he was then emotionally attached (and who herself had a thwarted wish to be an artist) that he had proposed to God 'a bargain—that I should become the perfect "heygate" [family code for "conventional"] on condition of being returned to health and vigour', adding the coda: 'Be careful not to miss the pathos of this letter.'[129] He now fell in with the family assumption that he would join the army, his only resistant effort being to ensure he would be posted abroad.[130] Apart from a few months leave, he served in India and then South Africa from autumn 1910 till the outbreak of the war. His attitude oscillated: at times (especially in India) he embraced the officers' life of riding, hunting and flirting; at others, he advanced plans to leave the army. His mother opposed this, to the extent of misrepresenting his attitude to potential patrons of an alternative career.[131] When, on home leave in 1912, he mentioned the possibility of training as an artist, family mockery again defeated him.[132] On the eve of war, he was still considering plans to leave military service.[133]

The next generation were prevented from proceeding straight from school to university or career by the outbreak of the war. Of these, Brenan alone had fiercely defied parental expectations before the war intervened. In his later years at school, he had begun to reject the values of his family and school (especially religion), and to cultivate a love of literature, and of nature mediated through literary writers.[134] In his efforts to separate himself from familial values, and consolidate his own identity, he made use of his desire to travel to remote foreign countries. This desire had its roots in his early life: the family had lived in India and South Africa because of his father's army career.[135] The subsequent casting of his foreign experiences into story form, helped by his reading of the Bible and travel literature, and in intimate co-operation with his mother, made them an integral part of the young Brenan's identity.[136] During his school years, he developed a passion for making maps and planning journeys around the world, strengthened by further reading.[137] Two cycling holidays in France at the ages of seventeen and eighteen in 1911–12, and a chance meeting with an ambulant knife grinder which suggested a way of making his living, confirmed his resolution. This growing sense of independence was linked to a first affirmation of his sexual desire, for a chambermaid at his hotel.[138]

Brenan's own interests were increasingly moving in an idealistic and literary direction. He desired emancipation from material possessions, and consequently a nomadic life, the ups and downs of which would, he believed, give rise to the moments of inspiration and ecstasy which were needed for the writing of poetry. Linked with this was a belief, derived from religious reading, that poverty was in itself a blessed thing.[139] The potential conflict between these new values which he was working out for himself, and his parents and their values, came to a head over the issue of the career for which his education had destined him. His father wished him to enter the army; this fitted the family tradition ('four generations of my paternal ancestors, by taking the Queen's commission, had decided this for me'); his mother supported this decision. Brenan's efforts, and those of his form master, to suggest that he was not cut out for an army career met with abrupt rebuff: 'they had fixed long before on the pattern I must conform to'.[140] Faced with this future, Brenan sought to find his own destiny abroad; by doing so, he could in a sense return to an identity which had already been formed and nourished in childhood, one in which his mother was an ally of his rather than an accomplice of his father.

In turning these dreams into a reality, a key role was played a recent acquaintance, John Hope Johnstone, a bohemian traveller and writer who had come to live nearby. They shared various interests—in poetry, Oriental languages and religion, and the taking of herbs and drugs; and Johnstone, eleven years older than Brenan, became a mentor.[141] With entry to Sandhurst imminent, Brenan now outlined a plan to run away from home, walk across Europe to the Pamir Mountains in Central Asia, and there settle among the nomadic peoples and live a life of voluntary poverty. He invited Johnstone to join him, and his friend accepted.[142] Disguised as a gas fitter, Brenan managed to get away from home, and meet up with Johnstone in Paris. During the autumn and winter of 1912, they travelled together on foot as far as Fiume on the Adriatic, and then Brenan pressed on alone through the Balkans. After reaching Montenegro, poverty and bitter weather forced him to turn back, and eventually to return home.[143] His father had not altered his view of Gerald's proper future; accepting his son's rejection of the army, and reviewing the other available options, he offered him the choice of the Indian or Egyptian Police. Swallowing his own current wish to become an art blacksmith, Brenan opted for the former, since it required him to study French and German.[144] He spent the next eighteen months, until summer 1914, preparing for the examinations (including a lengthy stay in Germany), while still entertaining continual dreams of escape to far-away lands.[145]

For both Graves and West, it was their wartime experiences which proved crucial in fuelling an effort to escape. Graves gives no indication that his parents had a specific career in mind for him, though it is clear that they intended his public-school education to lead on to the sort of career his brothers followed. What he does record, within a sardonic dialogue with a friend on the day they left school in summer 1914, is the sense of a narrowly ordained educational route with automatic progression to university, from which—despite thought of seeking one—there is apparently no escape. West records no signs of youthful rebellion. By his own account previously largely conformist to the values his father represented, the radical shift in attitudes he underwent during the war led to a struggle with his father over career choice once his delayed education was resumed in 1918.[146]

Several of these men were unable to accept the choice of career which their families' (and especially their fathers') wishes had prepared for them, and which their schooling had prepared them for. Instead, there was a moment of challenge to the pattern laid down for them. When the son resisted or rebelled against the future mapped out for him, this resistance could extend to opposing the role for which he was destined as well as the father who sought to determine that destiny. For some of these men, this challenge took the form of a literal withdrawal, a move abroad to escape the demands of an upper-middle-class British identity, and to find the space in which to forge a different identity felt to be their own. Brenan offers a straightforward exemplification of a refusal of parental direction, leading to flight abroad to seek new values and opportunities. Macfie in his early twenties rejected his family religion, and then twice attempted to escape both his destiny in the family firm and his wider class position. West can be understood as turning a period of involuntary exile (wartime internment) into an experience of moratorium.[147] Graves, by contrast, embarked on an early marriage and acceptable career, only to break from family and country in his thirties.

What is also crucial to note about such rebellion is that it can never be simply a sloughing off of inheritance. Often, at the level of behaviour and values derived immediately from parents or parental figures, there is a process of sifting and recombining: Brenan reanimating a part of his mother's personality which she had tried to repress in herself and in him, or West seeking to inhabit his father's craftsmanship and sense of purpose. The periods which I have read as moratoria represent particularly intense and charged phases of this inner conflict.[148] In initiating and carrying through such a rebellion, the influence of a close friend or group of friends was often crucial. Whereas during school years, the help of friends was mostly channelled into mutual survival of a hostile system, in early adult life such help was used in the search for a separate identity.

3

The First World War: Structures, Experiences and Responses

The Conditions of Warfare

Societies educate boys to become men with the expectation that, among other tasks, they may be required to defend their society at risk to their own individual lives. In the modern nations which emerged in western and central Europe from the sixteenth centuries, as the state increasingly sought to monopolise control of the legitimate exercise of (internal and external) violence, such an obligation became formalised. Following the profound impact of the French Revolutionary armies, with their *levées en masse* which mobilised unprecedented numbers of citizens into an all-conquering force, most continental European nations opted for regular conscription. Each age cohort of young men, as they entered adulthood, underwent a compulsory period of full-time military service. Once this was completed, they formed a trained reserve who were then required to undertake short periods of refresher training at intervals until they passed the age for active service. Only in this way, it was believed, was it possible for an army of sufficient size and proficiency to be raised in defence of the nation. Such compulsory enlistment was seen both as a component of citizenship, offering recognition in return for service, and (especially in newly unified or emergent nations) as a school for turning 'peasants into Frenchmen'.[1]

Britain, alone among the major European powers, did not follow this pattern. The reason lay primarily in political geography. Britain was concerned above all to defend its far-flung Empire, and the sea lanes which connected that Empire with the motherland, and along which the growing body of import and export trade flowed. Protected by the English Channel, it had no need for a large army to defend against land attack by a neighbour. Its armed forces were configured accordingly. Pride of place was given to the Navy. The Army, intended primarily for garrison duty in the Empire to keep internal order and protect against external threats or incursions, was small and professional. An officer corps drawn primarily from a traditional landed and gentry background commanded NCOs and men recruited mostly from the urban poor.[2] In the event of any major European conflict, British policy maintained its traditional aim of preventing the emergence of a single, dominant continental power; while expecting to achieve this through a combination of naval blockade, financial support for allies, and at most the contribution of a small expeditionary land force. Indeed, it was with this configuration and these expectations that Britain entered war in 1914.[3]

These two factors—the absence of conscription, and the tradition of a small standing army fighting distant colonial wars—contributed to the specific shock which the First World War caused. Following the overwhelming German triumph in the Franco-Prussian War of 1870, which demonstrated the power of a well-trained and well-led conscript army supported by a growing industrial economy, concerns about a continental threat began to grow in some political circles. This was reflected at the turn of the century in a popular literature which—sometimes explicitly—referred to fears of a German invasion.[4] The poor performance of the British Army against the Boers in the South African (Boer) War (1899–1902) raised anxieties both about the future defence of Empire, and about the implications for Britain's involvement in any future European conflict. These anxieties led to a restructuring of British reserve forces in the 1900s, with the existing Yeomanry and Volunteers being replaced by the new Territorials, and the Militia by the Special Reserve.[5] One further consequence was the development of political campaigns, supported by pressure groups, to introduce conscription in Britain.[6] Although these campaigns made little headway in shifting public policy before 1914, one arena in which they elicited a practical response was the public schools. Here, the development of the Officers' Training Corps (OTC), launched by Haldane in 1908, nominally voluntary but often effectively compulsory, provided initial military training which could then be extended at university. Edward Spiers notes that '[their] appeal had flourished in the wake of the Boer War and on account of the general anxiety about Britain's relative standing in the international arena. New corps were formed, more boys enlisted in them, and a surge of keenness was evident in the field days and annual camps.'[7]

On the outbreak of war in 1914, this development proved highly effective.[8] Very large numbers of young men who were just leaving or had recently left public school applied for and were granted commissions in the regular army—among them Robert Graves and Charles Sorley.[9] They paid a very heavy price.[10] In a class society, the long-term advantages of relative wealth and comfort usually ensure that those in the more privileged social classes (enjoying better diet, healthier living and working conditions, access to superior health care) on average live longer and healthier lives.[11] The First World War temporarily, for a specific cohort of young men, reversed that pattern. Of 247,061 British officers who served, 37,484 (15.2 per cent) were killed; whereas of 4,968,101 other ranks, 635,891 (12.8 per cent) died. Officers had an almost one-in-six chance of being killed, one-in-three of being wounded.[12]

The reasons for this are well known. Mechanisation of defence had preceded that of attack: the machine gun and barbed wire were perfected before the tank's usefulness had been thought of. Moreover, command and control of huge bodies of men advancing from the front line, and the co-ordination of artillery and infantry in attack, was extremely difficult. Since the Germans had seized and still held considerable Belgian and French territory in their initial invasion in 1914, the Allies including Britain felt obliged to try to recapture it and drive the invader out. The result, on the Western Front, was an infantry war fought from trenches in which (German) defence held a considerable advantage over (Allied) attack. Until radical advances in shell and machine-gun production, artillery targeting, the use of tanks, artillery infantry and ground-air co-ordination, and command procedures altered this balance by 1918, generals drew upon ever larger masses of men as the prime *matériel* for attack in this 'semi-industrialised' warfare.[13] Verdun, with its one million casualties on both sides, initiating the metaphor of 'bleeding the enemy dry', and acquiring nickname of the 'meat-grinder', was the *reductio ad absurdum* of such warfare.[14]

Junior Officers: Conflicts of Role

A cohort of British young men, including several literary figures, were virtually catapulted from adolescence into adulthood by the onset of the war. The impact of the First World War profoundly affected their experience of, and attitude towards, British society and the British state—whatever their role during the war itself. The character of the war as it unfolded placed exceptional strain on the mechanisms whereby upper-middle-class men were socialised to be, among other things, defenders of the nation. The range of responses from different groups within the army comprised forms of adaptation to or refusal of the new conditions. Especially important here are those of officers fighting in the front line, as well as of army doctors dealing with the physical and mental casualties of that service. These responses in turn illuminate the structure and functioning of mechanisms of class and gender which remained largely concealed in more normal times.

The initial success of those socialisation mechanisms is shown by the fact that, at the outbreak of war in August 1914, Graves and Brenan—despite their earlier intended or attempted breach with the paths mapped out for them—volunteered for the army to meet the national emergency.[15] So too did Sassoon and Sorley, as did Graeme West a few months later.[16] Graves, Sassoon and Brenan fought during the war on the Western Front, being wounded and receiving commendations for bravery.[17] Sorley and Graeme West were killed. Yet their wartime experiences tested to breaking-point important elements of their received national identities and loyalties. The experiences which Graves, Sassoon and Graeme West (among many others) underwent, and the manner in which they recorded them, help to lay bare the ways in which such men had been positioned as loyal and patriotic British subjects.

For most of those who served as army officers, the war called upon their previous class training, typically the loyalty to the values and practices of immediate and wider reference groups (team spirit), and the capacity to suppress emotion (manliness), inculcated in public school. As Spiers notes, the army had always valued such schools as much for their moulding of character as for any specifically military training. Within the landed and gentry communities from which the officer class continued to be significantly recruited, 'an uncomplicated patriotism and sense of duty flourished alongside an unbridled enthusiasm for field sports. These instincts and aptitudes seemed all too relevant for a pre-technological army. By offering abundant opportunities for sporting and social enjoyment, regiments sustained their appeal for the sons of county families.' Within the army, the regiment was the traditional source of identity and focus of loyalty, and hence a natural successor to the school. Officers led a controlled life, centred on the mess with its strict rules as the main site of socialisation and the regulation of conduct, and on regimental tradition.[18]

Just as their behaviour among themselves was shaped by their class training, so too was their relationship to the men they commanded. The British army was no less strongly structured by class than the society it sprang from. As Jay Winter and others have indicated, working-class men in civilian life knew untimely death, as well as hard labour, long hours, subsistence wages. This helps to explain how they could cope with the discipline, danger, monotony and drudgery of army life. Especially for those drawn from the traditional recruitment levels of the unskilled working class, their food and clothing in the army were better, and their accommodation away from the front often no worse, than they were accustomed to.[19] The gap, of both experience and current circumstances, separating them from their officers was profound.[20]

This is not to say that it was completely unbridgeable. 'In attempting to realize his role, many a young officer drew on ancient concepts of paternalism and almost forgotten habits of deference.'[21] British society around 1900 retained significant ideologies of paternalism, of duties and responsibilities owed by those with privilege to those without. The exercise of paternalism could occur in the traditional setting of rural areas, or take the newer form of urban paternalism with the factory owner or civic worthy taking the role of the village squire or landlord.[22] A still newer form, attempting to adapt paternalism to the less favourable setting of the large impersonal city, were the university settlements, sometimes religiously inspired, which enabled young students and recent graduates with a social conscience to live and work in working-class districts. Charles Sorley had considered such social work as an alternative to going to university; and both Macfie and Chavasse undertook voluntary work with working-class boys.[23] Gary Sheffield claims that 'by 1914 virtually all Regular officers were thoroughly paternalistic. The core of the officer's creed was…the belief that privilege entailed responsibility for the well being of their men.' The character of this paternalism is vividly conveyed by a pair of paintings displayed together in the Officers' Mess at Sandhurst. 'The first depicts a squire and groom standing beside a horse.

The squire is saying "Well, Jim, has he fed all right?" The second shows a group of soldiers sitting round a campfire. An officer is asking "Dinners all right, men?"' They share the same caption: *Noblesse oblige*.[24] This peace-time paternalism was combined with a strongly hierarchical structure, and distant relations with men. The Territorials, which as a part-time amateur force had a greater social mix and difficulties in enforcing rigid discipline, had an easier relationship between officers and men. Sheffield suggests that the war brought a pattern of officer-men relations closer to the Territorial pattern, while retaining the paternalism of the Regulars.[25]

Some officers had few expectations of their men, looking upon them with enormous condescension as 'like children', 'definitely inferior beings', and having little if any concern to connect with them. Others resented the barrier between them, and looked for opportunities to cross it.[26] Sheffield notes that a theme of many wartime officers' diaries, letters and memoirs is 'devotion, even love, for their men. Faced with similar conditions, '[m]any officers came to see their men as partners in adversity'.[27] Such care took the form both of what he terms 'institutionalised paternalism' (the many returns which the army required to be made about the men's health, clothing and other conditions); and of a high level of individual paternal care. A few even risked their careers to try to protect their men against hopeless demands; more took what steps they could at a very local level to protect them from the rigours of the disciplinary code.[28]

Paul Fussell has emphasised the homoerotic, though nearly always sublimated, bonds of affection which could develop between officers and men at the front. He suggests they represented a transfer of an earlier emotional pattern, 'like the "idealistic", passionate but non-physical "crushes" which most of the officers had experienced at public school.' They could be inspired by good looks, innocence, vulnerability and charm. 'The object was mutual affection, protection, and admiration. In war as at school, such passions were antidotes against loneliness and terror.'[29] Sometimes the affection would be concentrated on a particular individual, sometimes generalised to whole groups of men. 'Although the usual course of protective affection was from superior to subordinate, sometimes the direction was reversed, with men developing hero-worshipping crushes on their young officers.'[30] In later remembrance, these men (even when they were dead Germans) were often recalled as blond, after the romantic Galahad model which was part of Rupert Brooke's attraction.[31] Fussell has traced the poetic traditions and tropes which allowed such young men—boys or lads, as they were often referred to—to represent (in a mode of ruptured pastoral) the destruction of humanity by war. Of one particular set piece, the scene of watching one's own men bathing, he writes: 'The quasi-erotic and the pathetic conjoin in these scenes to emphasise the stark contrast between beautiful frail flesh and the alien metal that waits to violate it.'[32] Many of the middle-class volunteers considered in this book formed such strong attachments: generalised into self-sacrificial service for their men with Chavasse and Macfie, but taking the form also of intense friendships with individual fellow officers for Sassoon and Graves.[33]

Eric Leed lays emphasis on a different element of the officer-soldier dynamic. He stresses that their bond at the front was inextricable from their both being under the compulsion of technology and authority. It was a function of 'military subordination that—in the best of circumstances—acquired a moral and ethical force, and...of the common subjection of both men and officers to the overwhelming power of fire.'[34] The conditions of trench warfare, as they evolved during 1914–15, profoundly challenged the ideal image which the line officer had been offered of himself and his role; and thereby induced crises of identity. The challenge was partly directed at the officer's social class role. Large-scale, bureaucratically organised trench warfare brought about deskilling, as Martin Stone has stressed; the task of the line officer now was simply to give (i.e. pass on) orders from above.[35] Leed refers to this process as a form of proletarianisation of such junior officers. The profound 'disillusionment' so characteristic of much First World War literature he sees as especially the response of the ardent upper-middle-class volunteer, who had hoped to find in war freedom from the constraints of modern society, and scope for individual initiative, but who instead was reduced to the role of a military 'foreman'.[36]

Another potentially disturbing aspect of front-line service was the necessity to kill. It required from many a radical reversal of the inhibitions on individual violence on which contemporary civilisation was built. For someone like Grenfell, a regular soldier brought up in the hunting and shooting ethos of country sports, there was no such shift. Before the war, he had written poems in celebration of hunting as an experience in which man felt most alive.[37] In the early months of the war, he continued to view his experiences through this frame. 'It is all *the* best fun. I have never never felt so well, or so happy, or enjoyed anything so much...The fighting excitement vitalises everything, every sight and word and action. One loves one's fellow man so much more when one is bent on killing him.' It was in this spirit that he went 'hunting' Pomeranians.[38] By early 1915, his experiences under artillery bombardment provoked a different perception, about his fellow soldiers and himself: man as victim rather than hunter.[39] Nevertheless, his love of battle persisted; and in April 1915 he wrote his famous poem 'Into Battle' which again celebrated fighting as central to life.[40] For the volunteers, however, the requirement to kill—army instructions to a platoon commander placed 'Being blood-thirsty, and for ever thinking how to kill the enemy' on a par with 'Looking after his men's comfort before his own'—might be more troubling.[41] Recent research has laid more emphasis on (some) soldiers' readiness, even eagerness, to kill; but Joanna Bourke also cites work suggesting that many men in wartime avoid shooting at the enemy, and that armies are aware of this.[42]

The new conditions of warfare also threatened the officer's military aggressive (masculine) identity. The static nature of trench warfare, by immobilising troops in a prolonged situation of great fear, deprived them of that activity (motility, to use a psycho-physiological term) which is a way of mastering and defusing anxiety.[43] Military training was designed to reinforce the general repression of the expression of fear among men, established in peace time, so as to meet the specific conditions of wartime.[44] Yet the unprecedented demands of a mass manpower, semi-industrialised, static war worked to break down the effectiveness of that training, and to undermine some of its core values.[45]

As the war and the accompanying slaughter dragged on, wider forms of imagined community, such as the nation, became less prominent as repositories for loyalty. There was a regression of focus, even from the regiment and the battalion, towards the immediate face-to-face collectivity (such as the company or platoon) which lived and fought together in such proximity. The line officer could see his duty as being to the men immediately under his command, whose conditions he could strive to alleviate, and whose safety he would protect as best he could—as much from those back at base as from the enemy.[46] It was the increasing slaughter among these face-to-face groups from the Battle of the Somme (July 1916) onwards, and hence the continual rupturing of newly formed bonds, which began to erode in turn the strength of this new locus of morale.[47]

I want to suggest that the experience of the trenches on the Western Front—especially for volunteer junior officers, as opposed to regulars or conscripts—displayed some of the aspects of liminality, in a highly contradictory (and hence potentially explosive) combination with a heightening of social structure. On the one hand, there was a intensifying of hierarchy and rigidifying of norms through the command structure and mess culture of the regiment. On the other, among the junior officers themselves, and to a degree in their relations to their men, there were some elements from Victor Turner's characterisation of communitas within millennial religious movements: 'the wearing of uniform apparel, sexual continence... [s]uspension of kinship rights and obligations (all are siblings or comrades of one another regardless of previous secular ties)...acceptance of pain and suffering (even to the point of undergoing martyrdom)'.[48] Another element of the liminal stage in formal rituals which Turner identified was the use of monstrous forms. 'Elements are withdrawn from their usual settings and combined with one another in a totally unique configuration, the monster or dragon. Monsters startle neophytes into thinking about objects, persons, relationships, and features of their environment they have hitherto taken for granted.'[49] The Western Front, and especially the trenches, were full of monstrous forms. The shattered, fragmented body parts which the literature repeatedly presents the soldier as stumbling over, walking on, being greeted by, could be experienced as such a unique configuration, which might startle a neophyte into thinking about what they had hitherto taken for granted.

For a line officer in such circumstances, various responses were available. One could passively hope for a 'blighty'; or actively try to wangle a safe job back at base, in a training camp, or behind a desk in England. Among those for whom such modes of escape were unavailable or unacceptable, and yet for whom direct protest seemed impossible, one outcome was the phenomenon initially described as 'shell shock': the inability—expressed in a mixture of physical and mental forms—to continue obeying orders, or functioning as a soldier.[50] Though shell-shock cases first appeared before the end of 1914, the numbers of shell-shock victims increased substantially during the Battle of the Somme from July 1916.[51] Shell shock posed a considerable problem of discipline for the army when it first appeared. Many officers, and some doctors, refused to accept it as anything other than a shirking of duty resulting from cowardice; but soon the sheer numbers of shell-shock sufferers made it seem preferable to deal with them as individuals with symptoms requiring medical treatment, rather than as possible cases of mutiny to be treated judicially. Though a medical diagnosis of and explanation for 'shell shock' behaviour remained unacceptable to many in the army (including medics) throughout, during the later years of the war official policy had grudgingly accepted such a classification.[52]

Among officers and men deemed to be suffering from shell shock (or related or alternative diagnoses), patterns of both diagnosis and treatment were shaped by class perceptions.[53] In the line, officers were more considerate with each other than with their men when responding to apparent signs of shell shock.[54] This pattern was repeated in the differential diagnoses offered by doctors behind the lines or at hospitals in Britain. These reflected the class-divided medical practices of the pre-war period.[55] Other ranks were always investigated for supposedly pathogenic prior circumstances (instances of madness in the family, or of drunkenness). They were often diagnosed as hysterical, and still suspected of malingering.[56] Officers, by contrast, were almost never diagnosed as hysterical. Symptoms which in other ranks would have been described thus were redescribed as 'cloudiness of mind', 'exhaustion' or neurasthenia. Officers' problems were attributed to the pressures of their role; and doctors almost never looked for evidence of a hereditary taint.[57]

Consequently, the neat contrast between men typically suffering from grossly 'physical' symptoms such as temporary paralysis, and officers suffering from 'psychological' symptoms such as depression and anxiety—originally reported by wartime medics, and subsequently repeated by historians may be, at least partially, an artefact of these class-bound diagnostic procedures.[58] This does not invalidate the analyses such doctors offered of the causes of officers' war neuroses, but it does undermine the crude distinction between their experiences and those of their men.[59] According to Peter Barham, there were plenty of examples of ordinary soldiers just as regretful of their 'failures' or breakdowns as were their officers.[60] Officers were disproportionately represented among shell-shock sufferers: though there was one officer to every thirty other ranks at the front, there was one to every five treated for shell shock.[61] These casualties were concentrated among the ranks of junior officers, who because of their role as leaders in the field were responsible to those above them as well as below.[62]

Once diagnosed, shell-shocked officers and men were also treated separately.[63] The men were (usually) placed in non-specialist wards of General War Hospitals. They were treated by an eclectic mixture of remedies: physical therapy (including hydrotherapy and mild electric shock), suggestion (including 're-educational' pressure or persuasion to resume duty), and (occasionally) psychological treatment.[64] Officers were sent to specialist hospitals, at first private, then state run.[65] Here, they were usually offered rest and recuperation, re-socialising activities (sports, gardening), and psychological help.[66]

Elaine Showalter emphasised the gendered dimension of shell shock, describing it as a form of male hysteria. In the trenches, fear expressed itself through the body: men flinched, ducked and trembled like mere women.[67] Yet they were compelled by the codes of masculinity to suppress this fear, to maintain a stiff upper lip. In addition, army discipline demanded that they give no direct expression to their often immense hostility against those directing them, their senior officers and the General Staff. Where in peacetime oppressed, powerless, silenced women could articulate their protest against the intolerable only through the indirect language of symptoms, in wartime men too had perforce to communicate in this way.[68]

A crucial contemporary figure in elucidating the working of the traditional social mechanisms underlying army morale, their modification in the new conditions of the trenches, and their disruption in cases of shell shock, was the Cambridge physiologist, anthropologist, and wartime medic W.H.R. Rivers.[69] Rivers, with his development of a modified Freudian theory and therapy which he put into practice at Craiglockhart Hospital near Edinburgh, represented the most liberal element of the army medical service's response. He argued that the typical officer victim of shell shock, far from being a coward or malingerer, was over-conscientious.[70] It was the effort to live up to his sense of duty, including the need to care for the welfare of others and to show no fear, in a constantly life-threatening situation, which led to the disabling impact of what Rivers defined as anxiety neurosis.[71] Rivers, and Craiglockhart Hospital as a key site of intersection between three of the leading literary figures of the war

(Graves, Sassoon, Owen), have become the focus of considerable scholarly and literary attention.[72] His role and actions and their meaning will be considered again below in Chapters 4 and 7.

Divergent Responses: Noel Chavasse and Siegfried Sassoon

The structural situation of the junior officer, and its potential for role conflict, produced a wide range of responses. Here I will contrast two strikingly different examples: Noel Chavasse, a military doctor in the Liverpool Scottish; and Siegfried Sassoon, a junior officer in the Royal Welch Fusiliers.

Chavasse's life history represents almost an ideal type of the model of individual class reproduction set out in Chapters 1 and 2. He was born in 1884, the son of Francis Chavasse, an Evangelical clergyman and later Anglican Bishop of Liverpool (1900–23). His father was a strong-willed man of powerful and publicly articulated views, of whom Chavasse's biographer, Ann Clayton, comments: 'He was always utterly convinced that his views were the right ones, and that he was given the strength and eloquence to persuade others to his way of thinking by a God who could likewise never make a mistake.'[73] Chavasse was brought up within a powerful family ethos, with strong beliefs in particular Evangelical concerns such as Sunday observance and temperance, as well as a sense of responsibility for helping those less fortunate than themselves. '[L]ike his brothers and sisters, Noel acquired the strongest possible belief in and commitment to the family, and the beginnings of an earnest and unwavering patriotism'.[74] He accepted completely the interlinking of class, religion and nation, together with the ethic of service, and a respect for sporting prowess which later helped in the practical exercise of his social concern. He scarcely modified the strict Evangelical moral code in which he was brought up: a little on the subject of drink, but not at all about sex or Sabbatarianism.[75]

He was educated at public day school in Oxford, and then at grammar school in Liverpool where he took a leading part in sports including rugby and athletics. Here, in 1903, he became involved, at a Industrial School in Toxteth, with the welfare of local boys living in poverty and poor conditions. He drew on the full range of his interests, leading bible-reading sessions and sing songs, organising sports and taking the boys to summer camps.[76] Deciding to become a doctor, he studied medicine at Oxford (1905–9), where he also excelled at sport, representing Britain at the 1908 Olympic Games. In 1907, he read about and was deeply impressed by the life of General Gordon, a strongly committed (if idiosyncratic) Christian, with a powerful sense of duty (expressed both in his military career in the Empire, and his philanthropic work with poor boys) combined with disregard for his own comfort and even safety. Clayton comments:

> Gordon became Noel's hero thereafter, for he had not only been a great general, he had also applied a passionate zeal to his work among destitute boys in England. Noel's letters from 1907 onwards frequently reiterated the theme of duty, the keynote of his admonitions to deprived boys as well as to the men under his command in war.[77]

At the same time, he continued his work with the Industrial School during the summer holidays.[78] He also took a wider interest in social questions, attending meetings addressed by the socialist leaders Keir Hardie and George Lansbury.[79] In May 1907, impressed by the Oxford Bermondsey Mission which worked to raise money and resources for the children of that district, he wondered whether he should arrange to do a hospital placement there.[80] Another aspect of his sense of duty prompted his decision to join the University OTC in 1909. He wrote to his mother: 'I don't like the thought one little bit, except that I think it will be a good discipline and help to make a man of me (as the Industrial boys say)'; and a week later: 'I feel very virtuous being a Territorial as I feel that at last I am really doing my duty and am not a mere "flannelled fool" or "muddied oaf".'[81]

He completed his medical training at Liverpool University (1909–12), and then secured a placement at the Liverpool Royal Southern Hospital. Situated also in Toxteth, this charity hospital treated mainly poor people from deprived areas of the city, and so the appointment enabled him to continue to exercise his practical social concern.[82] In the later years of his medical training he had given up his involvement in the Territorials. Now, in June 1913, he rejoined, becoming medical officer to the Liverpool Scottish (the 10th Battalion, the King's [Liverpool] Regiment), the same battalion in which Macfie served. He took part in their summer camp, as well as attending their church parades.[83]

The battalion was one of the first Territorial units to reach the front, in November 1914; Chavasse had been eager to be with them.[84] 'He was the possessor of an unquestioning patriotism and an unshakeable belief that God was on the side of England, and his efforts for the welfare of his men soon became legendary.'[85] This commitment is vividly expressed in the closing sentence of his letter to his father when first departing for France: 'I am going to do my best to be a faithful soldier of Jesus Christ and King George.'[86] The central dynamic of his efforts in the war seems to have been his quasi-paternal concern for his men. The influence of his religious upbringing is apparent in this comment before embarkation: 'When I go out with the Scottish boys I feel quite paternal, and love keeping them fit and dressing their minor injuries. I think it is the pastoral spirit, for the care and cure of bodies instead of souls, although I do care for their souls too.'[87] After eighteen months at the front, he wrote: 'I seem to love my poor men, and to feel for them more than ever.'[88] In June 1917, he was offered a surgical job at a base hospital, which would have meant safety and a chance to develop his professional skills. Though tempted, he felt 'it is too comfortable. Such jobs are for the older men, young fellows like myself ought to be with the fighting men', and eventually turned the offer down: 'I thought I had better stay with the lads'.[89]

He drove himself repeatedly, at considerable risk, to try to ensure that all wounded men were rescued from the trenches and no man's land.[90] As well as offering first aid and when necessary performing surgery on the wounded, he also introduced valuable innovations in the transport and treatment of the injured near the front line, as well as in hygiene.[91] He also made considerable practical and financial efforts to improve recreational facilities for the men both in and away from the trenches, arranging supplies of books and magazines and a canteen, and eventually bending his principles enough to organise a beer garden.[92] Clayton comments: 'his concern for the men's welfare went far beyond the usual scope of a battalion Medical Officer. As the war went on, this aspect of Noel's interpretation of his role was to become legendary.'[93]

His role as an army doctor meant that Chavasse could successfully combine service to both God and King: his task was to save lives not to take them. There is nothing to suggest that either dimension of his faith came close to breaking. He gave increasing value to his own religious observance at the front. There was an outburst of anger, when he had to attend a High Church service, against the 'hermaphrodite' who celebrated it; 'out here one does like a plain and simple religion to help us through very blunt and plain truths and tragedies'.[94] His patriotism gave rise during the war to occasional outbursts of conventional conservative anger: against striking munitions workers, or critics of the war such as George Bernard Shaw.[95] While not tolerating men whom he regarded as malingerers, he was compassionate towards those he felt had genuinely broken down; he once helped to cover up the self-inflicted wound of a British soldier, and regularly had others who were near to collapse assigned to light duties with him while they recovered.[96] But he was not afraid to criticise those among his equals and superiors who he felt were not meeting the demands of the war. His targets included the inadequacies of other units of the Royal Army Medical Corps (RAMC), such as the Field Ambulance Service which he thought often failed the injured.[97] On occasion criticism extended to his superiors, both over the wider handling of the war, and over specific issues where he felt strongly, such as the measures they took against the spread of sexual diseases among the troops.[98] He could also be scathingly critical of his fellow professionals—doctors and chaplains—for their failure to get close to and communicate with the men. 'One does not go to the Medical or Religious professions to look for self-sacrifice. That old fable has been exploded.'[99]

His persistent and outstanding courage in rescuing wounded men under fire was recognised by an exceptional roster of medals: the MC (June 1915), the VC (August 1916), and—uniquely for the First World War—a bar to his VC awarded posthumously after he was killed by shellfire at his first-aid post in a dugout near the front (August 1917).[100] In coming to terms with the deaths of both Noel and another son at the front, Bishop Chavasse expressed a continuing faith, unshaken by the war, that in the end God (who 'cannot make a mistake') would make all things good: 'we keep praising and thanking God for having given us such a son. We know that he is with Christ, and that one day—perhaps soon—we shall see him again.'[101]

Siegfried Sassoon was born the son of a sculptor whose wealthy Jewish family had broken with him after his marriage to the Gentile daughter of an artistic and land-owning family. When Sassoon was barely five, the marriage collapsed, and his father died four years later.[102] Brought up by his mother with his two brothers, he was educated at Marlborough (1902–4)—where he was a member of the Rifle Volunteer Corps, and then for a year at Cambridge (1905–6) which he left without taking a degree.[103] Between then and the outbreak of war he lived a life divided between the conventional pursuits of a country gentleman (especially hunting and cricket), and the lifestyle of an aspirant but amateur poet (he had nine pamphlets of poems privately published between 1906 and 1912).[104] He had rejected the conventional Anglicanism in which he had been brought up, but retained a strong sense of the spiritual to which he had access especially though his passion for music.[105] In 1911, he wrote to Edward Carpenter, a socialist, homosexual and writer on homosexuality. Carpenter acted (through correspondence and in person) as a mentor for many homosexual men and women at a time when their sexuality could be discussed in public, if at all, only obliquely.[106] Sassoon's letter is revealing of this atmosphere of secrecy, ignorance and confusion.

> ...your words have shown me all that I was blind to before, and have opened up the new life for me, after a time of great perplexity and unhappiness...I knew absolutely nothing of that subject (and was entirely *unspotted*, as I *am now*), but life was an empty thing, and what ideas I had about homosexuality were absolutely prejudiced, and I was in such a groove that I couldn't allow myself to be what I wished to be, and the intense attraction I felt for my own sex was almost a subconscious thing, and my antipathy for women a mystery for me.

He concluded: 'of course the misunderstanding and injustice is a bitter agony sometimes'; and a few days later wrote again asking to visit Carpenter since 'I feel that you *could help me a lot*.'[107]

In their studies of the war poets, both Adrian Caesar and James Campbell point to the importance of Carpenter's model of homosexuality for the self understandings, and hence actions, of Sassoon (and Graves). In *The Intermediate Sex* (1908), Carpenter sketched a model of the homosexual man as having a female soul in a male body; this gave rise both to the artistic sensibility which he argued was common among homosexuals, and to the cleanliness of male comradeship.[108] Within this perspective, Sassoon (and Graves) could each accommodate both their devotion to poetry, and their erotic desires which were sublimated into chaste friendship. Such a psychic structure was, however, potentially fragile. It was subject to external (hypermasculine or homophobic) attack if the artistic sensibility were to be seen as unmanly. Sassoon dealt with this by a form of splitting, through the pre-war division of his life into two spheres which he kept carefully separate—the sporting and the aesthetic (the latter centred increasingly in 1913–14 in a world of homosexual writers). But it was also precarious internally, since it demanded the repression of any sexual expression.[109] The costs were evident in the pre-war years, when Sassoon was plagued by a sense of purposelessness, an inability to mobilise his creative powers as he wished.[110]

The war altered this accommodation by offering new challenges and new opportunities. Caesar suggests that the immediate volunteering of both poets (Sassoon some days *before* the declaration of war by Britain) reflected their enthusiasm for this escape from their dilemmas. It afforded a means of integrating the man of action with the creative artist, the potential for intense experience, an arena for self-sacrifice, and the company of men; while also demonstrating incontrovertibly their courageous manliness.[111] Sassoon hastened to enlist in the Sussex Yeomanry, part of the Territorial Force—initially as a private since he did not want the responsibility of being an officer. He volunteered for overseas service, but in October he broke an arm badly following a fall from a horse. By the time he had recovered in February 1915, he had decided to apply for a commission in an infantry regiment, so as to see action sooner. An old family friend encouraged and supported his application to the Royal Welch Fusiliers (RWF). He joined in May 1915, underwent his training at Litherland near Liverpool, and was posted to France in November.[112]

Sassoon's attitude towards the war underwent significant change between 1915 and 1918 as a result of his service at the front, so that it is possible to trace a trajectory from willing self-sacrifice in a just cause, through protest against slaughter in a cause he no longer found convincing, to determined commitment to support his men in a war to which he could envisage no end. Nonetheless, at each stage of this trajectory he displayed a range of different and sometimes contradictory attitudes and behaviour. He developed several ways of coping with his experiences of war, in particular the repeated loss of friends he was close to, and the more general suffering of the troops in the trenches.[113] A first was to throw himself wholeheartedly into the war, motivated initially by the aim of proving himself, then also by the desire for revenge, but increasingly by the wish to lead and help his men.[114] A second was to escape from and forget the war, which he did when on leave by taking up again with enthusiasm his pre-war passion for hunting, or by writing lyric poetry.[115] A third was to embrace the opportunities for self-sacrifice (his own and others') which the war offered, and the suffering which it inflicted, as valuable both in themselves and through the poetry they inspired.[116] And a fourth was to protest against the war, which he did publicly in July 1917. The ensemble of such attitudes and forms of behaviour at any given stage represented in part means of coping—sometimes involuntary, sometimes deliberately cultivated—with an otherwise intolerable situation, in part consciously perceived internal contradictions about what was right. Consequently, no one response viewed in isolation can be taken to represent Sassoon's view even for a single moment of the war.[117]

My suggestion is that Sassoon's stance towards the war comprised not only the transformative trajectory that took him from enthusiastic volunteer to bitter protester, but also the oscillations—marked in extent, and differentiated in their sources—around the trend line of this trajectory. Together, they represented his attempt to respond to and manage his cognitive and emotional experiences of the Western Front. The oscillations were fuelled not only by Sassoon's inner conflicts of judgment and value, but also by the immediate environment in which he found himself—one where his choices were highly constrained. At the front, his options were effectively limited to modifying the degree of enthusiasm with which he pursued the war (choosing whether to play safe, or take risks); Sassoon's values (as well as, at one time, the desire for revenge) drove him to the latter. Open protest, of course, would have been met with military discipline. When on leave, and in the company of pacifists and others who could show him a different way of looking at the war, he could reorientate his loathing of the front into a considered protest against its continuation. Or, he could fall back on a deep-rooted pleasure of his pre-war life and throw himself into hunting, where the immediacy and concentration of the hunting field could take his mind away from the war.

During his first year of active service, 1915, Sassoon viewed the war from within the framework of willing sacrifice, one strengthened by the loss of his brother. 'I have lived well and truly since the war began, and have made my sacrifice; now I ask that the price be required of me. I must pay my debt. Hamo went: I must follow him.'[118] Yet on leave during March 1916, Sassoon began to discuss the war with his literary mentor

Robbie Ross, who strongly opposed it and would later encourage, and assist the publication of, his critical and satirical anti-war poems.[119] Less than a fortnight after his return to the front came the death of his (and Graves's) close friend, David Thomas, the first of a series of such losses.[120] The continual deaths of so many close friends would affect all soldiers serving at the front. But the impact may have been more intense when the friendships were erotically tinged or charged, as was Sassoon's for Thomas.[121] At first, and for a while, Thomas's death added hatred and the desire for revenge to Sassoon's motives: 'I used to say I couldn't kill anyone in this war: but since they shot Tommy I would gladly stick a bayonet into a German by daylight.'[122] Yet it may also have opened up a space for later thinking critically about the war—for recognising that: '[t]he boy, a beloved object, was not only forbidden by law to be loved by an adult male but was legally sacrificed by the same laws in the service of his country.'[123] Sassoon now introduced in his diary the theme of upholding the honour of the poets as a further reason for persisting with the war.[124] Soon after this, in May 1916, he was awarded the MC, for his courage in rescuing the wounded under fire.[125]

In July 1916, during the opening days of the Somme, he found himself for the first time amidst the dead and decaying corpses of a recent battle. Although this was the occasion of his second heroic exploit (for which he was again recommended for a medal), it was also the action in which he came across the recently dead young German soldier who was to be the subject of 'A Night Attack'. 'He was a Prussian with a decent face, / Young, fresh, and pleasant, so I dare to say / No doubt he loathed the war and longed for peace, / And cursed our souls because we'd killed our friends.' This poem recognises the common humanity which links the dead German with Sassoon's own recently dead friend Thomas. His sense of waste was reinforced by sympathy for the new battalion of the RWF who joined the front line, and who were to be slaughtered days later when he himself had been relieved.[126]

Soon after, he was invalided home with trench fever. During his recovery in summer 1916, his attitude towards civilian perceptions of the war began to harden, and combined with a growing sympathy for the Germans (adumbrated in 'A Night Attack').[127] In September, together with Graves, he paid his first visit to Garsington, the home of Lady Ottoline Morrell to whom Ross had earlier introduced him. It was here that he first met the group of pacifists and conscientious objectors who were based there.[128] Later the same month, his distress and anger were increased by the accounts he received of the slaughter of the 1st Battalion, RWF at Delville Wood.[129] By the end of the year, convalescing at Litherland with Graves, and further alienated from what now seemed the complacent social circles in which he had grown up, he had begun to question the ethos of self-sacrifice: 'the thought of death is horrible, where last year it was a noble and inevitable dream'.[130]

Once he returned to active service in February 1917, his attitude became more visibly conflicted.[131] He was still attached to 'the feeling of self-sacrifice—immolation to some vague aspiration' (which he felt distinguished him from 'the commonplace grossness of the majority'); but as the immediately following phrase—'whether our cause be a just one or not'—indicates, he was no longer confident in its value.[132] In one of the occasional semi-fictionalised autobiographical sketches which appear in his diary, he had depicted himself in the third person—an officer lunching in a hotel in Rouen, who monitors the shift in his own feeling from anti-war sentiments such as Sassoon had recently shared with Graves.

> He had loathed the business of 'coming out again', had talked wildly to his pacifist friends about the cruel imbecility of the war, and the uselessness of going on with it. He came out with his angry heart, resolved to hate the whole show and write down his hatred in words of burning criticism and satire. Now he is losing all that; he has been drawn back into the Machine; he has no more need to worry...And through his dull acquiescence in it all, he is conscious of the same spirit that brought him serenely through it last year; the feeling of sacrifice.[133]

As soon as he moved towards the front line, he felt 'absolutely happy and contented...something even stronger than last summer's passionate longing for death and glory.'[134] He recognised that: '[s]omething in me keeps driving me on: I must go on till I am killed. Is it cussedness (because so many people want me to survive the war)—or is it the old spirit of martyrdom...'[135]

Yet it was barely four months later that he was to make his famous protest. What changed? His earlier doubts and anger were reinforced by a fresh exposure to the horrors of the front, in particular during the battle of Arras in which he took part in mid-April. Sassoon himself performed courageously; wounded in the shoulder, he was yet again recommended for a medal.[136] But in a diary entry headed 'Things to remember', written while awaiting evacuation to England, he included: 'stumbling along the trench in the dusk, dead men and living lying against the side of the trench—one never knew which were dead and which living. Dead and living were very nearly one, for death was in all our hearts. Kirkby [his CO] shaking dead German by the shoulder to ask him the way.'[137] The fivefold repetition of dead/death, the dead inextricably mixed with the living, drives home the sense that the border between death and life has been breached.[138] It was these 'horrors from the abyss' which led him to declare, in his poem (written in hospital in April) addressed 'To the Warmongers', 'You shall hear things like this'.[139] That seepage of the dead into the world of the living also existed within Sassoon's consciousness, shown in his sketch 'In the Ward' a week later. Here, at night, the ward is littered with dead bodies who 'look at me reproachfully, because I am so lucky, with my safe wound, and the warm kindly immunity of the hospital is what they longed for when they shivered and waited for the attack to begin, or the brutal bombardment to cease.'[140] There could not be a clearer statement of survivor guilt.[141] As he convalesced, his distress at the continuing slaughter intensified, while his friends encouraged him to seek a safe training post.[142]

Three further sets of experiences now came together to trigger Sassoon's protest. First, his stay with Lord and Lady Brassey in May during his convalescence confronted him forcefully with views which intensified his anger against the values he believed were prolonging the war. In another sketch, 'A Conversation', he recalled a discussion with Lady Brassey of his dilemma: whether to accept the opportunity to stay in England.

> For a while he thought that she understood. He spoke without reserve of his longing for life and the task that lay before him, setting against it his mystical joy in the idea of sacrifice and the disregard of death. 'But death is nothing', she said...'And those who are killed in the war—they help us from "up there", *they are all helping us to win.*'...'It isn't as if

> you were an only child, with a big place to inherit. No; I can't see any excuse for your keeping out of danger.'[143]

Her remarks combined an insouciantly aristocratic view of duty—ensuring the continuity of the family estate might outweigh the need to fight—with a version of Ettie Grenfell's denial of the reality of death. Second, Sassoon received letters from his friend Joe Cottrell, the battalion Quartermaster, detailing the RWF's heavy losses in the most recent action; as well as news of the death of E.L. Orme, the latest in a series of fellow officers to whom Sassoon had become attached, and who had been killed.[144] And finally, his renewed and now intensified round of meetings with friends of Ottoline Morrell who were pacifist or critical of the conduct of the war, including Russell, H.G. Wells, Middleton Murry and H.W. Massingham, gave him the intellectual framework, and practical encouragement, to determine on, formulate and enact a protest against the continuance of the war.[145]

In June 1917, with the help of Russell and Murry, Sassoon drafted a public statement as 'an act of wilful defiance of military authority, because I believe that the War is being deliberately prolonged by those who have the power to end it.' He emphasised that he spoke 'as a soldier, convinced that I am acting on behalf of soldiers....I have seen and endured the sufferings of the troops, and I can no longer be a party to prolonging those sufferings.' He also believed that his protest might 'help to destroy the callous complacence with which the majority of those at home regard the continuance of agonies which they do not share and which they have not sufficient imagination to realise.'[146] He then deliberately overstayed his leave; when summoned by his Commanding Officer, he sent him a copy of his statement, and then circulated it to his friends.[147] Most of his friends disapproved of his action, even when they agreed with his sentiments.[148] Ordered to rejoin his regiment in mid July he did so, but refused to withdraw his stance. His friend and fellow poet Robert Graves then took the decisive action in defusing the protest (discussed further below in Chapters 4 and 7). Meanwhile, his statement was read out in the House of Commons by a sympathetic MP, and then published in various newspapers.[149]

The nature of warfare on the Western Front generated potential role dissonance for volunteer junior officers. The model of heroic military masculinity which had been held out to them at school proved largely irrelevant in the trenches. Their conditions, and the threats they faced, placed them in some respects in a more dangerous situation than the men they led. By contrast, the model of paternalistic concern for others proved both highly relevant and eminently possible. The enforced proximity and shared danger intensified affectional and erotic bonds, thereby strengthening the motivation for paternalistic care. But this in turn heightened the contradiction between the two aspects of their role. On the one hand, they cared for their men, sometimes in the most intimate bodily way (from helping their blistered feet to dressing their wounds). On the other, they had to lead those same men over the top into withering machine-gun fire (and potentially, at the worst, shoot their own men if they refused to attack). And they had to kill young Germans, whom they might come to recognise as the counterparts of their own young men. This conflict, as well as fear for their own safety, could produce the shell shock or neurasthenic breakdown which Rivers and other psychologists understood as a solution to an impossible conflict of duties. More broadly, it tested to breaking point some of the ideologies which sustained and gave meaning to the war. The collapse of the model of martial manhood led to the rejection of the rhetoric of glorious, ennobling warfare ('war has made us wise') and the 'happy legion'.[150] The conflicts between killing the enemy, leading men to their death, and caring for them, exposed contradictions within conventional Christian models of sacrifice.[151] Noel Chavasse, because of his particular role as a military doctor, was not faced with this conflict: he could serve both Jesus Christ and King George. All his efforts (save perhaps his chivvying of malingerers) were bent towards saving lives; and the self-sacrifice he made could be entirely subsumed in his father's conventional but correct claim that he 'literally laid down his life for his men'.[152] Siegfried Sassoon, as a fighter who also displayed a passionate concern for his men, was brought starkly up against the contradictions: even to kill a German was to kill another blond youth of the kind whose death he mourned. His complex attitudes lay bare the forces pressing upon men in his situation, and his responses—courageous, confrontational and escapist—illuminate the moral and political dilemmas which the war posed. They provide a template against which to set the case studies of Graves, Macfie and West in Chapters 4–6.

Part II
Case Studies

4

ROBERT GRAVES

In 1929, the break up of his marriage, and the urgent need for money to start a new life, provided the impetus for Robert Graves to write his autobiography.[1] He completed it in a rush, under intense personal pressure, over the summer of that year. *Goodbye to All That* was one of the wave of war memoirs which appeared between 1928 and 1933.[2] Its publication both marked the end of a phase of Graves's life and enacted the moment of transition. As well as the concealed personal ending (he mentioned the break up of his marriage, but none of the circumstances leading to it), he was also saying an angry goodbye to the society into which he had been born and socialised, which had brought him and his cohort to the war. The autobiography was not only a psychic but also a financial means of leaving, selling 30,000 copies within the first month of publication and providing through its success the material base for the move to a new country and a new relationship.[3]

The text opens with Graves addressing—pointing a finger at—you and you and you and me and all that.[4] These are the representatives of what he is rejecting (including his former self): his family and the moral code in which he was brought up, his school and the masculine and imperial values which it inculcated, his society and the war into which it plunged him. The para-suicidal experience which precipitated the final break up of his marriage and his flight abroad was a moment of profound rupture; except when forced to return by the Spanish Civil and Second World Wars, Graves lived abroad for the rest of his life. It is explicitly from the perspective of this moment of rupture—'backward from where you are', as he addressed his dedicatee Laura Riding—that Graves depicted his earlier life.[5]

This chapter will explore that life history, drawing on his own narration as well as other biographical evidence, so as to bring out both the sustained effort at a critique of and distancing from his upbringing which Graves undertook, and the ways in which he was still constrained by its shaping power.[6] The first two sections will focus on his socialisation through his family and schooling, examining how he was brought up and trained in key religious and moral values concerning individual and national identity, and sexuality. The third section will examine the ways in which Graves coped with his wartime experiences at the front: the continuation of some values and practices (especially in his attachment to his regiment), the fragmentation and recycling of others (especially his religious beliefs), and the rejection and critique of others (especially what he later came to term 'innocence'). The final section, an account of his developing friendship with Siegfried Sassoon, will help to define their respective responses to the war, as soldiers, citizens and poets.[7]

Family and Household

Graves came from an upper-middle-class professional background. He was the third child, and first son, of Alfred Graves and his second wife Amy. The Graves family was conventionally Anglican. Their direct line was Irish ascendancy, and included both literary and religious men. Alfred's first marriage had been to a woman of an equally old-established Irish family, and they had five children. On his wife's death, Alfred married a woman of the distinguished German von Ranke family from which Robert received his second name.[8] Alfred Graves was an inspector of schools for Southwark, who in his spare time was a poet and song writer, and a local literary figure in Wimbledon where the family lived.[9] Amy, the eldest of ten children, had come to England at the age of eighteen as a live-in companion to an elderly relative—a post she held for fifteen years. After the old lady's death, she had inherited a large sum of money, and planned to train to be a medical missionary in India; but she was introduced to the recently widowed Alfred, and a rapid courtship and marriage followed. After her marriage she acted as companion and hostess for her husband while bringing up their children with the help of servants.[10]

Goodbye to All That can be read in part as an indictment of 'innocence': an innocence cultivated by Graves's upbringing about the realities of life, including sexuality and war. Published while both his parents were still alive, it is not surprising that his portraits of them are brief and largely neutral, somewhat remote figures, claiming that as the middle child of a second marriage: 'The gap of two generations between my parents and me was easier in a way to bridge than a single generation gap. Children seldom quarrel with their grandparents, and I have been able to think of my mother and father as grandparents.'[11] However, this account serves to distance and understate both their impact on him, and his reaction. The chief values which Graves notes as coming from both his parents are a moral seriousness and earnestness bound up with the Protestant religion. This earnestness, which was to stay with Graves in many ways through his early life, was also to cost him dear during his first days at public school.[12]

His mother held a firmly Victorian view of a woman's role; Graves notes that in consequence he too accepted unquestioningly 'the whole patriarchal system of things...the natural supremacy of male over female'.[13] Amy had a powerfully internalised sense of duty and responsibility, which had carried her through her years of service as a live-in companion.[14] Religious instruction was in her hands, and she took a stronger and less forgiving line in matters of morality than her husband.[15] She 'used to tell us stories about inventors and doctors who gave their lives for the suffering, and poor boys who struggled to the top of the tree, and saintly men who made examples of themselves'.[16] In the context of her own family, this meant that she set very high standards of achievement for them, and exerted intense moral pressure to live up to these standards.[17] Together she and Alfred trained their children in habits of moralism and self-examination which left them with no sense of how the world really was.[18] Graves's treatment of his father is faintly patronising about his career as a writer, and his lack of influence on Graves's own writing.[19] His response to his mother is more guarded and indirect. His text is at times openly critical of the moralistic upbringing she imposed, but the full force of her impact on him becomes more apparent in his struggles to make a new life in the post-war years.[20]

The family followed the typical pattern of an upper-middle-class servant-keeping household. They had live-in servants, though Graves believed his mother would have preferred to do without. His father was a busy man, occupied with his work, his writing, or the running of local literary or Temperance societies. His mother's household and social duties meant she saw less of the children than she might have. Consequently, they spent much time with each other, and also with their nurse. 'In a practical way she came to be more to us than our mother.'[21]

The servants formed an important element in Graves's growing sense of class. His parents were Liberal Unionists. 'In religious theory, at least, they treated their employees as fellow creatures. But social distinctions remained clearly defined.'[22] When he was four, Graves caught scarlet fever, and was sent to a public fever hospital. There, most of the children were working class; and while Graves accepted as natural the spoiling he himself received, it struck him forcefully as different in the case of the only other middle-class boy, a clergyman's son. On his return home, he was reproved for his 'vulgar' accent. A year later, he met one of his fellow patients, who turned out to be a ragged errand boy. 'I suddenly recognised with my first shudder of gentility that there were two sorts of people—ourselves, and the lower classes…I accepted this class separation as naturally as I had accepted religious dogma.' The servants' bedrooms, at the top of the house, were by accepted convention uncarpeted and poorly furnished. 'All this uncouthness made me think of the servants as somehow not quite human.'[23]

School, Religion and Sexuality

In his retrospective narrative of his adolescence, Graves exposes the mechanisms through which the public-school system worked, and the values which it attempted to inculcate. He offers, in his usual blackly comic style, an extended exploration of the ambivalent power of the school as institution to evoke loyalty, to become an object of worship. He attended a mixture of local and prep schools (at several of which he was already unhappy); from the last of these he successfully won a scholarship to Charterhouse.[24] His account of his unhappy time there (1909–14) includes many of the characteristic themes of such autobiographies. At the same time the form and content of the text both address and exemplify the ways in which such traditional loyalties can be successively, or simultaneously, rejected and re-embraced. Before he tells anything of his experiences at the school, Graves opens his narrative with a story which acts as a framing device. On the day he left Charterhouse, just before the outbreak of war, he discussed it with his friend Nevill Barbour, then Head of the School.[25] They agreed that there was no possible remedy for it, because 'tradition was so strong that if one wished to break it one would have to dismiss the whole school and staff and start all over again'. Even this would not be enough, since the very buildings were 'so impregnated with what was called the public-school spirit, but what we felt as fundamental badness.' They nevertheless agreed that, in twenty years' time, they would have forgotten, or would repudiate, these views ('I was a young fool then, insisting on impossible perfection'), and send their own sons there for sentiment's sake. Through this prefatory story, Graves neatly undercuts, or at least ironically distances himself from, the account he is about to give of his school and its apparent impact on him. In doing so, he sardonically acknowledges the power of institutions to instil, and then evoke, a form of loyalty which cuts right across any individual's actual experience of them.

As with some other public-school educated literary intellectuals at this period, one major difficulty Graves encountered was the hostility to book learning dominant among the other boys whose 'chief interests were games and romantic friendships'. As a scholar who had little spending money, as someone not particularly good at games, as a boy 'prudishly innocent' about sex, Graves was an easy target for teasing and bullying. His German middle name, once discovered, gave a further point for attack.[26] Under this pressure, he came near to a nervous breakdown. Half way through his second year, he wrote to his parents describing in confidence some of what was happening, and pleading with them to take him away.

> They were unable to respect this confidence, considering that it was their religious duty to inform the housemaster of all I had written them. They did not even tell me what they were doing; they contented themselves with visiting me and giving me assurances of the power of prayer and faith; telling me that I must endure all for the sake of...I have forgotten what exactly.

Their visit to the school, and the housemaster's subsequent denunciation of both bullying and informing, made clear to the other boys what had happened; and Graves's life became even harder. His next resort was to sham insanity; this largely succeeded, and soon his school fellows simply avoided contact with him.[27]

Key to Graves's more successful negotiation of his later years at Charterhouse was his discovery of two mentors; a slightly older fellow pupil

Raymond Rodakowski, and a new young master George Mallory. These like-minded friends made his survival easier. At the end of his second year he was invited to join the Poetry Society, consisting of a master and six other boys. Through the society he met Rodakowski, who befriended him at this lowest point in his school career.[28] He persuaded Graves to take up boxing, reminding him of the example of some senior members of the Debating Society, also renowned for their boxing prowess, who two terms earlier had stood up to and defeated the sporting 'bloods' who had disrupted a debate.[29] Graves's action here represents a successful defiance of the prevailing ethos of the school: he aligns himself with the intellectuals of the Debating Society against the philistinism of the bloods. Yet the form of the preceding moral exemplar mimics that of the popular public-school story, reproducing precisely the values which the public-school code supposedly promoted (the marrying of physical courage with moral and intellectual strength, the willingness of a brave few to stand up to bullies), and ensuring their triumph within the narrative.[30]

His relationship with Rodakowski (like that with Mallory) enabled Graves to bring together both intellectual and physical elements of his burgeoning masculinity in a constellation that was acceptable to, while modifying, the dominant code within the school. It also contained an element which he came to recognise as sexual: 'in the annual boxing and gymnastic display, I fought three rounds with Raymond. There is a lot of sex feeling in boxing—the dual play, the reciprocity, the pain not felt as pain. This exhibition match to me had something of the quality that Dr Marie Stopes would call sacramental. We were out neither to hurt nor win though we hit each other hard.' This successful boxing appearance won him a degree of acceptance.[31]

His last years at the school were made a little easier by entry into the sixth form, further success in boxing, and a growing friendship with Mallory. This unusual teacher treated Graves, like other boys, as a companion and equal. He introduced him to modern writers (including Shaw and Wells), and sent some of his poems to Edward Marsh, the influential literary editor who was to play a crucial role in developing Graves's career.[32] Besides encouraging him and Rodakowski in the literary endeavours, and introducing him to Samuel Butler's attack on the Victorian family, Mallory also inspired Graves to take up rock climbing and then invited him to join climbing parties in Snowdonia in 1913 and 1914.[33]

For members of the upper-middle class, national identity was not invariably single or unproblematical: their Englishness might be mixed with other, sometimes conflicting, national and ethnic identities. Graves came from a part-Irish family. There was considerable intermarriage between the English and Irish aristocracy and gentry; but with the rise of the Home Rule campaign in the last decades of the nineteenth century, and the potential threat it posed to the Union, the different (and perhaps problematical) status of the Irish within 'British' Englishness was highlighted.[34] Even more problematically, Graves, in addition to being part Irish, was also part German; his middle name—von Ranke—signalled his relationship to a German family which included the famous historian. As a young boy, he and his family spent summers on his grandfather's estate near Munich; and he later claimed a stronger sense of the German language than of French which he spoke more easily.[35] At one of his prep schools, German culture was revered, and this family connection was to Graves's credit. But his German ancestry, once his second name was known, came to haunt him at Charterhouse. He became the target for hostility, since 'Germany', to his schoolmates, meant economic rivalry, military threat and boring scholarship. His attempts to deflect this, by stressing his Irish blood, were unsuccessful.[36] Graves wrote: 'My history from the age of fourteen, when I went to Charterhouse, to just before the end of the war, when I began to realise things better, was a forced rejection of the German in me.'[37]

Graves was brought up in a family where Christian moral teaching was taken very seriously; and attended schools in which the Christian faith was part of the official system of belief and instruction.[38] It is clear that aspects of Christian teaching especially Evangelical morality, bit very deeply into him; and that he struggled for many yearsto free himself from them. Perhaps in consequence, the account he gives in *Goodbye to All That* of his relationship to religion, both before and during the war, is fractured, incomplete, contradictory, and in places chronologically inaccurate. It seems likely that at the time of his Confirmation (spring 1911), vulnerable from its lack of spiritual impact, and faced with arguments from his ally Rodakowski (an avowed atheist), he came to doubt the validity of the Christian faith; but that he nevertheless continued to hold on to it—even at the cost of thereby weakening, though not breaking, that key friendship.[39]

As well as the pressures to conform with the ethos and ideology of the school, Graves also emphasises the disturbing and hypocritical treatment of his sexuality.[40] His autobiography was unusually full, for its time, in its treatment of sexual matters, and had a complex narrative purpose. Just as, within the text as a whole, his critical account of the school as an institution prefigures, and prepares the way for, his criticism of the army, and of the society which propelled Britain into the war, so in that picture of the school its hypocritical treatment of sexual matters stands as paradigmatic. Within an atmosphere of ignorance and hypocrisy, sexual feeling, whether homosexual or heterosexual, is repeatedly linked in the text with death or murderous impulse.

Graves first goes out of his way to emphasise that his early upbringing had left him frightened of girls.[41] Then the atmosphere of furtive, guilty secrecy around homoerotic feelings in the schools he attended is established in an account of the headmaster of one of his prep schools, about whom there is a 'somehow sinister' secret known to the older boys. '[H]e came weeping into the classroom one day beating his head with his fists and groaning: "Would to God I hadn't done it! Would to God I hadn't done it!"' Graves was taken away a few days later, while the headmaster had to leave the country.[42]

Graves encountered a similar atmosphere when he entered Charterhouse.[43] When he deals with his time there, he has to negotiate the fraught issue of his own intense involvement with a younger boy. His narrative seeks to acknowledge this relationship and its importance to his younger self, to defend its innocence, to criticise the interference and sometimes hypocrisy of the masters, to recognise his own involvement in that confused emotional and moral climate, and yet finally to distance his current self from all that the relationship involved (in particular its homoerotic element, and its symbolic falseness). Graves prepares these complex manoeuvres by commenting on the results of such schooling:

> In English preparatory and public schools romance is necessarily homosexual. The opposite sex is despised and hated, treated as something obscene. Many boys never recover from this perversion. I only recovered by a shock at the age of twenty-one. For every one born homo-sexual, there are at least ten permanent pseudo-homo-sexuals made by the public school system. And nine of these ten are as honourably chaste and sentimental as I was.[44]

He then endorses a distinction made by the headmaster of Charterhouse between 'amorousness' (a sentimental falling in love with younger boys), and eroticism (adolescent lust). The former relationship involved romantic illusion, the latter (between boys equal in age) sexual convenience.[45]

The acceptance of these distinctions—'born' and 'pseudo' homosexuals, 'amorousness' and 'eroticism'—offers Graves a framework in which to present the story of his own homoerotic attachment at Charterhouse, and his complex interaction with the masters. In his fourth year there (aged seventeen-and-a-half), during the Christmas holiday in 1912, he had been deeply embarrassed by the attentions of an Irish girl who had been attracted to him: 'I was so frightened I could have killed her.'[46] Perhaps partly in reaction to this shock, in the next term back at Charterhouse he fell in love with a boy three years younger 'who was exceptionally intelligent and fine spirited. Call him Dick.' G.H. Johnstone was a fellow choir member and scholar, also interested in poetry. 'I was unconscious of sexual feeling for him. Our conversations were always impersonal.'[47]

The story Graves tells of this attachment is first of his spirited defence of the purity of his feelings, and refusal to give up the friendship, despite pressure from masters and merciless ragging from his fellows. 'Finally the headmaster took me to task about it. I lectured him on the advantages of friendships between elder and younger boys, citing Plato, the Greek poets, Shakespeare, Michel Angelo, and others, who had felt the same way as I did. He let me go without taking any action.'[48] Such arguments were then a standard justification for the value and innocence of close male-male friendships. Graves had in fact been reading the works of Edward Carpenter, and wrote to him in May 1914 to say that they had 'absolutely taken the scales from my eyes and caused me immense elation: you have provided a quite convincing explanation for all the problems doubts and suspicions that I have been troubled by in my outlook on sex, and I see everything clearly'.[49] This suggests that his assertions of innocence and unconsciousness of sexual feeling are, at least with regard to this stage of the relationship, overstated.[50] The public school system, with its segregation of adolescent boys at the time of their sexual maturing, made it likely that, for some, erotic feelings would be directed towards fellow pupils. In Graves's case, this was intensified by the family emphasis on purity of motive and action. This seems to have produced a sublimation of sexual feeling into intense idealised friendship, with any physical expression both feared (hence provoking murderous rage if evoked) and repressed (except indirectly and occasionally, as when sparring with Rodakowski).

In the second phase of the story, matters took a more serious turn, and Graves felt compelled to defend his beloved. One of the choir boys told Graves that the master who had initially warned him off this friendship had been seen kissing Dick.

> I went quite mad. I asked for no details or confirmation. I went to the master and told him he must resign or I would report the case to the headmaster. He already had a reputation in the school for this sort of thing, I said. Kissing boys was a criminal offence. I was morally outraged. Probably my sense of outrage concealed a murderous jealousy.[51]

(What may have been at stake here was not simply jealousy, but the fracturing of repression implicit in the recognition that Dick could be desired physically.) The master denied the allegation, and summoned Dick to give his account of events; Dick said that the claim was true.

> So…the master collapsed, and I felt miserable. He said he would resign at the end of term, which was quite near, on grounds of ill health. He even thanked me for speaking directly to him and not going to the headmaster. This was the summer of 1914; he went into the army and was killed the next year. I found out much later from Dick that he had not been kissed at all. It may have been some other boy.

The tragic end of this confrontation is just one example of the associative links established in Graves's text between such exploitative 'eroticism' and death or destruction.[52] At the same time, the narrative renders Graves himself both responsible (for his murderous jealousy), and not (since the master has a reputation, and Dick lied to protect him).[53]

Goodbye to All That offers a critique of the values of the world in which Graves was brought up.[54] He handled his school neither with the relative confidence of Sorley and Sassoon, nor with the outright rebellion of Brenan, but by developing something closer to the self-protective carapace which Woolf vividly described. With difficulty, and the help of mentors, did he manage to develop a version of masculinity (embracing both physical and intellectual skills) which enabled him to survive emotionally. By his final year, with his exhibition to Oxford secured, Graves was able to use his position as co-editor (with Barbour) of the school magazine to snipe at school traditions, launching an ironic, and eventually successful, campaign for the introduction of tennis as a 'manlier and more vigorous game' than cricket.[55] His account of his schooldays offers a severe critique which nevertheless (as he self-mockingly recognises) retains many of the values, and responds to many of the loyalties, which the institution itself had sought to instil, and from which he had suffered. Such was the price of survival. As Patrick Quinn comments: 'Perhaps only an individual who had been so fully imbued with these ideals could be as strongly affected as Graves was, when the authenticity of these ideals began to unravel as it did at Charterhouse and on the western front.'[56]

Coping with the War

Before the war, Graves had opposed militarism. In December 1913, he had spoken, alongside his school allies Barbour and Rodakowski, against a Debating Society motion supporting compulsory military service; and the following spring he had secured himself an exemption from military drill with the OTC.[57] But when the war broke out, just after he had left Charterhouse and gone to North Wales on holiday he had decided to enlist. This was partly out of dislike of German bullying, he claimed, and partly as a way of postponing going up to Oxford.[58] But it was also the expected response, 'I can't imagine why I joined: not for sentiment or patriotism certainly and I am violating all my most cherished anti-war principles but as D.N[evill].B[arbour]. says "France is the only place for a gentleman now," principles or no principles.'[59] His family were delighted at his decision: 'I immediately became a hero.'[60] In addition, suggests Adrian Caesar, it offered an escape from the inner conflicts he had been facing. Carpenter had written of the value of blood brotherhood (influenced in part by Whitman's celebration of male comradeship in the American Civil War); writing to Carpenter, Graves had eagerly taken up this theme, adding the Ulster band of brothers to the standard reference in contemporary homoerotic writing to the Theban Sacred Band of warriors. Graves could hope that the war would offer him a similar experience of male comradeship, and a continuation of the balance between masculine endeavour and artistic creativity which he had achieved in his last years at Charterhouse.[61]

Two important themes can be traced through Graves's narrative of the war: his immediate response to, and ways of coping with, his wartime experience; and the ultimate impact of that experience on both his beliefs and his relationship to institutions of his socialisation. Central to coping with the war was the role of the regiment. It was the accident of his being on holiday in Harlech that decided which regiment he was to join.[62] Nevertheless, despite this accidental start Graves was soon caught up in the spirit and tradition of the Royal Welch Fusiliers (RWF), to which he devotes a chapter of his book. He reports that in discussions with fellow officers this sense of loyalty to the regiment, or some more immediate group (one's own battalion or company), was of crucial importance in helping men to survive in the trenches; its importance grew by comparison with wider, more abstract focusses of loyalty such as patriotism and religion.[63] For all that the regiment as a military unit coerced its members into a situation of danger, it also served to defend and provide for them once there, and to afford them recognition as brave soldiers loyal to their fellows. This immediate collectivity also became an imagined community through the diachronic stress on its history and traditions.[64] Loyalty was maintained in part by continual reflection on the respective quality and qualities of the various groups in which one served.[65]

Graves developed this attachment to the regiment despite the way he was himself treated. In part, his treatment was routine: as a junior he was subjected to the normal snubbing administered to the 'new boy'; and as a newly arrived, temporary volunteer officer, he received a distant when not hostile reception from the regulars in the mess.[66] But he as an individual suffered more than many. He was half German; and his less-than-wholehearted embrace of the officers' mess culture, with its masculine (sporting and sexual) ethos, meant he was perceived as somewhat awkward or eccentric, priggish and bumptious.[67] This led to his first posting to France being repeatedly delayed.[68] His eventual arrival at the Second Battalion late in July 1915 was painful, since in R.P. Graves's words 'they maintained a tiresome degree of snobbery towards any soldiers who were not regulars'.[69] This becomes the occasion for one of his textual set pieces, in which a fellow wartime officer, already there on secondment from another regiment, acts as guide and explicator to a naïve Graves bemused by his reception. As he was taken through the various customs maintained as if the Battalion were still in India (where it had just finished an eighteen-year tour of duty), Graves protested: '"But all this is childish. Is there a war on here or isn't there?" "The battalion doesn't recognise it socially", he answered.'[70] When he was transferred to the First Battalion in December 1915, he had a better time. It had been in England since the South African War, and was therefore 'less old-fashioned in its militarism and more human…a much easier battalion to live in'.[71] But on his return to the Second Battalion in July 1916, he again encountered hostility.[72]

Graves's attitude towards the regiment, and more broadly the army, is divided. As with his account of his public school, so too here the text combines a sharp critique of many aspects of the regiment to which he belonged, and especially of the legacies of its (now seemingly archaic and cruel) pre-war practices, with both an explicitly positive valuing of it as a framework for survival in the war, and an attention to its history, rituals and comparative status which in part reproduces the very structure being criticised. He registers the parallels with his earlier school experience: the miserable fate of the new boy, the obsession with tradition and rituals including precise codes of dress and address, the sense of an imagined community extending across generations, the struggle for bragging rights over neighbouring units.[73] He is critical of several key aspects of its ethos: its clinging to snobbish practices at the expense of efficiency, and its treatment of junior officers which at times became callous.[74] Nevertheless, he also presents himself as caught up in that ethos.[75] He is proud of its history and fighting record, eager to record the ways in which this has been upheld in the current war. 'I have to live up to my part here as I have learned to worship my Regiment: in sheer self-defence I had to find something to idealize in the Service and the amazing sequence of RWF suicides in defence of their "never-lost-a-trench" boast is really quite irresistible.'[76] Despite the apparent fatuities of traditional discipline, he first records a discussion about the value of drill in promoting tactical fighting capacities, and then relays an admiring report, from an officer of a different regiment, of how the RWF had conducted themselves in just such an admirable textbook fashion under extreme circumstances.[77] He continued to idealise the regiment: preserving its good name, through his own and others' self-sacrifice, was held to justify the losses incurred.[78]

Graves began the war in much the same optimistic spirit, grounded in ignorance, as many of his contemporaries.[79] His subsequent attitude towards the war, and his ways of coping with his front-line experiences, both fluctuated and shifted. As R.P. Graves shows, his retrospective narrative is not always accurate in recording the complexities of his contemporary feelings.[80] As I have argued in Chapter 3, such contemporary fluctuations of feelings are unsurprising: they reflect both the impact of each immediate situation and the unfolding internal conflicts about what it is right to do.[81] Nonetheless, two major turning points can be detected in the period of Graves's front-line service. His first shocking experience came at the first offensive he was involved in, the battle of Loos in September 1915. Here he experienced some of the most brutal fighting, while at the same time he felt his own ability to cope with it being undermined.[82] Shortly after the battle, he wrote to Marsh: 'Oh Eddie, there were so awful scenes that morning of the 25th!...I am the only survivor now of five 3rd Battalion officers who came up together five months ago'. He now began to hope for a cushy wound or transfer to base, 'for tho' still loyal and willing I've ceased to feel aggressive'.[83]

As well as the direct impact on him of his front-line experiences, which eventually produced neurasthenic symptoms, he also had to cope with wider knowledge of what fighting such a war involved. This included atrocities, about which he reports the conversations in which he and his fellow soldiers worked out their own moral calculus.[84] Graves, like other junior officers, also had to face the constant deaths of men who had become comrades and often friends.[85] Just as he felt he was recovering from Loos came the death of his (and Sassoon's) close friend David Thomas in March 1916—a loss which was to provoke one of Graves's most powerfully critical war poems. 'Goliath and David' is an explicit inversion and hence repudiation of the Biblical story: the heroic David 'Holds his ground, for God will save', but the promise of God's protection is vain ('God's eyes are dim, His ears are shut'), and he is slain by the giant wearing a Prussian helmet.[86] This blow undid his recovery; at that moment, when he feared a 'general nervous collapse', he was sent back to England for an operation.[87]

As he recovered from the operation, his feelings again fluctuated. Unhappy with his base posting, he wrote to Sassoon inverting the meaning of the ubiquitous words of *Tipperary*: '"I want to go home"—to France.'[88] But once back at the front with the Second Battalion, faced with the spy rumours, and homesick for the more welcoming First Battalion, he asserted that: 'Contrary to my usual principle I'm at last looking out for a cushy wound'.[89] Two days later, facets of his fluctuating feelings were embodied in two poems included in the same envelope to Sassoon. One elaborated the fantasy of their post-war escape to distant lands where 'God! what poetry we'll write!', while the other recorded what he had just found on the battlefield, 'A certain cure for lust of blood', a 'dead Boche…Dribbling black blood from nose and beard'.[90] Five days later, during the battle of the Somme, he was hit by a shell fragment and left for dead. After his survival and recovery, he suffered continuing lung damage which prevented all but one brief further period of front-line service.[91] Graves's verdict on the front is perhaps represented by his framing of his own entry into and departure from it: each is marked by his seeing the body of a British soldier who has killed himself rather than continue.[92]

The experience of the trenches undermined many of the beliefs with which Graves had been brought up; and he had to find new ways of coping and making sense. R.P. Graves points out that his retrospective narrative oversimplifies his attitude to religion during the war; in it he dismisses Christian belief as difficult to sustain, whereas in fact it had continued to provide him with moments of meaning and comfort.[93] Though calling himself an agnostic, he continued to read the Bible while in the trenches.[94] Nevertheless, as 'Goliath and David' suggests, the movement was fundamentally away from faith. When he and his fellow officers analyse morale, religion is dismissed along with patriotism as worthless for sustaining it; this claim is supported in part by contrasting the behaviour of chaplains (especially Anglican) who supposedly stayed well behind the front line, with that of doctors.[95]

Instead, what is present in *Goodbye to All That* is a shattered edifice of religious belief, in which fragments are picked up and used for whatever immediate and temporary purpose they may serve. Here too, Graves is reporting a wider pattern of behaviour. Religion features alongside superstition, which he claims he like everyone became subject to through pessimism. Such superstition allows one man to predict the precise manner of his death; and another to "bring about"—by a careless remark which "tempts fate"—the deaths of three battalion officers (including David Thomas) in one night.[96] Graves follows his account of this shocking loss by recalling phrases from religious anthems which he used to repeat over and over in his head as charms. These included 'He that shall endure to the end, shall be savéd'; and 'Through faith unto salvation, Ready to be revealéd at the last trump'. This last, he reports, the soldiers always sang as 'crump': '"The last crump" was the end of the war and would we ever hear it burst safely behind us.'[97] During the war the landscape and hills around Harlech began to assume crucial importance in Graves's mind as a place of respite from the front (much as the activity of hunting was for Sassoon).[98] He bought a cottage there from his mother 'in defiance of the war'. At first, while recuperating from an operation, he found he could walk the hills around Harlech to restore his sanity; reciting, as a 'charm against trouble', the psalm verse 'I will lift up mine eyes unto the hills, from whence cometh my help.'[99] But after his near fatal wounding in 1916, 'the immediate horror of death was too strong for the indifference of the hills to relieve it'.[100]

Patriotism, too, presented particular difficulties for Graves in view of his divided heritage. Before the war teasing about his German lineage was a painful annoyance, now the rumours of his being a spy were a potential threat.[101] Worse still, members of his extended family were fighting and being killed on both sides. R.P. Graves records that late in his life, Graves lamented over the Germans that he had 'murdered'.[102] Nor, after the Easter Rising of 1916, was it so easy to take refuge in asserting his Irish identity.[103]

Like many soldiers, Graves employed humour as a coping mechanism. One of his characteristic textual moves is to present some of the horrors he encountered as comic anecdotes; this serves as a way of buffering the potential emotional impact on both the reminiscing narrator and the reader.[104] But this comic presentation is often a precursor to a textual repetition or elaboration in which the incident is presented more starkly.[105] During the preparation for an attack at Loos, a harassed storeman, rushing to the front with the rum ration that is to be drunk before going over the top, trips; as he falls the stopper comes out of the jar and the precious rum pours into the ground. The officer, deeming this an offence worthy of death, treads the offender into the mud; the rest of the platoon then march over him. This is presented in a narrative form which closely resembles an animated cartoon.[106] However, the anecdote also contains two further levels of meaning. One is situational. The rum, initially introduced as a jokey element, in fact proves an essential aid to fighting. When Graves himself, after intense combat, is near to a breakdown, he finds a water bottle full of rum, drinks it, and is able to pull himself together.[107] One of the bitter contemporary criticisms of *Goodbye to All That* concerned its reference to officers at the front relying on drink to get themselves through. But Graves is here presenting himself too as needing such support at times.[108] The other level is visual metaphoric: the rum spilled and body trampled in the mud echo the bloodshed and deaths of the battlefield.

Goodbye to All That offers a repudiation of the lethal 'innocence' which had been inculcated in Graves by his upbringing, both his mother's unworldly moralism and the ethos of his school. This innocence encompassed both the nature of sexual desire and the reality of warfare.[109] Some poems written at Charterhouse, or in the early wartime months before active service, had shown a continuing struggle between puritanism and sensuality in which the former dominates: self-sacrificial death in battle is more civilised than (hetero)sexual expression. Graves carried these attitudes with him through the war. Preserving his own sexual purity, and his belief in that of Johnstone, and thereby sustaining the image of Carpenter's comradely warrior and chaste lover, acted as a protective talisman.[110] The loss of this double innocence is expressed textually through his disillusionment about his ideal friend Johnstone ('Dick'). During the early years of the war this relationship, maintained through letters and occasional visits, and despite obstacles, had been very important to Graves as another way of coping, a counterbalance to the trenches. He idealised his friend as intelligent, better read, many times the poet he himself could hope to be; and the nature of their emotional bond as pure (that is, Platonic, asexual). 'Dick's letters had been my greatest stand-by all these months when I was feeling low; he wrote every week, mostly about poetry. They were something solid and clean to set off against the impermanence of trench life and the uncleanness of sex life in billets.'[111] Graves wrote a letter, to be sent in case of his death, to 'you who mean infinitely more to me than myself', hoping that perhaps he himself 'may live in you when my body is broken up, and have a share in all your doings'.[112] Gradually, this image was to be undermined. In June 1915, during Graves's first period of service at the front, a cousin at Charterhouse wrote to him that Johnstone was 'not at all…innocent…as bad as anyone could be'. At first shocked and bitter, Graves eventually convinced himself that his cousin had written out of spite; and Johnstone reassured him.[113] The next blow came nearly a year later, when Johnstone's mother found some of Graves's letters to him; troubled by their affectionate tone, and quotations from Butler and Carpenter, she had forced her son to agree not to see Graves until he had left Charterhouse. Graves described himself to Sassoon as 'widowed, laid waste and desolate'.[114] Three months later, recovering from his near fatal wound, Graves was encouraging Johnstone to use this turn of events to press his mother to be more amenable. By December 1916, he was arranging for his youngest brother John, now at Charterhouse, to be introduced to Johnstone as an older boy who could help him at the school; and he himself continued to enjoy and value the friendship.[115]

However, in July 1917, just as he heard of Sassoon's protest, Graves also received news that Johnstone had been convicted of a sexual offence with a Canadian corporal. In *Goodbye to All That*, Graves misdates this event to nearly two years earlier, immediately after the disastrous failure at Loos.[116] Fussell suggests that the false chronology serves a function within the text, expressing a thematic link between the two events: 'The shock was his discovery that he had been deceived by pleasant appearances: a relation that he had thought beneficially sentimental now revealed itself to have been instinct with disaster. It was like the summer of 1914.'[117] This connection is plausible, since the Loos offensive represented an emotional turning point for Graves. Referring to the ten years of disturbing memories and day dreams he endured after the war, he said: 'the scenes were nearly always recollections of my first four months in France; it seemed as though the emotion recording apparatus had failed after Loos.'[118] As well as creating the symbolic link with the failed offensive, as Fussell suggests, there may be another reason for the shift of date. In reality, it came after Graves had had his first (very brief) romantic involvement with a woman, when (the month before, convalescing in Oxford) he met and fallen in love with Marjorie, a probationer nurse.[119] By placing the break with Johnstone earlier, Graves could present his encounter with Marjorie as the second stage of a transfer from homo- to hetero-sexuality, rather than there being a period of overlap between the two forms of feeling.[120]

What is striking throughout Graves's account of his struggles with his sexuality in childhood, adolescence and into early adulthood is its association with feelings of violence in himself, and damage or death for others. He himself at the age of nine had been terrified by the bodies of older boys, by young girls exploring his body, and by sitting outside the girls' cloakroom at his sister's school. Then he had wished to kill the Irish girl who flirted with him, and in reaction began his idealised relationship with Johnstone.[121] Now, faced with evidence that Johnstone (and hence by implication their relationship) was not innocent, his response was: 'I decided that Dick had been driven out of his mind by the war. There was madness in the family, I knew...It would be easy to think of him as dead.'[122] This reflects Graves's repudiation of an aspect of himself. Before the war, in corresponding with Carpenter, he had understood himself as homosexual. This was certainly an element of his friendship with Sassoon, to whom he had written his belief (in fact, misplaced) that the recently dead Sorley was 'so', on the basis that at the age of twenty his poems included no love lyrics.[123] What Johnstone's arrest signalled was not simply the legal danger attached to any homosexual act, but the possibility of physical desire which Graves's homoerotic attachments had hitherto excluded. Graves's moralistic and prudish upbringing, together with a public-school adolescence, produced a repressed sexuality, whose physicality was denied and whose emotions were channelled into an idealised same-sex friendship. When its energies threatened to break through, they proved frightening and had to be violently expelled.

Graves and Sassoon

The loss of Johnstone was offset in part by his major new friendship of the war years, with Siegfried Sassoon, a fellow poet, and member of the same regiment. They first met in December 1915.[124] Their changing relationship, both during the war and in the post-war years, helps reveal the complex and shifting nature of their respective attitudes towards the war and their wider society. When they first met, each was a little wary of the other.[125] Graves was the less illusioned, having already served six months at the front; while Sassoon still adhered to the heroic vision. When Graves showed Sassoon some of his early war poems, Sassoon rebuked him for being 'too realistic'; whereupon Graves told him, as an old soldier, that his attitude would change.[126] Nevertheless, their literary interests (in the face of the indifference or hostility of their fellow officers) drew them together, as did their common idealistic homosexuality.[127] They began to meet when they could, correspond, and comment on the drafts of one another's poems. Sassoon became a confidant for Graves's feelings about the war, and his relationship with Johnstone. The bond was strengthened by their shared friendship with fellow-officer David Thomas, and grief over his death in

March 1916. Graves's fantasies about his life after the war included the suggestions, first that Sassoon should join him at Oxford, and later that they should travel far afield together, to Russia and the Caucasus. When Sassoon received the false news that Graves had been killed, he expressed a sense of loss because he thought he had found 'a lifelong friend to work with'.[128]

During the second half of 1916, when they spent a considerable amount of time together while convalescing, their attitudes towards the war became close.[129] After Graves had been wounded, he invited Sassoon (then invalided home with trench fever) to join him in Harlech in August 1916. This landscape—together with travel to remote countries—became an image of a world of escape after the war where he and Sassoon would write together.[130] They had begun to have serious doubts about whether the war should continue. They discussed the offer supposedly made to the Allies in 1915 of peace on the terms of returning to the pre-war status quo. Both, especially Sassoon, thought the terms should have been accepted. They no longer saw the war as a struggle between trade rivals, but as 'a sacrifice of the idealistic younger generation to the stupidity and self-protective alarm of the elder'.[131]

When they left Harlech, Sassoon arranged for them both to visit Lady Ottoline Morrell, whom he had recently met for the first time. Her Garsington house was a centre for pacifists, and here he and Graves were exposed to different views about the rightness of the war. As Jean Moorcroft Wilson comments, to Sassoon's emotional revulsion from the war was now added a reasoned critique.[132] However, his attitude towards their responsibilities fluctuated; and it seems that Graves followed his lead.

> We decided that it was no use making a protest against the war. Every one was mad; we were hardly sane ourselves. Siegfried said that we had to 'keep up the good reputation of the poets', as men of courage, he meant. The best place for us was back in France away from the more shameless madness of home service. Our function there was not to kill Germans, though that might happen, but to make things easier for the men under our command.

So in November 1916, Graves abandoned his existing plan to seek a posting to Egypt because of his damaged lung, and rejoined the battalion in

Litherland; he was followed shortly by Sassoon, and they shared a hut. Graves and Sassoon were now committed to two imagined communities—their front-line company, and the company of poets. After they were separated again early in 1917, when each returned to active service, their views began to diverge.[133]

Weakened both by his lung injury and by the persisting effects of shell shock, Graves was invalided back to England, after a brief return to the front, in February. He again visited Morrell, and maintained his anti-war position.[134] Then in April Sassoon was seriously wounded. As he convalesced again back in England, his distress at the continuing slaughter intensified. Haunted by visions of the dead, he was torn between fantasies of assassinating the Prime Minister, refusing to continue to serve (but 'they would only accuse him of being afraid of shells'), and taking a safe job at home ('but he knew that it was only a beautiful dream, that he would be morally compelled to go on until he was killed').[135] In June, however, he determined that he must make some protest against the continuance of the war. After consulting Bertrand Russell and other pacifists, he prepared and circulated publicly his refusal to serve further in the army. When this produced no immediate response, he deliberately overstayed his leave, and sent a copy of his statement to his Commanding Officer.[136]

Graves, who had been given a hint that Sassoon was planning some protest, was horrified, writing anxiously to Marsh:

> It's an awful thing—completely mad—that he's done....his friends, especially in the Regiment....all think he's mad....Personally, I think he's quite right in his views but absolutely wrong in his action....you can be quite assured that I'm a sound militarist in action however much of a pacifist in thought. In theory the War ought to stop tomorrow if not sooner. Actually we'll have to go on while a rat or a dog remains to be enlisted...[137]

The terms in which he justified his ensuing actions, and the debate which then opened up between himself and Sassoon, reveal the degree to which Graves embraced and was held within the public-school code of the gentleman. Sassoon had already rejected an offer by his Commanding Officer to bury the matter if he withdrew his protest; he wanted to be court martialled so as to gain full publicity for his stand. Graves now acted decisively to try to prevent this outcome, so as to save his friend from the likely consequences of what he saw as a futile if justified protest, and one which would be seen by their fellow soldiers as a betrayal.[138] He made strenuous efforts to persuade Sassoon to appear before a medical board, swearing (falsely) that the War Office was determined to avoid a court martial, and would instead send him to an asylum. Faced with this apparent out-manoeuvring of his protest, Sassoon gave way and agreed to the medical board.[139]

The board, at which Graves gave evidence, sent him to Craiglockhart Hospital, where he was treated by W.H.R. Rivers.[140] After some months there, Sassoon decided that, though he maintained his pacifist views, he had no choice but to return to the Front and secured via Rivers a promise that he would be sent back immediately.[141] After Graves visited him at Craiglockhart in October, Sassoon wrote criticising him (in Graves's words):

> for the attitude I had taken in July, when I was reminding him that the regiment would only understand his protest as a lapse from good form and a failure to be a gentleman. It was suicidal stupidity and credulity, he said, to identify oneself in any way with good form or gentlemanliness, and if I had real courage I wouldn't be acquiescing as I was.

Graves in reply pointed out that he had never been 'such a fire eater as [Sassoon] was....the direction of Siegfried's unconquerable idealism changed with his environment; he varied between happy warrior and bitter pacifist.'[142]

Graves was right to point out that Sassoon's attitude had oscillated, though he here omitted his own role in maintaining this situation by helping to defuse the protest. He offered a complex defence of himself against Sassoon's criticism, pointing out that the very people he wished to influence were those whom he would most hurt by: 'turning round in the middle of a war, after having made a definite contract, and saying "I've changed my mind"; they'll only think it "bad form" and that you're "not acting like a gentleman" which is the worst accusation they can fasten on a friend.' To keep their respect, it was necessary to be 'ready for pride's sake to finish your contract whatever it costs you, yet all the time denouncing the principles you are being compelled to further.' While this might be taken simply as a pragmatic point (this is not the way to convince such people), in the next paragraph Graves associated himself too with need to keep to a contract. This lost sight of the belief which he and Sassoon had discussed the previous year: that the aim of the war had changed since the original 'contract' of enlistment was signed.[143]

Equally important were the terms in which Graves responded to Sassoon's concern about the phrase 'anti-war complex' which Rivers had used of him: 'of course you're sane. The only trouble is you're too sane which is as great a crime as being dotty and much more difficult to deal with. That's the meaning of an anti-war complex. You see what other folk don't see about the rights and wrongs of the show. Personally I think you see too much...Your conscience is too nice in its discernment between conflicting forces.'[144] Graves's explanation of the difference between them is revealing. As with his volunteering at the beginning of the war so with his opposition to overt protest towards its end, the notion of gentlemanly conduct is invoked to explain his actions. At first he attributes these expectations to others, but then acknowledges that he too feels bound by this code. At the same time, he recognises both Sassoon's greater intensity of feeling (the idealism which could drive him in either direction), and his 'excess' of insight (too sane, seeing too much, too nice a discernment).[145]

Thereafter, Sassoon remained the more radical in his attitude towards the war. By November 1917, when Sassoon was preparing to return to the front, Graves highlighted this difference: 'you're so obsessed with the idea of the perpetual horror of this war that you can no longer...make plans for after the war, and can never conceive, as I still can, of a new world, emptier but wiser and happier than anything that has gone before.' Graves, now in love, had his dream of the post-war world (couched here in terms which echo the patriotic-sacrificial poetry of 1914–15), while Sassoon was trapped within a 'nightmare' of war from which he could not wake.[146] Graves felt some guilt about their respective decisions; but by July 1918, he was defending himself against Sassoon's criticism for not 'writing deeply' in his new poems.[147] Sassoon was sent first to Palestine, and then again to France, where in July 1918 he was injured and sent home for the final time.[148]

From spring 1917 Graves served as a training officer in Britain. Thereafter, his attitude towards his own involvement in the war fluctuated between wanting to return to the front, and a growing sense that this was unrealistic, that he had done his bit and now wished to survive. At first, with the war apparently endless and protest seen as futile or self-defeating, loyalty to his immediate fellows once again came to seem the only acceptable course. So during the second half of 1917, as both his lung condition and his more severe neurasthenic symptoms gradually improved, he manoeuvred to work his way back to an overseas posting to Palestine (better for his lungs, and with much less threat of heavy artillery bombardment and gas).[149]

The idealised love for Johnstone had formed for Graves a necessary counterpoint to the 'filth' (physical, sexual, moral) of trench life, a bond (like Harlech and poetry) to a different set of values. Its collapse opened an emotional space which was soon to be filled by a different kind of love, and a consequent relocation of the centre of gravity of his life. Shortly after the break with Johnstone, he had renewed his acquaintance with seventeen-year-old Nancy Nicholson, a young woman from a similar middle-class artistic background whom he had first met the previous year. He began a correspondence with her about some children's poems of his which she wanted to illustrate. Children had been one of his contrasting definitions of peace in his poetry, and 'my child sentiment and hers...answered each other'.[150] Soon he fell in love with her; and by December had decided to marry.[151] An anxiety to put a distance between himself and overt homosexuality may have been one element in what drove this sudden courtship and marriage; certainly, he went to some lengths to explain his decision to close friends.[152] But the marriage also represented an affirmation of the possibility of life in the face of the continuing deaths of the war.[153] They married in January 1918.[154] As a condition of the marriage, her parents had insisted upon a consultation with a lung specialist, who told Graves that his nervous condition meant he should not undertake any active service. Reconciled to this idea, he became content to continue as a training officer for the rest of the war.[155] With this final turning point, the centre of gravity of his life shifted; he now wanted to survive into the post-war world. As he later put it, he used Nancy 'as a way of forgetting the war'.[156] By August 1918, he was writing to Sassoon that: 'Worrying about the war is no longer a sacred duty with me: on the contrary, neither my position as a cadet instructor nor my family duties permit it. I am no longer fit to fight and I am out to get as healthy as possible for the good I can do in England.'[157] By mid-December, within a month of the Armistice, he had applied for demobilisation with a view to taking up a government grant to study at Oxford.[158]

Graves's response to British society before the war is represented chiefly through his portrayal of his public school; his critique is in part also directed against the later adult world for which it was preparing its pupils. Yet his ironic narrative also depicts the power of the school ethos to contain and reabsorb even the uncomfortable and protesting misfit. Hence it is not altogether surprising that, in the crisis of August 1914, the incipient rebel who had protested against compulsory military service and withdrawn from the OTC should volunteer in obedience to the code of the gentleman. After all, so too did Sorley, a considerably more mature contemporary with greater experience of the world and a more independent judgment. Graves's wartime experiences, and especially his periods at the front line between May 1915 and February 1917, put the class-and-gender ethos of family and schooling under immense strain. At the same time, his means of coping drew on that same ethos. The patterns of emotional affiliation which carried him through the war—to the institution of the regiment, to the fellow soldiers with whom he was arbitrarily thrown together, and to a small community of mentors and intimates ('the poets': Marsh, Ross, Sassoon, Nichols)—had their roots in those formed at school. He was integrated into the imaginary community of his (arbitrarily chosen) regiment, absorbing and taking pride in its history and traditions, and doing his part to uphold them. Yet the regiment replicated many of the features of the school which he had rejected (its treatment of newcomers, or anyone who fell outside a narrow pattern of interests and behaviour; its preference for hierarchy and tradition when faced with unprecedented circumstances). The strongest bonds which held him at the front, those of friendship and even love for fellow soldiers, were constantly ruptured by the rate of killing. His own life was continually under threat. And around him were scenes of devastation, 'a certain cure for lust of blood'.[159]

This resulted in an uneven pattern of fluctuations between rejection of the demands of such a role and of the ideologies which underpinned it, reassertion of them, and a compromise in which the requisite actions were performed while (most of) the justifications were abandoned or negated. Religion, in particular, ceased to make sense of what he was seeing and being asked to do; it fragmented into a handful of magical tokens and incantations, indistinguishable from superstitions. He had to repress the German aspect of himself, while fighting against members of his own family; the Irish identity which he had claimed in its place was threatened by the Easter Rising. The rebellious impulse, and the sense of grief for lost friends which helped to fuel it, brought him together with Sassoon in later 1916. But from early 1917, their paths diverged. Graves, physically and mentally battered by the war, was no longer capable of fighting at the front. He gradually reconciled himself to serving as a training officer at home, having 'done his bit'. Sassoon, meanwhile, his anger and despair at the slaughter intensifying, and given political form by his conversations with pacifists, protested against the continuation of the war. Whereupon Graves played a key role in defusing Sassoon's protest, even publicly supporting what he knew to be fundamentally false—that Sassoon was shell shocked. He took this action to protect his friend from what he feared would be serious consequences; because he believed the action would have no effect; but also (as became clear in their November 1917 correspondence) because he too, like the fellow officers to whose opinions he initially referred, felt that Sassoon's protest was a breach of the gentlemanly code and contract. As he acknowledged, Sassoon saw too much.

Both Graves and Sassoon developed ways of coping with the war by temporarily escaping it: through literature, through writing, through Harlech or hunting. A key escape for Graves was his love for Johnstone: an idealised figure, many times his own worth, and safe at home. Into this relationship could be channelled the intense erotic and affectionate energies of late adolescence. Before the war he had understood himself as a chaste homosexual. This was a not uncommon response to the single-sex, highly moralistic education he had received, which provoked and was in turn intensified by revulsion from the more coarsely physical sexual talk and behaviour of his fellow pupils and soldiers. It certainly strengthened his bond with Sassoon and (in his fantasy) Sorley. The good reputation of the poets as men of courage, which Sassoon wished them to uphold, may have contained a subtext that homosexuals too should show themselves fighters. The collapse of the relationship with Johnstone, and the potential 'sullying' of all such relationships which it might be taken to imply (the very possibility which he had argued so firmly against, thereby costing a master his job and possibly his life), left Graves doubly bereft: of an ideal, and of an emotional anchor and haven. The abrupt shift to a heterosexual love therefore performed several functions. Graves again had a love (now publicly recognised) to set against the cruelties of war, and one which—through their shared desire for children—could counter the endless sequence of deaths and provide an alternative focus for his loyalties and commitments. As his exchanges with Sassoon in 1918 made clear, he was now intent on surviving the war and making a new life.

5

Scott Macfie

Wartime service on the Western Front forced upon Graves and Sassoon unprecedented experiences which opened the possibility for a liminal fracturing of received frameworks, unsettling the values and expectations with which they had been brought up. This chapter considers a reverse case. It traces the trajectory whereby a man who (like Brenan) had attempted—by running away—to reject the course mapped out for him by his family, and who on his return had developed a pattern of life which placed him liminally between the demands of his social role and his own desires and identifications, found in the war a different liminal time/space in which he could reconcile and meet the demands of both society and self.

Family, Career and Voluntary Endeavour

Robert Andrew Scott Macfie was born in 1868 into a comfortably off upper-middle-class family, of Scottish origins, who had owned and operated sugar refineries in Scotland since 1788. His paternal grandfather, Robert Andrew Macfie (1811–93), creator of the Liverpool refinery in 1838, was co-founder of the Liverpool Chamber of Commerce and its chairman for many years. An active evangelical Presbyterian, and enthusiast for empire, he was Liberal MP for Leith Burghs (1868–74).[1] Macfie was educated at Oundle, and from 1886–91 at the universities of Cambridge, Göttingen and then Edinburgh where he received a BSc in Chemistry. He then joined the family firm.[2]

During the 1890s, in his twenties, Macfie went through some experiences of doubt and perhaps even personal crisis which significantly affected his sense of his identity. The first of these concerned religion. He was brought up as a Scottish Presbyterian.[3] At Cambridge, he was drawn into religious circles which were concerned that the Christian gospel should be socially relevant. Macfie himself taught a class for poor boys.[4] During one of the summer holidays, he went to America with the famous American evangelical preacher Moody. Something happened there, which his biographer refers to simply as: 'some shock which he appears to have received, a shock which left him uncertain of his position, and insecure in his faith…Macfie went out full of zeal and eager to undertake evangelistic work. Then came reaction and disillusionment.' On his return to England, Macfie told his father it would be hypocrisy for him to attend church. As a result he became estranged from his father for a long time; to his mother's distress, he moved out of the family home.[5] Whatever had provoked this 'shock' in Macfie, it had a profound effect on his attitude towards the Christian religion.

The second set of troubling experiences concerned Macfie's role as a upper-middle-class businessman. In 1895, some four years into his career, at a time of difficulties for the family firm, he suddenly left, went to London, and enlisted in the army as a private.[6] While joining the army in itself would have been acceptable socially, doing so as a private soldier certainly was not. Some weeks after enlisting, Macfie bought his way out of the army, and returned to the family firm.[7] The significance of this episode was reinforced the following year when his mother died, a loss which affected him strongly.[8] His biographer described his reaction thus:

> Uncertain health and the sorrow caused by his loss brought out once more that 'strain of eccentricity' which made him such a strange compound.…He wanted to know what the life of a working man really is from the inside. The opportunity presented itself in this way. One of the men in his employ had enlisted in the Army and, having got into the bad books of the Serjeant Major, deserted. He and Scott went to London, where they worked as labourers 'in the East End at 30*s*. a week', until their whereabouts were discovered by one of Scott's aunts.[9]

Following this escapade, uncertain what work the firm would require him to do, Macfie continued to live in workmen's lodgings. He wrote: 'Very often I go about in workman's clothes: it is rather disagreeable but very cheap.' His family then sent him on a Mediterranean cruise, ostensibly because of fears about tuberculosis, but perhaps also for more general purposes of convalescence and recovery.[10]

For a member of the British upper-middle class to dress up in this way and "play" at being a worker was not without precedent in the late nineteenth and early twentieth centuries. But usually it was associated with a claim to some wider purpose, often that of social investigation. Macfie was unusual in offering no such justification, but undertaking the adventure unashamedly for his own benefit.[11] Joining the Army as a private was even more unusual.[12] Seth Koven, in his study of slumming in the later nineteenth century, discovered that 'the widely shared imperative among well-to-do men and women to traverse class boundaries and befriend their outcast brothers and sisters in the slums was somehow bound up in their insistent eroticisation of poverty and their quest to understand their own sexual subjectivities'. He argues that both occasional forays of exploration into the slums (whether for purposes of social investigation or personal excitement), and more lasting periods of commitment as a settlement worker, provided such middle-class visitors with 'an actual and imagined location where...they could challenge prevailing norms about class and gender relations and sexuality', and 'stages upon which they enacted emancipatory experiments in reimagining themselves'. Within this liminal time/space, they could for a while 'throw all aside' in their 'critique of the illusory virtues of bourgeois codes of male conduct, which cut men off from their deepest selves and sympathies'.[13] Taken together, Macfie's successive acts of transgression, in response to work and personal crises, suggest a considerable degree of discomfort with the role expected of him by his family and society—a role from which he too could be considered a "deserter".

By the end of the 1890s, however, Macfie seems to have found an acceptable way of living his life. In his resumed managerial role in the family firm, he took on a wide range of responsibilities, while displaying (in the words of his biographer) 'characteristic humanity and consideration' for the workmen.[14] His role in a month-long strike which broke out at the refinery in 1913, however, makes it clear that this paternalism (not unusually for an employer) related more to his treatment of individual workers, or the workforce as individuals, than to his approach to their collective institutions.[15]

Alongside his role as a businessman, Macfie now began to channel substantial energy into other voluntary activities.[16] He became an early and very active member of the Liverpool Scottish, a Volunteer infantry battalion formed in 1900 in response to concerns about the strength of the British Army provoked by the crisis of the South African War.[17] The battalion, which recruited its members primarily though not exclusively from the upper- and lower-middle classes, was one of the institutions through which the Scottish in Liverpool retained and expressed their distinctive national identity, having some of the characteristics of an 'elite social club'.[18] This work was Macfie's central interest for several years. He devoted a great deal of attention to the training of his battalion, raising its standard so that the men won shooting competitions.[19]

In 1907, the focus of Macfie's voluntary efforts shifted. As one of the first members of the University Club at the recently founded (1881) University College in Liverpool, he had met several keen Gypsiologists, and through them developed an interest in Gypsy Studies and the Romani way of life. In 1907 John Sampson, a pioneer scholar of Gypsy language, and David MacRitchie, another Gypsiologist, persuaded him to revive the Gypsy Lore Society (GLS) which had been defunct for the previous fourteen years. On taking up this task he resigned from the Volunteers.[20] He became the inspiration and driving force behind the research published in the *Journal of the Gypsy Lore Society*. He worked tirelessly as secretary of the GLS and editor of the *Journal* until 1914, dealing with both the editorial and business sides. He commissioned and edited articles, and chivvied colleagues to undertake new work, filling gaps in Gypsy studies, or making the results of their own enquiries known. Although the focus of the *Journal* was primarily philological, and then historical, he paid some attention to current events affecting Gypsies both in Britain and abroad. He became one of England's leading authorities on Roma/Gypsies and their language, recording dialect, folk tales and songs from various bands of Roma/Gypsies in Britain.[21]

Macfie's engagement with British working men, as paternalist employer and as army Volunteer, was now paralleled by his strong attachment to Gypsies—both as individuals, and as a group whose language and culture he worked tirelessly to record and analyse.[22] This identification with Gypsies was a complementary if subordinate aspect of his identity, a form of romanticism which counterbalanced and in part mitigated the demands on him, as a businessman, of capitalist rationality and bureaucracy.[23] The work of Macfie and his fellow Gypsiologists in Britain arose from a particular cultural context. The Gypsy appeared regularly in nineteenth-century British writing as a figure who represented resistance to the increasing pressures of industrialisation and urbanisation, someone not tied to regular waged work or a fixed home.[24] The founders of the GLS in 1888 aspired to innovate within this tradition. They saw themselves as placing Gypsy studies on a new, more scientific, basis, connected to the well-established discipline of comparative philology, and the emergent discipline of folklore studies.[25] At the same time, this generation also displayed a strong strain of romanticism, celebrating while re-interpreting the mid-nineteenth-century writings of George Borrow on Gypsy life.[26] This romanticism was a reaction against the trammels of bourgeois life. More specifically, it embraced a distinctly rural, 'healthy life' (as opposed to decadent, urban) ethos, quite widespread in progressive cultural circles in late-nineteenth-century England—an ethos into which a life of caravanning and the 'open road' fitted well.[27] David Mayall comments: 'The Gypsy, to the lorist, provided a touch of an idealised past in the modernising, industrialising and urbanising world of the late-nineteenth and early-twentieth centuries.' Gypsies' ways 'contrasted with the gravity and sombre formality of day-to-day life.'[28] Moreover, he notes an analogy between the social position of many who became Gypsylorists, and the Gypsies themselves: 'Their image of the Gypsies was also created out of the attributes which they shared as a group and reinforced in each other: their love of freedom and nature, their bohemianism and romanticism, and their marginal position in society as academics, scholars and vicars, removed from urban industrial life.'[29] Interest in the Gypsies and their culture could simultaneously promote an engagement with an Other people and their language, and provide a bohemian space in the interstices of daily life where the constraints of middle-class convention—from formal dress to sexual mores—could be to a degree evaded.[30] It is clear that for some of its members, the GLS provided such a milieu within commercial and academic Liverpool around 1900.[31]

This founding generation of Gypsiologists undoubtedly displayed enthusiasm for and empathy with Gypsy life and culture, as a result of which they identified, collected and preserved significant materials towards its history.[32] But there were also substantial elements of stereotyping and patronage in their presentation of the Gypsies and their way of life.[33] Outsiders, such as Gypsies in late-nineteenth-century Britain, can be positioned as superior, objects of desire or envy because invested with qualities felt to be absent from those who thus define them.[34] Such a positioning of the outsider as Other nevertheless renders them a screen onto which the subject's desires (rather than their fears) are projected.[35] Macfie certainly shared this perception, viewing Gypsies as absolutely different in nature from *Gadzho* races. 'They manage to live in our idiotic civilisation without being affected by it. We poor slaves can't move a finger without hearing the chains rattle which we have spent centuries in forging for our own limbs.'[36] In 1913, replying to a correspondent who had asked him why Gypsies regularly told lies which had no instrumental value, he wrote: 'Gypsy lies—the motiveless ones—seem to me simply the manifestation of an uncurbed imagination. We don't tell lies of that kind because in youth our imaginations were put in irons: we couldn't do it if we wanted. So, like you, I enjoy and admire them rather enviously.'[37] Here is the romantic trope of the child's unfettered imagination, 'put in irons' by the process of education, from which Gypsies are happily free—a freedom which provokes envy as well as pleasure in others.[38]

In the crisis of his twenties, Macfie had attempted to 'flee' from his expected life-course, to desert his own class and enter the way of life of another. But he seems to have had no fixed intention of abandoning definitively his own status; rather, he seems to have "tried on" a different way of life much as he dressed in working-men's clothes. As he entered his thirties, he developed a more sustainable pattern of living through positioning himself liminally. During office hours an efficient Liverpool businessman, in his spare time he immersed himself first in the male world of the Volunteers, and then in the mixed scholarly and bohemian milieu of the GLS. This liminal positioning extended to his teasing and sometimes antinomian relationship to the law. On occasions he sided with, even identified himself with, those who had broken it.[39] Inviting one correspondent to visit him, he even presented his house as liminally situated on the margins of respectability. 'If you stay a while in Liverpool you will find me almost in the slums and under the shadow of a huge new cathedral which is gradually growing up. I live in half an old house which some rich merchant built a century ago.'[40]

Encountering the Other: Gypsies and Mohammedans

In 1912 Macfie received a pressing invitation to visit Bulgaria from Bernard Gilliat-Smith, the British Vice-Consul at Varna who, since 1909, had been contributing to the *Journal* a substantial series of Bulgarian Gypsy folk tales which he had collected. In May-June 1913 Macfie travelled to the Balkans and spent four weeks in Bulgaria.[41] He seems to have treated the visit as a much-needed holiday and break from hard work, rather than a serious attempt to gather information about Gypsy life and language in Bulgaria.[42] When the government took control of the railways in the weeks before the start of the Second Balkan War, Macfie, not wishing to be trapped in the country if hostilities broke out, seized what he himself termed this 'pretext' to arrange to travel from Varna to Rustshuk (modern Ruse)—and thence to cross the Danube to Galatz in Romania—in the company of a band of Gypsies, disguised as one of them. He subsequently wrote an account of this seven-day trip entitled *With Gypsies in Bulgaria*.[43]

This book is pervaded with desire for a romantic Other of contemporary western society. This desire structures two central strands in the text: its representations of Mohammedans and of Gypsies. The first of these comprises Macfie's constant reiteration of the superiority of the (clearly idealised) 'Mohammedan' religion and practical ethic over the Christian; and, linked to that, the superiority of Turks and Turkish rule over the other peoples of the Balkans. Macfie's views of the Balkans were largely the product of prejudgment and ignorance. His overriding admiration for the Turks long preceded his visit to Bulgaria.[44] Starting from that basis, together with his admiration for the Gypsies, he dismissed all the other nationalities he met in 1913, despite not speaking their languages.[45] He showed no sympathy whatever for the post–1878 Bulgarian nation-building project, nor recognised it as having secured any significant achievements.[46] Hence it is not surprising that he regarded only Turks as able to be trusted to rule a divided people.[47]

Nevertheless, his understanding of the peoples of the Balkans was also shaped by two distinct concerns of his own. First, his preference for the Turks was closely linked to, perhaps largely founded on, his admiration for Islam. He found Mohammedanism superior to Christianity in its tolerance, and the continuing ability of its traditions and principles to have 'an extraordinarily powerful influence on conduct'.[48] He displayed a marked antipathy to Balkan Christianity.[49] The mutual hatred of the various Christian peoples meant that they could not be trusted to rule one another, and would have been better off under a continuation of Turkish rule—which Macfie perceived as equitable and not onerous.[50] The virtues with which Macfie associates Islam, apart from tolerance, are concrete, practical ones: refreshment and cleanliness.[51] He praises the provision of drinking fountains (a blessing due to 'not western civilisation, not the Bulgarian sanitary board, but the despised Turk'), and lavishes similar praise on the 'noble dignity' of the Turkish bath at Razgrad. Under Ottoman rule, every Balkan town had its public *hammam*; once Christian rulers arrived, however, 'cleanliness, an easily dispensable adjunct of Christianity, gradually vanished, and godliness with it'.[52] This admiration for Islam rested in part on Macfie's rejection of many aspects of contemporary western society; but it may also have been fuelled by whatever the shock was which he had received during his period of Christian religious enthusiasm.[53] On his return to England, he flirted briefly with the possibility of converting to Islam, though ultimately he took the matter no further.[54] (However, although in later life he seems to have returned to attending church as a form of social duty, it is recorded that it was a Koran which he carried with him in the trenches.[55])

Second, Macfie's perception of Turkish rule was reinforced by a preference for what he saw as a more leisurely way of life under the Ottomans, in contrast to the commercial hustling of the West. 'The ideals and aims of our western civilisation are wholly different from those of the east—commercial prosperity is everything, factory chimneys, bustle, wealth that we have not time to use, and all the rest. The East aims more at leisure and meditation; and although it is different, I'm not convinced that it is inferior.'[56] Complementary to the splendour of the Turkish bath is the simplicity of a Turkish café. '[It] was as typical of the temperance and frugality of Islam as are the plate glass, coloured tiles, carved wood, vulgar decoration, polished metal—and drunkenness—in our taverns, of the feverish luxury of a western civilisation, which denies its slaves time for thought, kindness or reflection.'[57]

The second central theme of the book is Macfie's representation of Gypsies and Gypsy culture. If Mohammedans stand for tolerance, cleanliness, moderation—supposedly Christian virtues, but actualised by an

Other religion—Gypsies by contrast are positioned as outlaws. At first he planned to travel with a group of Zagundzhis, Mohammedan Gypsies whom he celebrated as colourful outsiders.

> They are Gypsies *par excellence*: in them the Gypsy character, which among more sophisticated tribes is wrapped in a habit of Gentile (*Gadzho*) respectability, stands proudly forth, naked, unconscious, unashamed. They are, as the poetic instinct of Franz Liszt discerned, children; with a child's indifference to public opinion, a child's unquestioning acceptance of destiny, a child's instinctive timidity, a child's sudden outbursts of rage and equally sudden recovery of temper, and at the same time a child's unreasoning happiness and a child's responsiveness to sympathy....Lithe as panthers, strong as lions, playful as kittens, affectionate as dogs, one loved them as one loves a dog, caring not one whit whether they have read Shakespeare, can play golf, or are capable of admiring Turner. They are scarcely human—but they are the most beautiful of animals.[58]

Here is the romantic Other fully fledged: instinctive and natural as children or animals, the Gypsies are located in fantasy outside the bounds of humanity.[59] The refusal of the Mohammedan Gypsy community leader to allow the Zagundzhis to escort Macfie seemed likely to prevent the trip. However, he then met a group of Christian Gypsies, comb makers, who were willing to take him.[60] At first, Macfie accepted this chance 'sulkily' and with disappointment, seeing them as boringly respectable and lacking in colour. He began to warm to them only when he discovered that Totana, the wife of their leader Petrika, stole chickens for their dinner.[61] His sense of involvement grew as the rest of the party, inspired by Totana's example, gradually revealed to him that they were also horse thieves.

> Their real calling, they almost boasted, was the ancient and lucrative, if dangerous, profession of horse stealing. Now horse stealing in Bulgaria is a science, and by no means an easy trade to be recommended to the bungling younger sons of suburban Philistines...Far from being a degrading trade, the theft of horses is a vocation in which an intelligent Gypsy can take an honest pride, and those who follow it

> with any success retain, like certain Britons who borrow umbrellas and smuggle cigars, the sentiment of honour intact.[62]

Macfie's text engages in a complex negotiation with his readers on this theme. He celebrates, in jibing and teasing manner, the Gypsies' law breaking, while refusing an invitation to join them (in case he faced a prison sentence). He seeks simultaneously to defend Gypsies against claims that they are all criminals, while recounting and enjoying their various law-breaking escapades.[63] At the same time, in doing this he is also negotiating between different impulses within himself.

What is then revealed in the text is Macfie's homoerotic desire. This is figured in his relationship with Turi, the son of the Christian Gypsies' leader. His attitude towards Turi changes markedly in the text: from indifference at the start of journey, it shifts to cautious interest and then blossoms into an intensely felt relationship.[64] When the two men visit the Razgrad Turkish bath together, there occurs an erotic epiphany. Macfie's lyrical account envisages his friend's 'dark and muscular body' as 'an ancient bronze statue...one of the three thousand...erected at Olympia to commemorate athletes'. As Turi stands 'under the great vault, pouring warm water over himself from a silvered cup', Macfie's imagination transforms him into a guardian spirit, lamenting the present fate of the once great baths. His desirability mitigates his criminality: 'to one who could be so beautiful, much must be forgiven—even horse stealing'.[65] In this quasi-baptismal scene water and beauty together transform Turi, a Christian Gypsy horse thief, variously into a Mohammedan *genius loci*, a victorious Greek athlete, and a redeemed sinner—at once a religious and a pagan ideal. The bond between them intensified, and the two men agreed to go through a formal ceremony of blood brotherhood.

As the narrative makes clear, this involved a valuing of fraternal over paternal bonds. From the beginning of the journey, Macfie was irritated with the Gypsies' leader, Turi's father Petrika, whom he found boring.[66] The start of this cardinal episode in his relationship with Turi, was signalled by their breaking away from Petrika's company: 'Turi and I shook the tiresome old gentleman off and escaped alone. We behaved like children released from school.'[67] For Macfie, an aspect of the meaning of that relationship seems to be an adolescent bonding in rejection of a father, a joint enactment of the status of outlaws.[68] This escape, however, proved only temporary. Twice, Turi's sense of filial duty, the need to protect his father from (the effects of) heavy drinking, broke the bond with Macfie: first by interrupting a night on the town together, and then by preventing them completing the formal ceremony of blood brotherhood.[69] If one aspect of their bond was rebellious, fuelled by an adolescent sense of outlawry, another was solicitous, marked by a sense of mutual concern. In Razgrad, Turi took upon himself responsibility for protecting Macfie from the dangers of dissipation, while after his return to England, Macfie did all he could to assist Turi when he later faced a murder charge.[70] It seems that both the rebellious and the solicitous aspects of their relationship were embodied in their blood brotherhood.[71]

Macfie's text has now become a story of thwarted love and painful parting. It was his growing attachment to Turi, as much as his discovery of the Gypsies' horse thieving, which had brought about Macfie's changed attitude toward his initially dispirited journey. For an Englishman of this period, to act on homoerotic desire was to break the law as much as was stealing a chicken or a horse. So while the ambivalence towards the law which Macfie's text reveals and revels in explicitly concerns laws of property, it is also infused with the power of forbidden desire. That desire, transmuted through Macfie's perception of Islam, becomes the baptismal water which washes away Turi's, and the Gypsies', crimes; no longer an outlaw, it is Turi who now in the narrative protects Macfie from those who would cheat and rob him.[72] That concern in turn enables Macfie to sublimate his outlawed desire into the intense and romantic bond of blood brotherhood. Both Turi and the author, Macfie's text asserts, are not truly outside the law; their love is redeemed and cleansed through beauty and mutual concern.

Recognition of Macfie's homoerotic desire casts new light on his rejection of proffered identities. His wish to escape from his class of origin, and identify with the working class, can be read precisely as a wish to identify with working *men*. The desire to escape is not merely from the boundaries of a class identity, but also from a prescribed pattern of sexual desire. The connection between the two—an identification across the boundaries of class, fuelled by erotic desire—was one which other British men of Macfie's social status experienced and explored in the 1890s.[73] Increased legal repression after the Wilde trial in 1895 may have intensified the existing tendency for such encounters to involve partners abroad—for reasons partly pragmatic (to avoid British law) and partly psychological (to evade a repressive sexual code).[74] It was in this context, in the late 1890s, that Macfie had to create a viable pattern of life for himself. Throughout his life, Macfie displayed a concern for younger, often working-class, men. This is evident in several of his activities: his class for poor boys at Cambridge; his later weekend club for lads in Liverpool; and his friendship with the deserter with whom he went to London, and whom he worked to help during his subsequent court martial.[75] His eventual choice had been to adopt liminal positions: to locate himself psychically, and at times practically, between classes and between nations.[76] Now in Bulgaria the intensity of Macfie's bond with Turi, and through him the Gypsies, meant that he had for the moment left his existing position of liminal poise, for a stronger identification with his romantic/rebellious other self.[77] On his return to England, Macfie registered the impact of his journey through the two works he wrote. But this did not absorb all the energies and desires the experience had aroused. His letters contain frequent references to his wish to return to Bulgaria, strikingly so as the anniversaries of different stages of the journey brought back memories. Though he sketched various travel plans, the outbreak of war precluded any possibility that they would be realised.[78]

Fraternal Bonds: the War as Liminal Space/Time

In his celebration of the Turkish café in Razgrad, Macfie recorded the following incident.

> But we were not long allowed to forget that western civilization which seemed so distant: there was suddenly the sound of firearms, with a mad rush of horses, and the officers of the detachment we had just seen drove past at breakneck speed, supremely drunk, rolling about in the carriages, and firing their revolvers recklessly in the air. Sad must be the lot of troops under such commanders: I felt glad that I was sitting in a Turkish café, and not in a Bulgarian restaurant.[79]

This vignette serves to secure Macfie's preference for temperate Turkish values (and rule) over Bulgaria's aping of the western civilisation which it aspires to join; and thereby underlines the message of the whole book.

Moreover, it is consonant both with his constant jibing at the supposed superiority of that civilisation, and what is known of his more specifically political attitudes.[80]

However, when—barely a year later—war broke out in the west, Macfie's response was very different. He immediately joined up, and despite the horrors which he saw continued to support the war to the end. His stance was revealed clearly in his actions and writings of the first few months. The first element is his imperative sense of his own duty. Immediately on the outbreak of war, he decided to re-enlist, intent on active service—even though he was then forty-six years old and already in indifferent health.[81] Having hastily completed and despatched the manuscript of *With Gypsies in Bulgaria*, and undergone necessary medical and dental treatment: 'I went to the Liverpool Scottish prepared to enlist as Andrew Scott, aged 30, no previous service. But they said I needn't bother to swear lies, took the responsibility of accepting me…and swore me in…I intend to volunteer for everything and perhaps ultimately in spite of all blemishes I may get away.' This abortive attempt to sign on as a private has a partly rational explanation (he was too old to volunteer), but perhaps also indicates a resurgence of his earlier desire for complete identification with the working man. Instead, he was reassigned to his old Volunteer position of Colour Sergeant, and in January 1915 was made Company Quarter Master Sergeant (QMS), in charge of stores and feeding.[82]

Macfie's sense of the demands of duty, which he embraced so immediately and fully himself, was far reaching. It was directed first towards his fellow Territorials. They were committed only to the defence of Britain at home; to be called up for service overseas, which the war now seemed to demand, they had to make a fresh undertaking.[83] Macfie played an active part in encouraging this; three weeks into the war, he wrote to his father:

> There was a miserable response to the request for volunteers for service anywhere (we are enlisted only for service in the UK). Today the Colonel (rather a silly old ass) appealed for more, and each man was asked individually. At the end we were still 70 below the minimum with which we could be taken as an independent battalion. Moffat—an old sergeant of mine—and I went round the company and got 20 more

> from E. Co. alone in about ten minutes. The other companies did nearly as well and we must be well over the necessary number now.[84]

His sense of the imperative duty to serve extended from himself to all other able-bodied men.[85] At times it expressed itself in ugly outbursts against those (such as strikers) he regarded as shirking, or otherwise undermining the war effort.[86] It was not modified by his encounter with the most brutal aspects of the war, which he reported in clear-eyed terms to members of his family.[87] These included extremely heavy casualties suffered by his battalion at the Battle of Hooge in June 1915, which clearly distressed him.

> [At a dressing station] we waited, and as we waited men of ours stumbled down the road to have their wounds dressed. We did not believe their stories—one officer, possibly two, was left: the total strength of the battalion could not be more than ninety: so and so is killed, so and so wounded…after a while there passed through our gate a handful of men in tattered uniforms, their faces blackened and unshaved, their clothes stained red with blood or yellow with lyddite. I shouted for Y Co.—*one man* came forward! It was heart breaking. Gradually others tottered in, some wounded, all in the last stages of exhaustion; and when at last I went to lie down at about 5.30 am, there were in the camp only 25 of my 130 men who had gone out thirty-six hours before…All my sergeants are gone, eight of them…It is terrible: the regiment is practically wiped out.[88]

He also reported British officers and NCOs being prepared to shoot their own men to compel them to launch an attack in appalling conditions.[89] Macfie's stance—an acceptance of the war, and of its human costs which he recognised, regretted, but regarded as unavoidable—seems to have survived till the end.[90] Even during his last months of service, following the armistice, he was contemptuous of those who had failed to serve, or had sought a safe berth.[91]

This stance arose from a deep personal commitment, for the sake of which Macfie was prepared to put himself fully at risk. Given his age and health, he would not have been liable to conscription once it was introduced, and certainly not for front line service.[92] Yet he volunteered on the outbreak of war, refused to apply for a commission, and repeatedly sought to avoid being sent for service away from the lines or worse still back at base.[93] In the first few months of the war, he fought in the trenches.[94] Once it was made clear that quartermasters were not expected to be fighting in the front line, Macfie still interpreted his role in an unusual way. While many Quarter Masters carried out their job a mile behind the front line, well away from danger, he made frequent visits to the trenches—to see that his men were receiving the supplies they needed, and to support and encourage them.[95] It was on one such visit to the front that he organised and led a rescue party for a group of men buried by a shell explosion—an action which led to his being awarded the Military Medal.[96] When he was not involved with immediate problems of billeting and supply, he devoted himself to other activities on behalf of the men, from fighting to secure arrears of back pay, to keeping up-to-date the company roll of dead, wounded and missing, and writing letters to the bereaved relatives.[97] In August 1917, he was promoted to Regimental QMS. Though he feared this might take him away from the men, he seems to have continued his role much as before.[98]

Apart from a few weeks of home leave, and three periods of hospitalisation, Macfie was on active service throughout the war, mostly in the Ypres sector. He clearly drove himself very hard.[99] His third hospitalisation, for trench fever and then heart weakness, was precipitated by his returning too soon to active service from his second, in an effort to avoid being sent for base duties. It lasted four months, with the doctor describing him as 'emaciated'.[100] His health was permanently damaged by his wartime exertions.[101]

This degree of personal sacrifice indicates a profound investment by Macfie in Britain's wartime cause. It stems from that part of him which identified with Britain, with his maternal family's military traditions, perhaps with the Turks as fellow defenders of empire. This is the Macfie who joined the Liverpool Scottish as soon as they were formed, served energetically for seven years, was proud to be the first Volunteer to take a parade of the Black Watch regiment in Edinburgh.[102] Yet this raises the question: what had become of his ambivalences, of his investments in the Others of class, nation, and desire? Two of these were clearly assimilated into Macfie's interpretation of his wartime service. As a QMS, he lived out more intensely—much more directly and at real personal cost—the role he had played before 1914 as a paternalist employer. This comprised both his own service, and his concern for the men he served with. Such concern comes out strikingly in the incident at the start of the war when he helped persuade young men to sign on for overseas service. While convinced this was the right course, Macfie was acutely aware of the potential costs of what he was encouraging them to do. His letter to his father describing his actions (cited above) continues:

> It was rather a terrible business persuading these men to go. Some of them are in pitiable circumstances—quite young lads, without parents, who support a family of younger brothers and sisters: recently married boys with a little baby: and fellows who had aged parents, beyond work, who will be left alone. They were pathetically anxious to go, but anxious about their dependents [*sic*] too, and I felt it a very heavy responsibility to urge that it was their duty. Almost every one decided to volunteer, and some have telegraphed home for permission.

His response to this anxiety is a classically paternalist one: he appeals to his father to find some way in which 'we' (meaning the family and/or the family firm) can agree to offer financial and other practical help to the men of his Company should the need arise. 'It is horrible to think of all the suffering that may follow our mobilisation…The poor fellows come to me and explain their circumstances and ask what is their duty—and I tell them, with misgivings, go. But it is all very dreadful.'[103]

Macfie's performance of this role was also fuelled by his homoerotic desire, here sublimated into concern for his men.[104] In this context, his emphatic choice not to serve as an officer, refusing the commission to which his class and experience would entitle him, but as a sergeant is crucial and revealing. This role allowed him once again precisely to position himself liminally, and hence mediate, between officers and men.[105] This was recognised very clearly by his fellow sergeant, J. G. Coltart Moffat, who had known him since the Volunteers, and served alongside him for periods throughout the war. He reported that Macfie had been told by his Commanding Officer, when he first joined the Volunteers, that he might count on commanding the Liverpool Scottish within ten years if he took a commission. 'But Macfie would have sacrificed very many things had he gone into that restricted circle. He knew that the radius of his influence would have been terribly foreshortened, so he very wisely chose the middle rank, where, as serjeant, he was in effectual touch with both officers and men.' Moffat deduced from several conversations with Macfie that: 'association with the average subaltern would have been a great strain on his charity of soul. A commission had no attraction for him: he was happier when rubbing shoulders with everybody.'[106]

Macfie's attitude towards officers shared much of the suspicion and even contempt to be found among those who served at the front.[107] But in his case it is there from the very outbreak of war; it is expressed quite sharply, and sometimes in ways which suggest a hostility not solely rooted in experiences of actual ineffectiveness.[108] Moreover, it is evident in his account of the initial scene where volunteers are being sought for overseas service. The story as he tells it is that the officer was incompetent in his attempts to recruit the men; it took Macfie himself, supported by another sergeant, to bring the men to recognise where their duty lay—which they did in a bare ten minutes. Behind the modesty of declining the officer's role lies a sense of superiority: he can do their job better than they can.[109]

In the war, Macfie's role—the liminal one, in respect of both authority and class, of sergeant—was characterised by a strong suspicion of paternal figures (officers), and an equally strong commitment to fraternal figures (his men), towards whom he adopted the role of a solicitous elder brother (though one who was in fact more competent than the father). This can be linked to Macfie's attitude towards his own father. The letters he wrote to his father during the war were quite equable in tone, framed in the same formal epistolary manner he used towards his siblings.[110] But some of the letters to his siblings betray impatience and even anger with his father, both over his selfishness vis-à-vis the demands of the war, and more generally about his excessive caution in business and the difficulties he made for his family.[111]

That the negative figure of his father as object of attachment and identification was partly offset by that of his mother is suggested by Macfie's account of an elderly French widow, Madame Dauthieu-Houllier, with whom he was billeted in late spring 1916. A peasant, she had stayed behind in a ruined and almost deserted village to protect her (as yet little damaged) property.[112] He formed a strong friendship with this woman (asking his family to send her suitable presents, and keeping in touch by letter once the battalion moved on), and after the war published an admiring and affectionate account of her.[113] The portrait he draws is doubly revealing. On the one hand, he depicts her in relation to her (somewhat rebellious) son as the understanding mother he had once had (or, perhaps, wished he had had). 'She had...a son who had caused her anxiety. He inherited, I suppose, his mother's energy and enterprise, and finding life in the small village monotonous and cramped, had kicked over the traces.'[114] On the other hand, the qualities he admires and praises in her are those he also valued in himself. She was independent, hard working and economical; bore a hard life while retaining a lively sense of humour and interest in the world; and, confronted by the dangers of war, displayed an untroubled courage and determination in staying and defending her property. Towards the British troops, she had mirrored to a degree Macfie's own (quasi-maternal) role as billeting officer.[115] These generally acceptable virtues support the framework of wartime values within which Macfie locates his portrait. His closing sentence—'Such are the mothers of French soldiers'—echoes his opening trope of the shared courage of British troops and French peasant women.[116] Yet this conventional depiction is inflected, made more complex and individual, by other qualities which Macfie is equally keen to insist upon. Her behaviour and language were plebeian, not polite. Comparing her, tellingly, to a soldier who had reported the death of a comrade in the foulest language, Macfie commented: ' No greater mistake can be made than to judge folk by their vocabulary; some of the best of men swear horribly; some of the worst talk like archbishops.'[117] She also displayed a sceptical attitude towards figures of authority, in both church and army. Macfie's booklet celebrates a figure who displayed tenacious courage and humour in defence of property, livelihood and country, and whose values derived from inner qualities, not social position or polish. That this figure was an unconventional woman aligns her with the positive maternal, rather than the negative paternal, figures in Macfie's universe.[118]

His most explicit and revealing statement of his relationship with his father, and its effects on his wider attitudes, came in a letter of September 1917. Macfie's sister Shiela, then twenty-nine and unmarried, undertook the traditional role of the youngest daughter in her class and generation—living at home and looking after her widower father. She had recently lost her voice, and told the family that the only cure was for her to go away.

Her eldest sister had written to Macfie apparently asking him whether she should remind Shiela of her duty. He responded with a trenchant negative. He linked this to his own childhood when, he claimed—citing the hunting and riding which he might have so much enjoyed as a boy, 'every pleasure was so artfully converted into a disagreeable duty that I was quite unhappy at the time and have hated all such things ever since'. He pointedly asserted: 'You must remember that there is not one of us who has not taken the first available opportunity to escape from the position in which Shiela now is, and from which she cannot herself escape simply because she happens to be the last.' The loss of voice, he suggested, was psychological; and commented: 'A few days at Rowton [the family home] plunge me into the depths of melancholy, and I think it is wonderful that Shiela has stood it for so long without a breakdown.' Rather than preach duty at her, the rest of the family should be grateful that she carried out 'a disagreeable task' which would otherwise be their responsibility, and accept that she needed to get away to recover. Macfie also generalised his response: 'I'm afraid I hate the word "duty"—it is mostly used by people who are unwilling to do their duty and applied to others who are already doing more than their share. Chavasse would never have used it: the series of contemptible persons we have had as chaplains always did.'[119]

Macfie's extension of the critique from his family to the army chaplains is significant.[120] They, who are figures of both paternal and religious authority, receive (together with officers) repeated criticism in his wartime letters. One such comment makes a particularly pointed reference.

> I was the first man of the division to meet Father Pike, who was Brigade Roman Catholic chaplain at the time of the St Andrew's day catastrophe, and who being, where he should have been (though in defiance of orders), in the trenches, became a prisoner in Germany for 3½ months. I claimed him at once for the Liverpool Scottish, and he is now officially attached to us. It is a great catch, as our indolent and cowardly Presbyterian chaplain does nothing for the men, and is always absent from places where he is most wanted. He baptized (Major) Bertie Macfie's infant...If I were Bertie, I'd have that kid baptized again![121]

The admired Roman Catholic was 'where he should have been (though in defiance of orders)', that is—behaving as Macfie himself did, obeying a true sense of duty by defying orders if necessary; the Presbyterian, by contrast, has through laziness and cowardice undermined his power to admit members of the family to the Christian community. Macfie's earlier disillusion with Christian preachers had been reawakened.

Yet there is a profound contradiction in Macfie's stance here. He deprecates the preaching of duty by his sister, and by the chaplains, while he himself was very willing to enforce on others, if necessary harshly, the duty to serve in the war. In this contradiction may be located the whole meaning of the war for Macfie. It allowed him, for the duration, to reconcile the conflicts within himself. By doing (more than) his duty to his country he embraced to the full the dictates of established values. Doing so allowed him to criticise those who in his eyes failed the challenge: able-bodied men who did not volunteer, workers who struck for higher wages, soldiers who looked for a safe berth, chaplains who preached duty but did not put themselves at risk, old men who continued to insist on their own comforts. At the same time, by refusing the paternal role of officer, and taking on the fraternal role of sergeant, he was able to embrace as an equal a commitment to the welfare of his fellows in a way impossible, earlier in his life, even for the most generous of paternalist employers. The love of his brothers could be practised with an unconstrained freedom impossible in peacetime. At the same time, he could also enact the rebel in himself: joining the other ranks in voicing a widely shared contempt for officers and (Christian) padres...and revelling in the superiority of his Gypsy tent over army accommodation. In the eyes of authority, and more importantly in his own experience, Macfie had a "good war".

In the war, then, Macfie's ambivalence about his class and nation was much less marked. His predominant response was to fight to defend his country: criticisms of western civilisation were largely set aside. His ambivalent or contrary impulses were channelled practically into his role of QMS, and rhetorically into his criticisms of officers (offset, perhaps, by his criticisms of shirkers). The desire for Romantic Otherness survived primarily in the muted form of his repeated pleasure that his skill in erecting a Gypsy tent frequently enabled him to enjoy a more pleasant night's bivouac.[122] Nevertheless, he did find one opportunity to reassert, at least rhetorically, this desire. In his preface to *With Gypsies in Bulgaria*, written while serving in the war, Macfie connected his experiences in Bulgaria with those in the trenches, his bond to his fellow soldiers with that to Turi;

while linking both to a romantic opposition to contemporary (Christian) civilisation.

> [Those who volunteered with me] have been my comrades for more than a year in…camps and bivouacs, enjoying that peculiarly tender intimacy and unselfishness, exercising the wonderful forebearance and tolerance, which, rare alike in the city streets and country mansions of so-called civilization, attain their majestic perfection, the universal brotherhood which Mohammedans both preach and practice, through long association in the field, and after common trials—summer's heat and dust; winter's cold and mud, discomfort, thirst, fatigue, sickness, danger, and often heroism.
>
> …To my treasure has been added the love of men from every walk of life, who are—or were, for many will never again shake me by the hand—'more than brother' to me.[123]

In later-nineteenth-century Britain, the borders of class and gender/sexuality were strongly marked, and those who blurred or crossed those boundaries closely policed. Marriages, and other romantic relationships or intimate friendships, across the boundaries of class, were relatively rare and liable to provoke anxiety as transgressive.[124] Same-sex relationships, especially those between men, became the subject of a moral panic. Macfie seems to have found himself, in his twenties, unable to live within the received constraints of class (and perhaps also sexuality), unable to follow in his father's footsteps or comfortably inhabit his family's milieu. Initially, he sought to escape from his proffered social identity via attempts at direct identification with the Other, by 'becoming' a working man—a private soldier, or a labourer. His second such desertion—running away to London, to dress, work and live as a member of the working class alongside an actual worker—was both transgressive and, at that particular moment following the Wilde trial, unusually risky.

For individuals subject to such policing of identity and desire, liminal moments, spaces or positioning could provide a (permanent or temporary) opportunity for oppressive structures to be evaded, forbidden emotions experienced, new possibilities explored. Macfie eventually developed a more manageable strategy for resolving his conflicts of identity. That solution involved repeatedly positioning himself liminally in relation to some of the major structuring elements of his society—class, nation, the law, religion, sexual orientation. From that liminal position, he could act out some of the ambivalence he felt between his ascribed social identities, and alternative identities to which he was drawn: between social classes, between Anglo-Scottish and Gypsy identities, between Christianity and Islam, between law and outlaw, between sexualities. Seen in this light, his journey to the Balkans was a temporary expansion and intensification of that liminal space. For six weeks he could move freely among Gypsy communities, speaking their language, sharing their meals, revealing his other identity; and for one of those weeks he could immerse himself in the travelling life, dressing, living, camping, 'passing' as an Other to his Anglo-Scottish bourgeois self. Living an alternative identity more intensely in this way allowed Macfie to experience and express more fully his love of men.

The war provided Macfie with an exceptional opportunity to bring the various elements of his identity into closer alignment. He could lay aside his daily responsibilities to his family and the family firm for unimpeachable reasons of a national duty. His love for men could be lived out in a whole-hearted and self-sacrificing way, this new family absorbing all his time and energies. No longer separated from working men as an employer, his crossing the boundaries of class could be enacted through his precise liminal positioning as sergeant. In this role he could act as brotherly advocate for his men to the officers, father figures from whom he distanced himself and towards whom he evinced a general contempt. Yet, since he felt wholly at one with the British cause, he could still preach duty to others. In this way, he could both avoid and enact his father's example. It is not surprising that his fellow soldiers claimed Macfie enjoyed the war; it gave him an unequalled opportunity to channel all his energies into a role and for a goal with which he was psychically at ease, at once dutiful and a rebel.[125]

6

Alick West

When war broke out, Alick West (like Graves and Sorley) was due to go to university. Like Brenan and Sorley, he had spent the first half of 1914 studying in Germany. Like Sorley he was arrested as war was breaking out—but a few days later, so that he was interned. His response to the war had to be formed in a very different setting, the enforced seclusion of a prison camp. Meanwhile his older brother Graeme, already at university, was moved to volunteer, and like Sassoon, Graves, Brenan and Sorley fought on the Western Front. The reactions of the two brothers emerged in a growing conflict with their father's Christian and imperial values.

Family and Education

Alick West's father, Arthur Birt West, born in 1859, was the son of a Nonconformist clergyman. Arthur had always wanted to be a doctor, but his mother forbade this; instead, he was apprenticed in his early teens to an engineering firm. He left them in his early twenties to become a missionary, training in New Zealand and then working in India; but subsequently he returned to England and resumed work as an engineer. In 1890, he married the daughter of a Baptist minister; they had three sons—Graeme, Cecil and Alick—and then a daughter, Constance. Arthur had considerable private means, enabling him to give up the small engineering firm which he had taken over, and move his family to a Warwickshire village where he led the life of a leisured gentleman—reading, writing, studying, and music making. In 1900, when Alick was five, his mother died.[1] Alick's autobiography opens with a scene of the young West trying to ease his dying mother's pain by 'helping my brothers to cut off from her bread the crust which irritated her throat'.[2] This is one of the very few direct memories of his mother to appear in the text. Thereafter, she features as an absence rather than a presence, until his later involvement in psychoanalysis begins to touch on this loss.[3] The loss had a profound effect on both Arthur West, described as 'clinging to a grim religious faith which seems to have been a burden to him and his family', and his children.[4] The family then moved to Highgate. West's father began to work for the Charity Organisation Society in the East End, continuing this until the war.[5] In 1905, when West was ten, his father married again, a settlement worker whom he had met in the East End.[6]

In West's autobiography (as in Brenan's), his father appears as a dominating figure against whom his son has to wage a classically oedipal struggle to establish an independent identity. West's attitude to his father was characterised by a profound ambivalence. The text presents this in several ways: by an explicit struggle to assimilate various elements of his father's legacy, by a conflict between seeing his father as an individual man and as a representative of a social role, and by the splitting of his father's qualities across several mentors and companions, thereby making them available for further exploration and re-assimilation.

First, his father was the source of some values which were of great importance to West—such as his craftsmanship, displayed in his engineering, carpentry and building. This came back to West in later life when:

> I began to read Marx's *Capital*, and was pleased when I felt that I had grasped the distinction between the concrete work which creates use value and the abstract work which creates money value. As I thought about them, I associated concrete work with the memory of standing beside my father in his workshop and of how I had helped him when he was building the house at Ruislip and my cold, clammy hands had been warm and dry.[7]

Important too was a sort of sturdy independency arising from and expressed in the language of Nonconformity. Two sayings of his father which West records are: 'They say! What say they? Let them say!', and 'A man must make others listen.... He must speak out the truth that is in him.'[8]

Nevertheless, there was an ambivalence between love and fear clearly expressed in this memory of father's daily return from work. The three brothers:

> ...would ask each other 'What sort of mood is he in?' If the report was that he was 'in a wax', with trepidation we entered his study to do our homework...From time to time our father came and looked over our shoulder at our exercises and sums. If we had done them wrong and he was 'in a bait', our wits deserted us. The bureau was opened, the strap taken out, and the helpless one was whipped round the calves. He blundered more, and was sent to bed.

When he was not in a bait, he would rumple our hair and lay his firm hand on our shoulders, and I would catch the loved smell from his brown Norfolk jacket.[9]

Second, though, this ambivalence opened the way for West to present his father as also a Father, a transmitter of social authority. This is expressed first through the complex relationship between father, son and servants. West conveys a sense of the freedom from stifling and constricting convention, from the rules and limitations of upper-middle-class domestic life, which could be associated with servants and the working class, by contrasting the closed-in isolation of his own house and its neighbours with the open doors of lower class households.

> Privacy was inviolable. My father said that I must never look in at other people's windows...But the row of slummy cottages, with their doors always open, which I passed on my way to school—these were not private. In the back garden we could play Robinson Crusoe and Red Indians, and make a noise; but between us and the world before the front windows there was a separating silence.

West contrasted this with his memories of the farm where they were taken by their nurse every summer holiday. 'The red-brick timbered house was friendly...Here there was no division and no separating privacy. The door usually stood open, and we all ate together.' He recorded too its inevitably temporary nature: 'I used to cry bitterly when we had to go back...'[10]

The contrast between the relaxed world of the servants, and the more rigid constraints of upper-middle-class respectability, highlights the transitional status of the son: 'the house had two entrances. Like the tradesmen and the servants, I had to use the side entrance; but I knew that this was because I was a child, and that one day I should go in and out of the front door, as I already did with my father.' His father was both 'the authority who maintained the division and the difference', and also the dispenser of justice (intervening when the housekeeper mistreated the nurse).[11] His position within the household mirrored that in the wider world. 'We were not very rich, I thought; but there was the same distance between us and the poor as between us and the servants; and again my father embodied this order. He went to the East End to help the poor if they were deserving; but he had no need of anyone to help him.' Yet he too was subject the higher authority. 'The throne stood above us all. So did the law. One day my father took me down a turning where a notice said "Private Road". I said, "It says Private Road". My father laughed, but I was still afraid.'[12]

West's father is presented here as the mediating figure of authority, who by imposing obedience and dispensing justice maintains the hierarchies of class and generation within the household, yet is himself subordinate to wider societal power. The child's uncertain position, one of temporary subordination which will come to an end one day when he enters into his inheritance, is captured in the last exchange. His actual father could set aside the rules of exclusion when he chose; but the young West remained fearful of the power that stood even higher. 'Just as I felt for my father both love and fear, so also I loved God and dreaded His anger. "Two women shall be grinding the corn; one shall be taken, the other left."' God's, apparently arbitrary, anger had taken West's mother; where else might it not strike?[13]

Much of West's early adult life can be seen as a struggle to work through this ambivalence, as it affected not only his relation to his father, but also his political stance, and his choice of career and partner. He presents himself as having been in childhood a conformist who sided with his father. By contrast, he writes of his eldest brother:

> I think Graeme did what he could to stand between us and our father. I remember him saying to me that when my father was whipping Cecil or me in the study at Talbot Road where in fearful silence we had all been doing our homework, he wanted to throw himself on our father and tear the strap away from him, which made me aware that I felt no such anger, but rather watched with pleasure and went over to my father's side.[14]

This conformism is present in the earliest political stance he reports. He recalls, in his teens, walking through a Hampshire village with his stepmother during the constitutional crisis of 1910. '[W]e stopped on the edge of a crowd round an open-air meeting in the market place. The speaker was attacking the House of Lords. After we had listened for a little while, I sang out in my treble voice "God Save the House of Lords". My stepmother said, "Well done, Alick!"'[15]

Though his elder brothers boarded at a public school, Blundell's, Alick stayed on as a dayboy at Highgate School till he was eighteen, leaving at the end of 1913. He recorded no painful experience comparable to those of Graves, Woolf or Brenan; but he did display strong loyalty to his own school (proud because it had been founded by a knight, where his brothers' had been founded by a draper), to the public school and Christian ethos and code as purveyed in popular fiction, and through that to king and country.[16]

Both West's grandfathers had been Nonconformist ministers, and his father a missionary, so it was hardly surprising that the family atmosphere was always religious.[17] As a child West associated God closely with his father: 'Just as I felt for my father both love and fear, so also I loved God and dreaded his anger.'[18] Religion was very much part of his father's being, and they often talked together about it. However, the religious atmosphere of the family lost its intensity after his father remarried, its Nonconformist rigour modified by his stepmother's membership of the Church of Ireland, just as the tone of the household became more self-consciously cultured.[19] Like Graves and Brenan, West began gradually to lose his faith in his later teens, troubled by a growing sense of inauthenticity in his religious practice, and then by awakening sexual desires which conflicted with religious teaching of purity.[20]

Like his brothers, he was due to go to university; the intention was that he would enter Balliol College, Oxford in 1914, read Classics, and then sit the examination for the Home Civil Service.[21] The First World War was to disrupt this plan, and change the course of Alick West's life. Early in 1914, he was sent to stay with a school master's family in Germany to learn the language; after a spell in Paris, he returned there in July to meet his family for a holiday. Still there when war broke out, he was arrested and interned.

Wartime Internment

A third aspect of West's ambivalent relation to his father can be traced in the presentation of his experiences during the war. His internment for the duration, at a period of his life (aged 19-23) when he would otherwise have been leaving home for university and then a career, provided an opportunity for him to differentiate and explore aspects of his father's (and also his stepmother's) character. The context, however, was one in which issues of affiliation and loyalty had to be settled under unusual pressures, which demanded the taking of symbolic stances while precluding to a considerable extent their testing out in direct action.

Through the accident of being in Germany on holiday when war was declared, West—unlike his exact contemporaries Graves and Brenan—did not have the opportunity to fight.[22] He was held at Ruhleben, an internment camp for 4000 British men of military age or above.[23] After initial weeks of uncertain policy towards enemy aliens, on 6 November 1914 the German government extended internment to all British subjects aged 17–55.[24]

The first weeks and months at Ruhleben were uncomfortable, disturbing and disorienting for the internees. The conditions in which they were kept—the stables of a converted disused racecourse on the western outskirts of Berlin—were at first quite inadequate: overcrowded, barely sanitary, lacking any resources for recreation. The internees had little privacy (West was fortunate to be one of those kept in a horse box arranged to hold six bunks), and suffered from cold and shortage of food. Those who did not receive food parcels or money from family or friends in Britain might have to work in the camp to earn money to supplement the inadequate diet.[25] The prisoners set out to make life as bearable as possible in these difficult conditions. They were eventually allowed to establish their own system of administration, under German supervision.[26]

These physical difficulties were made worse by their uncertain and confusing status: civilians had never been interned in wartime before, and it was not clear what Germany intended to do with them. This uncertainty led to frequent rumours in the early weeks that they were about to be released. Only gradually and obliquely did it become clearer that they were likely to be interned for the duration—itself an indeterminate prospect. Such rumours therefore continued, though sporadically, throughout the first two years of the war.[27]

In his analysis of life in Ruhleben, J.D. Ketchum notes two marked responses in those early months, which he suggests determined the way in which the camp inmates as a group responded to their plight. The first was an intense patriotism. The internees were drawn from several distinct social groups—predominantly merchant seamen, businessmen, professionals (including students and travellers), and workmen—who had little in common between them.[28] It was Germany which had brought them together by interning them as British: they responded by enthusiastically embracing and accentuating this identity and its supposed characteristics.[29] First, this gave them resources to cling on to in the face of uncertainty, providing both popular slogans around which to rally in the chaos and fear of the first days (hence the regular call-and-response 'Are we down hearted? NO!'), and the basis for a code of conduct by which to begin to regulate themselves.[30] Second, it gave them a negotiating position vis-à-vis their captors: it enabled them to mobilise themselves, and eventually make connections via the American Embassy with the British government, through which they were able to press for and secure considerable improvements in their conditions.[31]

The second response was a strong communal bonding, an assertion of solidarity through collective actions, including mutual concern and practical support in the face of severe logistical difficulties and personal anxieties. So intense was this bonding that it remained a nostalgic reference point for inmates throughout the years of internment, and underpinned the later feeling of some internees that these had been the richest years of their lives.[32] Ketchum argues that by breaking down many of the conventional barriers of class and custom which would otherwise have continued to divide the very diverse group of internees, it provided an essential basis of shared values which allowed their later constructive activities to flourish.[33] What Ketchum is describing here relates closely to Victor Turner's definition of liminality in modern societies as communitas. In some way secluded from the norms of their originating culture and environment, people in such a liminal state become 'neither here nor there; they are betwixt and between the positions assigned and arrayed by law, custom and convention'.[34] '[I]f liminality is regarded as a time and place of withdrawal from normal modes of social action, it can be seen as potentially a period of scrutinization of the central values and axioms of the culture in which it occurs.'[35] The group of men in Ruhleben were cut off both from the structures and expectations of their previous life, and from a role within the new reality of the war. They were secluded in a special place, and (to a large degree) stripped of the social status which they had enjoyed before the war.[36] What emerged in the early months was an intense feeling of equality and solidarity as they sought to support each other through the crisis of the first winter and discover a new identity for themselves.[37] This new identity was double: drawing on traditional tropes of national identity (Britisher), they nevertheless reworked them into an idealised egalitarian and co-operative form (Ruhlebenite). This involved both a significant degree of levelling (at least in social habits and mores), and the opening up of new spaces for creativity. This led to the later efflorescence of educational and recreational activity. It is clear from Ketchum's account that this helped the internees to the discovery of new interests and capacities, and for some men life-long changes of values or careers.[38]

A significant change came in the spring of 1915.[39] By now, it had become clear that the internees were unlikely to be freed without lengthy negotiations; and so, despite continuing rumours of possible releases, they settled down to making life in the camp tolerable and even valuable.[40] There followed a major flourishing of sporting, recreational and especially educational activity.[41] An Arts and Science Union (ASU) had been founded in December 1914, which arranged lectures and assisted private study and creative work, as well as putting on concerts and plays.[42] A split eventually opened up in its activities. The Ruhleben Camp School, originally an offshoot of the ASU, soon became a separate organisation, meeting the substantial demand for straightforward instruction with an ambitious series of educational classes ranging from elementary to first-year university level. The ASU, by contrast, regarded themselves as self-consciously Nietzschean 'Supermen'; they were, in Ketchum's view 'young intellectuals with a passionate belief in education, but little experience of teaching and no patience with fools'.[43] By the winter of 1915 they had handed over their lectures to the Camp School, and thereafter restricted themselves to Monday evening cultural activities (from June 1915), specialist study circles, and the allotment of space for private study.[44]

Drama was prominent among these cultural activities. In March 1915 'a band of enthusiasts, who had been rehearsing under fantastic difficulties, produced Ruhleben's first play, George Bernard Shaw's *Androcles and the Lion*.' The play was a success, and initiated a series of increasingly ambitious efforts which extended eventually to 128 productions over three-and-a-half years. When in full swing, there were theatre performances four nights a week, with a new production every Wednesday.[45] Drama was, however, another site of the tension between the so-called 'Supermen' and the rest. The group who had produced *Androcles* organised themselves into the Ruhleben Dramatic Society; and launched a programme of serious drama. Though their next proposed production, Shaw's *Arms and the Man*, was banned by the German authorities, they managed an ambitious effort in the late spring of 1915, including Galsworthy's *Strife*, Shaw's *Captain Brassbound's Conversion*, and scenes from Shakespeare.[46] Conflict arose with those who wanted less serious theatre, and more pure entertainment.[47] The 'Supermen' continued to stand out for their avant-garde views.[48]

This was the context to which West had to adjust and within which he had to find his way. His development during the war can be understood diachronically in terms of how he handled the intellectual and emotional legacies of his upbringing, and synchronically in terms to his responses to the different phases of camp life and the opportunities they offered. His reaction to this experience of involuntary internment, I would argue, was to treat it as a form of moratorium. Ketchum's analysis of the camp's development in its early months stresses the importance of patriotism and comradeship, and their mutual reinforcement. But, since that strong comradeship resulted partly from a breaking down of pre-existing values, there was also the potential for emerging conflict. He notes the antinomian effects on existing identities of this crisis, in which 'the past no longer counted'.

> if social uprooting was disturbing, it was also exciting and liberating. No one knew what norms should apply, no one expected the prisoner to play his previous role; he was therefore free to conduct himself almost as he chose...the footloose youngster exulted in his freedom, and most of the prisoners were markedly affected by it. Through the shock of internment they were in some measure reborn; their set habits were broken down and their behaviour became fluid and plastic. They were thus able to act in new ways in the new situation, to assume new roles and develop somewhat different selves.[49]

Thus the internees were in a liminal place, in a moratorium in their lives which bore some analogy both with the trenches and with university.[50] The result was an astonishing sense of freedom: 'all found themselves suddenly free to behave, talk, and think almost as they chose'.[51]

At first, West took the straightforward patriotic stance of most internees, in line with the attitude he had adopted in friendly debates with his German hosts earlier in the year, and immediately on the outbreak of war: 'we British prisoners must say to ourselves "They also serve who only stand and wait".' This phrase signalled an attitude which endowed their (otherwise frustrating or futile) internment with a patriotic meaning.[52] Ketchum suggests that this patriotic feeling was a response to pressing emotional needs. Though the internees were strangers, from different backgrounds, 'they were yet one and all *British subjects*...The solidarity that resulted was therefore a national solidarity, deeply infused with patriotism.'[53] The chief source of their high morale was 'pride in belonging to a traditionally free and indomitable nation. Conscious identification with Britain had been greatly heightened by internment.'[54] He notes that the resultant morale was internalised, but that there was also peer-group pressure—'Never down hearted!' was an attitude 'achieved by individual effort, and guarded by an unwritten law'.[55] Hence, surrounded by patriotic pride, the individual internee 'was compelled to try to emulate it, for the only alternative—ceasing to regard himself as British—was inconceivable. It would destroy his very identity.'[56]

External circumstances also reinforced their stance, and added to the motivations for patriotism. There was pressure on both governments to negotiate the release of these civilian internees, but the issue was a contentious one. Germany had offered a straightforward swap, but Britain ('coldly realistic') would consider only a man-for-man exchange since it held 26,000 men compared with the 4,000 held by Germany. Hence, willingness to endure internment, thus endowed with value and meaning, became a touchstone of patriotism within the camp.[57] It was particularly important in allaying the guilt (felt by many) which arose from recognition that, however uncomfortable the conditions in Ruhleben, the internees were safe while their male family members and friends were in danger.[58]

Nevertheless, despite these pressures, West's experiences during his internment, and in particular the process of questioning the values and attitudes of his family, gradually swayed him away from his initial unquestioning support for the British cause. Describing his years in the camp, West introduces four fellow internees who can be seen to embody, in varying ways, different aspects of his father's personality. His relations with them constitute a form of working through or testing of these qualities, especially with regard to religion, art and politics.

Initially, he came under the influence of two men in particular—David More a music student, and Thompson a scientist who had been working in Germany. More was his first acquaintance in the camp, and they shared with two others one of the 'cells'. There was an early growth of social ties between men thrown together in the same box (or loft section).[59] By the end of November, almost all internees were living, not on their own, but in close relationship with a few others with whom they ate, slept and shared anxieties.[60] In some cases, these turned into lasting and close, even transformative, friendships.[61] More was a deeply devout man, who organised the religious life of the camp, forming a choir and arranging regular services of worship.[62] In the early difficult months at Ruhleben, Ketchum noted, repressed emotions such as fear found their outlet in religious services, which were crowded and afforded comfort in a time of considerable anxiety and personal distress.[63] A close friendship developed between the two men, in which West showed More his poetry, and received musical instruction in return. The intimacy of the friendship is represented through an incident when More had had a fainting fit.

> I had the bunk beneath David's, and presently I heard him stretch down his hand through the space between the edge of his bunk and the wall, and knew that he wanted me to take it. So I raised my arm and took it, and held it for a long time. When I felt that he was asleep, I pushed his hand up through the crack and felt it drop limply on the blanket. The next day he was better.[64]

West wrote about More to his stepmother, who wrote back that she had included him in her prayers; but he felt guilty because at the same time he had kept silent about another friend.[65]

This was Thompson, the scientist who had been employed by a firm in Berlin. 'He was about fifteen years older than I, though to me the difference was like that between generations.'[66] Thompson's real name was H. Stafford Hatfield; 'an electrochemist of much originality and wide interests' with a powerful literary and humanist bent, he was the outstanding figure among the Supermen.[67] Thompson and West shared a study, and Thompson rapidly became an influential figure, talking to West about his own early lower-middle-class life and education, introducing him to drama and European literature including Nietzsche, and questioning the moral basis of the war, seeing it not as a crusade to save Belgium, but instead as a struggle for commercial supremacy.[68]

The conflicting influences of these two men, between which West felt himself to be torn, became a model for his future self-understanding—as a somewhat passive figure pushed this way and that. Just as he had 'gone over to his father's side' during the caning, so too here he adopted a passive stance, symbolised in the female parts he played on the stage. The first of these was Lavinia in Shaw's *Androcles and the Lion* (with Thompson playing the Emperor).

> ...I had to maintain, as I had tried to do when I received Holy Communion, an intensity of concentration in which I, as Lavinia, would live. When I spoke, imagining my heart beating beneath my breasts and my mind aware of my coming death, I had to hold the audience in the same intensity....The play was a success; and so was I, the first appearance of a woman.[69]

Later, in a production of Ibsen's *The Master Builder*, he played the role of Hilda Wangel, the young woman who urges the master builder to overcome his fear of heights and to dare once again to climb to the top of the spire.[70]

The Arts and Science Union came under attack from other internees for its productions of Shaw and Ibsen, which were regarded as highbrow and pro-German.[71] David More criticised West, and argued that Ibsen's Master Builder lived on the strength he drained from his wife; West replied with the political and artistic creed he had learned from Thompson: 'the talk about the war being a war for freedom and democracy and the rights of small nations was deception, in which the artist must have no part'.[72] Here arose an issue which was to haunt West again and again—that of the discrepancy between the evaluation of individuals and structures: 'But when David replied that the men who were fighting believed in the ideals for which they fought, I felt what had been in my own mind as I listened to Thompson in silence: my brothers were fighting, and I wronged them by making them into the mindless instruments of politicians and financiers.'[73] A final break between them came when More said, '"It's no use…You won't let yourself be what you are."' More moved out to another cell, and West stopped attending religious services.[74]

The third important figure through whom West explored aspects of his father was a man called Arch. The son of a printer, who was a leading Baptist in a small provincial town, 'he himself had the same kind of dignity as a good craftsman. He was grave and pale, and had grown a thick dark beard, so that he looked like an Old Testament patriarch.' Arch appears only infrequently in the text; but as even this opening physical description makes clear, he features as a "good father", sharing certain characteristics of West's own father, but free to make his own choices in relation to them. Thus he was a craftsman, who had been apprenticed as a carpenter, but hated it and lost his job through reading poetry in the workshop in his spare time. He later became a lay preacher, though subsequently he lost his faith overnight. 'He was without bitterness, but capable of intense anger against injustice to others; and he felt more than anyone I knew in the Camp the untold misery of a senseless war.'[75] The text recognises this role as "good father", by subsequently presenting the two men as able to "feed" one another. In 1919, when Arch was starving, West sold out £50 of war loan for him. Nearly thirty years later, when West was longing to live in the country, Arch recalled this occasion, and acted to repay the loan by offering West space in his house and 'giving me my food at what it cost to cook'.[76]

Under Thompson's influence, West made a decisive break with the patriotic stance, accepting a German invitation, early in 1917, to apply to be released from the camp and work in industry. 'Not to do so was to take my place with the herd, standing and waiting and serving my country.' Though Thompson's application was soon accepted, in West's case his services were not required, and so he remained in the camp till the end of the war.[77]

With Thompson gone, West spent more time with the fourth important figure from the camp, Paul Farleigh, a French teacher at a school in Edinburgh, to whom Thompson had introduced him.[78] Farleigh was the son of a deeply religious Catholic mother who had wanted him to become a priest. In the camp he too had changed; while at the beginning he still practised his religion, he had now become an atheist, devoted to art as what gave meaning to life. West admired him for what he regarded as Farleigh's impersonal respect for values, expressed in his criticisms both of West's poetry and of his character—as a 'born compromiser' and 'receptive to the point of weakness'.[79] From this point in the text, Farleigh is used as a sort of double, both positive and negative, of West himself. He is deployed to voice the judgments of West's stern, even harsh, conscience on himself.[80]

As West presents them, his relations with these four men offered him different ways of relating to, exploring the tensions between, and identifying with, aspects of the personalities of his father (and stepmother). Various stances towards religious adherence are represented by More's continuing fidelity; by Thompson's critique; by Arch's earlier commitment to both art and religion and his later loss of faith set alongside a hatred for injustice; and by Farleigh's equivocal rejection of belief. Under the influence of Thompson, and later of Farleigh, art became an alternative to religion as a source of value; yet West remained uneasy before the criticism he felt implicit in More's valuing of religion above art. The romantic and Nietzschean versions of art which West was drawn into reinforced a politics oppositional to the 'herd instinct' of patriotism, yet left him unable to disregard his brothers' continuing service.[81]

Graeme West's War

West was released at the end of the war and returned home.[82] Once back in England, conflict with his father and his father's values, which had hardly emerged before the war, but had begun to be explored in symbolic ways in relation to his fellow internees, came into the open over the issue of the war. His eldest brother, Graeme, had been killed at the front in 1917. At the end of the war, a close friend, Cyril Joad, had published Graeme's wartime diaries, letters and poems, together with a brief memoir. These revealed that he had come to believe the continuance of the war pointless, and had wished, but had lacked the courage, to refuse to continue serving.[83] Their father was bitter over the publication of the memoir, making public what he regarded as a moment of weakness under stress; and did not want Alick to read it.[84] Alick, however, went to see Joad, got a copy of the book, and learned of his brother's experiences.[85] An exploration of Graeme West's experience is of value, both for the importance it came to hold for Alick, and because of its connections—personal and structural—with that of Sassoon.

Graeme, born in 1891, had been sent like Alick to Highgate School and then at the age of fourteen as a boarder to Blundell's. His experience there, according to his fellow-pupil Joad, was a familiar story: he was bookish, unathletic, a little unpopular, and hence relegated by his school fellows to the category of 'worm'. He won a scholarship to Oxford in 1910, where he read classics and developed a passion for literature.[86] Joad described him as being notably self-contained as an undergraduate, so that at first the outbreak of war made no impact; he returned to Oxford in autumn 1914 to read English. However, at Christmas he applied for a commission; he was refused because of his eyesight, but then managed to enrol as a private in the Public Schools' Battalion in February 1915.[87] In November 1915 he was sent to France, then in December up to the front.[88] Graeme's responses to his army experiences over the next eighteen months, recorded contemporaneously in his diary and letters, make a significant comparison with those of Graves and Sassoon.[89] Four aspects in particular may be highlighted: the impact of these experiences in making him critical of the war; the links between this and his growing alienation from patriotism and religion; his struggles to find the courage to protest; and his search for a figure of authority to validate his stance.

A letter to Joad in February 1916 shows that his first spell in the trenches had brought him remarkably quickly to a familiar position.[90] He claimed to hate only soldiers in general and a few NCOs in particular, while feeling 'amiable fraternity' for the Germans in the trenches opposite. The troops were stuck there until their respective governments were ready to talk peace.[91] He continued to pursue a commission, and finally had his eyesight passed by a private doctor. From March to the end of August 1916, he went through officer training in Scotland.[92] This experience seems to have had the disruptive effect on him which much longer service, at the front, had on others.[93] According to Joad, he had joined the army from a feeling of duty and patriotism, while abhorring violence. He was an individualist who hated routine and system, and hence the whole mechanism of officer training with its mindlessness, callousness, and enforced group discipline. This inner revolt is recorded in stark detail in the diary account of his training.[94]

Once it was completed, in August 1916, he spent the several weeks of the usual pre-posting leave divided between his family in London and the Joads and other friends in Surrey.[95] Here the feelings of revulsion from his army experiences crystallised, and changed his attitude to the war.[96] What is striking in Graeme's account is the explicit link he makes, in rejecting them, between religious faith and patriotism; and between them and other smaller loyalties.[97] Already during the period of training, he had evolved a philosophy of nihilism, that nothing had any value. Viewed from the long perspective of past civilisations whose relics were to be found in the British Museum, 'Even the decision of this war is nothing; what does England matter, or whether she wins or not?...Mankind is perpetually puffing itself up with strange unearthly loyalties and promised rewards. Man goes out to fight for a delusion, to defend what he has tricked up as his Fatherland.'[98] He had adopted a new philosophy, that to bring happiness into the world was the only aim which mattered.

> all other creations that are supposed to have a claim on my life and time I spurn. I spurn the idea that I am naturally enthusiastic for the success of my hut or Platoon or Company or Battalion; that I am necessarily fonder of my own country than any other, and most of all, now, I reject the presumption that I worship a God by whose never wronging hand I conceive all the present woe to have been brought upon the now living generation of mankind.[99]

From this individualist perspective, collective loyalties were destructive: 'What right has anyone to demand of me that I should give up my chance of obtaining happiness—the only chance I have, and the only thing worth obtaining here?...I asked no one to form societies to help me exist. I certainly asked no one to start this war.'[100] Religion in particular came under critical scrutiny; at the start of his stay with the Joads, he noted in his diary that he now disbelieved completely in Christianity, and in the historical figure of Christ.[101]

Reflection on his experience had made him critical of the war and the ideologies used to justify it. This criticism now crystallised under the pressure of his imminent return to the front. Spending his leave in civilian company, he recorded, he had done fundamental thinking about the war and the army.[102] He moved among conscientious objectors (Joad was a pacifist); and read and was influenced by liberal writing.[103] In the light of this new understanding, he felt that his decision to enlist had been mistaken: 'I was under so many delusions when I joined at first; most of those have faded, especially religious ones.'[104] There followed what proved to be the crisis of his life—an agonised weekend in which he tried but failed, first to tell his family that he felt continuing with the war was wrong, and then to refuse to report back for service.[105]

His account reports a classically obsessional process of hesitation, of making and undoing resolutions. One aspect is worth tracing in detail—the use he made of Bertrand Russell's writings in his inner struggle. Of his Saturday with the Joads, he wrote: 'Never was the desire to desert and to commit suicide so overwhelming, and had it not been that I knew I would pain many people, I would certainly have killed myself that night.'[106] That night, having returned to London, he read Russell's essay 'Justice in War Time', and was so impressed by it that the desire to kill himself was replaced by the determination to stand out against the war. On the Sunday morning, he did not accompany his family to church, but re-read Russell, and decided to announce his decision to them at lunch. Again, he failed to do so. On Sunday night, he wrote a letter setting out his decision to his superior officer (in terms similar to Sassoon's of a year later), took it to the post box, but then could not post it. The same unavailing struggle was repeated the following day.[107] On the train to rejoin his regiment, he read Russell yet again, hoping it would help him maintain his beliefs back in the army, even if he could not acknowledge them openly.[108]

Graeme had not disowned his criticism of the continuance of the war. An hour before leaving the house to rejoin his regiment, he had written to Joad: 'I am *almost* certain I do wrong to go on—not quite certain, and anyhow, I question if I am of martyr stuff.'[109] In his inner conflict over what stance he should take, he seems to have used Russell's writing as a support, a vindication from a voice carrying authority of his own moral judgment about the rightness of the war, and the ideologies and loyalties which supported it. But it was not enough. As Samuel Hynes notes: 'The conflict between duty (or social pressure, or fear of authority) and hatred of the war was intense and deeply disturbing—and more so in the first years, when there were not yet any examples of opposition by soldiers, no bitter poems, no public gestures.'[110] Graeme did, however, find one way to make a form of protest. Responding to a posthumous volume of poems by another Volunteer officer (and Oxford student) of his own generation, Rex Freston, killed in January 1916, he wrote an angry riposte to its heroic idealising. Beginning 'God! How I hate you, you young cheerful men, / Whose pious poetry blossoms on your graves', it cites Freston's 'Oh happy to have lived these epic days' and then combats it with a realistic account of the trenches ('his head / Smashed like an egg shell, and the warm grey brain / Spattered all bloody on the parados') in the style which Graves and Sassoon were also developing. A version of the poem was published in the radical journal *New Age* in October.[111]

In September 1916, Graeme was sent to France, where he continued to serve at the front (believing the war to be sheer cruelty and waste) until he was killed in April 1917.[112] During this period, his experience (once again comparable to that of Graves and others) confirmed the judgment he had come to. He now wrote his most vivid and powerful accounts of the cruelty and destructiveness of what he saw in the trenches.[113] He struggled to justify to himself his own vision of the war, and his right to hold that vision. Reflecting on his very rapid shift of understanding and affiliation in the light of his experiences during the eighteen months since joining up, he recognised that further profound changes might lie ahead.[114] Nevertheless, he felt respect was due only to those 'poets and philosophers' who thought critically. Like Sassoon, he sought to understand why his fellow officers did not question themselves about the war. Noting that their response to his avowed atheism was either to question its genuineness, or to view him as morally suspect, he suggested that independent judgment was the rarest thing in the world.[115] They would fight on, patiently if not happily, sure that this was both necessary and useful, a stance he had once accepted but could no longer.[116] With a fatalistic attitude of 'It had to be!', they could not imagine that Britain might have any share of responsibility, nor that conscientious objectors could be worthy of respect. 'The maddening thing is the sight of men of fairly goodwill accepting it all as necessary; this angers me, that men must go on. Why? Who wants to?'[117] Even men who had come to regret joining up had strong reasons for not admitting it.[118] He did, however, record one officer who, returning from a training course, 'remarked, half-ashamedly, that he had really come to the conclusion since he had been away that the war was really very silly, and we all ought to go home. Nobody took any notice of what he said, or else treated it laughingly.' Graeme felt this officer was serious, and resolved to get to know him.[119]

During this period, he corresponded with Russell, who seems to have become for him a father figure who through his writings both validated Graeme's own view of the war, and represented the possibility of building a better future after it. Graeme first wrote to him from camp in Dorset shortly after reporting back for service, offering sympathy over Russell's eviction from his Cambridge fellowship for his anti-war activities.

> I know you must have many friends in the army, and are aware that it, too, contains men of good will, though it is through it and its domination that England finds herself as she is...Were I back in the Ranks again—and I wish I were—I could have picked half-a-dozen men of our platoon to have signed with me: here, it is not so.[120]

He wrote again from the Somme in December, having read Russell's *Principles of Social Reconstruction.* His language is striking for its religious resonances, informing Russell that for some 'the hope of helping to found some "city of God" carries us away from these present horrors', and assuring him there were those who after the war would commit their energies to 'the creative work that peace will bring to do'.[121] The religious imagery here served a double purpose: it mitigated the breach with Christianity which would be doubly hard for this son of an ex-missionary (as shown also by Alick's continuing struggle with religious questions both in the camp and later), and it provided a buttress for the otherwise frail hope of overcoming the destruction of war.[122]

Graeme West, as much it seems from his officer training as through his previous experiences in the trenches, came to find the war unjustifiable. Closely linked to this was his developing criticism of religion and patriotism as delusions. In so doing, he was turning against voices of authority, both those of the state and that of his own patriotic and religious father. Yet, for fear of hurting his family, he held back, opting instead for a form of inner exile. As he himself partly indicated, through his invocation of Hamlet, he shrank from overt action. He concealed his conflict within himself, not sharing it with his conscientious objector friends, revealing it only in the dumb show at the letter box to which he was the sole witness. Thereafter, through reading and writing, he turned to Russell as mentor and alternative authority, who could afford both confirmation of his own views and materials towards a vision of the future. Through their service as line officers, Graves and Sassoon had come to share similar attitudes: the war was madness, its patriotic and religious justifications empty; the government should work for a negotiated peace; but till then they must see it through. Then, in July 1917, Sassoon broke with this consensus. In an uncanny mirroring, he *enacted* the scene which West had only *envisaged*. In making his protest, he directly sought help from the conscientious objectors, including Russell. Thereafter, however, his protest was to be recuperated and neutered, in a form of undoing which again mirrored that of Graeme West.

For Alick, once he learned of it, Graeme's stance—from the position of a soldier who had served in the front line—offered a vindication of his own opposition to the war, formed through intellectual questioning in the isolation of the camp. It also provided an alternative focus of identification within the family to his father's continuing patriotism. During the following decade and more, as West struggled to define his own political position, he was to continue to hold to Graeme's rejection of the war as both a touchstone, and a justificatory talisman, of his own oppositional stance.[123]

This emergent conflict with his father came to its peak as West tried to decide on a career.[124] His father wanted him to continue with the prewar plan to go up to Oxford; West himself was now determined to become a writer. As the tension between them grew, so did the conflict West perceived between the individual man and the bearer of a social role. As his father helped him recuperate from the war, and they shared their respective wartime experiences, 'At first there were moments of nearness between us'.[125] But then his father began to press him to a decision: why not, he argued, get a degree first, as a safeguard for a career in case writing proved unsuccessful. Alick replied with a defence of poetry and an attack on Oxford as a school for gentlemen.

> Even if I was right, my father said, why should I be afraid of Oxford? Why couldn't I go there and get the degree I needed, and stick to my guns? 'A man ought to be captain of his soul', he said. If I didn't go, I should be cutting myself off from life. 'A man must make others listen',

he said. 'He must speak out the truth that is in him.' Those words stuck.[126]

Thompson, now returned to England, encouraged West's resistance. 'Your father has all the possessive instincts of the middle class; he thinks of a son as a piece of property.'[127]

In an effort to resolve the conflict, his father drew on the full resources of his paternal role. First, he threatened to cut Alick out of his Will ('Theobald Pontifex, I thought, in *The Way of All Flesh*, shaking his Will at Ernest'), and then: 'there was a note from him beside my plate, saying that I must either obey him or leave the house by the end of the week.'[128] As the time for decision neared, even moments of intimacy came to seem to West an unfair weapon in the struggle. Faced with this ultimatum, he persisted in his refusal to go to Oxford; but at the last moment he accepted a compromise suggestion of his stepmother and went instead to Trinity College, Dublin.[129]

When, during the war, he was held in the internment camp, West for the first time began to question his father's values and oppose his political stance. That questioning became one of the central elements in West's own subsequent political evolution. The way he dealt with the ambivalence he now felt towards his father was to present him as also a 'Father', a transmitter of social authority; that is, to split him between an individual person whose qualities could be valued and absorbed and a social figure who could be challenged and repudiated. His ambivalent relationship to his father then helped to shape his attitudes to wider focusses of authority

His father's values, and the authority with which he preached them, put Alick West (and perhaps also Graeme) into a form of double bind. He urged his sons to take the stance of the proud, independent and outspoken Nonconformist conscience: '"They say! What say they? Let them say!", and "A man must make others listen....He must speak out the truth that is in him."' Yet in practice he could brook no contradiction of his own point of view. Graeme felt himself unable to articulate his rejection of the war, and when Alick refused to follow the career path planned for him, he was expelled from the family home and cut out of his father's Will. So it is perhaps not surprising both that these sayings became for West a touchstone by which he sought to measure his own actions—and that he then often found those actions wanting.[130]

Part III
Divided Identities: The War and Its Aftermath

7

The Encounter of Siegfried Sassoon and W.H.R. Rivers

This chapter looks in more detail at the celebrated encounter between Siegfried Sassoon and W. H. R. Rivers at Craiglockhart Hospital in 1917, following Sassoon's abortive protest against the continuation of the war. A reconsideration of the reciprocal impact of the two men on each other will reveal in more detail how the nation state policed its citizens during wartime, how they in turn policed themselves through internalised ideologies of and attachments to the nation and subordinate institutions within it, and what was at stake in their respective struggles to free or discipline themselves. Examination of the wider role of psychotherapy during the war will illuminate how a particular professional ethos and practice could become subordinated to the demands of the nation.

Sassoon at Craiglockhart

The large numbers of soldiers, especially officers, diagnosed as suffering from shell shock during the war made it seem better to treat them individually as medical rather than judicial problems.[1] As a result of Graves's intervention, Sassoon's political protest was defused by being deemed medical, assimilated into the category of shell shock where it clearly did not belong (even if it originated in the same trench-warfare conditions as gave rise to shell shock).[2] As a result, Sassoon was sent for treatment with Rivers. The effect of this treatment was to lead Sassoon to doubt not merely any possible effectiveness of his protest (which the army's acceptance of Graves's intervention had already muffled), but also in the longer term his own capacity to form the judgments on which the protest was based. If shell shock can be seen as a form of *silent* protest (whether through the mutism of the soldier, or the disorientation of the officer), to be equally tacitly dealt with by therapy, then the application of that same therapy to Sassoon rendered his political action a *silenced* protest.[3]

Rivers was one of the medical personnel who had been involved in developing a form of psychotherapeutic treatment for shell-shock victims. He joined the staff of Maghull Military Hospital in July 1915, was commissioned Captain in the RAMC in 1916, and in October of that year was transferred to Craiglockhart Hospital for Officers, where he remained till the end of 1917.[4] In his theoretical writing, Rivers combated the notion of these patients as cowards; instead he stressed their sense of duty which, by forbidding them to desert their task or their men, gave rise to the inner conflicts which issued in their symptoms.[5] His treatment, though therapeutically innovative, remained within the framework of that same army discipline to which he himself was also subject.[6] Neither in theory nor in practice did he question the rightness of the need to enable such men to return to active service. However, the nature of his exchanges with Sassoon (and perhaps with other shell-shocked soldiers) opened up a consideration of the morality of the war.

Rivers was quite clear that Sassoon was not suffering from shell shock, or any neurotic symptoms. This is set out in the report he prepared after his first meeting with Sassoon.

> There are no physical signs of any disorder of the Nervous System. He discusses his recent actions and their motives in a perfectly intelligent and rational way, and there is no evidence of any excitement or depression. He recognises that his view of warfare is tinged by his feelings about the death of friends and the men who were under his command in France.[7]

Sassoon wrote to Ottoline Morrell: 'My doctor is a sensible man who doesn't say anything silly…He doesn't *pretend* that my nerves are wrong, but regards my attitude as abnormal. I don't know how long he will go on trying to persuade me to modify my views.'[8] However, when asked by Sassoon if he thought he was suffering from shell shock, Rivers replied: 'You appear to be suffering from an anti-war complex.' His use of the term 'complex' (as opposed to, say, 'attitude' or 'point of view') hinted at a psychologising of Sassoon's stance. Retrospectively, in *Sherston's Progress*, Sassoon commented that they had both laughed, as if at a shared joke.[9]

But his contemporary letter to Graves suggests that the implication had nevertheless got under his skin. 'He says I've got a very strong "anti-war complex", whatever that means. I should like the opinion of a first-class "alienist" or whatever they call the blokes who decide if people are dotty.'[10]

After three months at Craiglockhart (in many ways very productive for Sassoon, both for his own poetry and through his meeting with Wilfred Owen), he became very unhappy with his situation. With his protest effectively squashed, he began to feel guilty that he was betraying his fellow soldiers, keeping himself safely at home but for a suitably high-minded reason. This guilt was expressed in the poem 'Sick Leave', in which the dead 'whisper to my heart; their thoughts are mine. /..."When are you going back to them again? / Are they not still your brothers through our blood?"'[11] In addition, he felt both uneasy at being categorised with true shell-shock victims, and distressed at the atmosphere which their suffering produced. While he could express profound sympathy for the 'finer types of men' whose 'humanity had been outraged', he felt an urgent need to dissociate himself from 'a tacit understanding that we were all failures', reassuring himself that: 'After all, I haven't broken down; I've only broken out.'[12] He seems also to have been coming under increasing pressure from Rivers, writing to Morrell: 'he practically told me to-night that I am a pernicious person'.[13]

Sassoon was trapped. As he explained to Morrell:

> if I continue my protesting attitude openly after being passed for General Service they will call it a 'recrudescence' or relapse and keep me shut up here or elsewhere. They will *never* court martial me. The only chance would be—after being passed fit—to get an outside opinion from a man like Mercier [a mental health specialist]. I don't know how they'd act if *he* said I was normal.[14]

Despite mentioning this option of an independent assessment to both Graves and Morrell, Sassoon does not seem to have taken it seriously. Once it had been made clear that any further protest would be muffled in the same way, he felt that the only course open to him was to apply to return to active service, without withdrawing his views. He demanded a guarantee that he would be allowed to rejoin his battalion on the Western

Front, which Rivers negotiated on his behalf. Justifying his decision to Morrell, he wrote: 'After all I made my protest on behalf of my fellow fighters, and (if it is a question of being treated as an imbecile for the rest of the war) the fittest thing for me to do is to go back and share their ills. By passing me for General Service…they admit that I never had any shell shock…'[15] Sassoon maintained this stance, and—after he had deliberately missed a medical board in October—was passed fit for General Service at the end of November.[16]

Sassoon was quite clear about what were the costs of this (to him necessary) decision. In *Sherston's Progress*, he records the internal dialogue which preceded his decision. In addition to his conflict over the rightness of the war, and despite his growing sense that he should be with his men, he also recoiled from this likely 'renunciation of life' in favour of a 'potential death sentence', since 'the fact that it was everybody's business to be prepared to die for his country did not alter the inward and entirely personal grievance one had against being obliged to do it.'[17] After he rejoined the battalion at Litherland, he wrote: 'It is the only way by which I can hope to face the horrors of the front without breaking down completely. I must try to think as little as possible.'[18] When his posting to Egypt came through in late January, he made initial efforts to get himself transferred to the French or Italian fronts, against the urgings of both Graves and Rivers.[19] Thereafter, for the last six months of his war, until he was wounded again in July 1918, he tried to concentrate all his energies into helping his men. 'Nothing matters now but the welfare of the company I am with.'[20] This attitude had to be maintained, at times with difficulty, against both external and internal pressures to be a warrior.[21]

However, Sassoon did not in fact stop thinking. His diary records his continuing effort to understand why most of his fellow officers did not protest, but carried on with the war. Already the year before he had interpreted it in terms of the comfort of being relieved of all responsibility. Now, trying to understand the psychology of the 'average officer', he speculated: 'I am beginning to suspect that their mental deadness is an effective protection for them against the impending disasters. They refuse to *face* facts. And their mental atrophy makes it easy. They know they are "for it", and hope for luck and a Blighty wound or a cushy job. It is every man for himself.'[22]

Elaine Showalter, in her analysis of their encounter, sees Rivers as treating Sassoon by playing on his fears about his masculinity; in particular, that his attitude to the war was emotional/feminine, in contrast to Rivers's own which was rational/masculine. Sassoon, she argues, 'found himself overwhelmed by guilt and humiliation at being "dumped down among nurses and nervous wrecks", the women and non-combatants he had always despised....he needed to dissociate himself from them and to affirm his own sanity—in a way his own masculinity.'[23] My reading of Sassoon's account emphasises another dimension of anxiety about masculinity—what Rivers played on, in my view, was Sassoon's fear of being thought childish/adolescent, as much as feminine. It is clear that Sassoon formed a classical transference to Rivers as a father figure. Apart from the structural aspects of the doctor-patient relationship, and the age gap between them (Rivers was twenty-two years older), Sassoon's family constellation may well have contributed. His Jewish father, who had been disowned by his family for marrying outside their faith, had left his wife when Sassoon was five, and died soon after; the young boy was brought up by his mother. Richard Slobodin comments: 'Sassoon was not only fatherless but cut off from his father's line'.[24] While in his actions and letters of 1917 his attitude to Rivers is a little distant, by the time of his return to the front in 1918 he had formed a deep and lasting attachment.[25] Although Sassoon left Craiglockhart still holding to his position that the war should be brought to an end, by the late 1920s his stance had changed. His autobiographical writings both incorporate his post-war revision of his views about the possibility of a negotiated peace with Germany (thereby bringing him closer to Rivers's wartime standpoint), and include a marked degree of idealisation of and identification with Rivers (perhaps partly due to the loss represented by his premature death). Rivers now features as a source of wisdom and security, an authoritative voice on the politics of the war and its continuance.[26]

This view then overshadows the retrospective narrative of his protest and its outcome which Sassoon offers in his autobiographical trilogy. *Memoirs of an Infantry Officer* consistently ironises the episode, mocking the protest itself, the supposed political ignorance on which it was based, and its bathetic outcome. The text stresses the contrast between the naïve young Sassoon's expectations of martyrdom, and the reality of how he was actually treated.[27] In *Sherston's Progress*, Rivers represents adulthood, sanity and wisdom, while Sassoon clearly internalises this valued father figure. Again he mocks his own stand, especially via his depiction of the anti-war character Macamble and his attempt to 'rescue' Sassoon from Craiglockhart to resume his protest; he is seen (both when first encountered and in retrospect) as a (foolish) tempter.[28] Showalter notes the extraordinarily apt symbolic role of the Macamble figure (who has no counterpart in Sassoon's contemporary letters); she comments: 'It is really as if Macamble is the negative side of Rivers, the evil version of the benevolent authority; and the pacifist plot a test.'[29] The experiences of both Sassoon and Graeme West show clearly the psychic importance of the father, and of the wider authorities he both represents and is succeeded by, in validating or undermining the formation of the capacity to make judgments.

Rivers as Wartime Doctor

Rivers's encounter with Sassoon, and the values on which it was based, have to be placed in the wider context of the treatment of shell shock during the war. Eric Leed suggested doctors recognised that, in treating shell shock, they had assumed certain judicial and political functions.[30] He divided their therapeutic approaches into two groups, those of the moralists (who used primarily physical and persuasive techniques) and the analysts (who used psychotherapeutic methods).[31] The former adopted what he terms a 'disciplinary' approach, where for example electric-shock apparatus was deployed to determine:

> whether the patient could be persuaded, once more, that the survival of the public self, the nation, was a more pressing obligation than the survival of his individual ego. The basic conflict in therapy was conceived as a moral conflict between private and public selves in which the therapist was responsible for the total, unremitting assertion of the demands of duty.[32]

For analysts, by contrast, he suggests, the moral issue ceased to be one simply enacted in the medical encounter (with the doctor representing the demands of collective duty). Instead, both analyst and patient were brought to consider the moral and psychic implications of the continuing slaughter, and beyond this the tolerability of the war itself.[33]

However, Laurinda Stryker's detailed study of British shell-shock theories during the war calls this conclusion into question. She asks why those theories did not in fact anticipate the questions about the human costs of the war which modern scholarship sees as central. It was, she suggests, because they 'framed soldiers' breakdowns in ways which served to militate against such understandings and forestall such reflections'.[34] The default assumption behind all treatments (both physical and psychological) was that the sufferers retained a strong and conventional sense of duty, based upon both the military ethos and civilian models of masculinity. It was not the circumstances of the front, but men's responses to them, which needed to be addressed. This was done by simultaneously modifying the traditional code of masculinity, through acknowledging that fear was a natural response, not to be denied; while also invoking an underlying continuity of values. The intensity of such hysterical symptoms as paralysis or mutism was evidence of the strength of commitment to duty in its conflict with the instinct of self-preservation. 'That the unconscious had to adopt such extreme measures was itself proof of the soldiers' mettle.'[35] She concludes: 'A moral conservatism prevailed even amongst the most radical of the Freudians; the potential political and ethical implications of shell-shock theory were overwhelmed by the pull of conservative values which were shared by psychologists and their patients alike.'[36]

Yet this general moral conservatism, and the specific recuperation of Sassoon's protest into continuation of war service, is not the whole story. Both Showalter and Samuel Hynes, in their discussions of Rivers's work at Craiglockhart, note that despite maintaining his pro-war stance, he was nevertheless affected by his encounter with Sassoon.[37] Their discussions focus mainly on what Rivers terms his 'Pacifist' Dream, in analysing which he makes explicit reference to his most famous patient.[38] However, this focus may have the effect of misrepresenting the impact of this now iconic meeting, by treating it in isolation from Rivers's continuing work with war-damaged patients. By situating this dream in its wider context in his posthumous book *Conflict and Dream* (1923), it is possible to gain a fuller picture of Rivers's attitude to the war and his responsibilities during it, and how he handled the dilemmas to which these gave rise. The purpose of the book is to defend Rivers's own interpretation of the function of dreams. Unlike Freud's view that all dreams are wish fulfilments, he sees them as attempted solutions to inner conflicts, which display both psychic contents and modes of mental functioning deriving from earlier phases of life.[39] He avoids any depth psychological approach, emphasising instead the relevance of dreams to current conflicts in the dreamer's life.[40] To expound his theory, Rivers analyses several dreams of his own, as well as some of his patients'. Three of these dreams are directly relevant to the war; I shall consider them in their chronological order.

The first, that of the 'Reproachful Letter', Rivers dates precisely to 20/21 March 1917, five months after he had arrived at Craiglockhart, and four months before Sassoon did.[41] In it he had received a letter from a friend, which strongly reproached him for his political views. In analysing the dream, Rivers recognised that the reproach arose from his reading, the previous day, the *Cambridge Magazine*, one of the main publications which carried anti-war writing.[42] At the time, he took the affect of reproach as the key element of the dream, and saw it as referring to a self-reproach of the previous day about his insensitive handling of a particular patient. At this point in his dialogue with Freud, he was coming to think that dreams could express other affects than those of desire; the dream seemed to prove this point. Hence, he rested content with this explanation of the dream.[43] Four years later, his view had shifted to seeing dreams as attempted solutions to conflicts. As he was writing this chapter of his book, he interrupted it to re-analyse his dream in that light. He then detected:

> a conflict which I supposed might have been going on in my mind concerning the continuance of the war. At the time of the dream (1917) I was manifestly adopting the orthodox attitude, and any such pacifist tendency as might have been aroused by reading the *Cambridge Magazine* would have been repressed, thus providing exactly the conditions by which such a dream as that with which we are dealing would have been produced.[44]

All this was expressed in the conditional form: such a conflict 'might have been going on'. However, the night after the initial re-analysis, a new dream brought back to him what he had:

> completely forgotten, that I had had a definite conflict in my mind at the time (i.e. March 1917) whether I was right in subscribing to the *Cambridge Magazine*. The conflict was between the view that it was right

> to know the truth, to know what the people of other nations, enemy or allied, were thinking, and the view that in time of war nothing should be done to make people doubtful about the absolute justice of the cause for which they were fighting.[45]

Two aspects of Rivers's re-analysis are striking. First, once he has accepted such a conflict really existed in 1917, then in accordance with that aspect of his theory which expects the dream to make reference to an earlier stage of his mental life, he suggests that 'the former attitude would appeal more to my adult intelligence, while the second point of view would have appealed more to me in my youth'. It is from that youthful self that he imagines the reproach for his political views emanating.[46] Second, following an image in his new (1921) dream, of taking some books into his bedroom, he has the idea that:

> it might have been right to read the *Magazine* in private, but that it was not suited for general circulation. This certainly fitted with an element in the old conflict, according to which it was thought that such knowledge as was being provided by the *Magazine* should be accessible, but that such accessibility had its dangers, especially in connection with the army, where it might lead to a lowering of *morale*. The bedroom of the dream thus seems to have served as a symbol for privacy as opposed to publicity in relation to this publication.[47]

The text leaves it unclear whether this idea of reading the magazine only in private is a thought of 1921 or of 1917.[48] But what it reveals is the depth of Rivers's investment in the nation's cause. He is torn between his commitment as a scientist to seeking out, publishing and circulating truth, and as a patriot and soldier to preserving morale at all costs. As a citizen, he may contemplate dissenting views about the war; but as an army medic, he must protect his patients from such troubling questions. In 1921 he splits these attitudes between his older and his younger selves; but it is not clear that in 1917 the division was so neatly diachronic rather than synchronic. The solution to this conflict which he considers (or considered)—curiously abstracted in the passive 'it was thought'—is that such knowledge should remain private. The anti-war *Cambridge Magazine* is thus figured as though it were an early twentieth-century book of sexual knowledge—also too dangerous to public morality to be read except in the privacy of the bedroom.

Already in the spring of 1917, then, Rivers was experiencing inner conflict over his attitude towards the war. But, although by now he had extensive knowledge from his patients of their experiences at the front, any doubts were expressed in intellectual questions over policy and strategy.[49] He does not date his 'Pacifist' dream, but it was during his treatment of Sassoon, almost certainly before the latter decided to return to the front (that is, between July and September 1917). In line with his general theory that dreams always contain an egoistic motive, Rivers analyses it as a personal conflict between social duty and individual desire.[50] 'Though my manifest attitude was definitely in favour of war to the finish, I had no doubt about the existence of a very keen desire that the war should end as soon as possible for the egoistic motive that I might get back to my proper studies, which had been interrupted by the war.'[51] In order to understand his patient better, he had been reading—on Sassoon's suggestion—both Henri Barbusse's anti-war novel *Under Fire*, and articles in the *English Review* which suggested that Germany's economic position was so critical there was now the possibility of a negotiated peace.[52] 'There were thus the grounds for a definite conflict in my mind between a "pacifist" tendency dictated by my own interests on the one hand, and, on the other, opinions based partly on reasoned motives, partly on conventional adherence to the views of the majority, in favour of a fight to the finish.'[53] Rivers interprets the dream as an attempted solution to this conflict. It reinstates him as a civilian (symbolised by his finding his bowler hat and umbrella), and takes him back twenty years, to when he was pursuing medical research in Germany, and had strongly believed in the value of scientific co-operation for promoting international friendship.[54] It thereby opens up the possibility of peace, and the resumption of co-operation between scientists, which the *English Review* article allowed him to believe might now be realistically possible.[55]

In its own terms, this analysis is convincing. However, in positing the fundamental conflict with which the dream is concerned as one between public duty and egoistic wish to return to civilian life and scientific research, it marginalises another possibility obliquely acknowledged in the text: of a conflict between perceived public duty and an emergent belief that the war should not continue—a belief to which discussions with

Sassoon and a reading of Barbusse might both have contributed, and which if embraced might constitute a countervailing duty. Rivers first touches on such a conflict flippantly. In recalling his reading of the *English Review* article, he remembered that:

> I had thought of the situation that would arise if my task of converting a patient from his 'pacifist errors' to the conventional attitude should have as its result my own conversion to his point of view. My attitude throughout the war had been clearly in favour of fighting until Germany recognised defeat, and though the humorous side of the imagined situation struck me more than its serious aspect, there can be little doubt that there was a good opening for conflict and repression.

The following sentence, however, immediately switches to the egoistic motive of returning to his studies; and the potential conflict here mentioned vanishes.[56] However, the possibility continued to trouble Rivers. He acknowledged that his support for a fight to the finish was based 'partly on reasoned motives, partly on conventional adherence to the views of the majority'.[57] In analysing his dream, he was uncertain whether or not he had been in uniform. This question:

> had a definite connection with the conflict which I suppose to underlie the dream, and especially with my relation to the patient B [Sassoon]. So long as I was an officer of the RAMC, and of this my uniform was the obvious symbol, my discussions with B on his attitude towards the war were prejudiced by my sense that I was not a free agent in discussing the matter, but that there was the danger that my attitude might be influenced by my official position. As a scientific student whose only object should be the attainment of what I supposed to be truth, it was definitely unpleasant to me to suspect that the opinions which I was uttering might be influenced by the needs of my position, and I was fully aware of an element of constraint in my relations with B on this account.[58]

Here again is the conflict of the earlier dream. The strain of the tension between the demands of science and nation, knowledge and morale, is now heightened: Rivers can acknowledge that his support for the war is partly conventional, and at least entertain (if only jestingly) the possibility of changing position. However, ultimately his conception of his duty ('no one can be a free agent during a war') limited the degree to which he could allow himself to question his own adherence to conventional views: the very same question which Sassoon and Graves were to debate between themselves after Sassoon left Craiglockhart.[59]

However, I suggest that the potential conflict marginalised in Rivers's account of his own dream, and in particular its missing emotional content, surfaces in a displaced form elsewhere in the text.[60] He reports the post-war 'Suicide' Dream of a patient who had been a captain in the RAMC.[61] His patient had been so horrified by his experiences at the front, and especially the circumstances surrounding the death of a French prisoner who had been wounded escaping from the Germans, that—despite pressure from his family to resume his profession—he could not face returning to medical practice. Rivers had suggested that he take up public health, where he would not encounter scenes likely to revive his wartime memories.[62] The patient then recorded for Rivers a dream which vividly dramatised his dilemma. He was to give a speech on 'The Present Struggle' at the Golders Green Empire. Supported by Rivers, he took the stage, whereupon his vacated seat was occupied by a man who was clearly his *alter ego*, the self he had once hoped to be.[63] The hall was flanked by two stewards, one a Canadian (who represented the patient's family and the medical profession), the other Dr X (a friend who had recently committed suicide).[64] As speaker, he took a strongly pro-war line: '"We must continue the struggle to the last man. Better let us die than lose our manhood and independence and become the slaves of an alien people."'[65] His *alter ego* cheered, whereupon he was threatened by the Canadian and became intensely depressed.

> [H]is eyes became dark and filled with infinite suffering and he seemed to be almost another person, for his hair had become dark and his skin was no longer fair. He so affected me that I became less confident. 'I know', I said, 'that we have suffered and are all suffering dreadful agony'. At this the man...still dark in eye and face, groaned aloud in agony. 'What rest would peace bring us all', I continued. The man's eyes now showed such agony that I felt it would be merciful if I killed him immediately...[66]

After a repetition of this same cycle—of rousing speech met with enthusiasm and then despair by the *alter ego* and with threat from the Canadian—'[a]gain he was suffering dreadfully and I could not bear to see it. His eyes showed such agony that I felt I must kill him. Dr X smiled grimly and approvingly at me and shouted: "This way for the Angel of Peace".'[67] Rivers then intervened, to say that the *alter ego* was ill but would get well. Disregarding him, the patient prepared to shoot him. 'I was just raising the revolver when I heard the voice of my son saying, "Don't do it, daddy, you'll hurt me too."' He awoke ill and depressed from the worst dream of his life.[68]

Rivers interprets this threatened dream homicide as a veiled threat of suicide, with the voice of the child representing the stigma which would attach to the patient's family in such an event. He treats it as expressing the conflict between the strong family pressure to return to medicine, and the patient's horror at that prospect even in the modified form of Rivers's suggestion.[69] This then becomes the centre of Rivers's focus, marginalising his recognition that '[t]he speech of the dreamer was a direct indication of a conflict which I knew to be actively present between manifest opinions that the war must be fought to a finish and deeper feelings that a struggle involving such horrors as those which he had experienced should continue.'[70]

It seems clear that the *alter ego*'s responses, alternating between enthusiastic support for the speaker and profound sadness, reflected the patient's intense inner conflict. A stirring and even shrill rhetoric for continuing the war (telling the audience that 'despite our intense suffering we must go on. "There must be no surrender. We must not give in."'—rhetoric which is perhaps simultaneously a parody of what the patient feels he is fighting against) elicits initial keenness, but then despair and agony.[71] Moreover, since the proposed mode of death of the *alter ego* echoed that of the French prisoner, the patient seems also to be identified with this dead comrade.[72] What he has experienced at the front leads him to prefer the peace of death to continuing in his profession. This aspect of the case against the war (expressed forcefully by both Sassoon and Barbusse) is expelled by Rivers in his analysis of his own 'Pacifist' dream, only to resurface elsewhere—in the dream of his fellow RAMC officer. In analysing both these dreams, Rivers concentrates on the professional dilemma (shall I return to my research/medical practice?), while evacuating them of their potential political critique.[73] In this, he was firmly within the consensus of Britain's First World War shell-shock practitioners, as Stryker has depicted it. Showalter quotes Rivers writing in 1920 about how ideal military training should produce a soldier who would hardly notice 'even the utmost horrors and rigours of warfare...so inured is he to their presence and so absorbed in the immediate task presented by his military duties'. She comments acidly that this could be a description of Rivers himself, 'so perfectly conditioned by his education, his class, his sex, and his professional role that he performed his duties—even if his dreams were sometimes a bit troubled and unconventional—with perfect aplomb'.[74] In fact, those troubled dreams reveal the work which he had to engage in to maintain that aplomb.

It is clear that Rivers did change in some ways after 1918. His circle of friends widened to include others radicalised by the war. This hitherto unpolitical man began to take a stance on political issues; Slobodin argues: 'It was...the logic of wartime and post-war events that was moving Rivers from an apparent unquestioning traditionalism in politics toward a labourite position and an anxiety about the fruits of imperialism.'[75] During the war he had come to know some Labour Party intellectuals, including Bertrand Russell; and through Sassoon, became a close friend of Graves after the war.[76] He also made links with trade-union educational organisations, and was planning to give courses for the Workers' Educational Trade Union Committee in summer 1922.[77] In April 1922 (two months before his sudden death), after some initial hesitation, Rivers allowed himself to be adopted, to the surprise and sometimes dismay of his academic colleagues, as prospective Labour Party candidate for the University of London seat. He began to write about his understanding of socialism.[78] Nevertheless, as Showalter points out, he never fundamentally questioned or reconsidered his military role during the war.[79]

Psychotherapy and the War

Stryker's analysis of shell-shock theory during the war, and its associated practices, suggests that—while there were significant differences in the treatments offered by different practitioners—what they shared was a common view of the overriding duty to return soldiers where possible to active service. This duty derived both from their status as citizens, and from their specific role as military doctors. Hence the distinction which Leed suggests—between the moralists with their disciplinary approach which dramatised the conflict between duty and self-interest within the medical setting, and the analysts who recognised that it was (the continuation of) the war itself which was the arena of moral conflict—seems to have been a potential rather than an actual one. The analysts may have developed a more humane, and ultimately more effective, treatment for the conflicts which lay behind shell shock; but they did so without questioning the rightness of the cause. José Brunner has shown that the same is true for the practice of military psychiatry among the Central Powers. The analytic/therapeutic approach of those influenced by psychoanalysis proved more successful, as well as more humane, than the disciplinary/punitive techniques of the psychiatric establishment; so much so that by 1918 the German and Austro-Hungarian governments were sending official observers to the Fifth International Psychoanalytic Congress in Budapest.[80] But only very rarely did analysts question the cause for which they worked—to restore soldiers to fitness for front-line service.[81]

Stryker offers an illuminating example of how shell-shock theories muffled aspects of war experience which might have prompted moral questioning of the sort Leed suggests. Fear, from which the shell-shock victim suffered, derived from the impulse to self-preservation. Hence it was at best an amoral element which could not be accepted as outweighing the demands of duty. It could command understanding, even sympathy, and hence appropriate treatment aimed at promoting the soldier's recognition that fear was inevitable and thus lessening their self-reproach; but it could not countermand the requirement to return to service if possible.[82] Horror, however, a distinct emotion, contained a more altruistic dimension prompted by concern for the sufferings of others (rather than the self), and hence might provide the basis for a questioning of the nature and purpose of the war. Stryker points out how shell-shock theories elided these two emotional responses to front-line conditions together, thereby removing the potential of horror to prompt questioning of the nature of the war.[83]

One example she cites is a case history reported by the pioneer British Freudian and wartime RAMC officer David Eder. The patient, a hitherto robust and brave soldier now suffering from acute fear, had since childhood worked closely with and been strongly attached to horses. He now suffered from a repeated terrifying dream, based on an actual incident in which a Frenchman had plunged a knife into a mule to make it go. 'He wept profusely when talking to me of the sufferings experienced by the wounded mules at Gallipoli, and when I suggested that human beings suffered more he would not have it so. Animals could not talk. No animals should be allowed there he said.' Eder interpreted this as the soldier protesting too much. 'He identified himself with the horse. He was the horse of the dream; it is he who ought not to have been in Gallipoli—it was too much for him and others.'[84] Stryker comments that in Eder's framing of the case, '[t]he patient's concern for horses was read as a concern for the self: it was not a concern for animals, and equally not a concern for other human beings.'[85] While this may somewhat overstate Eder's personal blinkeredness (he recognises that 'it was too much for him *and others*'), it nevertheless captures the effect of the *institutional* framing: concern for self, others and animals becomes, by a form of reductionism, ultimately only concern for the self. Any wider political implications (the metaphorical knife used to make the soldier go) are occluded. It is a close parallel to Rivers's finding of an egoistic motive for his wish for the war to end. This procedure had been foreshadowed in Freud's analysis of his own dreams in *The Interpretation of Dreams*, where all political references are repeatedly translated into representations of the oedipal scenario, the family constellation. That is to say, the political becomes an epiphenomenon of the intra/interpersonal.[86]

In that light, it is worth looking again at the 'Suicide' dream. This can be interpreted as a classic example of Freudian condensation.[87] On the surface, the dream as reported by the RAMC Captain concerns the war—'The Present Struggle' as the title of his address has it. And the dream can be read almost completely consistently in this light.[88] But if we perform a gestalt shift (as on an ambiguous duck-rabbit pictogram), and understand 'The Present Struggle' to refer not to the war, but instead to the conflict between the Captain and his family over whether he should return to being a doctor, then it can equally be read consistently. When the speaker in the dream says: 'We must continue the struggle to the last man. Better let us die than lose our manhood and independence and become the slaves of an alien people', this can now be taken as referring to the Captain's struggle for control of his life and career, his refusal to be a slave to his family. As my reference to a gestalt shift suggests, it is not necessary to chose between these two interpretations. Both are true simultaneously.[89] The

Captain both wants the war to continue (as a citizen and an officer), and wishes it to stop (in view of the suffering he has seen). He both wants to resume work as a doctor (to please the wife he loves, and because of his professional investment), and to flee from it (because it revives horrific memories, and represents submission to the wishes of others). Since the two sets of wishes are each internally incompatible, they generate an intolerable conflict to which suicide seems the only answer. There is no need to reduce this dream, and the conflict it encodes, to a crude dichotomy between (altruistic) duty and (selfish) fear.[90] Yet in effect that is what the shell-shock therapists did.

Thus the encounter between Sassoon and Rivers was not simply the meeting of two individuals, but was framed by state coercion, by ideologies of nation and duty, and by emergent psychotherapeutic techniques. These techniques were themselves the product of innovative theorising about human mental processes, but a theorising built on a repudiation of the political, and hence vulnerable to recuperation in the service of the state. Both Sassoon and Rivers were attached by powerful emotional bonds to nation, duty, and the men they cared for. Both struggled to accommodate these attachments to the realities of modern warfare. Sassoon had begun by oscillating between heroic aggression and escapist forgetting before consolidating his growing doubts and horror into protest. Once his protest had been defused, he returned to front-line service willing himself not to think (not to be too sane)—the same remedy which Graeme West had speculated his fellow officers relied on. Rivers, too, was torn between thinking and not thinking, his duty to science and his duty to nation. So long as his thinking told him it was necessary to continue the war, these two duties could be reconciled; but once his encounters with shell-shocked officers and his reading of anti-war literature made it possible to think that perhaps the war should not continue, the duties clashed. Rivers's solution was to institute a form of splitting: by day, in the consulting room, he acted to maintain (his and others') morale; while by night, in the privacy of his bedroom and his dreams, different thoughts were entertained and the harmony of his existence was disturbed. Meanwhile, Eder's soldier turned to an imagery drawn from his profound and lifelong attachment to horses to express what might otherwise be unthinkable or unspeakable—men should not be driven like this.

8

Fractured Loyalties: the Nation and the War

This book has been concerned with the interrelationship between the life courses of individuals, with the patterns of attachment to institutions and ideologies which formed their identities, and their experience of British society before and especially during the war. It is not the argument of this book that the responses to the war of Graves, Sassoon, Alick West—or in his different way Macfie—were *typical.* Rather it is that an understanding of the complexities and underpinnings of their different (and changing) attitudes, and in particular the role played by the mechanisms of their class and gender socialisation, can help to illuminate a key aspect of the formation of individual public and political identities.[1] A comparison of their respective trajectories through family, school and career preparation, their responses to religion, and their efforts to come to terms with their sexualities shows how these intersect with and affect their affiliations and loyalties to class, nation and political beliefs and movements. A comparison of their responses to the experience of war shows the interaction of their personal life histories with contradictions within the ideology of the nation state which the war exposed. This chapter will connect the themes raised by the case studies of Part II to the broader issues explored in Part I by drawing together material under three headings. The first section reviews the diverse responses to the war of the individuals whose life stories have been considered above, indicating how divisions within these responses are still echoed in current assessments of the war. The second section examines both the strength of the British nation as imagined community during the First World War, and the fissures which—for some—that war opened in its appeal. It will look in particular at the concept of self-sacrifice and its relation to religious teaching and national identification; and the "unspeakable" truths which began to be spoken by those whose identities were fractured by the pressures of war. The third section concludes by looking briefly at other imagined communities which became alternative focusses of loyalty during and after the war years. It will thereby offer a more nuanced way of conceiving the loyalties and commitments which shaped individuals' affiliations to the British nation state, and the fracturing and reshaping which took place during and after the war.

Diversity of Responses

As many commentators, historical and literary, have pointed out, responses to the First World War were diverse. In particular, two dominant popular late-twentieth-century images of the war are misleading if they are taken as fully representative of contemporary views. Neither the poetic view—the tragic/elegiac trajectory from enthusiasm through anger and disillusion to pity and compassion represented by the successive figures of Brooke, Sassoon, Owen and Rosenberg, nor the comic view—the 'lions led by donkeys' black farce portrayed in *Oh, What a Lovely War!* and *Blackadder Goes Forth*, forms an adequate, let alone a comprehensive, depiction of how those who lived and served through the war responded to it.[2]

The point is made forcefully by the military historians Robin Prior and Trevor Wilson in their critique of Paul Fussell's influential study *The Great War and Modern Memory*.[3] They demonstrate convincingly the narrowness of Fussell's focus (junior officers with a literary orientation on the Western Front), his cavalier way with details of chronology and geography, and his wayward treatment of the logic of causation leading him into analytical difficulties when this supposedly interminable war finally comes to an end.[4] By comparing the overall thesis of the book with that of his later study of the Second World War, they are able to suggest that Fussell is viewing both wars through a single, fixed interpretative frame.[5] Another way of expressing this would be to say that Fussell's study is compounded of his immersion in, perhaps identification with, the viewpoint of the key writers he has chosen, and his own experiences of the later war in which he himself served. Prior and Wilson acknowledge that Fussell has powerfully focussed on the war as a watershed in '[t]he capacity of governments to imperil life on the planet' (and on destructive dimensions of war fighting in general); what they wish to challenge is that this represents the whole, or even the dominant, truth of the war.[6]

To reach a more adequate understanding of individuals' engagement in and response to the war, it is necessary to consider both the range of explicitly formulated accounts of why British soldiers continued to fight, and—since these are not the only, and may not be the most important, reasons—the patterns of identification and attachment explored above.[7] Explicit, politically articulated stances towards the war, even among the younger generation of literary figures who survived beyond the first year—many of whom served in the war and as junior officers—cover a wide spectrum. At one end was the position of D.H. Lawrence, who was opposed to the war and stated explicitly that he would prefer a German victory to a continuation of the conflict.[8] Then might be placed Charles Sorley. He joined up at the outbreak of war and believed in the justice of the British cause. However, he continued to esteem Germany and its culture highly, and saw the war as a tragic paradox, rather than a simple clash of right and wrong.[9] Repeatedly from the moment of his enlistment, Sorley cast a sceptical eye over his own motivation and its relation to popular sentiment. At the recruiting office in the first week of the war, he asked: 'what can I do to have some reasonable answer to give to my acquaintances when they ask me: "What are *you* doing?"'[10] The central theme for Sorley seems to have been a strong need to preserve independence of judgment, and to scrutinise where it led him.[11] Recognising a tension between his admiration for Germany and his own joining up, he laments: 'What a worm one is under the cart wheels...of public opinion.'[12] My argument stresses that no one expression of opinion can be taken as definitive in isolation, even about a particular stage of the war. Although Sorley had begun to register the brutalising effects of the war before he died in October 1915, it is impossible to know whether his views would have changed had he lived longer.[13]

Perhaps the most common position was that which came to be held, with differing nuances, by Graves, Sassoon and Owen. All had deep doubts about the rightness of the war (in Sassoon's case issuing in open protest), but all felt that they had a duty to continue fighting for the sake of the men they led.[14] T.E. Hulme also recognised the cruelty of the war, but saw it as necessary though negative work, essential because a German victory would be disastrous for Europe. Moreover, Hulme also opposed what Bernard Bergonzi terms the 'life ethic' implicit in the work of Sassoon and Owen, continuing to affirm heroic martial values.[15] The furthest extreme at this end of the spectrum is perhaps represented by the work of the German writer Ernst Jünger, who continued to exalt war as an ennobling experience. In J. P. Stern's words, Jünger adopted an attitude of assent towards the war, embracing its evolution as a machine and demanding that men assimilate themselves to its mechanism.[16] Bergonzi makes a striking comparison between the responses of Edmund Blunden and Jünger to the replacement of the soft cap by the steel helmet: the former presents it as a dehumanising moment, while the latter celebrates the emergent man of steel.[17]

Reviewing the changing stances of my case studies and their contemporaries towards the war both helps to situate them within that broad spectrum, and underlines the point that for many their attitudes shifted in the light of their experiences. For Chavasse, the war produced no visible rents in the seamless fit between his commitments to father, family, faith, nation and profession. As a doctor, he was not confronted with the necessity to kill; instead, he could pursue his vocation of service to both King and Redeemer, enacted through a care for his men which was continuous with his previous care for poor boys and for patients.

Macfie embraced the war as offering a resolution of the internal conflicts which he had hitherto managed by a form of benign splitting. Whereas previously the creation of a liminal space—between the demands of family, class and career—had required a delicate balancing act, with one (bohemian) identity partially concealed within a (respectable) other, now the war provided a liminal time space in which he could integrate all aspects of himself: supremely dutiful yet hostile to authority, a uniformed soldier of the King who was also a Gypsy in his tent, living in a homosocial world in which his love of men could be expressed through strenuous service yet not flinching in the face of "necessary" killing of British soldiers by their own officers *pour encourager les autres*.

In an inverse way to the experience of Macfie, the war resolved Grenfell's conflicts. As he emerged into adulthood, Grenfell had identified contradictions within the value system of his family and class—contradictions which would emerge more starkly during the war. But once his effort at rebellion had been contained, he reverted largely to type; he became a hunter who felt most alive in the chase. He enjoyed the war, although there seem to be both ironic and questioning undercurrents to his apparently enthusiastic views.[18] Its early months, though shaking some of his naïve faith in British martial resolution, allowed him to exercise to good effect his cherished skills as a hunter and stalker, with the Germans as prey. He thereby became a model soldier hero, winning a DSO.[19] Nevertheless, what seem in 1914–15 to be the actions of an entirely conventional aristocratic young man fighting and gladly risking death for his country are in fact in a longer perspective those of someone who had struggled to reject the very values of competitiveness and self-sacrifice which would be used after his death in May 1915 to enshrine his memory. This disjuncture is poignantly revealed in what he wrote, on leave the previous month, while making his first visit to Paris (where he had hoped to study art). Praising its light heartedness ('such *artists* in fun'), he concluded: 'It was the biggest experience of New Things I've ever had in my life, bigger than India, because it's more like our things and more comparable—but really how much further removed from anything of ours!'[20]

The respective stances of Graves, Sassoon and Rivers mutually illuminate one another. Graves began as the knowing veteran putting right the callow and idealistic Sassoon. As the latter gained front-line experience, he too was shocked by the horror of the war. Together, they shared the view that the war was madness, but that they must nevertheless persist. As Sassoon's horror intensified, he moved to outright rejection of the war—in which Graves declined to follow him. Graves then gradually accepted his withdrawal from active service, satisfied that he had 'done his bit', and prepared for life after the war. He rejected Sassoon's continuing agitation against the war, while simultaneously recognising that it was based on too great a sanity. Finally, in the post-war years it was Graves who gradually reached, in part from his wartime experiences, a rejection of the society in which he grew up; while Sassoon withdrew from his own anti-war stance and the insights on which it was based.[21]

Meanwhile, Sassoon and Rivers were engaged in their own *pas-de-deux*. Sassoon took the exceptional step of challenging the direction laid down by the government, elevating his duty to his men above that to the nation's political leadership. Though not shell-shocked, he was sent for psychological treatment as a political expedient; Rivers accepted that he was of sound mind, while insinuating the slippery phrase 'anti-war complex'. He proceeded to address directly not Sassoon's emotions but his judgment—

are you in a position to assess the rightness of continuing the war? The coercive power of the state neutered Sassoon's protest; and once he had decided not to follow the path of an apparently futile persistence in protest, his sense of duty took him back to his men, without having renounced his beliefs. Only after the war, and partly under the emotional dynamics of his transference to the now dead and idealised Rivers, did Sassoon begin to distance himself from his wartime protest.

Rivers, having donned military uniform upon joining the RAMC, adhered to what he saw as his duty. In order to do this, in the face of what he learned from the soldiers he treated, he had to engage in various forms of splitting or marginalising. He divided his responses to the continuation of the war along an axis of duty/egoism; the forces compelling his continuing support of the war were assigned to the former category, those questioning that support to the latter. He avoided the possibility of an alternative duty emerging, one which might require him to question the war. Maintaining this split involved a further division of himself into public and private: a form of censorship was required to protect the morale of the public self from the full impact of the disturbing material being read in private. He also instituted a split between reason and emotion. The former sustained his support for the war, and enabled him to attempt to win over Sassoon. The latter was displaced, resurfacing textually elsewhere in the form of Rivers's own *alter ego*, the RAMC captain driven to the brink of suicide by what he had seen at the front. Nevertheless, Rivers was not untouched by the experiences of the war. While he was performing his duty in returning Sassoon to active service, Sassoon's doubts worked upon him to transform his support for the establishment. This previously politically disengaged man emerged as part of that Liberal intelligentsia which committed itself to Labour and social reform at the start of the 1920s. In doing so he began to follow the path which Graeme West had committed himself to—contributing to post-war reconstruction.

Graeme West's history has echoes of both Sorley and Sassoon. Like Sorley, he early detached himself from the nationalist assumption of the unequivocal rightness of Britain's cause. This seems to have been precipitated by the very process of making men into soldiers, as much as by what those soldiers then did. His detachment, however, took the form for a time of a nihilistic despair at the value of any human endeavour: imperial

Britain would one day be as distant and forgotten as Pharaonic Egypt. Having tried and failed to protest by refusing to continue to serve, he then recovered a sense of purpose through a commitment (supported by his reading of Bertrand Russell) to the project of post-war reconstruction. His brother Alick also freed himself from an unquestioning nationalism, through exposure to different values and perspectives in internment. In the post-war conflict of values with his father, which centred round choice of career, the words of his dead brother Graeme became the support for his new direction.

The dilemmas over action with which these men wrestled during the war retain an afterlife as dilemmas over interpretation. In *The Unquiet Western Front*, Brian Bond, a leading military historian, laments the continuing difficulty of studying the war 'simply as history without polemic intent or apologies'.[22] He claims that 'military historians have in general failed to present a positive interpretation of Britain's role in the war or, at any rate...their versions have been overwhelmed and obliterated by the enormous impact of supposedly "anti-war" poetry, memoirs, novels, plays and films.'[23] He traces this effect back to the literature of the war which emerged at the end of the 1920s; but argues that its effects were amplified (and in part distorted) when it was reappropriated and reworked in the very different social and political climate of the 1960s (in works such as *Oh What a Lovely War!*).[24] The further bastardised version presented in *Blackadder Goes Forth*, has, he suggests, now become at the start of the twenty-first century the received truth about the war.[25]

What, for Bond, has been lost sight of, and what he wants to reassert, is that the war 'was, for Britain, a necessary and successful war, and an outstanding achievement for a democratic nation in arms.'[26] It is this which he believes the dominance of anti-war literature (and caricature) has obliterated from popular memory. For Bond, this is partly explained by a structural feature. The writers who contributed most to the anti-war picture were predominantly front-line junior officers. They were in no position to understand the political and strategic dimensions of the war which alone gave meaning to it; and without which, he concedes, the front-line experience was indeed meaningless.[27]

The main goals he consistently invokes as having been worth fighting for are preventing German domination of continental Europe, and protecting/expanding the Empire.[28] For Bond, the policies of the inter-war years which failed to prevent the rise of Hitler and Nazism are separable from the war itself, and could have been avoided.[29] But it is at least as arguable that the price of victory was Pyrrhic, so great that it rendered reluctance to face another such war nearly inevitable. As for the empire, which as Bond notes reached its greatest extent after 1918, within fifty years it was gone; and yet the British nation continues to exist. This is not to say that the political leadership of 1914 would not inevitably have fought to defend the empire; it is to say that those who did not share that view were not necessarily wrong.

Suppose, however, that the war were both necessary and successful: Germany, a militaristic power which invaded a neighbouring country in defiance of treaty obligations, was defeated.[30] Suppose too that, except at the margins, the war could not have been won more quickly or with significantly less loss of life.[31] It is still arguable that the human price of this was excessive: that what it required of the men who fought it, and also of their families, was intolerable. In other words, that there was a categorial gap between what Bond terms British interests, and the interests of individual Britons. It is this evaluation which Sassoon sought to articulate.[32] The war, from this perspective, was truly a tragedy: (arguably) necessary, but intolerable.[33]

Ironically, Bond's own text shows that he himself recognises, if he does not share, this perception.[34] More than once, he notes that representations of the war had an effect beyond, or even contrary to, the intentions of their authors. He cites R.C. Sherriff's surprised response to the reception of *Journey's End* as anti war; his intention had been 'to stress the virtues of duty and perseverance in the face of fear and extreme danger, but in the long run…these ideas could not prevail over the play's claustrophobic setting in a trench and the deaths in action of all the main characters'.[35] He reaches a similar verdict on the BBC's famous 1964 series *The Great War* which had sought to rehabilitate the British military commanders. However, concludes Bond, 'the medium proved to be much more powerful than the message'; audience research revealed that 'the visual images of the ravaged battlescapes, the broken bodies and the faces of the haggard survivors had made a vastly greater impact than the text. Viewers were struck by the horrors of war and the appalling waste of young men.'[36] But for Bond, these conclusions constitute (continuing) misreadings of the war. Although he recognises that in Britain the view has prevailed that 'approximately one million deaths in combat (in all war theatres) was an unacceptable catastrophe rather than the high price that had to be paid to safeguard the nation's strategic interests in western Europe and the empire', he nevertheless wishes to separate this outcome of the events of 1914–18 from what he terms 'the "real", historical war' which 'abruptly ceased to exist in November 1918.'[37]

Leed, seeking to illuminate the difficulty troops in the trenches faced in grasping the war, offered an analogy between 'a text that, when written down, gains a certain autonomy from the motives, intentions, and purposes of an author, and an historical event which, for participants, gains an autonomy and a dynamic distinct from the intentions of those who make it'.[38] I would suggest that the same analogy can illuminate the efforts of both participants and later generations to make sense of the war. Bond's interpretation operates at the level of the intentions of those who went to war; the mis/readings he deplores arise—as he himself recognises—from an examination of consequences rather than intentions. It was the same reading which Sassoon proclaimed in 1917, and which Rivers sought to persuade him was a misreading.

Nation in Contradiction

Benedict Anderson and Ross Poole have stressed the almost unique power of the nation in the modern world to attract allegiance and willing self-sacrifice. The nation is a key element in individual identity, which is formed in part through identification with the nation—both directly, and through intermediate institutions. In particular, they argue, the nation holds out the promise of indirect immortality. By identifying with the supposedly eternal character of the nation, the individual can construe themself as part of a continuing stream of meaning which will extend beyond their own lifetime.[39] This view of the relationship between the nation and individual identity has similarities with that of Emile Durkheim, for whom the modern nation was not simply parallel to, but had replaced, god/religion. Like the historic religions, he suggested, the nation state defined a community to which the believer/citizen belonged, inculcated and enforced a set of moral values, inspired an attachment which could mobilise self-sacrifice, and offered a continuity beyond death.[40]

I want to modify Anderson's picture of the nation state by suggesting that (like Durkheim's) it is too benign and unconflictual.[41] This leads to a glossing over of contradictions in the nation's appeal, so that in some respects the analysis appears to repeat elements of the ideology of nationalism, rather than critically appraising them. A key instance is the stress which both Anderson and Poole lay on the nation's capacity to elicit self-sacrifice. Some countervailing points can be made here. First, the nation elicits murderousness as well as self-sacrifice.[42] Of course, both are aware of this aspect of the nation state and both (especially Poole) refer to it; but the murderousness is somehow treated *diminuendo*; it is the eliciting of self-sacrifice which is regarded as striking, even defining, about the nation's appeal.[43] Second, the terms they use are not adequate to describe the processes by which nations achieve these responses: I have suggested that coercion and provision also play a role, so that the response derives from obedience and self-interest as well as self-sacrifice.[44]

It is war which puts the identification of individual with nation to the greatest test and reveals some of its fault lines. As Poole has pointed out, in war the always latent conflict between the demands of the nation state and the claims of liberal morality are forced into the open; at time of crisis the nation will move to override subordinate values.[45] While provision and recognition continue to be important vectors of state action, coercion comes to occupy a more prominent place. All the debates, doubts and hesitations faced by these men during the wartime years were (except for Alick West) experienced under the sway of military discipline and censorship. The First World War raised acutely the question of the relationship between individual and society. The earlier chapters have shown how individuals are from birth constructed as members of society; in bourgeois liberal democratic societies, and especially for those from the upper-middle class in relatively privileged positions, this includes their construction to understand themselves as autonomous, self-motivating agents with a degree of control over their lives. Though sections of that class had well-established traditions of military service, and there could be strong family pressures (as on Grenfell and Brenan) to follow that profession, in peacetime few were driven by sheer necessity to fight.[46]

The war, by making exceptional and radically anomalous demands, exposed contradictions in this positioning, which might otherwise have remained obscured. It required men to do things which in normal peacetime conditions would be strictly forbidden or senseless: to be willing to die; to be so willing in unprecedented circumstances; and to kill.[47] Yet, as both Gilmore and Poole noted, for the individual this demand is potentially intolerable. To ensure men would accede to it, society had to combine the ideological and institutional preconditioning which prepared men to be "hailed" as proud sons of Empire with direct and indirect coercive pressures. The wartime military doctors (most of whom were themselves civilians with temporary commissions) who treated shell-shocked patients were quite clear about this. The needs of the nation now came ahead of those of the individual.[48]

For middle-class volunteers, however, the ideological appeal of the nation was initially more important. Poole suggests that: '[i]n nationalism, as in religion, the voluntary act of self-sacrifice establishes an identity which transcends that of the individual who dies. Death is the paradoxical proof of immortality. It is the achievement of a locus of meaning sought by, but denied to individuals in their ordinary material existence.'[49] To be prepared to sacrifice oneself for one's nation meant accepting that it was better to be dead than Prussian.[50] In other words, one had to put the imagined community of the nation (and the imagined communities of intermediate collectivities such as one's school, career or class) before oneself, and before the actually existing, face-to-face community of family and friends; or to accept that the latter was appropriately subsumed into the former.[51] At the outbreak of war many men, including Graves, Sassoon, Sorley and Graeme West, responded—in part at least—to the power of this call. The First World War, however, made this dilemma of self or country worse by plunging those who fought on the Western Front into conditions where individual agency in general, and traditional forms of military initiative in particular, were radically circumscribed.[52] The scale of killing called into question the fantasy of immortality through death when soldiers were confronted not only with the possibility of their own death (in circumstances where they were objects of slaughter, not subjects of heroic action), but that of hundreds and thousands around them. It thereby created, for some, an insoluble dilemma.[53] To accept the continuance of war meant accepting the unacceptable as a necessary consequence. Yet to resist the set of rationales centred on honour and duty which society presented them with was immensely difficult.

The initial response, and the continuing commitment, of these men were secured both by the summons which the nation offered, and by the pattern of identifications and loyalties which their upbringing had established. The grounds for inviting them to risk the paradox of immortality through death had been prepared, for men from this background, by their public school education. The concept of self-sacrifice was central. Fusing together the religious teaching of muscular Christianity, now inflected by social Darwinism, with the Classical and English literature of heroism, it provided a fundamental link with ideologies of the nation and the needs of the state.[54]

In his study of chivalry, sacrifice and the First World War, Allen Frantzen—drawing on the work of René Girard—explores the history of the Christian concept of sacrifice and its relationship to warfare. The manner of Jesus's life, and of his death on the Cross, are termed by Frantzen antisacrificial.[55] He is the scapegoat par excellence, designed to end the cycle of violence begun with the murder of Abel; his death is intended to underline the message given to Abraham, that God does not want human sacrifice.[56] Moreover, by not simply undergoing his Passion, but voluntarily embracing it, Jesus converted what would have been an antisacrificial death into a self-sacrificial one.[57] Frantzen then explores the ideological roots of chivalry in the early medieval period, tracing the ways in which this antisacrificial/self-sacrificial message—a death willingly embraced, which did not demand revenge—was reversed. Already by the time of Augustine, the Constantinian church had accepted the possibility of just war.[58] The ninth and tenth century poems *The Heiland* and 'The Dream of the Rood' had dramatised 'the tension between the warrior's duty to requite the enemy and Christ's call for the acceptance of abjection.'[59] From the beginning of the Crusades in the late eleventh century, the medieval church sacralised violence in an effort to exercise control over the knightly class. 'The most important presupposition of chivalry became the belief that one bloody death—Christ's—must be compensated by others like it.'[60] In this way, 'Christ's Passion supported a sacrificial system at variance with his teachings but essential to both ancient and modern ideas of war.'[61] At the heart of this system was the elision contained in the figure of the warrior martyr, typified by St George. Like Jesus, he was willing to sacrifice himself; unlike Jesus, he was willing to kill.[62]

By the early twentieth century, the Constantinian identification of the church with the secular power allowed bishops and priests to assert that Britain's cause was the cause of righteousness.[63] The Church of England displayed overwhelming commitment to the British cause.[64] Even Nonconformists, with their traditional distance from the state and opposition to war as an instrument of foreign policy, found ways to reconcile themselves.[65] Resolute opposition to war remained a minor and marginalised strand among the organised Christian churches.[66]

Elisions—of killing, of agency, of responsibility—are at the centre of state ideologies during the First World War. The insistent emphasis on *self-sacrifice*, on laying down one's life (for one's friends), hid the killing which necessarily accompanied it.[67] This was continued into the war memorials erected after 1918. The design of Reginald Blomfield's Cross of Sacrifice, to be found in all large British war cemeteries in Flanders, is an inverted sword centred on the face of a plain cross. Frantzen comments: 'Neatly suppressed is the body needed to wield the sword or bear the cross, but the outline of a body, arms extended, is easy to imagine as an invisible third element to the composition.'[68] The active agent of war is elided, in favour of the passive (self-sacrificial) victim who 'laid down' his life (as opposed to—had it torn from him).[69] Responsibility for such deaths could be attributed to those who offered themselves for sacrifice, independently of any actions of the state.[70] 'The transformation of sacrifice into self-sacrifice is facilitated—even mandated—by heroic masculinity, for two reasons. First, if the heroic male sacrifices himself, he alone is responsible for determining the significance of his death. Second, self-sacrifice requires the continuation of violence in the victim's name.'[71]

The demand to kill veiled behind the emphasis on self-sacrifice required, for civilian volunteers, that they be appropriately trained, both technically and ideologically. Leed comments:

> The purpose of training is to identify the soldier as an aggressor and to get the soldier to accept that identification. The purpose of propaganda is to place the act of violence within a moral universe by identifying the enemy as something that lies on the boundaries between the inhuman and the human, as...the proper object of hostility.[72]

Grenfell, a professional soldier imbued with the ethos of the hunt, could inhabit this moral universe. Yet it went against all the constraints on aggression which most men had previously had to internalise.[73] Sassoon commented sardonically on the mentality such training sought to instil when depicting bayonet drill in 'The Kiss'.[74] Once the new injunction had been accepted, it had the potential to come into conflict with the continuing recognition of the enemy as human. For that recognition, and any resultant unwillingness to kill, set the soldier at odds with what his society was now expecting of him: 'however admirable and humane was the "identification with the enemy", it was also the source of a profound, deeply felt conflict, in which the combatant was forced to repudiate self-conceptions sponsored by his society and often shared by himself'.[75] Graves, half-German himself, had to kill Germans, while members of his family fought on the other side. Sassoon was riven by precisely this conflict: first discovering within himself the capacity to hate, to desire revenge, and to kill (after the loss of his friend David Thomas); and then forced to confront a dead blond German whom he recognised as the other face of his own bereavement. It is experiences such as this which led him to his protest.

What Barnett and Bond regard as the whingeing of a too sensitive and imaginative individual can be interpreted differently. Individuals could come to challenge elements of national ideology and its religious underpinnings. I have suggested in Chapter 3 that service in the trenches was in some respects a liminal experience, one in which the conventional civilian world was fragmented and reconstituted in monstrous forms. A crucial dimension of this was the blurring, both literal and metaphorical, of the distinction between the living and the dead.[76] These monstrous forms could then continue to haunt men (such as Graves and Sassoon), in neurasthenic symptoms, daytime hallucinations or nocturnal dreams. But, suggests Victor Turner, liminal periods can also be the occasion for new thinking, when men are 'withdrawn from their structural positions and consequently from the values, norms, sentiments, and techniques associated with those positions. They are also divested of their previous habits of thought, feeling, and action.... [they] are alternately forced and encouraged to think about their society, their cosmos, and the powers than generate and sustain them.'[77] War, as a liminal experience, fractured and broke apart familiar, unconscious elements of the culture of Graves and Sassoon, and forced them to confront, through the new combinations, some of the realities of their society. They then tried to make sense of this new reality, Sassoon especially through his wartime satirical poems, Graves through his autobiography. The process was a difficult one.

> The knowledge and 'self' acquired in war could only with difficulty be integrated into a continuous self. It is significant that in combat men learned things that were not cumulative, things that did not enhance but devalued what they formerly thought they knew, things that made initial attitudes, truths, and assumptions into lies, illusions, and falsehoods.[78]

One particular object of this rethinking was the ideology of self-sacrifice, and the Christian teaching with which it was intertwined. The Christian tradition, as a powerful and enduring ideology, contained resources which enabled people to negotiate the experience of warfare. Hence it was entirely possible for men to come through the experience of the Western Front and retain their Christian beliefs. Bill Adams, author of a book about the RWF whom both Graves and Sassoon admired, did.[79] So too did Macfie's doctor hero Chavasse. Or, to take an unknown figure, Pte William Henry Campbell, also a volunteer in the Liverpool Scottish, who struggled to keep his faith amidst the mounting slaughter.[80] The wartime letters of Lt H. F. Bowser, a middle-class volunteer in 1914 who fought in France from 1916–18, give a vivid illustration of how this was possible. Though he was deeply shaken by the duration of the war and the loss of 'our best and most beautiful lives in hundreds', a combination of the Gospel narratives and Victorian poetry ultimately enabled him to retain his faith in both God and the war.[81]

Others, however, interrogated these beliefs more radically. Sassoon and Graves has already questioned the Christian faith before 1914; and Owen had lost his in the face of his experience of class society. During the war Graves could record that his fellow officers regarded God and Gott as no more than tribal deities; and Owen asserted that patriotism had no place in Christianity.[82] But all three found it necessary to go further, challenging and rejecting in their writing both the notion of the war as God's cause, and central Christian myths which their experiences rendered radically false.

As became clear in his confrontation with Lady Brassey, the war had destroyed any remnants of Sassoon's childhood faith, while leaving him with a sense of (unmet) spiritual need.[83] This process can be traced through his poems. Early in the war, Sassoon in his poetry drew readily upon the stock of Christian themes and tropes.[84] The most important of these poems is 'The Redeemer', begun in late November 1915, a few days after he reached the front line. As a working party struggles along a muddy trench at night, a flare lights up one of the heavily burdened men ('No thorny crown, only a woollen cap / He wore—an English soldier, white and strong') of whom Sassoon declares 'I say he was the Christ, who wrought to bless / All groping things with freedom bright as air'. As the flare fades and darkness returns, someone stumbles and drops what he's carrying, 'Mumbling: "O Christ Almighty, now I'm stuck!"' Though the colloquial curse of that final line brings the scene down to earth, the core of the poem equates the burdened English Tommy with the Redeemer.[85] By Christmas 1915, a month after he arrived at the front, Sassoon was beginning to question the easy equation between the nation's cause and the true meaning of Christianity. 'The Prince of Wounds', which begins with a seeming alignment of the two ('The Prince of Wounds is with us here'), ends on a doubting note ('Is he a God of wood and stone, / While those who served him writhe and moan, / On warfare's altar sacrificed?').[86] By April 1916, these doubts had strengthened. In 'Stand To: Good Friday Morning', an officer on duty in the darkest hours of a night of incessant rain greets the stand to at dawn by offering a bargain: 'O Jesus, send me a wound today, / And I'll believe in Your bread and wine, / And get my bloody old sins washed white!'[87] 'Christ and the Soldier', written during convalescence in August 1916, develops this scenario more fully, and in doing so undoes the equation suggested in 'The Redeemer'. It sets up an ironic dialogue between a worn-out soldier, and the Christ on a roadside Calvary. The soldier has a use for Christ only if he can be of practical help: a cushy ('Wounds like these / Would shift a bloke to Blighty just a treat!'), or an end to the fighting. When Christ asks him to believe, the soldier acknowledges that this might bring some comfort, but then poses the question: 'But be you for both sides? I'm paid to kill / And if I shoot a man his mother grieves. / Does that come into what your teaching tells?' The soldier and Christ inhabit different worlds, so that the values of the latter can bear upon the former—if at all—only through radical transformation (of the stigmata into a blighty).[88]

Self-sacrifice was at the heart of the ideological and emotional cluster which the experience of the war fractured. Already before the war, Grenfell had identified the incompatibility between the two virtues celebrated in his milieu, self-sacrifice and competition; but his effort to challenge this had been defeated.[89] During the war, Graeme West had rejected 'strange unearthly loyalties and promised rewards', adopting the view that bringing happiness into the world was the only worthwhile aim. Now Graves and Owen launched a head-on assault on two of the paradigmatic Biblical stories through which the value of self-sacrifice was instilled. The former reversed the story of David and Goliath: God was not found protecting the young, vulnerable and good.[90] The latter reversed that of Abraham and Isaac: offered the chance to slay the Ram of Pride instead, 'the old man would not so, but slew his son, / And half the seed of Europe, one by one'.[91] This trope might now seem extreme: there were plenty of old men to protest that their grief for their lost sons was profound and inconsolable.[92] But it seems less extreme when set against the view repeatedly proclaimed by Ettie Grenfell and her contemporaries: that it was not the dead who were to be pitied, but those who were left behind.[93] In critiquing these two Old Testament motifs, Graves and Owen were confronting central elements of the self-sacrificial ethos. A memorial window was erected in 1920 at St Nicholas, Rattlesden, Suffolk, in which the stories of Abraham and Isaac, and David and Goliath, flank a central St George. Frantzen comments: 'this window acknowledges, with perhaps unintended bluntness, the sacrificial meaning of chivalry...The outer images offer complementary visions of George's fate and hence the fate of the men whose sacrifice the window honors. It is righteous to ask the young to die in God's service, for God aids those who undergo danger in his name.'[94] And yet...even then, with its Christian framework challenged, the power of the demand for self-sacrifice retained its hold on Sassoon, Graves and Owen; each returned to the front.[95]

For some, the war also called into question the centrality of nationalism. From the start, Sorley recognised, and articulated a critique of, some of the hidden assumptions on which it rested. He had spent six months in Germany in 1914, learning the language, attending lectures at Jena, and acquiring a considerable respect for German society and culture.[96] In the months of training between his enlistment and posting to the front, he set out, in several letters which vary in tone between the serious and the semi-jocular, his view of the war. He did not see it through a nationalist lens. Two themes stand out. First, he admired several aspects of German culture: its thoroughness and enterprise, its Faustian seeking and energy.[97] He figured it as a rising power, determined to take its place on the world stage, and spread its culture like a missionary. 'They are a young nation and don't yet see that what they consider is being done for the good of the world may be really being done for self-gratification.'[98] In the battle between the virtue/vice pairings of German efficiency/intolerance versus British sympathy/casualness, he would fight for tolerance as the larger virtue; but this did not blind him to the value of German strivings.[99] In a daring comparison, he suggested that if the German bigots did conquer they would mend their methods with time, as had the Christian bigots when they had conquered.[100] In this respect he shared with Graeme West a historic perspective which could conceive of a world in which Britain was not the dominant power, without sharing his nihilism about the prospect. Second, he also argued that Britain, the power in possession, had a share of responsibility for the conflict. 'Germany must be crushed for her wicked and selfish aspiration to be mistress of the world; but the country that, when mistress of the world, failed to set her an example of unworldliness and renunciation should take to herself half the blame of the blood expended in the crushing.'[101]

I want to put this questioning alongside that of the shell-shocked soldiers whose history and voices Peter Barham has set out to recover and make audible.[102] In *Forgotten Lunatics of the Great War*, he traces the changing pattern of treatment which men who suffered wartime mental breakdowns were offered, arguing that it shifted from a previous biologically based either/or model, in which men were either sane and fully responsible for their actions or mentally defective, to a psychological model which recognised degrees of mental distress, much of which might be reactive, temporary and curable. While this shift was by no means total during the war, he locates it as part of a wider picture whereby wartime arguments on behalf of the citizen soldier were able to connect with and intensify pressures already present in Edwardian society to break down rigid barriers between classes, and between the sane and insane, and modify the unequal distribution of entitlement to care which followed from those divisions.[103] A consequence of this recognition of a continuum between mental health and distress, for the present-day historian if not for many of the wartime doctors, is that the shell-shocked also have truths to tell about the war.[104]

Barham cites several cases of distressed soldiers expecting to be killed, or offering to kill themselves, for their failure to make themselves good soldiers.[105] James Batchelor, a regular with twelve years' service, complained to a medical officer in summer 1918 that 'he was "quite sure that the officers of his Unit intend that he be shot", he expected Sir Douglas Haig to be present at the execution. He drew a map representing all the trenches in France on which he marked all the exits "Gates of Death", and suggested that the only way out was suicide.' In a striking example of internalisation, or parody/mimicry, of psychiatric lore, he added after considerable hesitation that 'he had masturbated since youth and thought that was the cause of his trouble'. He was diagnosed as suffering from 'delusions of unworthiness'.[106]

Barham interprets such behaviour as indicating the degree to which these soldiers had internalised both the ultimate sanctions of military discipline, and the views of at least some officers that it would be better if such 'malingerers' were shot.[107] I would take this interpretation further. While, in the asylum at Napsbury, no one was under literal threat of being shot, what their words symbolically express is the truth of what they faced at the front.[108] Their officers did wish them to be (at risk of being) shot, and on occasion would themselves shoot men who refused to take that risk. Hence it makes complete symbolic sense for a soldier to assert that Haig would attend at his execution. Where all exits lead to the Gates of Death, and both sides are threatening to shoot you, then suicide is only a form of (prematurely) obeying orders.

When Barnett and Bond describe Sassoon as whingeing, or him and his fellow literary junior officers as too sensitive and imaginative, they are unconsciously repeating the language used by both psychiatrists and military commanders, before and during the war, of those who did not live up to their expectations. I propose instead that Sassoon, Graves, Graeme West, Owen and others on the one hand, and the shell-shocked soldiers on the other, can be understood as speaking truths from the margins. Paradoxically, the shell-shocked soldiers who had broken down were in some respects in a position to speak such truths more bluntly. Charles Abberley gave as '"the reason for Britain engaging in war the belief that she wanted more colonies"'.[109] Isadore Brooks from Stoke Newington, formerly a postboy in the Colonial Office, '"a peculiar looking undersized youth"', had undergone a spiritual awakening in France, and saw religious portents everywhere. His behaviour troubled Major Stanford Read, wartime commanding officer of the asylum at Netley Clearing Hospital. 'He is self-satisfied and rather expansive…Instead of *answering* many questions, he *asks* me some in return, as "what is war", "what is a nation", what do I mean by this and that?'[110]

To suggest this connection is neither to idealise the shell-shock victims nor to locate them in an identical space to Graves, Sassoon and co. As Barham's material makes clear, the speaking of blunt truths about the war existed at Napsbury alongside acute self-abasement and feelings of worthlessness. The inner conflicts around duty, masculinity and identity took a different form for the junior officer poets. As Martin Stone has expressed it, the socialisation of volunteers to working life in the trenches was more than an internalisation of a mental representation of the firing squad; they also internalised a notion of duty, mediated via the concept of morale. He terms this the 'exploitation of courage': volunteers were attracted by an image of war, as an occasion of self-fulfilment and a test of personal qualities, which was in practice dysfunctional and (by 1917) viewed by veterans as a liability. This revelation—that, as Ivor Gurney put it, 'men do things not for courage or their country but because of discipline'—came as a deep personal disenchantment to Gurney himself and many others, and led to 'profound feelings of personal failure in spite of the fact that most had never shirked their duty'.[111] Such feelings—those which Sassoon perceived and sought to distance himself from in his fellow officers at Craiglockhart—represent an identification with the aggressor, a turning against the individual self of the collective madness that was trench warfare. Not "the war is wrong, inhuman", but "I am wrong, less than human".[112]

The officer poets queried aspects of nationalism (Sorley, Graeme West), they repudiated Christian images of self-sacrifice as justification for the war (Sassoon, Graves, Graeme West, Owen). Yet in the end, held in part by a powerful sense of duty to their men—that is to a face-to-face rather than an imagined community, they chose to continue to serve.[113] This was a form of what Stone terms the 'exploitation of friendship'.[114] In 'At a Calvary near the Ancre', Owen critiqued the priests, and the scribes who 'brawl allegiance to the state'. He concluded with the lines: 'Those who love the greater love / Lay down their life; they do not hate.'[115] But he continued to fight. Graves, in particular, exemplified the continuing hold of the interlocking pattern of loyalties established within family and school, and codified in the notion of the gentleman who did not let the side down. For Graeme West, too, it was his family whom he first failed to tell of his decision to protest, before he withheld his letter and telegram to the army.[116] The channelling of emotional and libidinal energy into relationships between men reinforced the acceptable dimension of self-sacrifice: Graves, Sassoon, Graeme West and Owen aimed to do all they could for their men within the parameters of the war. To survive, they confined their horizons to their immediate front-line community which they sought to serve, striving not to think where such thought led only to an impasse. Rivers, too, disciplined himself not to raise questions which might trouble the status quo; and set to work on similar goals, within the same parameters, as his patients Sassoon and Owen. The price which Graves paid was a disintegration of self, which it would take a decade—and a wrenching break with family and country—to begin to overcome.[117]

Individual responses to the war have to be located in the wider political context. Britain was not a dictatorial society, and it was possible within limits to express opposition to the war, or particular aspects of it (such as conscription).[118] But the government worked hard to neutralise such opposition, especially when it seemed it might be effective; and the pressures from civil society not to undermine the war effort were also substantial.[119] To oppose the war as an individual was immensely difficult, especially for those who had voluntarily placed themselves under military discipline. Whatever their private views, public opposition to the war rendered them liable to court martial. Hence the courage of Sassoon's protest, and the depth of Graves's concern for his friend's well being if he persisted. Graeme West tried and failed, the *reading* of Russell's texts not providing sufficient support. Sassoon, with the face-to-face support of Russell and other pacifists and conscientious objectors, did find the strength of purpose; and sustained his views despite the opposition of many friends and fellow officers, and the suasion of Rivers.[120] But sustained and large-scale opposition to the (continuation of) the war was more likely in the context of adherence to another imagined community, which could support the individual by weaving their beliefs and values into a wider network of meanings shared with fellow members. The final section will conclude by exploring some of the alternative imagined communities which played this role in Britain during the war.

Alternative Imagined Communities

The previous section identified contradictions which the First World War posed to members of the imagined community that was Great Britain, while pointing to the difficulties faced by individuals who were moved to oppose the war. I want to illuminate some possible sources of collective opposition by extending the range of application of the concept of 'imagined community' to other social collectivities, particularly social classes and political movements, which potentially formed competing locuses of identity; and to explore how different imagined communities can come into conflict. Anderson himself sees the developing bourgeois classes who were to be the prime movers of nationalism in this light.[121] A rising bourgeois class had to project an imagined future for itself and its demands, as it fought for economic, legal and political privileges. Once it had achieved a relatively stable position within a capitalist society, it developed a set of formal and informal institutions for reproducing itself, consolidating its power and cohesion regionally and later nationally.[122] Yet Anderson's figuring of class as imagined community seems to be rooted in, and to remain constrained by, its connection with nation building. Once modern nation states have secured their sovereign existence, he tends to treat them as almost unique in their power to evoke love and self-sacrifice, explicitly contrasting them with voluntarily adopted ideologies such as liberalism or marxism.[123] To challenge this, I shall borrow the term 'actually existing'.[124] My argument is that nation is a term which mediates between the actually existing and the imagined. A nation-in-formation had to effect a transition from one or more *actually existing* communities to another *imagined* community; while a nation-once-formed has to hold in tension its actually existing and its imagined realities.[125] Any polity offers to its subjects an actually existing social location, with specific accompanying political status, level of economic and cultural provision, and perhaps possibility of betterment. Would-be nation builders of the nineteenth and twentieth centuries had to persuade sufficient followers that the imagined community of the envisaged future nation would offer them more than their actually existing identity as subordinate people within a dynastic realm, or colonial people within a foreign empire.[126] Once a nation has been established as a sovereign state, then its nationalism entails (and can only be understood in terms of) the interaction of its reality as the now actually existing material force (coercive and providing) shaping the lives of its citizens, with its *ideologies* of imagined nationhood which stabilise its current identity, and project its existence back into the past and forward into the future.[127]

This delineation of a tension between the actually existing and the imagined in nationalism, with its different modalities before and after accession to nation statehood, can also be used to illuminate the character of other social collectivities. Modern individuals belong to a *variety* of imagined communities, ranging from the family through class to the nation and beyond. Such imagined communities overlap, sometimes reinforcing, sometimes coming into conflict with, the nation and each other. As Eric Hobsbawm has commented: 'we cannot assume that for most people national identification—when it exists—excludes or is always or ever superior to, the remainder of the set of identifications which constitute the social being. In fact, it is always combined with identifications of another kind, even when it is felt to be superior to them.'[128]

In certain circumstances, some of those imagined communities may attempt, or even succeed in, a mobilisation of their actual or potential inhabitants which challenges the currently dominant actually existing community. Such challenges often take the form of a separatist or irredentist nationalism; but they may also be inspired by religious or political ideologies. The success of their challenge depends on the degree to which, in comparison with the existing power, they are able to translate an imagined into an actually existing community.[129] This perspective views the mobilising power of nationalism as less unique than Anderson tends to suggest, and aligns its mechanisms in part with those of both class and political movements. It makes it necessary to explore concretely the relative powers of other potential focusses of loyalty in the modern polity.

Opposition to the war in Britain took several forms, each of which can be associated with an alternative imagined community. The most successful of these came from the republican tradition within Irish Nationalism. With Home Rule finally agreed by Parliament in 1914 (though then suspended for the duration of the war), a majority of the Irish Nationalists followed their leader John Redmond in supporting the war effort. They believed this would bring reward after the war for their conspicuous loyalty, by showing that dominion status for Ireland could work without threatening England's security. A minority, however, followed the older

Fenian tradition (harking back to the United Irishmen in 1798), that 'England's difficulty is Ireland's opportunity'. Regarding the British cause as no concern of theirs, they planned to exploit the opportunity through an armed uprising; hence Roger Casement's effort to secure German support and arms. Though the Easter Rising of 1916 was easily defeated by the British Army, the harsh repression which followed, and the threatened introduction of conscription (which Ireland had hitherto been spared) in 1918, undermined the constitutionalists. After the 1918 General Election, Sinn Fein, having won an overwhelming majority of southern Ireland constituencies, took this as a mandate for independence. They set about constructing a parallel state with its own legitimacy (the Dáil), and coercive and providing powers—a form of the dual power which Lenin theorised. This ultimately led, after several years of guerrilla war, to the formation of a (virtually independent) Irish Free State in 1922. Here there is clearly a clash of two nationalisms, in which those Irish republicans gave their affiliation to an imagined Ireland which drew on actually existing historical, cultural, religious and linguistic resources. Unionists in the north resisted, giving their continuing loyalty to the existing imagined community of the United Kingdom in accordance with Protestant traditions stretching back to the Glorious Revolution.[130]

Opposition to the war from conscientious objectors drew on a variety of subordinate and emergent intellectual traditions. They were inspired by a mixture of religious and political beliefs. Those who objected to all wars created the newly emergent identity of pacifist. A significant role in the pacifist movement was played by those minority Christians (especially Quakers and other radical religious groups) who held to a more literal reading of Jesus's teaching and practice of non-resistance to enemies.[131] Another cluster of opponents, who objected not to all wars but to this particular one, were more varied in their motivations: they might be opposed to imperial rivalry as the cause of war, or feel that this particular war posed no threat to Britain. They displayed elements of Durkheim's 'world patriotism', valuing the shared humanity of the populations of the warring nations over the integrity of existing nation-state structures, and not feeling justified in killing fellow human beings. Durkheim had been acutely aware of the tension between the patriotism of the nation state, and that of an emergent, wider form of identification which he termed 'world patriotism' (*cosmopolitisme*).[132] He warned lucidly of the dangers which this contradiction posed—a contradiction which the war dramatically revealed: 'we cannot make it a fact that international competition shall not have preserved a military form'.[133] The tension between the claims of nation and those of a wider humanity were felt in different ways by Sorley, Graeme West, Graves and Sassoon.[134]

A further source of opposition to the war came from those socialists who held to the original goals of the Second International. The International had, before 1914, pledged its affiliated parties to oppose such a war—understood as a product of inter-imperialist rivalry from which all workers would suffer—at all costs: the international general strike was to be their weapon. All these plans came to naught, as a majority of almost all socialist parties in the belligerent countries found reasons to identify their nation's cause with the defence of class interests or socialist progress, and voted for war credits.[135] Some of those socialists who remained opposed to the war drew on existing political traditions. One of the most striking in Britain was the loosely knit, but effective, political alliance of socialists, Liberals and religious activists whom Cyril Pearce has documented in Huddersfield, who made it a community resistant to the pressures to support the war effort.[136]

Others sought a more aggressive policy to combat the war effort. Revolutionary socialist activists made strenuous efforts to mobilise working-class protest against wartime conditions, and if possible to generalise this into protest against the war itself. They depicted the war as the slaughter of working classes on behalf of ruling classes, in a struggle from which they could never benefit (seeing war as an inter-imperialist conflict, in terms not so different from those of ruling-class theorists of inevitable imperialist rivalry), and as paving the way for a newer and more brutal capitalism after war (based on fear of the continuance of such wartime measures as the Defence of the Realm Act, suppression of a free press, deportation of political activists, dilution, and the conscription of labour for industry as well as the military). Against that, they tried to conjure the notion of an alternative imagined community, the working class, first British, then international. Class division, they argued, was greater than national unity; international class solidarity more important than national divisions. They achieved their greatest success in areas where large-scale industry was crucial to the war effort, with a strong trade-union base, and a tradition of marxist organisation and education before 1914.[137] Their efforts were caught in a dilemma: many of the successful protests were in practice waged to defend the privileged position of skilled workers, both against the 'dilution' of their skilled labour practices (with its apparent threat to future prosperity after the war) and against their own 'combing out' for army service.[138] In Britain, they did not succeed in generalising these particular, regional or sectional, grievances into an anti-war movement. Only in countries which towards the end of the war underwent total political collapse (Russia), or a major weakening of regime authority (Germany), did the pressures towards working-class unity (to end the war and near starvation) overcome these difficulties. Even here, the German elites quickly co-opted a section of the working-class movement, and established a democratised but non-revolutionary regime. The situation in Britain never came near to this degree of crisis.

But the war also gave rise to a striking, and radically new, political force—international Communism. The Bolsheviks, alone among the major socialist parties in 1914, had held to the Second International policy of opposing war. The collapse of that policy gave rise to Lenin's insistence on a highly centralised and tightly disciplined international movement to match the authority structure he had already constructed in the Bolshevik Party. The Bolsheviks' opposition to the war, and their conclusion of peace with Germany in 1918, assisted their appeal to many on the left in post-war world. Furthermore, by seeming to show the working class in power, the Soviet Union apparently demonstrated that socialism was no longer a utopian dream. Thus in the interwar years, it was seen by many as the actualisation of a class-based imagined community, the 'workers' own state'. The Communist movement drew substantial support across the borders of European nation states in a manner whose nearest precedents lay in popular enthusiasm outside France for the French Revolution in the 1790s, or in the wars of religion of the sixteenth and seventeenth centuries. In some respects, this created a tension scarcely known in British politics since the consolidation of the nation state at the end of seventeenth century. For the first time since the post-Reformation religious conflicts, there was potentially a body of British citizens owing an (ultimately primary) allegiance to an external power. In practice, the failure of the Bolshevik/Communist revolutionary movement to extend its power beyond Russia after 1918 meant that the Communist International soon became subordinated to the foreign policy needs of the Soviet Union as the new regime sought to consolidate its domestic rule.

However, this failure is not to say that it is impossible for there to be a different focus of identification and belonging, an alternative imagined community, than the nation state. The Communist movement, like the socialist, demonstrated some of the characteristics which Anderson and Poole identify as hallmarks of the power of nationalism: the capacity to elicit self-sacrifice, the sense of belonging to a community beyond the face-to-face which forms a part of one's identity, the creation of meaning which extends beyond the life of the individual.[139] In countries where the Communist Party was not in power, but gained large-scale popular support, the imagined community it created extended beyond a cadre of professional revolutionaries to a substantial section of the working class. To a considerable extent, however, even the largest of such parties remained—like the pre-1914 Social Democratic Party in Germany—a sort of mega-sect, confined to a position of institutionally powerful but constrained opposition within the political system.[140] Many nationalist movements of the nineteenth and twentieth centuries had also begun from positions of weakness. Among the reasons for the defeat of the socialist/Communist project is that, for a nationalist movement to turn the actually existing elements of a proto-nation into the projected imagined community of the future nation state, they needed to succeed only within a delimited socio-geographic space. The socialist/communist project, by contrast, imagined its reach as universal.[141]

9

New Attachments: Confronting the Post-war World

Those men who survived the war carried with them into the peace the legacy of their wartime experiences and whatever changes these had provoked in how they understood and engaged with their society. This chapter examines how that legacy led them to challenge the family expectations and social structures which faced them after 1918.

Macfie was already well into middle age when he volunteered. He returned from the war with his health permanently weakened by his efforts, but with a secure position in his family firm to resume. Sometime in the 1920s, his health declining, he withdrew from active involvement in both business and the GLS, retiring to a house with lands which he had bought near Lunds in the North Yorkshire Dales.[1] Here he recreated, partly through small-scale involvement in his local community, and partly in fantasy, that detachment from certain key inherited values which he had practised before 1914. Accounts of his last years stress how he fitted himself into the community, neither patronising nor romanticising the Dales way of life.[2] They emphasise his altruism, his wish to help this poor upland sheep-farming community in practical ways. He used his knowledge of science to devise and test ways of enriching the soil, and hence grass yield; published the results; organised lectures for local farmers to encourage other new farming practices; and offered essay prizes to encourage children's interest. He also identified the cause of, and a remedy for, an outbreak of canine hysteria which was killing local sheep dogs.[3] He also seems to have made his peace with the church, attending services regularly (though declining office on the grounds that he was a Presbyterian), paying for the construction of a road across the fields to the church, and undertaking considerable research to promote the case for Lunds becoming a separate parish.[4] He also devoted himself to researching the local history of the Dales.

These endeavours are clearly continuous with Macfie's earlier efforts on behalf of his workmen and soldiers. Part of the attraction for him of this community he worked for was the ideological frame within which he situated it, his (no doubt idealised) perception that there was: 'Not a gentleman, parson, or scholar within five miles; nothing but small farmers who have never had masters and speak a dialect founded on old Norse.'[5] The Gypsies represented one sort of alternative to western civilisation—a way of life with a nomadic and in some ways transgressive character. The people of the Dales represented a different alternative—profoundly rooted in a single locality, law abiding, but sharing with the Gypsies (and the Mohammedans as Macfie understood them) a form of primitive equality without rule by landowners or priests.[6] One of his fellow local historians commented of him: 'Lunds, we discovered, on several occasions in its history gave shelter to interesting fugitives. Mr Macfie escaped the twentieth century and found rest there.'[7]

Graves and West, by contrast, were in their early twenties as the war ended, with a place to find in the world and careers to make. Their lives in the post-war decade map some of the contours of the younger generation's reaction to the war. To a perhaps surprising extent, there was still a battle with Victorian legacies, even if these were overlaid with the recent and powerful effects of war. This is visible in their attitudes towards family (Graves first as an engaged father, then as an explorer of communal living; West by resisting marriage as an institution which would tie him to the values which he was seeking to resist), towards nation (West living abroad for most of the decade, Graves fleeing abroad at its end), and towards class and politics (flirtations with socialism and communism by Graves, membership of the Communist Party for West). Both made use of psychoanalysis (Graves briefly, West more elaborately) as a resource for exploring and trying to loosen or undo some of the emotional bonds which tied them to the past. Despite their rejection of Christianity, both felt a pull towards some form of religious belief as a net of signification to hold them: for Graves, this came in the 1930s with the first steps to elaborating a theory of primitive matriarchy as a source of poetic inspiration; for West, in his struggle to reconcile his new political faith with a continuing sense of the attraction of religious feeling.

Graves: Saying Goodbye

Goodbye to All That was a product not only of Graves's childhood and wartime experiences, but also of his struggles to come to terms with the post-war world—both by overcoming his own direct legacies of war, and by building a way of life free from those aspects of his upbringing he was now striving to reject. He described his autobiography as a story of 'gradual disintegration'.[8] That failure of integration, which persisted throughout the twenties, is explored in 'A Letter from Wales' (*c.*1924).[9] This troubled poem takes the form of an address by Graves ('Richard Rolls') to Sassoon ('Abel Wright'), apparently provoked by, and trying to explain, a post-war failure of communication between them. It concerns a crisis of identity, stemming from 24 July 1916 when Graves 'died, poor fellow, the day he came of age'. So too, the poem suggests, did Sassoon when 'something snapped and sent you Berserk'.[10] Thereafter two substitutes, sharing the same features as the dead men, 'Came up to Harlech pretending a wild joy / That they had cheated Death', writing, talking, smoking, enjoying life; 'but unless I now / confound my present feeling, with the past, / They felt a sense of unreality'.[11] Graves wants Sassoon to confirm one particular memory, yet knows he cannot: 'for who are you? or I' As they had walked in the mountains together the sun 'gild[ed] our face with heroic light'; the two men proceeded to perform a joint parody of Christ's Transfiguration.[12] Thereafter, he claims, the men's two substitutes returned to France, only for both to be killed once again (Sassoon by a bullet in the head, Graves 'after the Armistice / Pneumonia, with the doctor's full consent').[13] What this text expresses is the disruption of continuous identity brought about by wartime experience, and particularly the sequence of near deaths (from wounds, reckless actions, pandemic) which each man suffered. Is not the Graves of 1924 simply one in a series of substitutes for the man who died in 1916? He would like to appeal to his friend for confirmation, but he cannot since now a gap has opened between them.

This struggle against disintegration can be traced through several aspects of Graves's life. He had to deal with his own direct legacy of war. He suffered from continuing nervous reactions directly related to his wartime service—termed shell shock during the war, categorised as neurasthenia in its post-war manifestations—for nearly a decade after the

Armistice.[14] He experienced flashbacks to his military service. 'These day dreams persisted like an alternate life....they did not leave me until well on in 1928.' Various everyday activities, including travelling, and meeting.numbers of people at once, overstrained his nerves.[15] On occasions, these attacks reached a peak of intensity which drove him to seek psychological help or undertake efforts at self-cure.[16] He also suffered from survivor guilt, and guilt about the killing he had done.[17] This legacy was exacerbated by a series of post-war deaths among those close to him, which came to seem part of the same malign pattern as the wartime deaths of friends and acquaintances with which his text is saturated.[18] They began in the transitional year 1918, when he was trying to build his post-war future of marriage, family and rural life during the closing stages of the war itself. His marriage was followed shortly by the death of Nancy's mother from pneumonia (brought on partly by her effort, when already ill, to see her son off to the front), then of Nancy's brother himself on active service, and finally of his friend and literary patron Robbie Ross.[19] They continued with the deaths in close succession in 1922–4 of three men who had been key mentors: Mallory at Charterhouse, Rivers during and after the war, and Sir Walter Raleigh, his tutor, who had gone out of his way to adapt Oxford regulations to accommodate Graves's needs.[20] *Goodbye to All That* is scattered with references to other such losses, conveying the sense that Graves's life in the 1920s is still haunted by the apparent ubiquity of death.[21]

He was also dealing with the considerable demands of his growing family (four children were born between 1919 and 1924).[22] Graves's relation to his new family can be seen as part of his revolt against the conditions of his own childhood. Whereas he had been brought up in a traditionally Victorian framework, seeing his parents relatively little, with his day-to-day care delegated to servants and then school, he himself was a 'hands-on' father in a manner more characteristic of later generations. This was partly a matter of principle, concerning both the manner of child rearing and the intention that Nicholson too should pursue her career as an artist; and partly the result of a lack of money which made employing servants at first difficult and then impossible.[23] At the same time, Graves was determined to establish himself as a writer, in accordance with his vow on demobilisation never to be under anyone's orders again in his life.[24]

These principles contributed to his conflicts with his natal family in this period. His parents were horrified at some aspects of Robert's and Nancy's marriage and child-rearing methods: Nicholson's keeping her own name; her mode of dress; their refusal to have their children christened; and the way they included their housekeeper in their pattern of daily sociability. These matters were anxiously discussed among family members, and recorded in Alfred's diary.[25] At the same time, although Graves had published several collections of poetry and books of criticism, he had failed to establish himself as a professional writer. This, and his unwillingness to consider other jobs, meant that he repeatedly fell back on his family (and friends) for financial support.[26] There was a gap between Graves's expectations for his pattern of life (relatively modest though these were compared with his upbringing) and what he was able to earn for himself—something of which he was at times uneasily aware.[27] His family (and father-in-law) gave him continual and substantial financial support throughout the 1920s (though on occasion with reservations); but this intensified the unease of their relationship. Graves resented this continuing dependence, and the advice, reproval and pressure to obtain a secure job which it elicited from his troubled parents.[28]

Graves also strove to engage with wider problems of the post-war world. He began to question inherited values and assumptions concerning class, gender and race. Before the war, he records little sign of any political awareness. Though he dates his first consciousness of class difference to the age of four, he also says that he accepted it as he did religious faith, and only questioned it nearly twenty years later—that is, during the war. Politically, he and Sassoon had ended the war sympathetic to socialism, and to the post-war unrest. This was a result of the reaching across the barriers of class, erected by their upbringings, which wartime service alongside their men had made possible; as well as of the discontent with established leadership which arose from their criticisms of the conduct of the war.[29] At this point, Sassoon was the more active, campaigning on behalf of the anti-war Labour MP Philip Snowden in the 1918 General Election.[30] Graves was the more moderate: though sympathetic to the Russian Revolution, he set out clearly in 1918 his distance from its methods, which—he recognised—arose from his own class position.[31] His politics (and the more democratic pattern of daily living he and Nicholson adopted) caused tension with his family, which, though proud of his war service and sympathetic to his shell-shocked state, were horrified at his apparent revolutionary sympathies. His father tried to dissuade him, reminding him that his half-brother Philip, 'once a pro-Boer and a Fenian, had recovered from his youthful revolutionary idealism and come out all right in the end.' Several of his half-siblings were in the Near East, as British officials or their wives, and his father hoped Graves would join them, perhaps in the consular service, 'where the family influence would help me, and there get over my "revolutionary idealism"'.[32]

Sassoon's phase of political activism passed relatively quickly. After an abortive attempt to report the anti-unemployment riots in Glasgow in February 1919, he worked for a year as literary editor for the strongly left-wing and independent paper the *Daily Herald*; and during the confrontation between the Triple Alliance and the government in 1921 he tried to support the miners through journalism. But Sassoon's personality was not suited to politics; and his various efforts to become more politically engaged soon petered out. By the 1926 General Strike, though sympathetic to the miners, he was taking part in unofficial negotiations for a compromise.[33] Graves, however, indicated a growing disillusionment with the Labour Party, and a sympathy (if only rhetorical) with the Communists. He began a more active engagement in local politics after he and Nicholson moved to Islip outside Oxford in 1921; and she encouraged him in this stance. His strongest links of friendship there, and occasional public stances, were clearly with the working-class villagers.[34] He offered his house for meetings of the local Labour Party, and in 1924–5 became one of three Labour members on the parish council for a year, campaigning for better sanitation for the village.[35] Under Nicholson's influence, he also began to question the patriarchal assumptions with which he had been brought up; while his friendship with the Bengali philosopher Basanta Mallik led him for the first time to doubt the inferiority of non-European races.[36]

Intellectually, Graves began the post-war years interested in psychoanalysis, which he had first encountered through Rivers. He used it as a tool to explore the various conflicts he was experiencing. He turned to it, especially at moments of crisis, as a way of trying to understand and cope with his neurasthenia; though he was also hesitant to undertake a full treatment, fearing both that he would become dependent on a psychiatrist, and that any cure would also deprive him of the spur to write poetry.[37] He also used it to try to understand the internal conflicts created within him by his family and upbringing.[38] And he deployed it in his first attempts to develop a theory of poetry, arguing that a poem represented the writer's attempt to resolve his own conflicts, which could then appeal to readers who had experienced similar conflicts.[39]

Psychologically, the decade was marked by Graves's continuing struggle with the legacy of his upbringing and especially the pressure of his mother's intense moralism and high expectations. His struggle to free himself from his mother took the form of attaching himself to another figure with whom he could form a similar bond.[40] This pattern held for his intimate emotional life over this period. He formed relationships in turn with two strong-minded and strong-willed women, Nancy Nicholson and Laura Riding. From each of these relationships he gained substantial support in his efforts to free himself from his past; but each also imposed costs through the demands they placed on him.[41] Nicholson, an atheist, supported him strongly—against his family—in his continuing struggle to free himself from the legacy of religion, and especially the guilt which his wartime killing now evoked in him; and in not bringing their children up as Christians.[42] As a strong feminist, she continually challenged the patriarchal assumptions with which he had grown up, and which he had never hitherto questioned. And she supported the more democratic way of living which he had adopted.[43] The marriage had been for Graves a passionate assertion of the value of life in the midst of the carnage of war, as well as of the struggle for independence. However, by the mid-1920s, the difficulties within the relationship were beginning to erode the strength of that bond.[44]

These difficulties were themselves products of the couple's respective upbringings, of the circumstances which brought them together, and of their efforts to develop a new pattern of living. They had married when very young, under the pressure of war. As the marriage was ending, Graves's sister Clarissa sought to explain it to other family members in these terms: 'She married when she knew nothing and was no more than a child. I think this present separation is Nature's own protest that Nancy should have had no proper youth.' And, she suggested, war 'drives men into premature marriage in the hope of propagating themselves before sudden death.'[45] Graves had retained a puritanical anxiety about sexual passion, as he would do throughout his life.[46] Nicholson too suffered from the sexual ignorance imposed by her upbringing: she had been quite unprepared for the trauma of childbirth.[47] Her feminism, based partly on seeing her mother sacrifice her own artistic career to that of her husband, meant that marriage always had an element of compromise for her, and by spring 1920 she already wanted to be 'dis-married'.[48] It led her, in Graves's view, sometimes to underestimate his own wartime sufferings.[49] And their married life was made difficult by the constant shortage of money and a certain impracticality.[50]

In 1925 Graves began to correspond with the American poet Laura Riding, whom he invited to join him and Nicholson as they set out for Egypt.[51] Under increasing financial pressure, Graves had finally been compelled to complete his long-delayed degree and look for a permanent post. He was soon offered a professorship of English at Cairo University.[52] His parents were delighted, since this represented security and a good salary; but they were also anxious. One of Graves's half-brothers, Richard, held a senior post in the British administration in Egypt, and they feared that the presence of Nicholson, who still kept her own name, would damage his career.[53] Graves, on his arrival, saw the degree to which the British were in effect running Egypt; his role, as professor, was to uphold the British cause at the university. He quickly decided that the life of an expatriate academic was not for him, and—to his parents' consternation (over both the loss of income and the potential effect on his brother's career), but the 'undisguised relief' of his sister-in-law—resigned the post after just six months to return to England.[54]

During these months, however, the emotional centre of gravity of his life had begun to shift towards Riding. The next three years saw what proved to be the gradual unravelling of his marriage. At first, he and Riding developed an intense intellectual partnership, as they worked together on joint works of literary criticism, and Graves reconstructed his whole approach to the writing of poetry.[55] As well as sharing his intellectual and literary interests, Riding welcomed and rewarded him emotionally for his devotion to her.[56] The relationship soon became sexual as well. Over the next two-and-a-half years, they tried to live, together with Nicholson, a triangular, 'open', relationship (which Riding termed a 'three-life'), sharing between themselves emotional ties and the upbringing of the children. They developed a bohemian, semi-communal lifestyle, living in a flat and on a houseboat in London.[57]

However, in the spring of 1929, after Riding had invited the Irish poet Geoffrey Phibbs to join them in a 'four-life', the newly extended ménage rapidly blew apart.[58] Viewed from one perspective, the ensuing emotional complications (ultimately, Phibbs's wife was invited to join them to make a 'five-life'), and resultant flights-and-pursuits between England, Ireland and France, veer between the tragicomic and the farcical.[59] Looked at another way, they can be seen as an abortive attempt to find a new pattern of living outside the framework of conventional marriage, of a kind that was to become more common in the 1960s.[60] After considerable stress for all involved, Phibbs decided that he wanted an exclusive relationship with Nicholson. At the height of the emotional crisis this provoked in June 1929, Riding leaped from a fourth-floor window, and was lucky to escape alive and unparalysed (though with long-term injuries). Graves, shocked by her action, ran down one floor and then jumped himself, sustaining only minor injuries.[61] This near-suicidal dénouement finally rent apart the complex network of relationships. In its aftermath, Graves decided to leave England with Riding and settle abroad where they could live more cheaply. He then embarked on his defiant goodbye to family, friends, England, and his own earlier self.

The whole extended Graves family was intensely literary: several kept diaries (and later wrote autobiographies), and they conducted an extensive correspondence among themselves, parts of which were then recirculated by the original recipient (as enclosure or by quotation).[62] This correspondence can be regarded as the documentary archive or deposit, the material trace, of the family as an institution of the kind discussed in Chapter 2. It records the ways in which the dynamics of provision, coercion and recognition operated through interpersonal relationships. Graves's parents were torn between wanting to support Robert and their grandchildren, while deploring both the way of life on which he had embarked and its potential effects on themselves and their other children.[63] This was enacted through financial and moral support and pressure. Throughout the crisis of Graves's marriage and its aftermath, his parents and family once again reacted with a mixture of concern, disapproval, and attempts to understand and help.[64] Financial assistance continued to be offered, but was withdrawn when Robert's behaviour went beyond what was acceptable.[65] At the same time, Alfred and especially Amy expressed their pleas to their son in a Christian, moralising language which he had now firmly rejected.[66] Because in the post-war years Graves had not established himself financially, he remained in a situation of dependency, where his behaviour was monitored and commented on within the family. This made it harder for him to challenge their values or behaviour. Consequently, when the break finally came, it was the more violent. As R. P. Graves comments, alluding to Samuel Butler's excoriating critique of the Victorian family, *The Way of All Flesh*, to which Graves had been introduced by Mallory at school: 'The 1929 crisis meant that he became emotionally free to jettison as much of his family as he pleased, and in that sense to become a full-scale Butlerian of the kind to which he had previously only aspired.'[67]

Graves's and Riding's survival of their leaps concludes, outside the text, another strand of *Goodbye to All That*, one which works in counterpoint to the succession of deaths which otherwise permeate the narrative. Graves's first older mentor was Mallory, who had introduced him to mountaineering.[68] In describing his first efforts at climbing in North Wales in 1913–14, Graves recounts an episode in which, having slipped, he accomplished something impossible: he improvised a foothold in mid-air from which he regained safety. His framing of this event reveals two self-identifications. The first is with Mallory himself, about whom he tells a similar story of an impossible climbing feat. The second is with Christ: Graves describes himself as having been given what the devil offered Jesus—survival after casting himself down from a high place.[69] This episode can be linked to the events of July 1916. Graves, publicly declared dead on his twenty-first birthday—the beginning of his (adult) life, had been triumphantly resurrected to read his own death notice and letters of condolence.[70] Now, both he and Riding had survived potentially fatal falls; for each their old life had died and a new one was being born.[71] This interpretation helps to make sense of the surprising language which Graves then began to use to describe Riding, as someone 'living invisibly, against kind, as dead, beyond event'. By this, he seems to mean beyond the ebb and flow of daily life, a sort of Platonic Ideal figure. Increasingly under the sway of Riding's exalted estimation of herself as a goddess or figure of destiny, he was also reported to have described her as 'seamless, like the garment of Christ'.[72]

This strand of Graves's text, as well as having a quasi-blasphemous connotation which perhaps reflects his continuing struggle with the weight of Christian teaching, can also be linked to what was said earlier about movement and the masculine body. As Connell has argued, confident inhabiting and mastery of the active body is a key component of many masculinities.[73] And as Leed pointed out, one of the most stressful aspects of trench warfare was the inability of soldiers to master their anxiety through motility.[74] The omnipotence which Graves's narrative of his pre-war climbing episode contains represents an understandable (retrospective) psychic response to the helplessness induced by conditions on the Western Front.[75] At the same time, it represents an apotheosis of one strand of his mechanisms of survival during the war. Then, he (and his fellow soldiers) clung to (hopeful) fragments of hymn and scripture as a primitive defence against the randomness of the death and mutilation with which they were threatened by fragments of metal. In conditions of war, it proved impossible for Graves (as for many) to bring those fragments together into a sustainable whole; the Christian message proved an inadequate container for the fragmenting anxiety. Having survived the war, and the shell fragment which pierced his lung, Graves could figure himself (and now Riding) in fantasy as another Christ, reborn from the grave to live a new and transformed (Transfigured) life—an omnipotent reversal (confirmed by the further survival of the twin leaps) of the damage (physical and mental) the war had inflicted. Such a perception, moreover, also offered a way to manage the survivor guilt of being alive when so many of those he had been closest to were not, as well as the moral guilt of having killed men who shared a part of his identity. As well as this retrospective dimension, an overcoming of his past, his omnipotent fantasy also had a prospective role, helping him muster the necessary energy for breaking with family, friends and England, and saying *Goodbye to All That.* As such, it is a testimony to the power of the internalised forces from which he sought rupture.

Alick West: Seeking to Belong

West's life during this post-war period was characterised by several interrelated struggles. These centred round the authority which his father both exercised and represented: an authority variously translated into, and expressed through, the spheres of religion, nation, the choice of a career and the imperative to form a family. In rejecting the patterns of authority offered him, West excluded himself from existing frameworks of meaning and identity. Influenced by his readings of Nietzsche and Max Stirner, and by his friend Paul Farleigh's reworking of similar themes, he saw himself as an artist, one of those conscious of what they did, as opposed to the unconscious herd.[76] But this form of individualism proved hard to sustain; he gradually came to experience impulses to belong to a nation and a faith, to find a group into which he could merge his individual identity and an authority which he could obey willingly. Politically, he rejected England and went to live abroad; but then sought a way to return which would allow him once again to belong. Belonging could mean adherence to a nation, organisation or creed; but it could also involve forms of identification which were in part mediated through personal, including sexual, relationships.

Following the compromise resolution of his conflict with his father over his future career, West studied at Trinity College, Dublin, from 1919–22, first classics and then modern languages.[77] His political trajectory had begun with the questioning of his father's beliefs, through the influence of his various mentors in the internment camp, and his subsequent opposition to the war, retrospectively validated through discovering that his serving brother had come to the same stance. This rejection of the unquestioning patriotism of his family and his own youth now extended, through sympathy with the independence struggles which he encountered when living in Ireland and then Egypt, to identification with the opponents of British imperialism.[78]

In autumn 1920, while at university, he suffered a tubercular lung haemorrhage; so the following winter he was sent to Egypt for six months for his health, as a member of an archaeological expedition.[79] He stayed with his step-uncle, who was a professor of medicine at Cairo University. The leader of the expedition was an ex-Army officer, strongly pro-Empire; and of his step-uncle West wrote: 'He had rigorously excluded from his mind any questioning of his family's code of the English garrison in Ireland, and now, with a consciousness much stronger than my stepmother's had ever been, he was a part of the British garrison in Egypt.'[80] West felt himself trapped in this environment. His own attitude to the Egyptians assisting the dig was ambivalent: though drawn towards them, in situations of possible conflict he continued to act as an Englishman 'conscious of the separation between us and the Arabs'.[81]

During this visit, West had his first sexual encounter, with an Egyptian prostitute. He then recounts the following incident:

> Some days later, I was sitting on the balcony...when I heard shouting from the street. A dense column of Egyptians was approaching, and the purpose of their demonstration was heard in the anger of their multitudinous voice. Alone, some ten yards before the head of the column, was a young girl; every few yards she turned round to the marchers and flung her arms high into the air, shouting with all the passion of her being. I watched until the demonstration had passed. My uncle tapped me on the shoulder. 'Look at your cigarette', he said. I had left it burning on the flat arm of a garden chair. 'You've ruined that chair,' he said.[82]

The vision of the young girl leading the crowd condensed passion, foreignness, and hostility to Britain as ruler, in a way which transfixed West. For him, as for Macfie, exogamy, that is forming a sexual relationship with someone outside their class and/or nation, could come to take on the meaning of a rejection of the expectations of family and class, and an identification with some 'Other'.

After taking his degree in October 1922, Macfie moved to Switzerland where (except for two years in Berlin from late 1923 to late 1925) he was to live until 1935. He worked initially as a tutor to a young boy; and then, after a further attack of tuberculosis had led to a stay of several months in a sanatorium in the winter of 1925–26, as tutor to a businessman in Zurich. In September 1926 he became Lektor in English at Basle University.[83] During these years, he regularly visited his family, and also Farleigh, who now lived in Berlin.

Four intertwined themes can be discerned in West's account of his years in Switzerland: his efforts to comprehend the disjunctions between the personal and the societal within individuals, his search for the possibility of belonging to a nation or creed, his intimate relationships, and his engagement with psychoanalysis.

West repeatedly explored the tension—at times, the apparent disjunction—between the personal characters and qualities of family members, lovers, friends and acquaintances, and the social roles they occupied. Centrally, when trying to deal with his ambivalence towards his father, he sought ways of absorbing what he valued in his paternal legacies. But he was also sensitive to the same conflict in other people whom he encountered.[84] His acuteness in perceiving this tension in others derived from his struggle over it within himself. In particular, he was faced with a contradiction between his critical assessments of aspects of society, and the ways in which he saw that those criticisms could both arise from and mask his continuing inner conflicts. This theme dated back to his opposition to the war while in internment; but becomes more prominent in his account of his life after the war.

The tension between the personal and the societal realities of marriage and the family was one which West struggled to resolve in his own life. His autobiography makes clear that patterns of identification are formed not only with individuals and immediate family members, but also with social structures and institutions which, like them, can act as focusses of loyalty and identity. Two such focusses presented as central in the text are religion and the nation. With each of them, West's text explores the links between rational attitudes towards an ideology or social structure, and the emotional roots of such attitudes, and their adoption, in childhood experiences and family relations.

West's loss of Christian faith, which began in his later teens, was accelerated by his experiences in internment. These years had seen him explore conflicts over religion, through the figures of More (who was devout and remained so), Thompson (whose Nietzschean questioning challenged religious belief), Farleigh (who had rejected religion, but who West felt retained a fear which atheism masked), and Arch (who is presented as genuine both in his faith and in his loss of faith). Yet despite his rejection of formal religion, this issue had not been resolved for West as an adult. That very rejection itself remained a source of considerable tension. In 1931, he was offered the post of director of English teaching at a mission school in Basle. He refused on the grounds that he would not teach men English so that they could preach Christianity. His girlfriend (herself the daughter of a missionary) disputed his quoting Lenin's dismissive phrase for clergymen, 'policemen in surplices', since, she argued, the missionaries helped the Africans to a better life. 'Hospitals or no hospitals, I said, missionaries are there to make the people quiet with Christianity. "But your father was a missionary", she said; and I had the misgiving that my pleasure in Lenin's phrase...was a betrayal.'[85]

The conflict was also internal. West continued to be attracted by aspects of religion, in particular the feeling of awe it could inspire, and the sense of meaning it could offer.[86] It caused an undercurrent of tension in his relations with Farleigh throughout the 1920s. Farleigh had developed a theory of the 'three realities' characterising successive phases of European history: the unity of the organic group in the middle ages, individualism, and collective association. West resisted Farleigh's pressure to work with him on literary projects expounding the theory, and using it to offer a fresh, cultural, dimension to Communism; he came to criticise it as a reworking of Catholicism from which Farleigh had never freed himself.[87] Yet at the same time he was aware of a desire in himself to worship. Against this pull, he was grateful for opportunities to identify himself with some external reality, which could offer him a way out of isolation, and a relief from guilt, without drawing him back into the religious faith he had rejected.[88]

Another important focus of identity was the nation. During and immediately after the war, West had rejected the patriotism of his family and his own youth, and the Empire which members of his family had served. His attitude to his own country was then further explored through his involvement with his country of residence, Switzerland, and through the meanings attributed to his ultimate decision to return to England to join the Communist Party. As with religion, the central theme running through West's exploration of 'nation' is that of belonging: what does it mean to 'belong to' or identify oneself with a nation; and can he himself find a way of so belonging? In his early years in Switzerland, he presents himself as an observer of the strength of Swiss national feeling (evident in the First of August celebrations), who is gradually and hesitatingly drawn towards some participation in it, yet remains aware of tensions within Swiss society (revealed in the grotesque figures of the participants in the Basle Lenten Carneval and the savage political caricatures they carried) and of the conflicts within himself.[89]

Towards the end of the decade, this hesitant engagement with another nation was to be outweighed by West's gradual attraction to Communism. His first acknowledgement of post-war politics arose from concern about government responsibility for the 1926 General Strike. This was reinforced the following year as he began to research British trade-union history for his lectures. He then became interested in the Social Credit movement (1928), and attended a Communist lecture on the Soviet Union (1929). Planning his own lectures on 'The English Family in Life and Literature' led him first to Engels, and then Marx and Robert Owen—whose 'wrathful descriptions of private families shut up in boxes' reminded him of the stifling atmosphere of his childhood home.[90] In the lectures, he described the English family as 'one of the battle-grounds in the fight between capitalism and socialism'. The revolutionary role of the family during the rise of the bourgeoisie in the seventeenth century now exhausted, the middle class today: 'invested the family with that moral authority to which they had to be able to appeal in order to be able to restrain the individual member of their own class and to keep the working class in subjection.'[91] It is striking that West's first engagement with Marxism took the form of its analysis of the family.

This search for public forms of belonging was entangled with the development of his intimate relationships. Early in 1927 he met a Swiss woman, Sophie Huber (whom he called Sonja), a teacher of deaf children.[92] A relationship developed between them, often tense and difficult. From the start, he had associated her with the values of his home and family. Her father had been the head of a school for training missionaries, as West's father had been a missionary; and West (self-critically) appraised Sonja as someone his stepmother would approve of.[93] Two themes predominate in his account: their mutual oscillations between drawing close to, and backing away from, a permanent commitment; and his association of her, and the possibility of marriage to her, with the bourgeois world of his family and its conservative values. The two themes are intertwined with one another; at times West justified his reluctance to offer marriage in terms of a rejection of the bourgeois family, while Sonja came to criticise his politics of family and society as a form of emotional withholding.[94] They also intersect with West's public stances. The first holiday they spent together coincided with the First of August, and this provoked him at a celebratory dinner to publicly declare 'an Englishman also wished their country happiness'.[95] Conversely, when—after his critical lectures on the English family—Sonja challenged Engels's analysis of the family, West felt that his defence of Engels was forced and insincere. 'For I wrote home regularly because I was held in the relationship of father and son; and I wanted at moments to marry Sonja. The bourgeois character of the family as an institution was the cause neither of that desire nor of the sense of belonging to the family of my childhood.'[96] Fraught by hesitations, advances and withdrawals, from each of them, the relationship ended with her suicide in 1932.[97]

In dealing with these inter-personal and intra-familial conflicts, and the problems of identity and identification—cutting across the supposedly distinct arenas of the personal and the societal—to which they gave rise, West turned to psychoanalysis. Save for one key moment, he seems to have used it in an intellectualising way which left some central dilemmas of his personality unchanged. He had first read Freud while in the internment camp, and his early engagement with psychoanalysis took the form of a self analysis.[98] However, in the course of his relationship with Sonja he began a personal analysis with her Jungian analyst, Dr Schmid, which did enable him to break through to a powerful emotion linked to the death of his mother; but the potential of this moment was soon dissipated.[99] Despite the apparently limited therapeutic gains West derived from his analysis, he used psychoanalytic ideas to try to uncover, understand and depict the interaction between the personal and the societal; and—eventually—to explore the roots of his own political affiliations.[100]

Following his lectures on the English family, West had begun to take part in more detailed discussions about Marxism. As the political crisis of the early 1930s intensified, he drew closer to direct political engagement. In May 1931, he attended for the first time the celebration of Mayday. He watched the Communist band approaching:

> The pace gained a quick and firm beat as there came a band of fifes and drums, behind which followed a company of young girls in blue blouses, singing as they marched:
>
> Denn was wir singen
> Heisst Klassenkampf!
>
> In their high, ringing voices 'Klassenkampf' cut like the edge of a sword, as I stood among the onlookers.[101]

Yet when invited symbolically to join them, he refused. 'One of the girls in a blue blouse came up to me with a tray of red rosettes. She held one out to me. "Wollen Sie ein Mai-Banderli?" "Nein", I said, and turned away.'

Later that year, on a visit home during the general election following the fall of the Labour Government over the economic crisis, and the formation of a National Government, West encountered a Communist Party demonstration in central London.

> I heard shouting, repeated, and could distinguish 'Down with the National Government!'; and I could see, jerkily moving across Gower Street to the right, red banners. Then between the heads of the people watching I saw the faces of workers, some in caps, some bare headed, and beside them, every few yards, walked a policeman. They passed, and I looked after the loose end of the procession. I remembered the girls in their blue shirts wheeling on to the Marktplatz and their high voices singing. These marchers in a London street, they are Klassenkampf; and as I went on between the unbroken fronts of Georgian houses, the long vista leading to the heights of Highgate and the hazy spire, I imagined them still marching.[102]

This image forms a bridge between the two nations of Switzerland and England, the two cities of Basle and London. The marchers, and the class struggle they represent, offer an alternative focus of identity from nationalism ('Down with the National Government!'), while they seem also to hint at a potential link between West, his family, and the people.[103]

In autumn 1932, West prepared a lecture series on 'Socialism in English Literature', for which he began to read Marx's *Capital.*[104] By the time of his visit home in autumn 1933, after the Nazi seizure of power, he was struggling with the question of whether to join the Communist Party himself, believing that Graeme would have done so and that 'for him I must do what he would have done'. Another moment of vision completed the imaginary circuit whereby his Highgate home, his family and West himself were joined into one with the people.

> It had been raining, and the sun had come out, and we were having tea on the flagged terrace. You could see right across north-east London to the hazy distance of Essex, and two or three miles away the wet roofs of the houses in the sunlight were a pattern of shining rectangles on a blue ground. It was like a cubist picture, and as I wondered at it, I thought that in this picture there were people, and imagined how, looking toward us, they would see, as I had seen looking up Gower

> Street, after I had watched the demonstration crossing it with red banners, the brow of Highgate heights and the hazy spire of St Michael's. And at one pinprick in their picture, the reality which they didn't know was my father, stepmother and I, sitting here together. The meaning of 'I' changed: the people invisible for me in my pattern of bright rectangles were also living their lives; they also were all 'I' and 'I' and 'I', among the shining roofs of extending London.[105]

In this complex image, West envisages all the people of London, each a separate centre of consciousness, or 'I', linked together in an artistic whole. An aesthetic vision is used to draw all these people, unknown to one another, into a unity. Yet the image itself contains contradictions. Cubist painting breaks down classical one-point perspective, so that each subject, or 'bright rectangle', has equal power to live their own life, to be the centre of their own being. It offers a democratic version of Benedict Anderson's 'imagined community' in which 'in the minds of each lives the image of their communion.'[106] Yet this vision works against the more linear notions of the earlier passage, here picked up by allusion, of the march which binds people together in struggle, and the 'long vista' which links Gower Street and Highgate. Just as, after his encounter with Nietzsche, art had replaced religion as source of meaning, so here it seems to threaten to displace politics, being offered as the frame which can join all the separate 'I's into 'We'. The conflict between this (aestheticised) decentred democratic vision, and the centralised undemocratic realities of Communist politics, was to be an issue with which West struggled for the rest of his life.[107]

After Sonja's death, West began a relationship with one of his students, Claire Endrich. Where Sonja had always been, for him, associated with the world of his family, Claire was engaged in anti-fascist activities, and encouraged him to become active too.[108] She became an element in the commitment which West was to make soon after this visit home when, in 1934, he decided to join the Communist Party. On his return to Switzerland, 'Claire and I decided that we would marry in the spring. Then when she got her degree, we would leave and move to England, for I realized that I wanted to join the Communist Party in my own country.'[109] They made the journey back to England early in 1935.[110] As a foreign national, and a Communist, she was—in the terms sketched earlier—an 'exogamous' choice of partner for West; yet the commitment he made to her and to Communism was also to be the means by which he could return to his own country.

Finally, the text offers a further exploration of the wish to belong, and of the relation of the loyalty and identity demanded by an oppositional politics to that which it opposes and rejects. Joining the party was to be, West hoped, a way of identifying himself again with his own people, after his decade and more of living abroad. Committing himself to the Communist party and cause was to overcome that separation from life, and that division within himself between belief and action, which had so often troubled him. Yet, as in the image of London considered above, his account also presents this adherence as arising from a desire to merge his identity into a mass, of whom he could be an obedient member. His first encounter with communism had come in 1929, when one of his students invited him to a lecture. 'The speaker was a communist...He singled me out with his eyes and for a minute on end spoke directly at me. "The Soviet Five Year Plan", he said, "is the most stupendous event in history." Nobody, except my father in a religious mood, had I heard speak with such conviction.'[111]

During the family visit which preceded his decision to join the party, West attended a Communist meeting to call for the release of the imprisoned Dimitrov.

> The hall was packed to the roof. I had been at theatres and concerts in the Albert Hall; now for the first time I was one of a body of people who wanted not only to see and hear but to do. The excitement and unity mounted, and there was a storm of applause when Harry Pollitt got up from his seat on the platform and stepped forward, and in dead silence began.
>
> Never had I seen such a man, or heard such oratory. Drawn towards him, the whole hall, tier upon tier of people, became a great wave curving over to break, as his impetuous, unconquerable voice soared and struck and rang, 'Fight fascism'.[112]

Thus party membership allowed West to be obedient to a quasi-paternal voice speaking with near-religious conviction; but one which was dissident, which defied the system.[113] Earlier in that same visit, not yet decided whether to join, he comments: 'I read again Graeme's book, and at his words "To defy the whole system, to refuse to be an instrument of it—this I should have done" I thought that if he had lived he would have joined the Communist Party, and that for him I must do what he would have done.'[114] This stance enabled him simultaneously to identify himself with Graeme and his defiance, yet also partially to disown responsibility for the decision, which became not his own act but a dutiful doing of what his brother would have done.[115] If the upbringing of upper-middle-class men like West had led them from the intimacy of family relations to loyalties towards institutions, creeds and country, so the rejection of nation or ideology might carry as its price the disruption of familial relationships, creating a need for alternative bonds of intimacy.

Conclusion

For Graves, the story of the post-war decade was of the failure of his efforts to build a new life. He tried to bring up his growing family in a different way, more informal and less hierarchical in the relationship between parents and children, and between family and wider society. In this, Nicholson played an equal if not a leading role. But as a writer, despite substantial effort, Graves failed to establish himself as an independent professional, neither succeeding in finding a market, nor defining to his own satisfaction a style or a creative identity. As a result, he remained financially dependent on his family, from whose values he was simultaneously trying to distance himself. Underlying both these efforts was the struggle to recover from the trauma of war. This took several forms: specific symptoms related to immediate war experiences of gas, shells and the excruciating train journey from casualty clearing station to hospital; flashbacks and nightmares of the bodies of the nameless dead and the ghosts of lost friends and comrades; a pervasive sense of recurrent deaths reaching beyond the war into the supposed peace; survivor guilt; and the profound and unresolved question—in what sense was he himself alive? Had he not died before he became a man? If so, who or what was he now? Is he free to be forever a child? Or has he in fact transcended death, been Resurrected and Transfigured?

1929 was to provide, for the next decade, an answer to those questions. In the grip of, as well as in rebellion against, the pattern established in his bond with his mother—a powerful woman who was felt to demand both obedience and success as the price of love, Graves had first allied himself with Nicholson. Despite the eventual failure of the marriage, it had certainly helped him to loosen significantly inherited constraints of class and gender roles and religious ideology. But by 1926, it seemed as though he was being drawn back into an expected role, as an educational official of informal Empire. The developing relationship with Riding helped him to escape this outcome. At first as an intellectual partner, working intensely with him on his poetry and criticism, then as a lover, and finally as a manipulator of ties of intimacy, Riding created a new emotional constellation whose explosion generated the energy for his repudiation of England. Graves, one might say, recognised Riding as both goddess and Devil, leaped, and survived.

Alick West similarly struggled to free himself from his family's expectations. By living abroad, he separated himself physically from parental oversight (thereby replicating one aspect of his internment). But in itself this did not free him from the emotional and ideological attachments he brought with him from childhood. He ultimately sought membership of the Communist Party as a way of reconciling the tensions within and between his membership of both family and nation. Associating his father's physical skill of brick laying with the concrete work which creates use value in Marx's *Capital*, he could separate the father whom he loved from the father who was the representative of a class hierarchy, nation and religion which he had repudiated.[116] In the anti-fascist speaker whose voice gripped him, he sought and found an alternative authority figure to whom he could adhere with a clear heart. Yet, as his psychoanalytic explorations revealed, such an affiliation did not dissolve the conflicts from which it in part arose. The need to belong, and the consequent difficulty of speaking out in defiance of an authority to which one was attached, were to recur as crucial dilemmas throughout West's life as a party member.

The patterns of socialisation developed by the British upper-middle-class in the late-nineteenth century were intended to turn boys into men able to maintain or improve their family's social standing, through a successful career and marriage; and—if necessary—to defend the nation and its empire. The passage from family and household of birth, through the structure, ethos and curricula of the public schools, into manhood was directed to moulding intellect, character and sexuality into patterns of attachment and loyalty which would prove mutually reinforcing (Chavasse). Viewed sociologically, this system succeeded, as the volunteering figures of 1914 demonstrate (Macfie, Chavasse, Sassoon, Graeme West, Brenan, Graves, Sorley). But even in peacetime any individual—by reason of their own intellect, character and sexuality—might find the requirements of this trajectory impossible or unbearable, hence might break away or break down (Macfie, Grenfell, Brenan). The First World War subjected the structures of upper-middle-class imperial masculinity to unprecedented strain. For some who had previously rebelled, it created a socio-psychic space within which they could accommodate their sense of self to the demands of society (Macfie, Grenfell). For others it initiated a process of questioning and challenging what they had hitherto accepted (Sassoon, Graves, Graeme West, Alick West). These 'fractured loyalties' became evident in the babble of competing voices which proclaimed the conflicting demands of duty—voices which pulled Sassoon hither and thither, reduced Graeme West to paralysed silence, forced Graves to distance himself from what was 'too sane', and drove Rivers to lock them away. For some of those who survived the war, coming to terms with their experiences meant embarking on a process of questioning the structures and values through which they had become men (Rivers, Sassoon, Graves, Alick West). Peter Barham strikingly links such questioning to the development of psychoanalysis in Britain in the 1920s, writing of Donald Winnicott: 'One might say that he became a genealogist of shell shock, for whom the breaking shells are not so much artillery shells as the egg shells of emergent and contested identities.'[117]

Notes

Introduction: the Roots of Individual Political Identities

1. Carl E. Schorske, *German Social Democracy 1905–17: the Development of the Great Schism* (Cambridge, MA: Harvard University Press, 1955), 290. Cf. Eric Leed, *No Man's Land: Combat and Identity in World War I* (Cambridge: Cambridge University Press, 1979), 50–1. Haenisch (1872–1925), formerly an anti-revisionist and strong opponent of war, who as a radical had been frustrated and marginalised within the party machine in the pre-war years, supported the war from a position of 'belligerently anti-Russian nationalism'. This speech to the 1916 SPD conference recalled the 'August enthusiasm' of 1914. Schorske, 133–5, 250–1; Nicholas Stargardt, *The German Idea of Militarism: Radical and Socialist Critics 1866–1914* (Cambridge: Cambridge University Press, 1994), 138 (quoted).
2. Samuel Hynes, *The Soldier's Tale: Bearing Witness to Modern War* (Allen Lane, 1997), 34–42.
3. Hynes, *Soldier's Tale*, 38–41 (quoted at 39–40).
4. Jon Stallworthy, *Anthem for Doomed Youth: Twelve Soldier Poets of the First World War* (Constable/Imperial War Museum, 2002), 25, reproduces this entry. Grenfell's fuller account of the killings in his diary is quoted in Hynes, *Soldier's Tale*, 40.
5. Hynes, *Soldier's Tale*, 40–1.
6. Nicholas Mosley, *Julian Grenfell: His Life and the Times of his Death 1888–1915* (1976; Persephone Books, 1999), See further below p.66.
7. The term 'dissident' is also used broadly, to indicate that in their lives as intellectuals they adopted stances at odds with the dominant values and political positions of their class of origin.
8. T.G. Ashplant, 'Psychoanalysis in Historical Writing', *History Workshop Journal* 26 (1988), 102–19.
9. Sigmund Freud first addressed this issue in 'Group Psychology and the Analysis of the Ego' (1921), in his *Civilization, Society and Religion*, Pelican Freud Library vol.12 (Harmondsworth: Penguin, 1985), 95–178. Eugene Victor Wolfenstein, *Victims of Democracy: Malcolm X and the Black Revolution* (1981; Free Association Books, 1993), uses this essay to explore the dynamics of American racism.
10. For the work of Erikson, see n.25 below and below p.42. Feminist psychoanalytic theorists influenced by the object-relations school include Jessica Benjamin,

The Bonds of Love: Psychoanalysis, Feminism and the Problems of Domination (Virago, 1990). R. W. Connell, *Gender and Power: Society, the Person and Sexual Politics* (Cambridge: Polity Press, 1987), 206–7, suggests that patterns of masculinity different from Freud's oedipal model are explored in the works of Jung, Adler and other later analysts.

11. Dana Breen, 'General Introduction', in D. Breen (ed.), *The Gender Conundrum: Contemporary Psychoanalytic Perspectives on Femininity and Masculinity* (Routledge, 1993), 1, 36–7. For example, Freud's opponents in the 1920s' debates over female sexuality saw mind as very directly related to body unless psychopathology intervened; there was a return to this position among some analysts in France and America from the mid-1960s: 5, 9–10, 12–14.
12. Breen, 'General Introduction', 2, 19–20.
13. See, among many examples, the re-analyses of the Dora case-history in Charles Bernheimer and Claire Kahane (eds), *In Dora's Case: Freud, Hysteria, Feminism* (2nd., enlarged, edn, Virago, 1990), and Hannah S. Decker, Freud, *Dora and Vienna 1900* (New York: Free Press, 1991). In the 'Afterword' to the most recent edition of her memoir *My Kleinian Home: a Journey through Four Psychotherapies—Into a New Millennium* (Karnac, 2001), the psychoanalyst Nini Herman reflects critically on (her own) Kleinian tradition's lack of attention to the external world. By a nice irony, Freud's own early life is beginning to be explored in this way, leading to reinterpretations of the patterns of loyalty and conflict which helped shape not only his adult personality and professional identity, but also his construction of psychoanalysis itself. Key works here include William J. McGrath, *Freud's Discovery of Psychoanalysis: the Politics of Hysteria* (Ithaca, NY: Cornell University Press, 1986), and Decker, *Freud, Dora and Vienna 1900*. Consequently, particular psychoanalytic conceptualisations and explanations themselves need to be understood as historically located in a double sense: not only *internally* with respect to the development of the discipline itself (e.g. the enormously increased attention to the role of the mother in early childhood since Freud), but also *externally* with respect to changing social expectations (e.g. attitudes to women or homosexuals). Decker is exemplary in her treatment of both dimensions of historical specificity.
14. See the overview in Stephen Frosh, *The Politics of Psychoanalysis: an Introduction to Freudian and post-Freudian Theory* (2nd edn, Basingstoke: Macmillan 1999). For one such tradition, see Jeremy Holmes, *John Bowlby and Attachment Theory* (Routledge, 1993).
15. Thus this book engages with Michael Roper's emphasis on investigating 'how publicly circulating codes of masculinity relate to the behaviour and emotional dispositions of individual men', in order to 'pursue a properly grounded notion of "identity", which includes autobiographical experience'. He suggests, of revisionist accounts in the 1990s of how the First World War affected British masculinities, that: '[p]rioritizing ideology or discourse over experience, they fail to see how the effort to represent the war's profound personal effects might motivate the search for new forms of self-expression or encourage reflection on the old.' 'Between Manliness and Masculinity: the "War Generation" and the Psychology of Fear, 1914–1950', *Journal of British Studies* 44.2 (2005), 345. For a complementary approach, which addresses several of the themes of this

book via a Bakhtinian reading of Wilfred Owen's engagement with and challenge to dominant discourses within which he was educated, see Douglas Kerr, *Wilfred Owen's Voices: Language and Community* (Oxford: Clarendon Press, 1993).

16. David Gilmore, *Manhood in the Making: Cultural Concepts of Masculinity* (New Haven, CT: Yale University Press, 1990).
17. Connell, *Gender and Power*; R.W. Connell, *Masculinities* (Cambridge: Polity Press, 1995).
18. Connell, *Masculinities*, 11. He suggests that: 'the worth of psychoanalysis in understanding masculinity will depend on our ability to grasp the structuring of personality and the complexities of desire at the same time as the structuring of social relations, with their contradictions and dynamisms' (20–1).
19. Connell, *Masculinities*, 8–12, 15–18; cf. Frosh, *Politics of Psychoanalysis*, ch.6.
20. Connell, *Masculinities*, 19–20, 70–1 (Lacan); 45–66 (body).
21. Connell, *Masculinities*, 18; pt II; R.W. Connell, 'Class, Gender and Sartre's Theory of Practice', in his *Which Way is Up?: Essays on Sex, Class and Culture* (Sydney: Allen and Unwin, 1983), 63–79.
22. Connell, *Masculinities*, 23.
23. Benedict Anderson, *Imagined Communities: Reflections on the Origin and Spread of Nationalism* (1983; rev. edn, Verso, 1991); Ross Poole, 'Structures of Identity: Gender and Nationalism', in P. Patton and R. Poole (eds), *War/Masculinity* (Sydney: Intervention Publications, 1985), 71–9; id., *Morality and Modernity* (Routledge, 1991), 101–9; id., *Nation and Identity* (Routledge, 1999), chs 1–2.
24. Victor W. Turner, 'Betwixt and Between: the Liminal Period in *Rites de Passage*', in his *The Forest of Symbols: Aspects of Ndembu Ritual* (Ithaca, NY: Cornell U. P., 1967), 93–111; *The Ritual Process: Structure and Anti-Structure* (Routledge and Kegan Paul, 1969); *Dramas, Fields, and Metaphors: Symbolic Action in Human Society* (Ithaca, NY and London: Cornell University Press, 1974)
25. Erik H. Erikson, *Childhood and Society* (rev. edn, Paladin, 1977); *Young Man Luther: a Study in Psychoanalysis and History* (1958; Faber, 1972); *Identity: Youth and Crisis* (1968; Faber, 1971); *Life History and the Historical Moment* (New York: W.W. Norton, 1975).
26. Since my argument is concerned precisely to stress the interconnection of the external and the internal (the social and the psychic), these terms should not be understood here as comprising a binary pair, but rather as designating the respective centres of gravity of these elements. A political stance or (religious or national) ideology exists "externally" (independently of an individual), even if that individual internalises it; an individual's patterns of attachment are "internal" to them, even though shaped by, and crucial to how they engage with, the external social world.
27. 'Studies of a historical, political reality must work with the category of possibility. They grasp the world that is brought into being through social action in the light of the possibilities not realized. Such knowledge is based on a critique of the real, not just a reflection of it.' Connell, *Masculinities*, 44.
28. One founding text is of course E.P. Thompson's *The Making of the English Working Class* (rev. edn, Harmondsworth: Pelican, 1968), with its much-quoted aim to rescue marginalised historical figures from the 'enormous condescension of posterity' (13). See Jim Sharpe, 'History from Below', in P. Burke, (ed.), *New*

Perspectives on Historical Writing (Cambridge: Polity Press, 1991), 24–41. This perspective will be touched on at points in this book, for example through the work of Peter Barham in uncovering the *Forgotten Lunatics of the Great War* (New Haven, CT: Yale University Press, 2004), cited below p.202.

29. See below pp.68, 176; above p.1.
30. Glen Elder, 'History and the Life Course', in D. Bertaux (ed.), *Biography and Society: The Life History Approach in the Social Sciences* (Beverly Hills, CA: Sage, 1981), 77–115, provides a rich introduction to, and case-study example of, the intersection of the psychosocial and the historical. For the relation between life-stage and historical moment, see 79.
31. For the differential impact of historical events between, and within, age-cohorts, see Glen H. Elder, 'Family History and the Life Course', in T.K. Hareven (ed.), *Transitions: the Family and the Life Course in Historical Perspective* (New York: Academic Press, 1978), 34–9; Elder, 'History and the Life Course', 86–8, 97, and for the specific impact of the war, 91–2; and Chris Harris, 'The Individual and Society: a Processual Approach', in A. Bryman et al. (eds), *Rethinking the Life Cycle* (Macmillan, 1987), 24–8.
32. Robert Wohl, *The Generation of 1914* (Cambridge, MA: Harvard University Press, 1979), ch.3, discusses the post-war myths of the 'generation of 1914' and 'the lost generation' in relation to Britain; these are of some significance in understanding the atmosphere to which Graves and the other war autobiographers of the years around 1930 contributed.
33. Grenfell came from the aristocracy. For the sake of concision, I shall refer to the institutions and practices of the group's class of origin simply as 'upper-middle-class' except where it is necessary specifically to distinguish an elite or aristocratic 'upper-class' element. 'West' throughout refers to Alick West; his brother is referred to as 'Graeme West' (or 'Graeme' when other family members are also being mentioned).
34. Ken Plummer, *Documents of Life 2: an Invitation to a Critical Humanism* (Sage, 2001), 179–80, discusses the continuum in the interpretation of life histories between the subject's and the historian's 'pure account'; my approach attempts what he terms 'systematic thematic analysis'. Liz Stanley, *The Auto/Biographical I: the Theory and Practice of Feminist Auto/biography* (Manchester: Manchester University Press, 1992), pt II, explores some implications of the fact that any biographical narrative is always a partial (in both senses) reading of the life history it presents.
35. Such an approach to the selection of life histories is explored by George C. Rosenwald, 'A Theory of Multiple-Case Research', in D.P. McAdams and R.L. Ochberg (eds), *Psychobiography and Life Narratives* (Durham, NC: Duke University Press, 1988), 259–61. For a comparative approach to a related theme, see Ellen Kay Trimberger, 'Feminism, Men and Modern Love: Greenwich Village, 1900–25', in A. Snitow, C. Stansell and D. Thompson (eds), *Desire: the Politics of Sexuality* (1983; Virago, 1984), 169–89.
36. Questions of the representativeness and validity of (groups of) life histories are discussed in Plummer, *Documents of Life 2*, 153–4, 158–9; and Paul Bellaby, 'Histories of Sickness: Making Use of Multiple Accounts of the Same Process', in S. Dex (ed.), *Life and Work History Analyses: Qualitative and Quantitative*

Developments (Routledge, 1991), 21–2.

37. Robert Graves, *Goodbye to All That: an Autobiography* (Jonathan Cape, 1929), 17–23.
38. Frederick George Ackerley, 'Friend of all the world: a memoir of Robert Andrew Scott Macfie', *Journal of the Gypsy Lore Society* (3rd series) 14 [Special number] (1935), 7–8, 16.
39. Alick West, *One Man in His Time: an Autobiography* (Allen and Unwin, 1969), 7–8, 13, 15–16.
40. Mosley, *Grenfell*, 3–5; Ian Beckett, 'Grenfell, William Henry, Baron Desborough (1855–1945)', *Oxford Dictionary of National Biography* (Oxford: Oxford University Press, September 2004; online edn, May 2006; http://www.oxforddnb.com/view/article/335660)
41. Gerald Brenan, *A Life of One's Own: Childhood and Youth* (1962; Cambridge: Cambridge University Press, 1979), 1, 2, 13, 18–19, 21, 28, 31, 37, 170–2; *Personal Record 1920–1972* (1974; Cambridge: Cambridge University Press, 1979), 123, 127, 322–3.
42. Richard Slobodin, *W.H.R. Rivers* (New York: Columbia University Press, 1978), 3–17.
43. Ann Clayton, *Chavasse: Double VC* (Leo Cooper, 1992), 1–4.
44. Jean Moorcroft Wilson, *Charles Hamilton Sorley: a Biography* (Cecil Woolf, 1985), 9–15, 24, 84.
45. Jean Moorcroft Wilson, *Siegfried Sassoon: the Making of a War Poet: a Biography (1886–1918)* (Duckworth, 1998), 8–12.
46. Leonard Woolf, *An Autobiography 1: 1880–1911* (Oxford: Oxford University Press, 1980), 4–9 (quoted at 5).

1 Theoretical Perspectives

1. Poole, *Nation and Identity*, 44–5, suggests that the defensible core of the term identity is that: 'we come to understand who we are through the resources provided for us by the forms of social life within which we exist. More explicitly: we have an *identity* because we *identify* with figures or representations which are made available to us. The concept of identity implies that there is a constitutive linkage between forms of *subjectivity*, i.e. the ways in which we conceive of ourselves, and forms of social *objectivity*, the patterns of social life within which we exist.' (original emphasis)
2. Sally Alexander and Barbara Taylor have referred to this intertwining of psychic and social as effected by 'mechanisms through which patterns of authority and submission become part of the sexed personality itself'; see their 'In Defence of "Patriarchy"', in Raphael Samuel (ed.), *People's History and Socialist Theory* (Routledge, 1981), 370–2 (quoted at 372). My study focusses particularly on class, gender and nation; in other contexts, ethnic and religious dimensions might be equally crucial.
3. I have adopted the terms 'inhabit' and 'habitation' to refer generically to the range of relationships between individuals and social collectivities; terms such as 'belong' or 'membership' are either too narrow, or carry unwanted overtones.

4. My use of the term 'recognition' here is analogous to Louis Althusser's concept of 'interpellation': 'Ideology and Ideological State Apparatuses', in his *Lenin and Philosophy and Other Essays* (New Left Books, 1971), 127–86. The theme of a shared identity extending beyond the individual is taken up again in the discussion of imagined communities below pp.31–6. The three functions singled out here—coercion, provision, recognition—are also those which parents perform for their children.
5. See further the discussion of the power of imagined communities below p.35–6.
6. The nature of the hold in any particular case needs careful specification. For instance, the initial link between army and individual differs significantly for volunteer and conscript; but once under military discipline and in a war situation, the difference may be eliminated.
7. The idea of emotions 'bound' within patterns of loyalty and identification draws on Freud's notion of the 'binding' (*bindung*) of psychic energy within structures. See Jean Laplanche and J. B. Pontalis, *The Language of Psychoanalysis* (1967; Karnac Books, 1988), 50–2, especially the third aspect of the concept which they identify: 'a fixation in one place of a certain quantity of energy which can no longer flow freely' (52).
8. I deliberately use the term 'standard' here; 'normative' is, I believe, a product of those moments when psychoanalysis lends itself to the laying-out or even enforcement of a 'norm' of development.
9. This is clearly registered in any at all detailed case history. So Connell, *Gender and Power*, 209, comments that Freud's case-history of the 'Wolf Man' uncovers at least four distinct and conflicting aspects of his masculinity (cf. 221–2); while Barry Richards, 'Masculinity, Identification and Political Culture', in J. Hearn and D. Morgan (eds), *Men, Masculinities and Social Theory* (Unwin Hyman, 1990), 164–8, distinguishes two aspects of the formation of Ronald Reagan's masculinity.
10. For a sketch of some of these difficulties, see Ashplant, 'Psychoanalysis in Historical Writing', 111–16.
11. Erikson, *Identity: Youth and Crisis*, 24. He continues: 'In the meantime, we can only try to see where a historical instance or a bit of normative development, a fragment of case history, or an event in a biography becomes clearer when something like identity development is assumed to exist.'
12. Erikson, *Identity: Youth and Crisis*, 53, comments: 'A child has many opportunities to identify himself, more or less experimentally, with real or fictitious people of either sex and with habits, traits, occupations, and ideas. Certain crises force him to make radical selections. However, the historical era in which he lives offers him only a limited number of socially meaningful models for workable combinations of identification fragments.'
13. For fairy tales, see Bruno Bettelheim, *The Uses of Enchantment: the Meaning and Importance of Fairy Tales* (1976; Harmondsworth: Penguin, 1978). For the psychic importance to Freud of his identifications with figures from the Bible, ancient history, and the plays of Schiller, see McGrath, *Freud's Discovery, passim.* For the role of literary myths in inculcating models of desired masculinity; see below p.26. In contemporary society, fictions from popular culture may also provide figures for identification; see the analysis of comics in David Jackson, *Unmasking*

Masculinity (Unwin Hyman, 1990), 223–51.

14. Erikson, *Identity: Youth and Crisis*, 257.
15. See Carolyn Steedman, *Landscape for a Good Woman* (Virago, 1986), and Graham Dawson, *Soldier Heroes: British Adventure, Empire and the Imagining of Masculinities* (Routledge, 1994).
16. This structure may of course include ambivalence towards, or rejection of, a potential object of identification or loyalty.
17. Freud delineated definable phases of human psycho-sexual identity in infancy, childhood and adolescence, using the quasi-biological terms 'oral', 'anal' and 'genital' to emphasise that these stages linked experience of one's own body (weaning, toilet training, castration anxiety, puberty) to emotional relations with significant others. These maturational shifts constituted vicissitudes through which the growing individual must pass, and meant the developmental process was liable to disruption. See his 'Three Essays on the Theory of Sexuality' (1905), in *On Sexuality*, Pelican Freud Library vol.7 (Harmondsworth: Penguin, 1977), 39–169. Later analysts have built on and modified Freud's schema in relation to early life (see, e.g., Margaret Mahler's definition of the stage of separation/individuation, discussed by Benjamin, *Bonds of Love*, 17–36), just as Erikson has done for adolescence and adulthood. R.W. Connell, 'Men's Bodies', in his *Which Way is Up?*, 26–7, suggests a re-thinking of Freud's original emphasis on the oedipal crisis as *the* key moment of crisis in the consolidation of masculine identity, noting that more recent psychoanalytic work has placed the formation of a gendered sense of self earlier. He offers (31) a schema of three moments of potential crisis which is close to my own sketch.
18. It was this 'adhesiveness of the libido', which puzzled Freud when writing about grief in 'Mourning and Melancholia' (1917), in his *On Metapsychology: the Theory of Psychoanalysis*, Pelican Freud Library vol.11 (Harmondsworth: Penguin, 1984), 251–68. For a critique of historiography's frequent reliance on oversimplified notions of self-interest as motivating force, see Peter Gay, *Freud for Historians* (New York: Oxford University Press, 1985), 99–115.
19. See John Bowlby, *Attachment and Loss* (3 vols, 1969, 1973, 1980; Harmondsworth: Penguin, 1981). Poole, 'Structures of Identity', 77, notes of the individual within the capitalist market: 'the task of providing one's own meaning is a daunting one; and is constantly threatened both by the demands of ordinary living, and more significantly, by the actuality of mortality.'
20. See Connell, *Gender and Power*, 114 (ambivalence), 212–13 ('stickiness' of cathexis). For an extended study of such a process of shifting loyalties, see Wolfenstein, *Victims of Democracy*.
21. The quoted phrases form the titles respectively of Graves's and Brenan's autobiographies.
22. 'Rather than attempting to define masculinity as an object...we need to focus on the processes and relationships through which men and women conduct gendered lives. "Masculinity", to the extent that the term can be briefly defined at all, is simultaneously a place in gender relations, the practices through which men and women engage that place in gender, and the effects of these practices in bodily experience, personality and culture.' Connell, *Masculinities*, 71.

23. Connell, 'How Should We Theorise Patriarchy?', in his *Which Way is Up?*, 59; Gilmore, *Manhood*, 9–10.
24. Gilmore, *Manhood*, 22; Connell, *Gender and Power*, 78–87 (quoted at 79); cf. Connell, *Which Way is Up?*, 59–60, 75–6.
25. There is today no single psychoanalytic model of masculinity. Richards, 'Masculinity', 162–4, sketched three current psychoanalytic models of masculinity, which he suggested were not exhaustive. Nevertheless, it might be argued that work over the last few decades in psychoanalysis has been cumulative, with attention to the baby and infant boy's relationship with his mother defining a fundamental set of issues concerning separation and differentiation which precede and help to give shape to the oedipal conflicts which were the focus of Freud's original work. Breen (ed.), *Gender Conundrum*, brings together essays from a variety of psychoanalytic perspectives.
26. The societies Gilmore selects for closer attention are: Truk Island (South Pacific), Mehinaku (central Brazil), Samburu (East Africa), Sambia (New Guinea), Tahiti, Semai (Malaysia). He does, however, also draw brief comparisons with more complex societies, principally modern Andalusia (Spain) and rural Greece.
27. For Gilmore's own statement of his relationship to functionalism, which he terms 'dialectical functionalism', see *Manhood*, 3–4, 225–7. From my perspective, he works with a one-dimensional sense of the demands made by a society on its members, which omits a real sense of intra-societal conflict. However, I am sympathetic to the approach he sets out to the interaction of psychic and social: 'psychological theories must be applied in tandem with materialist perspectives, that is, taking into account the way that intrapsychic dynamics relate to the social organisation of production' (3). Connell, *Masculinities*, 32–3, is abruptly dismissive of Gilmore's work.
28. Gilmore, *Manhood*, 224: 'gender ideologies are social facts, collective representations that pressure people into acting in certain ways'; cf. 4–5, 9, 22–3. Cf. the parallel conclusion of Michelle Zimbalist Rosaldo, 'Women, Culture and Society: Theoretical Overview', in M.Z. Rosaldo and L. Lamphere (eds), *Woman, Culture and Society* (Stanford, CA: Stanford University Press, 1974), 17–42.
29. Gilmore, *Manhood*, 11, 17; for his use of the terms 'stressed' and 'pressured', 15–16.
30. Gilmore, *Manhood*, 1, 17, 106–7, 153–4 and *passim*. This is so, he claims, even in relatively gender-egalitarian societies (24; cf. 115). Michael Kaufman, 'The Construction of Masculinity and the Triad of Men's Violence', in Michael Kaufman (ed.), *Beyond Patriarchy: Essays by Men on Pleasure, Power and Change* (Toronto: Oxford University Press, 1987), 1–29, argues that men's violence, towards women, other men and themselves, is one of the major vectors of such proof of manhood.
31. Gilmore, *Manhood*, 41–6, 128–33, 222–3 and *passim*. In more complexly differentiated societies, it could also involve for some men artistic creativity, stressed as a form of masculine endeavour (113).
32. Gilmore, *Manhood*, 35–6, 77, 89–91, 140–1.
33. I use the term 'community' here, rather than 'society', because men could be

called upon to defend their particular clan or lineage, as well as their society as a whole.

34. Gilmore, *Manhood*, 69–70, 121–2, 148–51; cf. further below p.33.
35. Gilmore, *Manhood*, 93–5, 98, 158, 228. He argues that masculinity is no more simply psychological than it is biological (25–6; cf. 224). He regards regression as a more valuable psychoanalytic concept in understanding masculinity than the more often employed Oedipus complex, arguing that it is a greater threat to the functioning of society, and hence a more central concern in the social construction of masculinity. He is here drawing on the work of Dorothy Dinnerstein, *The Rocking of the Cradle and the Ruling of the World* (1976; Souvenir Press, 1978) and Nancy Chodorow, *The Reproduction of Mothering: Psychoanalysis and the Sociology of Gender* (Berkeley: University of California Press, 1978); see 25–9, 228–9.
36. Gilmore, *Manhood*, 36, 94–8, 104. This widespread identification of masculinity with activity and femininity with passivity has been carried over uncritically into psychoanalysis; cf. Stanley Fish's discussion of this theme in Freud's account of the 'Wolf-Man', 'Withholding the Missing Portion: Psychoanalysis and Rhetoric', in his *Doing What Comes Naturally: Change, Rhetoric, and the Practice of Theory in Literary and Legal Studies* (Oxford: Clarendon Press, 1989), 536–43. Connell, Gender and Power, 205, refers to 'the activity/passivity polarity that plagues psychoanalytic discussion of gender'.
37. Gilmore, *Manhood*, 37–40, quotes the *Odyssey* and the story of *Tannhaüser* as European examples of such myths; re-reads the Mehinaku myth of the 'Tapir Woman' as also a warning against regression (95–8); and interprets Melville's story 'Bartleby the Scrivener' in similar terms (108–9). He notes that *Koro* is a specifically masculine form of hysteria to be found in south and east Asia among men who cannot live up to the demands of the male role (173–5).
38. Failure to live up to the role condemned one as 'unserviceable' (Gilmore, *Manhood*, 35), a 'trash yard' or 'rubbish' man (92, 104; cf. 132–3). He offers case-studies of individual failures to perform the masculine role in Andalusia (32–5, 52–5) and Africa (111–12).
39. Gilmore, *Manhood*, 123–41 (Samburu), 141–5 (Masai), 154–62 (Sambia), 162–5 (Gisu), 165–6 (Mende). He comments of the Samburu rituals: 'the ritual cycle that makes men from boys is a kind of structural transformation by which children are changed into adults, narcissistic passivity is changed into selfless agency, and the raw protoplasm of nature is changed into finished culture' (140).
40. Gilmore, *Manhood*, 124–5, 133–4 (*rites de passage*), 152, 158–60 (separation). In New Guinea, these rituals also involved homosexual contact, in which boys fellated older men. The adult men's semen was believed to quicken into life and strengthen the incipient masculinity of the boys: 151, 154–5. For women's recognition of newly-achieved adult male status: 137–40, 143–4. For a critique of psychoanalysis's one-sided emphasis on the need for separation to secure individuation, especially in men, see Benjamin, *The Bonds of Love*, 148–52, 211–13.
41. Gilmore, *Manhood*, 56–7, cf. 123–4 (citing Erikson's work); and chs 3–4 *passim*.
42. Gilmore, *Manhood*, 220–1. The societies he examines are Tahiti (where food and land are abundant, and there are no hostile neighbours), and the Semai of

Malaysia (who flee deep into the jungle if attacked). He sees this atypical lack of concern about masculinity as nevertheless affording proof of the social rather than biological construction of gender roles (230).

43. It would be wrong to make easy parallels between the mechanisms of pre-industrial societies on which he mostly focusses, and those of more complex industrial societies. In western Europe *c.*1900, for instance, there were no fixed rituals for achieving adult male status; though such markers as entering secondary school, graduating from university, or completing national service, may have served such a role unofficially. See further ch.2 below.
44. Gilmore touches on clan or lineage conflict, and stresses the generational privilege of fully adult masculinity; but does not deal with power blocs within a society.
45. T. Carrigan, B. Connell and J. Lee, 'Hard and Heavy: Toward a New Sociology of Masculinity', in Kaufman (ed.), *Beyond Patriarchy*, 177. Cf. Connell, *Gender and Power*, 110, 183–8; *Masculinities*, 76–81 (hegemonic/subordinate masculinities).
46. John Tosh, 'Hegemonic Masculinity and the History of Gender', in Stefan Dudink, Karen Hagemann and John Tosh (eds), *Masculinities in Politics and War: Gendering Modern History* (Manchester: Manchester University Press, 2004), 53–4.
47. Connell, *Gender and Power*, defines the structures of labour, power and cathexis (96–116), and deals with their interactions (119–41). (In *Masculinities*, 74, he uses the term production instead of labour.) He borrows the term 'cathexis' from Freud, defining it (112) as: 'the construction of emotionally charged social relations with "objects" (i.e., other people) in the real world'. I would add that: first, in object-relations theory objects (or part-objects) are emotionally charged internal representations which are projected onto people in the real world; and second, that such objects can also be projected onto social collectivities, a point I develop below.
48. Connell, *Gender and Power*, 110, stresses the ordering of different masculinities into a hierarchy 'with at least three elements: hegemonic masculinity, conservative masculinities…and subordinated masculinities.' He further notes that: 'Hegemonic masculinity is constructed in relation to women and to subordinated masculinities. These other masculinities need not be as clearly defined—indeed, achieving hegemony may consist precisely in preventing alternatives gaining cultural definition and recognition, confining them to ghettos, to privacy, to unconsciousness.' (186) Some subordinate masculinities, by contrast, are temporary, based on age, such as boyhood, or apprenticeship. In *Masculinities*, 79–80, he replaces the term 'conservative' with 'complicit' masculinities.
49. Connell, *Gender and Power*, 185, argues: 'The public face of hegemonic masculinity is not necessarily what powerful men are, but what sustains their power and what large numbers of men are motivated to support.' Cf. Carrigan et al., 'Hard and Heavy', 174, 179–80.
50. Carrigan et al., 'Hard and Heavy', 182. That task has been pursued both through such positive reinforcements as promotion of a dominant pattern of familial heterosexuality (via fiscal, legal and welfare rules), and negatively by criminalisation of homosexuality. Connell, *Gender and Power*, 126–31, explores

the role of the state more fully, commenting (130): 'In managing institutions like marriage and motherhood the state is doing more than regulating them. It is playing a major part in the constitution of the social categories of the gender order.'

51. Connell, *Gender and Power*, 185; cf. Connell, 'Crisis Tendencies in Patriarchy and Capitalism', in his *Which Way is Up?*, 41; *Masculinities*, 79–80.
52. Carrigan et al., 'Hard and Heavy', 174–6, 178–9.
53. Connell, 'Crisis Tendencies in Patriarchy and Capitalism', 41; id., 'Class, Gender and Sartre', in his *Which Way is Up?*, 76; id., 'How Should We Theorise Patriarchy', 58; id., *Masculinities*, 81–6, 185–243; ibid., chs 4–8, offers case studies of contemporary restructurings of masculinity. Carrigan et al., 'Hard and Heavy', 178, 181, note that the groups who contend about the definitions of masculinities come into being in those very processes of struggle.
54. Gilmore's analysis of 'stressed' masculinity, though not critical in the same sense as feminist and gay accounts, also fits this pattern.
55. Connell, 'Men's Bodies', 22, argues that masculinity is in fact a rich character structure, but oppressive to women.
56. Carrigan et al., 'Hard and Heavy', 158–9, citing and critiquing the work of Joseph Pleck.
57. Kaufman, 'The Construction of Masculinity', 10–11, 18–19. This analysis, clearly consonant with Gilmore's (above p.26), could be supported by the example of same-sex practice in Classical Greece. It was acceptable for an adult man (active) to penetrate a younger male (thereby positioned as passive and feminine). This latter role was seen as a temporary phase on the way to full adult masculinity; see Gilmore, *Manhood*, 154–5. Kaufman, 18–19, thus explains one common male mode of friendly greeting, the punch on the shoulder which demonstrates activity, thereby pre-emptively neutralising the passivity associated with more tender affection. Cf. Graves's experience of boxing with a friend, below p.101.
58. Simone de Beauvoir, *The Second Sex* (1949; Harmondsworth: Penguin, 1972).
59. Connell, 'Men's Bodies', 28–30. Gilmore, *Manhood*, shows the widespread segregation in different societies of men's and women's space: see, e.g., 33, 51, 52–5 (Andalusia), 61–2 (Truk), 82, 91–3 (Mehinaku). This desire to separate not only serves to put a protective boundary around a potentially fragile gender identity, but is undoubtedly also fuelled by male hostility to women as simply different. See Connell's list of sources for such hostility (30). Fear of the feminine is also projected onto 'effeminate' men, into which category may be placed homosexual men, or those of another race: see Connell, *Masculinities*, 78–9; T.G. Ashplant, 'Dis/Connecting Whiteness: Biographical Perspectives on Race, Class, Masculinity and Sexuality in Britain *c.*1850–1930', *L'Homme: Zeitschrift für Feministische Geschichtswissenschaft* (Vienna) 16.2 (2005), 68–85.
60. Connell, 'Men's Bodies', 30–1; cf. Andrew Tolson, *The Limits of Masculinity* (Tavistock, 1977), 22.
61. Erikson, *Identity: Youth and Crisis*, 55, comments: 'The more subtle methods by which children are induced to accept historical or actual people as prototypes of good and evil consist of minute displays of emotions such as affection, pride, anger, guilt, anxiety, and sexual tension.'

62. See Connell, *Gender and Power*, 195–6, for a clear statement of the possibility of resistance, and its importance in testing the adequacy of any theory of gender formation; and *Masculinities*, pts 2 and 3 for detailed case studies. R. Sieder, 'A Hitler Youth from a Respectable Family: the Narrative Composition and Deconstruction of a Life Story', in D. Bertaux and P. Thompson (eds), *Between Generations: Family Models, Myths and Memories: International Yearbook of Oral History and Life Stories vol.II* (Oxford: Oxford University Press, 1993), 99–119, explores one example in detail.
63. Connell, 'Men's Bodies', 22–3; cf. Connell, *Masculinities*, 38. For a detailed exploration of the relationship between changing structures of work and class-specific masculinities, see Tolson, *Limits of Masculinity*, 47–133; cf. Jackson, *Unmasking Masculinity*, 57–9.
64. Connell, *Gender and Power*, 131, 180. Cf. Gilmore, *Manhood*, 46–7, 49–50; Connell, *Masculinities*, chs 4–8.
65. Connell, *Gender and Power*, 179.
66. Poole, *Nation and Identity*, 18–25, criticises on chronological grounds Gellner's claim that *industrialisation* is what necessitates nationalism, suggesting instead the widespread development of capitalist *market relations*.
67. Ernest Gellner, *Nations and Nationalism* (Oxford: Blackwell, 1983), 24 and ch.3 *passim*.
68. Tom Nairn, *The Break-Up of Britain: Crisis and Neo-Nationalism* (New Left Books, 1977), 348–50. Anthony Barnett, 'After Nationalism', in Raphael Samuel (ed.), *Patriotism: the Making and Unmaking of British National Identity:* vol.1, *History and Politics* (Routledge, 1989), 145–8, re-emphasises Nairn's argument that the progressive and regressive elements in nationalism cannot be separated.
69. Anderson, *Imagined Communities*, chs 4 (creole nationalisms in the Americas), 5 (new European nationalisms), 6 ('official' nationalisms of existing dynastic states), 7 (post-colonial nationalisms).
70. Anderson, *Imagined Communities*, 6; cf. his description of the nation as a 'community in anonymity', 36. Poole, in his critical appreciation of Anderson's concept (*Nation and Identity*, 10–18), points out (10–11) that all social relations (including those face-to-face) have an imaginative dimension. An 'imaginative community' in Anderson's intended sense, he suggests, requires 'both that people conceive of themselves as belonging to the community, and also that the conception of the community informs the way in which they live [and] relate to others'. Not all extensive networks of social relations take this form; e.g. the market is a counter example (11).
71. Anderson, *Imagined Communities*, contains a recurring critique of the marxist tradition's failure to theorise the nature and appeal of nationalism, and the source of its power: 'nationalism has proved an uncomfortable *anomaly* for Marxist theory and, precisely for that reason, has been largely elided, rather than confronted.' Anderson, 3–4; cf. 5, 141 and n.1, 161 (quoted at 3, original emphasis). The desire to correct this failure of perception leads Anderson to emphasise (I would say, overemphasise) both the positive dimensions of nationalism, its power to evoke love and sacrifice, and the almost unique nature in the modern world of its capacity to do so. My argument will sketch a critique of both these points (see below pp.35, 206–11).

72. Anderson, *Imagined Communities*, 4, 7 (quoted; original emphasis); cf. 141.
73. Anderson, *Imagined Communities*, 10. Elsewhere, Anderson notes that religion (like race) could also function as an imagined community: 124–6, 169–70. He treats religion traditions more fully as a source of identity at 10–9, 22–4; see also Gellner, *Nations and Nationalism*, 71–87.
74. Anderson, *Imagined Communities*, 11. As he puts it elsewhere, the nation was a new way of 'linking fraternity, power and time' (36).
75. Poole, 'Structures of Identity', 71–9.
76. Poole is here highlighting a central *tendency* of market relationships; in practice, such commitments to self-identities and relationships constantly come into collision with market drives towards impersonality. Cf. Connell, *Masculinities*, ch.7.
77. Poole, 'Structures of Identity', 73, 77.
78. Poole, 'Structures of Identity', 74. Cf. Gilmore's stress on society's need for a masculinity which encourages men to think of themselves as dispensable, above p.26.
79. Anderson, *Imagined Communities*, 143. For his discussion of the role of one's native language, which is also a contingent given, and extends before and after the lifespan of an individual, in the construction of the imagined community of the nation, see 141–6.
80. As with his positive revaluing of the nation, there seems to be an element of over-correction here. Anderson, *Imagined Communities*, 143–4, refers to recent work on 'the idea of the family-as-articulated-power-structure' as 'certainly foreign to the overwhelming bulk of mankind. Rather, the family has traditionally been conceived as the domain of disinterested love and solidarity.' However, these are not mutually exclusive perceptions.
81. Poole, 'Structures of Identity', 76–8; Poole, *Morality and Modernity*, 101–12.
82. Poole, *Nation and Identity*, 12.
83. Poole, *Morality and Modernity*, 101–2 (original emphasis).
84. Poole, *Nation and Identity*, 12–13.
85. See above p.19.
86. See Homi K. Bhabha, 'Introduction: Narrating the Nation', in H.K. Bhabha (ed.), *Nation and Narration* (Routledge, 1990), 1–8.
87. So eighteenth-century Britain used armies against the United Irishmen in the 1790s. Irish independence in the twentieth century was secured not only by Pearse's poetry, but also by his armed uprising.
88. Thus Anderson, *Imagined Communities*, writes (144): 'the great wars of this century are extraordinary not so much in the unprecedented scale on which they permitted people to kill, as in the colossal numbers persuaded to lay down their lives. Is it not certain that the numbers of those killed vastly exceeded those who killed?' The referents here are uncertain. In the First World War, fought predominantly between combatant armies, the numbers who killed (the fighting troops) certainly outnumbered those who were killed; and by no means all of the latter can be described as 'persuaded to lay down their lives'. In the Second, the vast numbers of civilian victims certainly outnumber those killing, but ever fewer of them laid down their lives willingly. Anderson's theorising here curiously replicates, rather than analysing, the claims of nationalisms. Cf. below p.194.

89. See above p.19.
90. Transnational imperatives could comprise religious, ethnic or racial components of identity; for instance, Kipling's poem 'The White Man's Burden' (1899) sought to implicate Americans in the imperial role already undertaken by the white races of the old world (pre-eminently Britain). Other, more local, elements could include the demands of occupational identities, or those which made up the 'Public School' man. For the wider international context of late-nineteenth-century British masculinities, see Connell, *Masculinities*, 185–98.
91. The various masculinities within a given social class may be either coexistent or conflicting. Pamela J. Walker explores the new masculinity offered by the Salvation Army to its urban working-class converts, in challenging their existing patterns of behaviour, in her '"I Live But Not Yet I For Christ Liveth in Me": Men and Masculinity in the Salvation Army', in Michael Roper and John Tosh (eds), *Manful Assertions: Masculinities in Britain since 1800* (Routledge, 1991), 92–112.
92. Connell, *Gender and Power*, 98–9, uses the terms 'gender order' to refer to the gender structure of a whole society, and 'gender regime' for that of a particular institution within a society.
93. Cf. above p.28 and n.48.
94. Connell, *Gender and Power*, 184. Graham Dawson, in his 'The Blond Bedouin: Lawrence of Arabia, Imperial Adventure and the Imagining of English-British Masculinity', in Roper and Tosh (eds), *Manful Assertions*, 113–44, at 118–19, talks about masculinities as forms of 'imagined identity', borrowing from Anderson's term 'imagined communities'.
95. Cf. n.12 and n.13 above. Freud's models included characters from high and popular literature (Faust, Sherlock Holmes), as well as recent and contemporary history (Wincklemann, Napoleon, Schliemann).
96. Dawson, 'Blond Bedouin', 121–37, brings out how the American journalist Lowell Thomas's 1920 narrative for *Strand* magazine presented Lawrence's story as a demonstration that adventure romance was still possible in modern war, away from the bungling bureaucratic nightmare of trench warfare on the western front. Lawrence, separated from the military establishment by his youth, scholarly background, shy and maverick personality, is offered as a superior model of masculinity (as he is also, in different ways, to his Arab allies and Turkish enemies).
97. Lawrence, already an archaeologist, became, during the writing of *Seven Pillars of Wisdom* (1926, 1935), a celebrated figure in intellectual circles; while the story of his adventures as told by others had already by 1919–20 been turned into a massively successful touring show, and serialised in popular magazines; see Dawson, 'Blond Bedouin', 113–14. Cf. General Gordon, below p.83.
98. Connell, *Gender and Power*, 185.
99. The diaries of Hannah Cullwick, in the 1850s and 60s, give access to a working-class woman's struggle to negotiate between definitions of herself in linked terms of class and gender; see Liz Stanley (ed.), *The Diaries of Hannah Cullwick, Victorian Maidservant* (Virago, 1984).
100. Prescriptions for masculinity (or femininity), and fantasy-identifications with hegemonic models, could cross class boundaries more easily than could lived

practices.

101. Connell, *Gender and Power*, 176–7, stresses the co-existence of different patterns of masculinity (and femininity) within the same social milieu. Some of these model masculinities would form close supports of the goals of hegemonic masculinity while others would fall into the category he terms 'conservative' masculinities, 'complicit in the collective project but not its shock troops' (110).
102. My formulation here tends to privilege class as the organising principle of gender regimes. Connell, *Gender and Power*, 103–4, argues that gender divisions, like those of race, should be seen as central to capitalism, which he argues is a system for extracting surplus for the benefit of a class/race/gender hierarchy.
103. Some such notion underlies the idea of a meritocratic society, in which roles are still distributed hierarchically but the allocation of individuals to those roles is decided by 'merit' (however defined) rather than birth.
104. Drawing on detailed statistical analysis of marriage patterns, Andrew Miles, in *Social Mobility in Nineteenth- and Early Twentieth-Century England* (Basingstoke: Palgrave, 1999), 162–75, concludes that by the late-nineteenth century among the upper-middle class 'the expansion of the professions led to a dramatic increase in endogamy' (173).
105. Connell, 'Class, Gender and Sartre's Theory of Practice', 70–2, arguing against the reification involved in referring to the 'class position' which a person or family occupies, asserts: 'Strictly, we should...speak of practices which are organised in a class way; which are constrained by, and oriented to, the larger class process...We need, in short, to speak of the class practices of units which are not classes, such as individuals and families.' (71). He sketches, as an example, the schooling of a ruling-class boy in contemporary Australia; and suggests that this vignette with its contradictions 'helps us to see...the different levels of mobilisation through which even so small a group as a family may pass, fleetingly, in its constant grappling with the problems endlessly posed by its class situation.' (72). Cf. the more extended case-study of 'Delia Prince' in *Gender and Power*, 1–6; and Carrigan et al., 'Hard and Heavy', 180.
106. Female challenges to various aspects of the powerful mid-Victorian prescription of 'separate spheres' gathered strength in the 1880s, and were widely-noticed and partly caricatured in the figure of the 'new woman' in the 1890s. See D. Rubinstein, *Before the Suffragettes: Women's Emancipation in the 1890s* (Brighton: Harvester, 1986), ch.2.
107. For upper-middle class women's pattern of life-cycle, familial and educational experiences in this period, see: Pat Jalland, *Women, Marriage and Politics, 1860–1914* (Oxford: Clarendon Press, 1986); Barbara Caine, *Destined to be Wives: the Sisters of Beatrice Webb* (Oxford: Clarendon Press, 1987); Carol Dyhouse, *Feminism and the Family in England 1880–1939* (Oxford: Blackwell, 1989); Eleanor Gordon and Gwyneth Nair (eds), *Public Lives: Women, Family and Society in Victorian Britain* (New Haven, CT: Yale University Press, 2003).
108. Gellner, *Nations and Nationalism*, 29–30, 32–8, stresses the importance of universal high culture in modern industrial society; and argues that the level of literacy and technical competence required is such that it cannot be provided by the kin or other local units, but only by 'centralized exo-education'. As will be seen

in ch.2, a class-specific version of such centralised education was becoming the norm for upper-middle-class boys at this period.

109. See ch.2 below.
110. Connell, *Gender and Power*, 112.
111. For divergent goals within socialising agencies see Connell, *Gender and Power*, 192. Roper and Tosh, 'Introduction', 3, argue for 'a marked shift in the codes of manliness current among the governing and professional classes during the latter half of the nineteenth century—from the moral earnestness of the Evangelicals and Dr Arnold to the respect for muscle and might so prevalent at the close of the Victorian era'; cf. 16–17. Cf. John Tosh, 'Domesticity and Manliness in the Victorian Middle Class: the Family of Edward White Benson', in ibid., 44–73.
112. Connell, *Gender and Power*, 116–17. Elsewhere, he argues (44) that social reproduction more generally is the object of a strategy, not a pre-given fact: there is 'the constant possibility that structure will be constituted in a different way. Groups that hold power do try to reproduce the structure that gives them their privilege. But it is always an open question whether, and how, they will succeed.'
113. Connell, *Gender and Power*, 194–6. Roper and Tosh, 'Introduction', 17, comment: 'One of the most precarious moments in the reproduction of masculinity is the transfer of power to the succeeding generation, whether it be within the family from father to son, by apprenticeship in the case of skilled workers, or by "palace revolutions" in the case of business. The key question is whether the "sons" take on the older generation's gender identity without question, or whether they mount a challenge, and if so how.' Cf. n.62 above.
114. In practice, these patterns of cathexis are frequently intertwined.
115. A career is clearly an institution in a somewhat different sense from a university, regiment or political party. Nevertheless, ideals attached to the idea of a career can attract and mobilise emotional energies whether that career is partially embedded institutionally (as in, say, the law), or is embodied largely through loose interpersonal structures (as with writers in this period).
116. Tolson, *Limits of Masculinity*, 45–6 (original emphasis).
117. Turner, 'Betwixt and Between', 97, 105.
118. Turner, *Ritual Process*; Turner, *Dramas, Fields, and Metaphors*. 'I have tried to eschew the notion that communitas has a specific territorial locus, often limited in character…For me, communitas emerges where social structure is not.' *Ritual Process*, 126.
119. Turner, *Ritual Process*, 127–8.
120. See Erikson, *Identity: Youth and Crisis*, and his *Young Man Luther*. His use of the concept reflects the particular context in its close relationship with the American pattern of school and college education.
121. Erikson, *Identity: Youth and Crisis*, 155.
122. Erikson, *Identity: Youth and Crisis*, 156–7.
123. Erikson, *Identity: Youth and Crisis*, 157–8.
124. Erikson, *Identity: Youth and Crisis*, 129.
125. Erikson, *Young Man Luther*, 38. Stephen Yeo, 'A New Life: The Religion of Socialism in Britain 1883–1896', *History Workshop Journal* 4 (1977), 5–56, vividly recreates the widespread experience of 'conversion' into socialism.

126. In Luther's time a monastery was for some such a psychosocial moratorium, 'one possible way of postponing the decision as to what one is and is going to be', since there were formal and acceptable ways to become an ex-monk. Erikson, *Young Man Luther*, 38–9.
127. So Erikson's claim, *Young Man Luther*, 40, that societies are apt to give such young people a moratorium. His is a liberal, functionalist model which, while fully aware of the possibility of the developing individual's entry into a new stage of the life-cycle resulting in conflict or catastrophe, through damaging interaction with their family and/or wider social environment, nevertheless employs a language which fundamentally emphasises the possibilities of mutual recognition between individual and society: e.g. Erikson, *Identity: Youth and Crisis*, 159–60. For a discussion of the politics of Erikson's work, see P. Roazen, *Erik H. Erikson: the Power and Limits of a Vision* (New York: Free Press, 1976), ch.3 and *passim*. Later critics have also argued for the fundamentally masculine character of Erikson's developmental model; for a more complex appraisal, see C.E. Franz and K.M. White, 'Individuation and Attachment in Personality Development: Extending Erikson's Theory', *Journal of Personality* 53.2 (1985), 225–56. The roots of the notion of moratorium lie not only in 1950s America, but also in Erikson's own early adult life in 1920s Europe: see Erikson, *Life History*, 17–47.

2 From Boys to Men

1. Nairn, *Break-Up of Britain*, 342–5.
2. Anderson, *Imagined Communities*, ch.6, esp. 88, 90–4.
3. Anderson, *Imagined Communities*, 88–93, sketches the changing pattern of British rule in India. See also K. Ballhatchet, *Race, Sex and Class under the Raj: Imperial Attitudes and Policies and their Critics, 1793–1905* (Weidenfeld & Nicolson, 1980), 121–2, 144, 164; and Ronald Hyam, *Empire and Sexuality: the British Experience* (Manchester: Manchester University Press, 1990), ch.5 (increasing need felt after 1857 to keep a wide social and sexual distance between rulers and ruled; see further n.19 below); cf. Ashis Nandy, *The Intimate Enemy: Loss and Recovery of Self under Colonialism* (Delhi: Oxford University Press, 1983), 4–7; Bernard S. Cohn, 'Representing Authority in Victorian India', in Eric Hobsbawm and Terence Ranger (eds), *The Invention of Tradition* (Cambridge: Cambridge University Press, 1983), 165–210.
4. Eric Hobsbawm, *Nations and Nationalism since 1780: Programme, Myth, Reality* (2nd edn, Cambridge: Cambridge University Press, 1992), 86.
5. Hobsbawm, *Nations and Nationalism*, 85.
6. Hobsbawm, *Nations and Nationalism*, 83; Tosh, 'Hegemonic Masculinity', 49.
7. Eric Hobsbawm, 'Mass-Producing Traditions: Europe, 1870–1914', in Hobsbawm and Ranger (eds), *Invention of Tradition*, 263–307.
8. Hugh Cunningham, 'The Language of Patriotism', in Samuel (ed.), *Patriotism*, 57–89. One effect of this development was to weaken and partially marginalise the 'little England' tradition in early/mid-nineteenth century politics, which had linked an avoidance of foreign, especially European, entanglements with a critique of unreformed or corrupt government at home. See Richard

Gott, 'Little Englanders', and E. Green and M. Taylor, 'Further Thoughts on Little Englandism', in Samuel (ed.), *Patriotism*, 90–109. This tradition revived during the Boer War, and was put to its sternest test in 1914.

9. David Cannadine, 'The Context, Performance and Meaning of Ritual: the British Monarchy and the "Invention of Tradition", *c.*1820–1977', in Hobsbawm and Ranger (eds), *Invention of Tradition*, 120–38.
10. For the development of Empire Day, which originated in a private initiative, see J.M. MacKenzie, *Propaganda and Empire: the Manipulation of British Public Opinion, 1880–1960* (Manchester: Manchester University Press, 1984), 231–6; and his '"In Touch with the Infinite": the BBC and the Empire, 1923–53', in J.M. MacKenzie (ed.), *Imperialism and Popular Culture* (Manchester: Manchester University Press, 1986), 168–79.
11. See below p.72.
12. Hobsbawm, 'Mass-Producing Traditions', 291, argues that this period saw efforts to establish a clear class identity by both 'the genuine national elite of an upper middle class' and 'the relatively large mass of [the middle class]...who neither belonged to this elite nor...to that clearly inferior order of the petty-bourgeoisie'.
13. Hobsbawm, 'Mass-Producing Traditions', 292–7.
14. Hobsbawm, 'Mass-Producing Traditions', 299, notes that 'the crucial informal device for stratifying a theoretically open and expanding system was the self-selection of acceptable social partners'.
15. Britain was by far the most prominent country in this development: Hobsbawm, 'Mass-Producing Traditions', 297, 299–300.
16. Hobsbawm, 'Mass-Producing Traditions', 297–8; and John de S. Honey, *Tom Brown's Universe: the Development of the Victorian Public School* (Millington, 1977), ch.4, esp. 238–41, 252–66. Hobsbawm, 300–2, notes the dominance of international sporting competitions by amateurism (i.e. the middle class) before 1914 He suggests that the middle class may have found 'subjective group identification unusually difficult', being neither small enough to establish it through personal contact (as the upper and upper-middle classes did via Oxbridge or the London Season), 'nor sufficiently united by a common destiny and potential solidarity, like the workers'; and speculates that they 'found it easier to establish a sense of belonging together through external symbols, among which those of nationalism...were perhaps the most significant'.
17. John Tosh, 'Masculinities in an Industrializing Society: Britain, 1800–1914', *Journal of British Studies* 44.2 (2005), 331.
18. George L. Mosse, *Nationalism and Sexuality: Respectability and Abnormal Sexuality in Modern Europe* (New York: Howard Fertig, 1985).
19. In the case of India, Hyam, *Empire and Sexuality*, 115–21, has shown how real or perceived military/political threats to the maintenance of British rule led to tighter controls over sexual propriety as a bulwark of imperial power; cf. Ballhatchet, *Race, Sex and Class*, ch.4. This pattern of regulation spread to other colonies: Ballhatchet, 145–55 (Burma); Hyam, ch.7 (sub-Saharan Africa).
20. Anderson, *Imagined Communities*, 53, writes of 'the ways in which administrative organisations create meaning'.
21. For the ways in which Macfie's identification of himself with Gypsies could

disrupt or modify conventional demands, see below pp.129–34; see also below pp.206–11.

22. Thus Bertrand Russell came from the heart of the Whig-Liberal section of the aristocracy.
23. The Liberals suffered major losses to the Conservatives following the crisis over Home Rule for Ireland in 1886; among those who left for the newly-formed Liberal Unionists (later to merge with the Conservatives) were Grenfell's and Graves's parents. Thereafter Russell's family were distinctly in the minority among the aristocracy.
24. See further below pp.209–11.
25. See n.33 below, and below pp.98, 146. For patterns of middle-class fatherhood in mid- to late-nineteenth-century Britain, see John Tosh, *A Man's Place: Masculinity and the Middle-class Home in Victorian Britain* (New Haven and London: Yale University Press, 1999) esp. chs 4–5.
26. See below pp.139, 146.
27. Brenan, *Life of One's Own*, 4–5, 11, 18–19, 34–5.
28. Brenan, *Life of One's Own*, 8, 17.
29. Brenan, *Life of One's Own*, 28, 83–4, 90–2; cf. *Personal Record*, 132.
30. Brenan, *Life of One's Own*, 8, 62–4, 66–7, 103–4, 118–19, 200; *Personal Record*, 121–3, 132.
31. See further below p.68.
32. See below p.218.
33. He shared his father's love of country life and hunting, but without his emphasis on mass killing: Mosley, *Grenfell*, 157–9, 223; Jeanne MacKenzie, *The Children of the Souls: a Tragedy of the First World War* (Chatto & Windus, 1986), 34–5.
34. Mosley, *Grenfell*, 90–1, 126–7.
35. Mosley, *Grenfell*, 135–6, 172.
36. Mosley, *Grenfell*, 172, 210–13, 216–19. He comments that Grenfell's questioning of 'love' in one such letter was 'a rejection of his mother's so-called love for him—which too was an attempt to stop him living his own life and make him guilty' (211); and notes how in her Family Journal, privately circulated after his death, she amended the text of his letters to increase 'the impression of how much *he* had loved *her* as a little boy' (213; cf. 238–9). MacKenzie, *Children of the Souls*, 26: Ettie 'felt her children as extensions of her own perpetually buoyant personality'.
37. Mosley, *Grenfell*, 214–15, 240–1, 243, 244–5, 248–9, 350.
38. Mosley, *Grenfell*, 172.
39. See below p.140.
40. Brenan, *Life of One's Own*, 28.
41. Brenan, *Life of One's Own*, 4–5, 11, 19 (quoted), 34–5.
42. Brenan, *Life of One's Own*, 25. He recalls an incident at the age of eight, which he interprets as arising from his fear that she did not respond enough to his love: 40.
43. Leonore Davidoff, 'Mastered for Life: Servant and Wife in Victorian and Edwardian England', *Journal of Social History* 7 (1974), 406–28; id., 'Class and Gender in Victorian England: the Diaries of Arthur J. Munby and Hannah

Cullwick', *Feminist Studies* 5.1 (1979), 87–141.

44. See below pp.98–9.
45. The simultaneously exciting and shameful sexual feelings attaching to servants, and by extension working-class women, were often registered/represented through the sense of smell: Davidoff, 'Class and Gender', 94–6 and n.32. Brenan associated unpleasant smells with the lower-middle-class household which for him symbolised a sexual world: *Life of One's Own*, 54–6.
46. Woolf, *Autobiography 1: 1880–1911*, 32–3.
47. See below p.147. This relaxation could be quite literal and bodily, since these children's upbringing required them to distinguish themselves from the lower classes by their erect and stiff bodily posture: Davidoff, 'Class and Gender', 97. Cf. Peter Stallybrass and Allon White, *The Politics and Poetics of Transgression* (Methuen, 1986), 164–8, for an account of how Freud's Wolf Man delighted in reversing the way social superiority was inscribed in the body and its behaviour.
48. Theresa McBride, '"As the Twig is Bent": the Victorian Nanny', in A.S. Wohl (ed.), *The Victorian Family: Structures and Stresses* (Croom Helm, 1978), 52–3.
49. See below p.99.
50. See below pp.147–8. Davidoff, 'Class and Gender', 97, notes ways in which house, body and society could be used interchangeably as images for one another, as West uses the front and side doors here, or Graves the servants' bedrooms (below p.99). Davidoff, 'Mastered for Life', 406–7, 417, 422 and *passim*, draws out analogies between the legal, customary and work situations of servants, wives (especially but not only working-class), and children, all subordinate to the paternalistic master.
51. Honey, *Tom Brown's Universe*, 146. This section draws in particular on Honey, and on C. Heward, *Making a Man of Him: Parents and Their Sons' Education at an English Public School 1929–50* (Routledge, 1988). Although the subject of Heward's study is at some distance from the schools considered here—it deals with the two decades after the First World War; and is based on Ellesmere College (a Woodard school founded in 1884) which, according to Honey, 269–71, was *c.*1902 in the outermost fringe of schools claiming recognition as public, and drew on a clientele ranging from the less secure and wealthy middle class to some aspiring members of the upper-working class—nevertheless it is particularly valuable comparatively both for her focus on masculinity and for the use she was able to make of school correspondence which enabled her to trace factors shaping individual boys' careers.
52. For the growth of such hierarchies, Honey, *Tom Brown's Universe*, 151–3; cf. Harold Perkin, *The Rise of Professional Society: England since 1880* (Routledge, 1989), 17–26; Heward, *Making a Man of Him*, 36, 39–44 (on the post-1918 period), 126, 171–4.
53. Heward, *Making a Man of Him*, 13. Lee Krenis, 'Authority and Rebellion in Victorian Autobiography', *Journal of British Studies* 18.1 (1978), 109–11, discusses the intense pressures on the sons of professional families before 1850 to secure their position through success in education.
54. For the growing provision of prep schools from the 1870s, see Honey, *Tom Brown's Universe*, 126.
55. In addition, Sassoon and Sorley boarded at Marlborough, Grenfell at Eton,

Graeme West at Blundell's, and Brenan at Radley; Rivers attended Tonbridge, and Woolf St Paul's, as day boys. All nine of these schools were among the elite public schools around 1900. (Honey's second tier of elite public schools includes Radley, for which he recognises a strong case for inclusion in the first tier, and Highgate; Blundell's is in his third tier, Oundle his fourth: *Tom Brown's Universe*, 263–5, 283.) Chavasse's Magdalen College School and Liverpool College, which he attended as a day boy, are both part of Honey's 'long list': 268. Macfie, Grenfell, Graeme West, Graves and Sorley attended boarding school for five years; Brenan for four; Rivers and Sassoon for three; of these all but Graeme West and Sorley had previously boarded at prep school.

56. Peter Parker, *The Old Lie: the Great War and the Public School Ethos* (Constable, 1987), 53–61.
57. For attitudes to friendships between masters and boys, and among boys, Honey, *Tom Brown's Universe*, ch.3, §12–13. For the damaging effect of the prohibition on friendships with boys outside one's own house, and its failure to prevent 'vice', see Harold Nicolson, 'Pity the Pedagogue', in G. Greene (ed.), *The Old School: Essays by Divers Hands* (Cape, 1934), 119–20. For emotional expressiveness, Honey, 106, 191–4; sexuality: nn.105–7 below; games: n.65 below.
58. Heward, *Making a Man of Him*, 51. For this complex community as the late-Victorian parental ideal, Honey, *Tom Brown's Universe*, 119–20, 146; for efforts to extend a similar degree of control to day school pupils, 149, 182–3.
59. John R. Gillis, *Youth and History: Tradition and Change in European Age Relations 1770-Present* (New York: Academic Press, 1974), 102–3, 108.
60. Heward, *Making a Man of Him*, 15, 69–72 (total system); 66–8 (uniform); 74–5 (daily/termly/yearly calendar); 75–6 (learning the 'form'); Honey, *Tom Brown's Universe*, 141–2.
61. Heward, *Making a Man of Him*, 73–4, 76–7.
62. Heward, *Making a Man of Him*, 126.
63. Honey, *Tom Brown's Universe*, 127–35; Heward, *Making a Man of Him*, 31–2 (classics); Honey, 34, 135–8 (Modern side of curriculum); Heward, 34, 36, 61, 82 (Ellesmere gave greater importance to modern studies).
64. Heward, *Making a Man of Him*, 35. At some schools, pupils were ranked, within form, by examination marks, often those in Latin.
65. J. de S. Honey noted that: 'there was a general tendency in public schools for games to become organised, by about 1860; and between 1880 and 1900 for them to become compulsory.' *Tom Brown's Universe*, 114; cf. 104–5, 110–17; Parker, *The Old Lie*, 77–84; Heward, *Making a Man of Him*, 52–3. J. A. Mangan, *Athleticism in the Victorian and Edwardian Public School: the Emergence and Consolidation of an Educational Ideology* (Cambridge: Cambridge University Press, 1981), chs 4–5, argues that the spread of games and the introduction of compulsion was gradual and uneven, but that once achieved such games became the focus of real enthusiasm for many boys.
66. Heward, *Making a Man of Him*, 72–3; Parker, *The Old Lie*, 71–4. Mangan, *Athleticism*, 146–54, offers a sophisticated analysis of the role of the house as an intimate focus of loyalty and emotion refracting the wider values of the school, as 'a symbolic crucible in which individuality was melted down into conformity' (150). Cf. the role of the regiment in the army, discussed below

p.75.

67. Mangan, *Athleticism*, 141–6, 179–85, discusses the ritual functions of key sporting fixtures (such as the Eton-Harrow match) and songs.
68. For the importance of reciprocal sports fixtures in defining a school's status, see Honey, *Tom Brown's Universe*, 115–17; Heward, *Making a Man of Him*, 36–7 (Ellesmere's early difficulties).
69. Heward, *Making a Man of Him*, 54–5. For tensions and contradictions within and between these hierarchies: 8, 132–3, 135–6, 172–3.
70. Honey, *Tom Brown's Universe*, 126–7, points out the narrowing of the age range of public school pupils after 1870.
71. For transfer of capacity for loyalty from school to adult institutions, see Mangan, *Athleticism*, 145.
72. J.A. Mangan, 'Social Darwinism and Upper-class Education in Late Victorian and Edwardian England', in J.A. Mangan and J. Walvin (eds), *Manliness and Morality: Middle-class Masculinity in Britain and America, 1880–1940* (Manchester: Manchester University Press, 1987), 135–59, argues that: 'What frequently characterised the public schools of this period was an implicit, if not explicit, crude Darwinism encapsulated in simplistic aphorisms: life is conflict, strength comes through struggle and success is the prerogative of the strong…The public school world was often a godless world of cold, hunger, competition and endurance.' (142) By the 1870s, agnosticism and positivism had spread among public school staff, and the attitudes they inculcated were more stoic than Christian.
73. Gillis, *Youth and History*, 111; cf. below pp.72–3.
74. Derek Verschoyle explicitly compared the structure of discipline within the public school to that between administrator and subject in the colonies: 'Indian Innocence, Ltd.', in Greene (ed.), *The Old School*, 200–3.
75. J.A. Mangan, *The Games Ethic and Imperialism: Aspects of the Diffusion of an Ideal* (Harmondsworth: Viking, 1986), ch.2; Mangan, *Athleticism*, 135–9.
76. Mangan, *Games Ethic and Imperialism*, ch.3; Mangan, *Athleticism*, 122–7.
77. Both Heward, *Making a Man of Him*, 88–9, 91, and Peter M. Lewis, 'Mummy, Matron and the Maids: Feminine Presence and Absence in Male Institutions, 1934–63', in Roper and Tosh (eds), *Manful Assertions*, 168, compare this with the prototypical narrative of *Tom Brown's Schooldays*.
78. Heward, *Making a Man of Him*, 178–9.
79. Heward, *Making a Man of Him*, 151. She gives an example of Ellesmere's efforts to build self-confidence in a deeply-unconfident boy (126–8), and explores the anxieties produced by exam failure (173–4). Cf. Lewis, 'Mummy, Matron and the Maids', 177.
80. Woolf, *An Autobiography 1: 1880–1911*, 38–59.
81. Woolf, *An Autobiography 1: 1880–1911*, 43.
82. Woolf, *An Autobiography 1: 1880–1911*, 44.
83. Woolf, *An Autobiography 1: 1880–1911*, 49. Mangan, 'Social Darwinism', 152, uses a different mechanical image: 'life was frequently a physical and psychological struggle for survival against hunger, cold and callousness in one form or another. It resembled the annealing process of an iron foundry: intense "heat" in the initial stages, gradually lessening in intensity. As such it was part

and parcel of a calculated toughening technique'. Cf. Brenan, *Life of One's Own*, 42–3, 45, 47.

84. Mangan, *Athleticism*, 103–11, describes the dominance of the games ethic and the resultant anti-intellectualism. For the squashing of early attempts at intellectual exploration by a future writer at Wellington, see Nicolson, 'Pity the Pedagogue', 111–17.
85. For an analysis of this masculine hierarchy based on sporting skill and commitment, see Connell, *Gender and Power*, 85, 177–8; for a vivid account of the emotional-erotic pleasure of such skill, Connell, 'Men's Bodies', 18–20. In my terms (see above p.37), the successful athlete constituted a 'leading masculinity' within the gender regime of the public school system. For activity as a core component of masculinity, see above p.29. Mangan, *Athleticism*, 103–10, notes that few alternatives to participation in games were permitted, and that anti-intellectualism was very powerful. On bloods, see also below p.101.
86. Woolf, *An Autobiography 1: 1880–1911*, 40, 55–9 (quoted at 56). Cf. Graves, below pp.100–1.
87. Honey, *Tom Brown's Universe*, 216–19 (quoted at 218). He goes on to compare the public school system with the initiation rites for transition to adulthood in pre-literate societies, and in ancient Greece: 219–22. Brenan's account of his schooldays highlights this double cycle, and indicates the different strategies he adopted to cope with each stage. *Life of One's Own*, 41–3, 45–8, 51–3, 60–1, 80–1, 83–4, 90–2, 126–7.
88. Honey, *Tom Brown's Universe*, 196–203, 216, 220–1, 223–4. Cf. Heward, *Making a Man of Him*, 76, 151–5.
89. See Honey, *Tom Brown's Universe*, ch.5 and *passim*, for examples; and Graves, *GTAT*, 42–3, for his brother who did this. The role of ordinary public school master would form, in Connell's terms (above p.37), a 'conservative/complicit masculinity'.
90. For the school as object of worship, Honey, *Tom Brown's Universe*, 138–41, 160 (despite hatred felt while there); Parker, *The Old Lie*, 203–8. Mangan, *Athleticism*, 179–86, 255–64, quotes a wealth of school poetry praising the moral virtues of sport and its role in inculcating loyalty. For the sacrifices this could help elicit in the First World War, Honey, 158–9, and cf. ch.6 n.42 below.
91. For the development of Old Boys' associations from the 1870s, Honey, *Tom Brown's Universe*, 153–7. 'Around this figure [the Old Boy] grew up what amounted to a religion. The schools represented places of worship, with headmasters and their staff...representing the priests, uniforms and old school ties provided vestments, and the verses of [school songs] serving as hymns.' Parker, *The Old Lie*, 19.
92. Honey, *Tom Brown's Universe*, 160–4, points to the school as a locus of dynasticism, means of social mobility and of intermarriage, and object of endowment to perpetuate the family name.
93. For the development of a system of public schools, and the accompanying notion of 'public-school men', see Honey, *Tom Brown's Universe*, 229–31. For the component schools of this community around 1900, ibid., ch.4. For the role of sports fixtures in helping to define this community, see above n.68.
94. Arguably the school itself was such an imagined community, built up from

personal contacts with individual masters and boys mostly of one's own house. For the intensity of the attachment to school which could develop, including its role during the war, see Parker, *The Old Lie*, 203–11. The desired integration of individual, school and nation, under the aegis of God, was expressed in the Memorial Cloisters at Winchester: 'In the day of battle they forgot not God, Who created them to do his Will, nor their Country, the stronghold of freedom, nor their School, the mother of godliness and discipline. Strong in this threefold faith they went forth from home and kindred to the battlefields of the world and, treading the path of duty and sacrifice, laid down their lives for mankind.' (203).

95. Heward, *Making a Man of Him*, 178–9. For the internal tensions to which this could lead, see Michael Roper, 'Maternal Relations: Moral Manliness and Emotional Survival in Letters Home during the First World War', in Dudink et al. (eds), *Masculinities in Politics and War*, 298–9, 311.
96. Heward, *Making a Man of Him*, 73–4, 93; Honey, *Tom Brown's Universe*, 207. This exclusive maleness was carried forward to university. Insofar as the school did replace the role of parents, it was Heward argued a better father than it was a mother: 181.
97. Heward, *Making a Man of Him*, 77, 157–8.
98. Heward, *Making a Man of Him*, 158, 193–5. In *Testament of Youth: an Autobiographical Study of the Years 1900–1925* (1933; rp. Virago, 1978), 77–81, Vera Brittain used an account of a public-school speech day to focus her critique of the dominance of such masculine values, and their role in helping to bring about the war. Cf. Lewis, 'Mummy, Matron and the Maids', 168–86.
99. For the ultimate expression of this exclusively masculine world, see the account of the Cambridge Apostles in this period by S. P. Rosenbaum, *Victorian Bloomsbury: the Early Literary History of the Bloomsbury Group, vol.1* (Macmillan, 1987), 164–75. For suppression of female identifications, see Connell, 'Men's Bodies', 20.
100. A paradoxical outcome could be an intensification of the bond with the mother, so that she could in practice continue to exercise considerable influence over the values and emotions of her son: see Graves and Grenfell above p.50.
101. Connell, *Masculinities*, 85.
102. Heward, *Making a Man of Him*, 125, 138–9; but such friendships would not yet have developed when most needed by newly-arrived younger boys: 194. For the contrast between the public impartial judgment of the school and the private warmth of the crush, Royston Lambert, *The Hothouse Society: an Exploration of Boarding-school Life Through the Boys' and Girls' Own Writings* (Weidenfeld & Nicolson, 1968), 336.
103. Jeffrey Richards, '"Passing the Love of Women": Manly Love and Victorian Society', in Mangan and Walvin (eds), *Manliness and Morality*, 100–6, 110–14, discusses the codes (especially Greek and medieval) and models of manly love offered within public schools of the period, stressing their appeal to an adolescent romanticism which could be channelled into imperial among other causes. Intense friendships between fellow-pupils were celebrated in popular fiction; it is striking that in two of the three novels Richards analyses (114–17) the friendship brings together an intellectual and an athlete. Cf. Parker, *The Old*

Lie, 105–15. For the potential closeness and warmth of an all-male community not divided by sexual competitiveness, Lambert, *The Hothouse Society*, 307–8; for masters as paternal figures, Jonathan Gathorne-Hardy, *The Public School Phenomenon, 597–1977* (Hodder and Stoughton, 1977), 172.

104. Mangan, *Athleticism*, 185–91. He comments: 'The elements of sexual identity and legitimate sensuality are inseparable from the worship of games...To be manly was a condition that exuded the physical, but, at the same time, it was an asexual "physicality" extended into early manhood, in which sexual knowledge and experience were taboo.' (186) Intellectuals, by contrast, were seen as effeminate (189).
105. Honey, *Tom Brown's Universe*, 7, 167–76; Gathorne-Hardy, *Public School Phenomenon*, 88–92. J. Chandos, *Boys Together: English Public Schools 1800–1864* (1984; Oxford: Oxford University Press, 1985), ch.14, also notes markedly greater anxiety about sex from the 1850s.
106. Honey, *Tom Brown's Universe*, 178–94.
107. Heward, *Making a Man of Him*, 155–7. Cf. Gathorne-Hardy, *The Public School Phenomenon*, 159–72; Lambert, *The Hothouse Society*, 318–30; Alisdare Hickson, *The Poisoned Bowl: Sex, Repression and the Public School System* (Constable, 1995). For Graves's experience of this conflict, see below pp.102–4.
108. For Graves, see below pp.99–106; for Woolf, *An Autobiography 1: 1880–1911*, 40–1, 50–1; for Brenan, *Life of One's Own*, 57–61. Alick West, too, found his school's vague warnings against sexuality during his confirmation classes as unnerving: *One Man in His Time*, 18–19.
109. The intertwining of religion with sexual repression led Brenan to reject the authority his schooling proposed to him in both areas: *Life of One's Own*, 84–6, 103–5, 120–1. For Grenfell's critique of conventional Christianity: Mosley, *Grenfell*, 225–7, 230–1; Sassoon's: Wilson, *Sassoon (1886–1918)*, 154–5; Sorley's: Wilson, *Sorley*, 42, 84–7. Chavasse alone held firmly to the faith in which he was brought up: below pp.82–5. Woolf makes no mention of any religious struggle or crisis in his life. He seems to have adopted as his own what he presents as his father's practice: a strong (secular Jewish) ethic without religious support. *An Autobiography 1: 1880–1911*, 12–16. For connections between the critique of religion and of paternal authority in nineteenth-century autobiographies, see Krenis, 'Authority and Rebellion in Victorian Autobiography', 122–4.
110. C. H. Sorley, *The Collected Letters of Charles Hamilton Sorley*, ed. J. M. Wilson (Cecil Woolf, 1990), 83–6, 92, 102–3, 108, 143–5 (quoted at 83, 85, 92).
111. For Woolf, see above p.58; Graves, below pp.101, 106. West, attending a public day school, recorded no painful experience comparable to those of Graves, Woolf or Brenan; but he did display powerful loyalty to his own school (proud because it had been founded by a knight, while his brothers' had been founded by a draper), to the public school ethos and code as purveyed in popular fiction, and through that to king and country. *One Man in His Time*, 16–18.
112. Heward, *Making a Man of Him*, 121–2; cf. 193: 'the reigning social principle was social Darwinism, the survival of the fittest'.
113. Honey, *Tom Brown's Universe*, 119–20, 151–3; public school education bestowed a right of entry to a status which would be maintained by achieving an appro-

priate occupation.
114. Heward, *Making a Man of Him*, 13.
115. Heward, *Making a Man of Him*, 10; for an example of such a parental strategy, 97–101.
116. Heward, *Making a Man of Him*, 14, 87 (quoted), 178; pressure from fathers to follow certain career paths: 61–2, 77–9, 83–7.
117. Heward, *Making a Man of Him*, 8–10, 13–14, 88, 177–8. The parents' spheres of responsibility were distinct: 179–81. Fathers dealt with fees and the management of their sons' education and future careers, mothers their health and welfare: 17. On the different role of widowed mothers, ch.5.
118. Heward, *Making a Man of Him*, 88.
119. Heward, *Making a Man of Him*, 177; cf. 88.
120. For West, see below p.164; Brenan, below p.68.
121. Brenan, *Life of One's Own*, 80–1.
122. See above p.42.
123. See below p.124.
124. Mosley, *Grenfell*, 221–33; MacKenzie, *Children of the Souls*, 93: 'Born into a family where competition was the watchword, the older he got the more he shied away from it.'
125. Mosley, *Grenfell*, 222; MacKenzie, *Children of the Souls*, 84.
126. They variously described this as him going about with 'his intellectual fly-buttons undone', producing 'a series of slashing essays on Today; airing rather petulantly all his many grievances against the outward forms and manners of modern society', which left one of Ettie's friends 'quite flummoxed by so profane an attack on that by which he lives and has his being'; an instance (in retrospect) of '[over-riding] his hobbies like he used to when he wrote his attack on the smart set'. Mosley, *Grenfell*, 147, 235–6; cf. MacKenzie, *Children of the Souls*, 92–3.
127. Mosley, *Grenfell*, 222–3.
128. Mosley, *Grenfell*, 250–1; MacKenzie, *Children of the Souls*, 96–7.
129. Mosley, *Grenfell*, 255–6; cf. 214–15; MacKenzie, *Children of the Souls*, 90–1.
130. Mosley, *Grenfell*, 256, 326–7.
131. Mosley, *Grenfell*, 314, 320.
132. Mosley, *Grenfell*, 306, 314, 318–19.
133. Mosley, *Grenfell*, 339–40.
134. Brenan, *Life of One's Own*, 89–90, 92–3, 103–5, 120–1.
135. Brenan, *Life of One's Own*, 1–2, 14–18.
136. Brenan, *Life of One's Own*, 4–7, 18–19.
137. Brenan, *Life of One's Own*, 48–9, 86–7, 89–90, 120, 180. Reading included Elisée Reclus (the French anarchist geographer/anthropologist), Shelley, Thoreau, W.H. Davies and Rimbaud.
138. Brenan, *Life of One's Own*, 102, 122–3.
139. Brenan, *Life of One's Own*, 124–6.
140. Brenan, *Life of One's Own*, 25–6, 80–1, 102–3 (quoted at 80, 102).
141. Brenan, *Life of One's Own*, 105–14, 143–7.
142. Brenan, *Life of One's Own*, 123–8.
143. Brenan, *Life of One's Own*, 134–68.

144. Brenan, *Life of One's Own*, 168–9.
145. Brenan, *Life of One's Own*, 173–82. Well into the post-war years, his father was threatening that he would discontinue the allowance he made unless Gerald settled to a career: Brenan, *Personal Record*, 70; cf. 123.
146. Graves: *GTAT*, 61–2, 67, 355, 435; and below pp.99–100, 216, 219. West: below p.164.
147. Woolf's period in the Ceylon Civil Service (1904–10) can be understood in similar terms: *An Autobiography 1: 1880–1911*, 135–301.
148. Erikson, *Young Man Luther*, 72–3, 87–92, 139–42, 237, saw Luther's decision to enter a monastic order, in defiance of his father's wish that he pursue the worldly career of a lawyer, as a retreat from familial pressure to a socially-sanctioned space where he could seek out his own sense of direction. Only through his experiences in the monastery and the Augustinian order was Luther able to find a career to which he could commit himself. That career was both a defiance, and an adaptation, of his father's values.

3 The First World War

1. Ian Beckett, 'The Nation in Arms, 1914–18', in Ian F.W. Beckett and Keith Simpson (eds), *A Nation in Arms: A Social Study of the British Army in the First World War* (1985; Tom Donovan, 1990), 2–3. Cf. above p.46; Eugen Weber, *Peasants into Frenchmen: the Modernization of Rural France, 1870–1914* (1976; Chatto & Windus, 1977), 298–302. For the relationship of this shift to codes of masculinity, see Connell, *Masculinities*, 192; John Horne, 'Masculinity in Politics and War in the Age of Nation-states and World Wars, 1850–1950', in Stefan Dudink, Karen Hagemann and John Tosh (eds), *Masculinities in Politics and War: Gendering Modern History* (Manchester: Manchester University Press, 2004), 28, 31. The spread and hold of nationalist ideals among subaltern classes may have been less than its advocates wished: Poole, *Nation and Identity*, 21; Weber, 292–8.
2. Edward M. Spiers, 'The Regular Army in 1914', in Beckett and Simpson (eds), *A Nation in Arms*, 39–46, 51–3; Keith Simpson, 'The Officers', ibid., 64–7; Gary Sheffield, 'Officer-Man Relations, Discipline and Morale in the British Army of the Great War', in H. Cecil and P.H. Liddle (eds), *Facing Armageddon: the First World War Experienced* (Leo Cooper, 1996), 413 (in 1913 unskilled and skilled labourers accounted for over two-thirds of recruits).
3. J.M. Bourne, *Britain and the Great War, 1914–1918* (Edward Arnold, 1989), 133–8.
4. The most famous of these was Erskine Childers's *The Riddle of the Sands: a Record of Secret Service* (1903; Harmondsworth: Penguin, 1978); cf. also H.H. Munro [pseudonym Saki], *When William Came: a Story of London Under the Hohenzollerns* (John Lane, 1913). See Beckett, 'Nation in Arms', 5–7; Parker, *The Old Lie*, 134–7.
5. Beckett, 'Nation in Arms', 6–7; Ian Beckett, 'The Territorial Force', in Beckett and Simpson (eds), *A Nation in Arms*, 127–63; Hugh Cunningham, *The Volunteer Force: a Social and Political History 1859–1908* (Croom Helm, 1975), 140–6.
6. Beckett, 'Nation in Arms', 3–5. Haldane, a Liberal Imperialist sympathetic to the idea of the nation-in-arms, found it impossible to move in this direction

given Britain's military profile. Spiers, 'Regular Army', 38–9. Anne Summers, 'Edwardian Militarism', in Samuel (ed.), *Patriotism*, 236–56, argues for the strength of popular militarism, linked to popular-Liberal support for liberation movements, before 1914.

7. Spiers, 'Regular Army', 41; Beckett, 'Nation in Arms', 5; Parker, *The Old Lie*, 55–6, 61–7. Cf. above p.46.
8. It had not been successful in Haldane's original intention of providing a fast-track into an expanded peacetime officers' corps: Spiers, 'Regular Army', 42.
9. Parker, *The Old Lie*, 31–5, 39–40. A quarter of pre-war officers were casualties in the first four months of the war, and needed replacing; 30,000 such commissions in the Special Reserve were granted in this period. Over 20,000 were commissioned from the OTCs in the first eight months of the war. Simpson, 'Officers', 69–72.
10. Parker, *The Old Lie*, 16–17.
11. Jay Winter, 'Army and Society: the Demographic Context', in Beckett and Simpson (eds), *A Nation in Arms*, 195.
12. Death rates were higher still among Oxbridge students: Gerard J. DeGroot, *Blighty: British Society in the Era of the Great War* (Harlow: Longman, 1996), 273–4; Simpson, 'Officers', 86–7.
13. Brian Bond, *The Unquiet Western Front: Britain's Role in Literature and History* (Cambridge: Cambridge University Press, 2002), 20–2, 97–9. Grenfell, after over four years as a regular soldier, could write in November 1914 after undergoing an artillery bombardment: 'one's nerves are really absolutely beaten down. I can understand now why our infantry have to retreat sometimes—a sight which came as a shock to one at first, after having been brought up in the belief that the English infantry cannot retreat.' Mosley, *Grenfell*, 361.
14. Jay Winter and Blaine Baggett, *The Great War and the Shaping of the Twentieth Century* (New York: Penguin Studio, 1996), 155–73
15. In both cases, class mechanisms came into play: prior experience in the school OTC, and in Graves's case a providential sporting contact with the local golf club secretary. Brenan was in fact "volunteered" by his father, whose own application for a commission had been rejected because of deafness: Brenan, *Life of One's Own*, 183–4.
16. Chavasse immediately volunteered as a doctor.
17. Robert Graves, *Goodbye to All That: an Autobiography* (Jonathan Cape, 1929; cited hereafter as *GTAT*), 125, 334–5 (no medal); *DNB 1981–85*, 169 (mentioned in dispatches). Brenan, *Life of One's Own*, 234–5 (medals). Both adopt a cynical attitude towards wartime awards. Sassoon: below p.89.
18. Spiers, 'Regular Army', 41–4 (quoted at 41). Grenfell was a prime exemplar of someone for whom field sports played this role.
19. Winter, 'Army and Society', 194–6; Bond, *Unquiet Western Front*, 15 (on disciplinary code).
20. Sheffield, 'Officer-Man Relations', 414–15; Parker, *The Old Lie*, 163–6; Graves, *GTAT*, 129 (Welsh miners).
21. Leed, *No Man's Land*, 27.
22. Patrick Joyce, *Work, Society and Politics: the Culture of the Factory in Later Victorian England* (Brighton: Harvester, 1980), 134–57; Stephen Yeo, *Religion and Voluntary*

Organisations in Crisis (Croom Helm, 1976), ch.2; cf. the Macfie family, below p.138.

23. On such settlement and social work with boys, see Parker, *The Old Lie*, 140–5; Seth Koven, *Slumming: Sexual and Social Politics in Victorian London* (Princeton, NJ: Princeton University Press, 2004), ch.5, and his 'From Rough Lads to Hooligans: Boy Life, National Culture and Social Reform', in A. Parker et al. (eds), *Nationalisms and Sexualities* (New York and London: Routledge, 1992), 365–91. Sorley: J. Moorcroft Wilson, *Charles Hamilton Sorley: a Biography* (Cecil Woolf, 1985), 91–2; Chavasse: below p.82–3; Macfie: below p.124.
24. Sheffield, 'Officer-Man Relations', 413. The paintings appear as plates in a 1913 book entitled *Pink and Scarlet, or Hunting as a School for Soldiering*: 422 n.5.
25. Sheffield, 'Officer-Man Relations', 414; anxiety on the part of Regular officers that the Territorial counterparts would not be able to exercise such paternalism proved misplaced: 415–16.
26. Simpson, 'Officers', 85; this was close to Graeme West's initial attitude to the men among whom he initially served as a private: [Arthur Graeme West], *The Diary of a Dead Officer, being the Posthumous Papers of Arthur Graeme West* (1918; rp. Imperial War Museum, 1991), 22 (20 May 1916). Sheffield, 'Officer-Man Relations', 418, suggests that the men's lack of initiative and 'dependency culture' arose inevitably from the paternalist structure within which they were placed.
27. Sheffield, 'Officer-Man Relations', 414; cf. 417–18; Roper, 'Maternal Relations', 306–7.
28. Sheffield, 'Officer-Man Relations', 416–17; Parker, *The Old Lie*, 166–8.
29. Paul Fussell, *The Great War and Modern Memory* (New York: Oxford University Press, 1975), 272.
30. Fussell, *Great War*, 274; Sheffield, 'Officer-Man Relations', 420; Parker, *The Old Lie*, 168–78.
31. Fussell, *Great War*, 275–6; cf. below p.89 and n.126. Parker, *The Old Lie*, 97–9, 107–15, 186–93, points to the public-school story as a source for the celebration of romantic friendship, and highlights the David and Jonathan theme.
32. Fussell, *Great War*, 276–306 (quoted at 299). On the varying erotic connotations of 'men', 'boys' and 'lads', see 282.
33. Sassoon's soldier servant told him that the company refused to do anything unless Sassoon went with them, and that he loved his officer 'like a brother': Siegfried Sassoon, *Diaries 1915–1918*, ed. R. Hart-Davis (Faber, 1983), 79 (26 June 1916).
34. Leed, *No Man's Land*, 27.
35. Martin Stone, 'Shellshock and the Psychologists', in W. F. Bynum, R. Porter and M. Shepherd (eds), *The Anatomy of Madness: Essays in the History of Psychiatry, vol.2: Institutions and Society* (Tavistock, 1985), 259–60.
36. Leed, *No Man's Land*, 75–6, 81–95; cf. Stone, 'Shellshock', 261–2. Leed's fuller exposition of this theme illuminates primarily the volunteer-officer/conscript-soldier relationship in the German army, as he acknowledges.
37. 'Hymn to the Fighting Boar' (1911): E.B. Osborn (ed.), *The Muse in Arms: a Collection of War Poems* (John Murray, 1917), 203–4, cf. Mosley, *Grenfell*, 284–8; 'To a Black Greyhound' (1912): ibid., 311–12; cf. ch.2 n.33, above.

38. Grenfell to Ettie Grenfell, 3 November 1914 (original emphasis), in [Ethel Grenfell, Lady Desborough (ed.)], *Pages from a Family Journal, 1888–1915* (Eton College, 1916), 480. Cf. above p.2.
39. About his fellow soldiers needing to retreat, above n.13; about himself: 'heard noise of bomb dropping on top of dug-out. Petrified. Lost self-control—lay still, clenching my hands, for 20 secs [*sic*]. Asked what it was. "Rum jar thrown away".' (diary, 15 February 1915): Mosley, *Grenfell*, 378.
40. Mosley, *Grenfell*, 383–5 ('And he is dead who will not fight / And who dies fighting has increase'.)
41. 'Instructions for the Training of Platoons for Offensive Action' (1917), reproduced in Siegfried Sassoon, *Sassoon's Long Journey: an Illustrated Selection from Siegfried Sassoon's 'The Complete Memoirs of George Sherston'*, ed. P. Fussell (Faber, 1983), 39.
42. Joanna Bourke, *An Intimate History of Killing: Face-to-face Killing in Twentieth-century Warfare* (Granta Books, 2000), 30–1, and Niall Ferguson, *The Pity of War* (1998; Harmondsworth: Penguin, 1999), 363 (killing); Bourke, ch.3 (avoidance).
43. Leed, *No Man's Land*, 96–105 (need for defensive personality), 164, 181–3 (immobility led to war-neurosis). This account of the importance of motility as a defence against anxiety draws on Rivers's 1918 work: cf. Slobodin, *Rivers*, 66; Leed, *No Man's Land*, 182. Cf. Brenan's adopting a policy of frequent, risky patrolling, first in no man's land and then behind German lines, as a way of dispelling his anxieties about his courage in facing personal combat: *Life of One's Own*, 219, 224–33; and Sassoon on his return to France in 1918: Siegfried Sassoon, *Sherston's Progress* (1936; Faber and Faber, 1988), 135–44.
44. E. Showalter, *The Female Malady: Women, Madness and English Culture, 1830–1980* (Virago, 1987), 169, 171 (masculine expectations); W.H.R. Rivers, 'War Neurosis and Military Training', *Mental Hygiene* 2.4 (1918), 515–17, 520–1 (war training built on earlier education; cf. above p.57).
45. For the impact of front-line service, see Barham, *Forgotten Lunatics*, 69, 71, 115–16; Ben Shephard, *A War of Nerves: Soldiers and Psychiatrists, 1914–1994* (2000; Pimlico, 2002), 33–7.
46. Rivers, 'War Neurosis', 522–3; Leed, *No Man's Land*, 93 (officers kept going by immediate duty); and see Brenan, *Life of One's Own*, 214, 234–5, 237, and Sassoon, *Sherston's Progress*, 33–5, 43, 107, 110, 112, 116, 121. This duty to soldiers under one's immediate command could be eroticised: Leed, 185; Showalter, *Female Malady*, 171–2; Fussell, *Great War*, 272–9. By marked contrast, there could be considerable bitterness against the staff (Leed, 94, 109–10; Fussell, 82–6), combined with an identification with the enemy who shared the same fighting conditions (Leed, 105–8).
47. See n.51 below.
48. Turner, *Ritual Process*, 111–12.
49. Turner, 'Betwixt and Between', 105.
50. For the origin of the term 'shell shock', and its subsequent formal replacement by other diagnoses, see Stone, 'Shellshock', 257–8; Shephard, *War of Nerves*, 1–3, 21–32, 54–8, 110–13; Peter Leese, *Shell Shock: Traumatic Neurosis and the British Soldiers of the First World War* (Basingstoke: Palgrave Macmillan, 2002), 32–9, 51–67; Barham, *Forgotten Lunatics*, 6, 17–91; Allan Young, *The Harmony*

of Illusions: Inventing Post-Traumatic Stress Disorder (Princeton, NJ: Princeton University Press, 1995), 49–60.

51. Shephard, *War of Nerves*, 39–43, 110–11; cf. 56 (Passchendaele); Barham, *Forgotten Lunatics*, 115–16. Brenan, *Life of One's Own*, 202–4. Craiglockhart Special Hospital for Officers was opened in October 1916 in response to the effects of the Somme. The number of officially recorded shell-shock cases rose to over 16,000 for the period June to December 1916, more than four times the previous highest six-month total. Leese, *Shell Shock*, 104. Stone, 'Shellshock', 250, 261–2, suggests that shell shock became a more severe problem after the further slaughter of Third Ypres and Passchendaele; but Shephard, *War of Nerves*, 53–4, cites official figures claiming that there was less shell shock after Passchendaele. The latter may be partly a result of more effective immediate treatment of casualties near the front, partly an artefact of new diagnostic labelling. Stone's evidence may refer more precisely to a decline in morale.
52. Leed, *No Man's Land*, 165–9; Stone, 'Shellshock', 248–53; Shephard, *War of Nerves*, 25–6, 29, 44–6, 54–7, 67–71; Leese, *Shell Shock*, 39–47, 55–9, 103; Barham, *Forgotten Lunatics*, 51–3, 58–60, 74–5, 83–7. This ambivalence persisted into the 1922 *Report of the War Office Committee of Enquiry into 'Shell-Shock'*: Ted Bogacz, 'War Neurosis and Cultural Change in England, 1914–22: the Work of the War Office Committee of Enquiry into "Shell-Shock"', *Journal of Contemporary History* 24.2 (1989), 238–51
53. Leese, *Shell Shock*, 85.
54. Shephard, *War of Nerves*, 37–8.
55. Barham, *Forgotten Lunatics*, 35–9, 77–8; Shephard, *War of Nerves*, 7–15.
56. Leese, *Shell Shock*, 93, 97; Shephard, *War of Nerves*, 114–18; Young, *Harmony of Illusions*, 54–5, 57–8, 62. The fear of malingering in pursuit of a post-war pension was linked to pre-war anxieties about physically-injured workers seeking insurance compensation: Leese, 71–2; Shephard, 16–17.
57. Leese, *Shell Shock*, 103, 109–14; Shephard, *War of Nerves*, 57; Young, *Harmony of Illusions*, 62–5.
58. Rivers, 'War Neurosis', 514–15; Leed, *No Man's Land*, 163–4; Showalter, *Female Malady*, 174–5 (who however notes the close fit between this distribution of symptoms and class–oriented attitudes to hysteria). Contrast Barham, *Forgotten Lunatics*, 76.
59. Leese argues that the surviving sources about individual patients are not adequate, in number or detail, to say whether there was a real difference in symptoms. He refers to: 'the near impossibility of recreating clearly the encounter between medic and patient that frustrates the historian's ambition to know what attitudes and expectations were brought to the consulting room, and how they shaped a peculiarly malleable form of hysteria such as shell shock.' *Shell Shock*, 70 (quoted), 90–1, 104, 107–8. He discusses (115–16) whether the clear difference in patterns of diagnosis results from perceptions of class or of army rank (since some officers, by the later years of the war, came from a working-class background); but this may be too subtle—ways of perceiving officers were determined by class presuppositions, and the working-class officer could be assimilated to the category of 'temporary gentleman'.
60. '[W]hat may have been carried over into the war from the peace was not so

much the social distribution of symptoms as the predispositions to code working-class reality. It is not that the signs and symptoms common to the officer class were not in evidence in the other ranks, rather that they were submerged, disavowed and trivialized by the attitudes and interpretations that were imposed on them.' Barham, *Forgotten Lunatics*, 6–7, 71–2, 76–8 (quoted at 77–8). His argument based on individual case notes is supported by Leese's examination of what soldiers wrote in hospital journals: *Shell Shock*, 100, 102. So Rivers's assumption that the other ranks enjoyed themselves once safely away from the front is class-bound, another version of the 'seeking compensation' anxiety.

61. Shephard, *War of Nerves*, 75.
62. The records at both Craiglockhart Special Hospital for Officers and Lennel Convalescent Home show that officers below the rank of captain formed the largest group (c75%). The incomplete Lennel Register for 1916–17 records 34 2nd Lieutenants and 11 Lieutenants (76%), the rest comprising 9 Captains and 5 Majors. Leese, *Shell Shock*, 105, 108–9.
63. Leese, *Shell Shock*, 69, 87–8, 106–7.
64. Barham, *Forgotten Lunatics*, 47–96; Leese, *Shell Shock*, 70–1, 73, 76–81, 90–8; Shephard, *War of Nerves*, 58–60 (initial treatment at the front), 73–5, 78–80, 85–7 (in hospital).
65. Leese, *Shell Shock*, 104, 116–17, 119–20; he observes (113) that officers' case notes were fuller.
66. Leese, *Shell Shock*, 106–7, 119–20; Shephard, *War of Nerves*, 85–95. A dichotomy whereby men were subjected largely to aversion therapies (often physically delivered, such as electro-shock), while officers were accorded forms of psychological treatment, was first suggested by Leed, *No Man's Land*, 170–80, and Showalter, *Female Malady*, 176–86; and later popularised in Pat Barker's novel, *Regeneration* (1991). It was symbolised by the polarised figures of Lewis Yealland using electric shock on soldiers at Queen Square Hospital, and W.H.R. Rivers using psychotherapy on officers at Craiglockhart: Young, *Harmony of Illusions*, 68–74, 81–2; Shephard, *War of Nerves*, xx. This has been shown by fuller research to be a substantial oversimplification. Yealland and Rivers represented opposite ends of the spectrum of (generally pragmatic and empiricist) shell-shock treatments practised in Britain: Leese, *Shell Shock*, 73. The frequently-cited (and disturbing) Case A1 was Yealland's most extreme (reported) case. He treated relatively few shell-shock sufferers, and his practice not followed elsewhere even in his own hospital: Leese, 73–81, esp. 74–5; Shephard, *War of Nerves*, 76–8. Although psychotherapy was predominantly used to treat officers, some other ranks were also treated at the pioneering centre in Maghull, and (in a much more limited way) at Napsbury War Hospital: Leese, 81–4, 88–90; Shephard, 80–3; Barham, *Forgotten Lunatics*, 78–82, 91,
67. See, for example, Shephard, *War of Nerves*, 33–7; Mosley, Grenfell, 361; West, *Diary of a Dead Officer*, 66–9.
68. Showalter, *Female Malady*, 171–5 (male hysteria); Rivers, 'War Neurosis', 521, and Leed, *No Man's Land*, 167 (hostility to senior officers).
69. For Rivers's life and pre-war career, see Slobodin, *Rivers*, 1–85; Allan Young, 'W.H.R. Rivers and the War Neuroses', *Journal of the History of the Behavioral Sciences* 34.4 (1999), 359–62. Stone, Leed and Showalter all draw on his

original work.

70. Rivers, 'War Neurosis', 516, 524–7; Leed, *No Man's Land*, 176–7.
71. Rivers, 'War Neurosis', 515, 529, for definition of war-neurosis.
72. See below ch.7; and Pat Barker, *The Regeneration Trilogy* (Viking, 1991–5); Sharon Monteith, et al. (eds), *Critical Perspectives on Pat Barker* (Columbia, SC: University of South Carolina Press, 2005).
73. Clayton, *Chavasse*, 2.
74. Clayton, *Chavasse*, 19. The family ethos of service was such that one of Noel's brothers also became a doctor, another a clergyman (and later bishop), and the third was about to study theology when the war broke out.
75. Clayton, *Chavasse*, 25–6, 35–6, 64, 113, 176, 184; cf. 169.
76. Clayton, *Chavasse*, 18, 29.
77. Clayton, *Chavasse*, 28; cf. Koven, *Slumming*, 375 n.202; Summers, 'Edwardian Militarism', 249. Richard Davenport-Hines, 'Gordon, Charles George (1833–1885)', *Oxford Dictionary of National Biography* (Oxford University Press, 2004; http://www.oxforddnb.com/view/article/11029) comments of Gordon's Khartoum journals that their 'insubordinate temper and air of doomed heroism have understandably attracted rebellious or idealistic readers'. Horne, 'Masculinity', 28, suggests that 'nation building required the construction of the secular equivalent of sainthood': Gordon, like Havelock (Dawson, *Soldier Heroes*, chs 4–5), could be seen as a combined secular/religious hero.
78. Clayton, *Chavasse*, 18, 29, 42.
79. Clayton, *Chavasse*, 35.
80. Clayton, *Chavasse*, 29–30.
81. Chavasse to his mother, 24 January, 30 January 1909: Clayton, *Chavasse*, 39–41 (quoted at 40).
82. Clayton, *Chavasse*, 49–50; during his training, he had continued his involvement with the Industrial school: 42–3; cf. 47.
83. Clayton, *Chavasse*, 42–3, 51–4.
84. Clayton, *Chavasse*, 58–60.
85. Ann Clayton, 'Chavasse, Noel Godfrey (1884–1917)', *Oxford Dictionary of National Biography* (Oxford University Press, 2004; http://www.oxforddnb.com/view/article/55355).
86. Chavasse to his father, 31 October 1914: Clayton, *Chavasse*, 67.
87. Chavasse to his father, 18 August 1914: Clayton, *Chavasse*, 60; cf. 31 October 1914: ibid., 66.
88. Chavasse to his parents, 28 March 1916: Clayton, *Chavasse*, 148. Clayton suggests (64) that he may in some respects have been more comfortable among the men than in the drink-centred culture of the officers' mess.
89. Chavasse to his parents, 15 June, 25 June 1917: Clayton, *Chavasse*, 185–6.
90. See, e.g., his account of the Battle of Hooge in June 1915: Clayton, *Chavasse*, 118–23; cf. 137, 200.
91. Clayton, *Chavasse*, 71, 174, 187–8; Helen B. McCartney, *Citizen Soldiers: the Liverpool Territorials in the First World War* (Cambridge: Cambridge University Press, 2005), 137.
92. Clayton, *Chavasse*, 68, 129, 134–5, 155–7, 164, 180, 184.
93. Clayton, *Chavasse*, 156; cf. 134–5; McCartney, *Citizen Soldiers*, 222.

94. Chavasse to his father, 22 October 1916: Clayton, *Chavasse*, 131–2 (quoted at 132).
95. Clayton, *Chavasse*, 113, 183.
96. Clayton, *Chavasse*, 73, 179–80; McCartney, *Citizen Soldiers*, 137–9.
97. Clayton, *Chavasse*, 121, 169–71.
98. Clayton, *Chavasse*, 181. He was violently opposed to licensed brothels: 171–2.
99. Chavasse to his parents, 30 May 1917: Clayton, *Chavasse*, 131–2, 181–3 (quoted at 182). There may be an element here of his hero Gordon's attitude to his colleagues and superiors.
100. Clayton, *Chavasse*, 125–6, 163–5, 219–21. Two of his brothers were also awarded the MC, while the third was killed at the front.
101. Clayton, *Chavasse*, 179, 205; cf. 209, 220.
102. J.M. Wilson, *Siegfried Sassoon: the Making of a War Poet: a Biography* (1886–1918) (Duckworth, 1998), chs 1–2; Egremont, *Sassoon*, ch.1.
103. His education included the familiar elements of puritanical Christianity, and imperial enthusiasm: Wilson, *Sassoon* (1886–1918), 88–106, 113–27; Egremont, *Sassoon*, 24–36; Adrian Caesar, *Taking It Like a Man: Suffering, Sexuality, and the War Poets: Brooke, Sassoon, Owen, Graves* (Manchester: Manchester University Press, 1993), 63.
104. Wilson, *Sassoon* (1886–1918), chs 6–7; Egremont, *Sassoon*, ch.3.
105. Wilson, *Sassoon* (1886–1918), 154–5.
106. Jeffrey Weeks, *Coming Out: Homosexual Politics in Britain from the Nineteenth Century to the Present* (Quartet, 1977), 68–83; Sheila Rowbotham and Jeffrey Weeks, *Socialism and the New Life: the Personal and Sexual Politics of Edward Carpenter and Havelock Ellis* (Pluto Press, 1977); Christopher Scoble, *Fisherman's Friend: A Life of Stephen Reynolds* (Tiverton: Halsgrove, 2000), 235–6; Stanley, *Auto/Biographical I*, 225–33
107. Sassoon to Edward Carpenter, 27 July, 2 August 1911 (original emphases), in *Fabian Economic and Social Thought Series One: The Papers of Edward Carpenter, 1844–1929, from Sheffield Archives, Sheffield Libraries and Information Services—Part 1: Correspondence and Manuscripts* (Marlborough: Adam Matthew, 1994), Reel 10, MSS 386–179, 181.
108. Caesar, *Taking It Like a Man*, 65–6, 192; James Campbell, '"For You May Touch Them Not": Misogyny, Homosexuality, and the Ethics of Passivity in First World War Poetry', *English Literary History* 64 (1997), 827–8.
109. Wilson, *Sassoon (1886–1918)*, 94, 151–5; Egremont, *Sassoon*, 46–7. Sassoon's idealising and puritanical attitude to his desires at this point fitted both the public school and Christian ethos around sex in which he had been brought up, and the emphasis on Platonic love which Carpenter deployed for strategic purposes in his writings but which Sassoon (like Graves) accepted literally.
110. Wilson, *Sassoon (1886–1918)*, ch.7; Egremont, *Sassoon*, ch.3. Caesar, *Taking It Like a Man*, 4–6, 8–9, further suggests that the pain which this sexual self-denial imposed found both expression and justification in Sassoon's (and Graves's) adherence to the ethic of necessary suffering and self-sacrifice promoted by both the Christian/imperialist ideology of their schooling, and the late Romantic model of creativity to which they subscribed.
111. Caesar, *Taking It Like a Man*, 67; Wilson, *Sassoon (1886–1918)*, 179–80.

112. Wilson, *Sassoon (1886–1918)*, 180–4, 188–96, 202, 207.
113. For such deaths, see n.144 below.
114. Wilson, *Sassoon (1886–1918)*, 244–5, 258, 269.
115. Wilson, *Sassoon (1886–1918)*, 302, 311–12, 429, 435, 437 (hunting), 254–5, 439–40 (poetry).
116. Caesar, *Taking It Like a Man*, 67–98, 107, argues that, for Sassoon (and Graves), self-sacrifice and suffering remained both imperative and valued. Alongside Sassoon's growing criticism of the war was a recurring emphasis on the value of such sacrifice and suffering, and its expression in poetry. See, for example, 'Secret Music' (December 1916; Sassoon, *War Poems*, 62) and 'Can I Forget?' (August 1918; *Diaries 1915–1918*, 278); Wilson, 309–10, 314, 494, provides more precise contextualisation for each poem.
117. For examples of short-term mood swings, see Wilson, *Sassoon (1886–1918)*, 243 (spring 1916, after the death of David Thomas), 254–5 (April-May 1916, at training school), 260 (May 1916, the action for which he won an MC), 308, 310, 318–19 (November 1916–February 1917, preparing to return to the front), 328, 341–2 (March–April 1917, approaching the front), 433 (January 1918, training at Limerick).
118. Sassoon, *Diaries 1915–1918*, 22 (3 December 1915); cf. 26 (10 December, 17 December 1915).
119. Wilson, *Sassoon (1886–1918)*, 235. For Sassoon's friendship with Ross, a fellow homosexual and defender of Wilde: 202–5; Egremont, Sassoon, 84–5.
120. Sassoon, *Diaries 1915–1918*, 44–5 (19 March 1916); Wilson, *Sassoon (1886–1918)*, 239–41. For later deaths, see n.144 below.
121. For Sassoon's friendship with Thomas, see Wilson, *Sassoon (1886–1918)*, 196–8. She notes (241) the censoring of an earlier, franker version of his poem 'The Last Meeting', which reveals the strength of his physical desire for Thomas. His reaction may also have included an element of delayed grieving for his brother Hamo, who had been killed in November 1915, and to whose death he had originally reacted with a degree of numbness (205–7, 239).
122. Sassoon, *Diaries 1915–1918*, 52–3 (1 April [quoted], 4 April 1916); Wilson, *Sassoon (1886–1918)*, 239–41, 244–5.
123. Timothy d'Arch Smith, *Love in Earnest: Some Notes on the Lives and Writings of English 'Uranian' Poets from 1889 to 1930* (Routledge and Kegan Paul, 1970), 223, writing about Ralph Chubb's reaction to the death of a seventeen-year-old whom he loved, at Loos in 1915; quoted in Fussell, *Great War*, 284. Cf. the army doctor weeping at the eagerness of young recruits to risk death: 276–7. Cf. Connell, quoted above p.60.
124. Sassoon, *Diaries 1915–1918*, 50–1, 53 (31 March, 4 April 1916). This is also a coded reference to the honour of homosexuals: see Sassoon to Carpenter, 27 July 1911 (as n.107 above) MSS 386–179/1v, on his involvement in cricket, riding and hunting: 'I am thankful to say I am as good as those others in their sports, and have some of their strength and courage.' The strength of this desire in Sassoon is vividly evident in his triumphant 'A Last Word' (Jan. 1919), where his 'Three wound stripes and a Military Cross' demolish the pre-war superiority of a jingoistic, philistine sportsman: Siegfried Sassoon, *The War Poems of Siegfried Sassoon*, ed. R. Hart-Davis (Faber, 1983), 138–40.

125. Wilson, *Sassoon (1886–1918)*, 258–60.
126. Wilson, *Sassoon (1886–1918)*, 268, 270–2; Sassoon, *War Poems*, 42–3. For the significance of the dead German's 'blond face' (Siegfried Sassoon, *Memoirs of an Infantry Officer* [1930; Faber, 1965], 64; Egremont, *Sassoon*, 106), see above pp.76–7.
127. Wilson, Sassoon (1886–1918), 290–1; Sassoon, 'The Stunt', *Diaries 1915–1918*, 101 (12 August 1916).
128. Wilson, *Sassoon (1886–1918)*, 294–6.
129. Wilson, *Sassoon (1886–1918)*, 299–300.
130. Sassoon, *Diaries 1915–1918*, 109, (27 December 1916); cf. 105–6, 24 December 1916; Wilson, *Sassoon (1886–1918)*, 312–13, 315.
131. For other examples of such conflicting attitudes in late 1916 and early 1917, see Egremont, *Sassoon*, 107–8, 112–13, 120, 123, 127, 133–4.
132. Sassoon, *Diaries 1915–1918*, 122 (21 January 1917); cf. 127, 133 (27 January, 22 February 1917); Wilson, *Sassoon (1886–1918)*, 324.
133. Sassoon, *Diaries 1915–1918*, 137 (27 February 1917); Wilson, *Sassoon (1886–1918)*, 325–7. This same lunch was permeated by the anger which gave rise to 'Base Details': *Diaries 1915–1918*, 139–40; Sassoon, *War Poems*, 71.
134. Sassoon, *Diaries 1915–1918*, 151 (7 April 1917); cf. 149, 156 (3 April, 17 April 1917).
135. Sassoon, *Diaries 1915–1918*, 162 (29 April 1917). Leed, *No Man's Land*, 137, notes that the wartime psychologist F. C. Bartlett 'felt that death and the desire for death as an "honourable escape" from war was a preoccupation particularly of those men who had "high ideals of duty"'.
136. Wilson, *Sassoon (1886–1918)*, 349–51. For Arras, see Trevor Wilson, *The Myriad Faces of War: Britain and the Great War, 1914–1918* (Cambridge: Polity Press, 1986), 450–6.
137. Sassoon, *Diaries 1915–1918*, 154–7 (14 April 1917, quoted at 156–7); cf. 159 (19 April 1917). Wilson, *Sassoon* (1886–1918), 345–6.
138. Leed, *No Man's Land*, 21, comments: 'The front is a place that dissolved the clear distinction between life and death. Death, customarily the "slash" between life/not-life, became for many in the war a "dash", a continuum of experience.'
139. Wilson, *Sassoon (1886–1918)*, 346; Sassoon, *War Poems*, 77. This haunting by memories of Arras is also recorded in 'Repression of War Experience' (written early in July): Wilson, 378–9; Sassoon, 84–5.
140. Sassoon, *Diaries 1915–1918*, 160–2 (24 April 1917, quoted at 162).
141. Cf. 'Death in the Garden', Sassoon, *Diaries 1915–1918*, 172 (25 May 1917).
142. Graves presents him as torn between fantasies of assassinating the Prime Minister, refusing to continue to serve (but 'they would only accuse him of being afraid of shells'), and taking a safe job at home ('but he knew that it was only a beautiful dream, that he would be morally compelled to go on until he was killed'). *GTAT*, 317–18; Graves to Sassoon, 30 June 1917, Robert Graves, *In Broken Images: Selected Letters of Robert Graves, 1914–46*, ed. Paul O'Prey (Hutchinson, 1982), 72.
143. Sassoon, *Diaries 1915–1918*, 165–7 (15 May 1917, quoted at 166). Wilson, *Sassoon (1886–1918)*, 364–6. Shortly afterwards he wrote a poem about this encounter, 'Supreme Sacrifice': *War Poems*, 81. The character of the

'Theosophist', a fellow-patient at Craiglockhart, is a comic rendition of the same theme: Sassoon, *Sherston's Progress*, 20–1, 30–1.

144. Wilson, *Sassoon (1886–1918)*, 367–8, 374–5. Deaths of friends and fellow officers: above p.89 (Thomas); Sassoon, *Diaries 1915–1918*, 184 (5 September 1917); Wilson, 397–8 (Harbord). Sassoon, *Diaries 1915–1918*, 267 (12 June 1918); Wilson, 477 (Dobell; rejecting the usual consolations about the dead). Cf. Wilson, 276 (false news about Graves: July 1916), 300 (Dadd, Newton and many other officers: September 1916), 331–3, 337 (Casson, Evans, Poore: Sept. 1917), 368 (Conning: May 1917).
145. Wilson, *Sassoon (1886–1918)*, 373–5.
146. Sassoon, *Diaries 1915–1918*, 173–4, (15 June 1917), cf. 175–7 (19 June, 21 June 1917); Wilson, *Sassoon (1886–1918)*, 373–6.
147. Sassoon, *Diaries 1915–1918*, 177 (4 July 1917); Wilson, *Sassoon (1886–1918)*, 377–80.
148. Wilson, *Sassoon (1886–1918)*, 380–1. Bobbie Hanmer, object of another of Sassoon's chaste but passionate friendships (201–2), whom he (almost enviously) admired for his simple faith and patriotism (Sassoon, *Diaries 1915–1918*, 135 [24 February 1917]), wrote: 'What is this damned nonsense…that you have refused to do any more soldiering? For Heaven's sake man don't be such a fool. Don't disgrace yourself and think of us before you do anything so mad.' Hanmer to Sassoon, *Diaries 1915–1918*, 178, July 1917.
149. Wilson, *Sassoon (1886–1918)*, 384–5.
150. Phrases from his poem 'Absolution', written between April and September 1915, while first training with the RWF: Sassoon, *War Poems*, 15; Wilson, *Sassoon (1886–1918)*, 193.
151. These themes are resumed below, Chs 5, 7–9.
152. Bishop Chavasse to his son Bernard, 16 August 1917: Clayton, *Chavasse*, 209.

4 Robert Graves

1. References to Robert Graves, *Goodbye to All That: an Autobiography* are to the first edition (Jonathan Cape, 1929; cited hereafter as *GTAT*) unless otherwise stated. It was reissued in a revised edition in 1957 (cited as *GTAT* 1957; my references are to the Penguin, 1960, version of this edition). As well as a general tautening and refining of the prose style, this made some significant changes, which are analysed in the 'Annotations' to Richard Perceval Graves's reprint of the 1929 original (Oxford: Berghahn, 1995), 327–82 (cited as RPG 1995, with his critical notes cited in the form: page number of his note, page number/line number of the passage in his edition to which he is referring). The whole text was reworked in detailed ways, not all in one direction. In some respects, Graves was now able to be more open: e.g. he included proper names, and the (previously censored) story of the parade-ground incident (Graves, *GTAT* 1957, 69): Fussell, *Great War*, 210–11. But he also excluded some sensitive material which had appeared in the first edition, such as a reference to his own homosexuality: 'Many boys never recover from this perversion. *I only recovered by a shock at the age of twenty-one.*' (italicised sentence later deleted). Graves, *GTAT*, 40; Fussell, 214. Relevant divergences are discussed below.

2. Richard Perceval Graves, *Robert Graves: the Years with Laura, 1926–40* (Weidenfeld & Nicolson, 1990; hereafter cited as RPG (2)), 100, 111, 116–19. He had started to write about his war experiences in novel-form during the war itself; after the war, he had tried but failed to finish the novel several times. Graves, *GTAT*, 289, 408; Brian Finney, *The Inner I: British Literary Autobiography of the Twentieth Century* (Faber, 1985), 165.
3. Finney, *The Inner I*, 166.
4. Graves, *GTAT*, 13.
5. Graves, *GTAT*, 443.
6. Throughout, attention will be given to Graves's textual narration of these experiences, in terms both of explicit statement, and metonymic and metaphoric representation.
7. For his life after the war, see pp.214–22.
8. Graves, *GTAT*, 18–24.
9. Graves, *GTAT*, 21–4, 27–9.
10. Graves, *GTAT*, 19–20, 27; Richard Perceval Graves, *Robert Graves: the Assault Heroic, 1895–1926* (Weidenfeld & Nicolson, 1986; hereafter cited as RPG (1)), 5–10.
11. *GTAT*, 27. His father was forty-nine, his mother forty, when he was born.
12. Graves, *GTAT*, 27–9, 68. His father set a strict example of rectitude, once buying and tearing up unused a train ticket because his son had (accidentally) made a journey without paying.
13. Graves, *GTAT*, 51.
14. RPG (1), 8–10; Miranda Seymour, *Robert Graves: Life on the Edge* (1995; Doubleday, 1996), 6.
15. RPG (1), 78–9.
16. Graves, *GTAT*, 53.
17. RPG (1), 37: her pride in their success and disappointment at failure meant that her children 'grew up feeling that they were loved by her not for themselves but for whatever special talents they possessed'; cf. 42, 79, 97, 284, 295; Seymour, *Graves*, 14–15, 33, 119.
18. Graves, *GTAT*, 27–9, 52–5; RPG (1), 53–4. See, for example, below p.100.
19 Graves, *GTAT*, 23–4; RPG (1) 47–9. RPG (2), 104, 134, 149–51, notes the unfairness of this depiction.
20. 'She allowed us no hint of [humanity's] dirtiness and intrigue and lustfulness, believing that innocence was the surest protection against them.' Graves, *GTAT*, 52. It is significant that he attributes to her moralism his father's decision to become a teetotaller, which was in fact taken for health reasons. *GTAT*, 24; RPG 1995, 329, 13/13. Cf. below pp.218, 220–1.
21. Graves, *GTAT*, 27–9 (quoted at 28), 31–2 (quoted at 32). For the remoteness of such mothers, especially from the physical care of their children, see Davidoff, 'Class and Gender', 94–5 and n.33; McBride, '"As the Twig is Bent"', 46–8, 51.
22. Graves, *GTAT*, 31.
23. Graves, *GTAT*, 30–2.
24. Graves, *GTAT*, 38–43; RPG (1), 50–2, 55–9.
25. Graves, *GTAT*, 61–2; name supplied in *GTAT* 1957, 36–7.

26. Graves, *GTAT*, 63–5. For similar school experiences, see Woolf, *Autobiography 1: 1880–1911*, 31–59; Brenan, *Life of One's Own*, 41–8, 51–3, 60–1, 81–4, 126–7. Sorley and Sassoon each negotiated school more easily.
27. Graves, *GTAT*, 67–8 (quoted at 67); *GTAT* 1957, 40, adds, at the end of the quoted passage, 'perhaps my career'.
28. RPG (1), 73–4. They shared the experience of being teased over their names, Raymond's father being an Austrian Pole. Cf. Woolf, *Autobiography 1: 1880–1911*, 55–9.
29. Graves, *GTAT*, 69–73. In this story, the intellectuals had unilaterally appropriated distinctive school dress previously the sole privilege of the bloods. For the symbols (of 'colours' and clothing) and rituals awarded to, or appropriated by, the 'bloods', see Mangan, *Athleticism*, 161–77.
30. Behind this story lie the values of Dr Arnold's Rugby, and of *Tom Brown's Schooldays*.
31. Graves, *GTAT*, 69–70, 75 (quoted). The 1957 revision replaced 'sex feeling' with 'love', and removed the coded sexual reference of the allusion to Stopes. Cf. ch.1 n.57 above on masculine desire. RPG (1), 85.
32. It was in this year's boxing that he won by using a blow, the swing, not taught by the trainers ('somehow neglected, probably because it was not so "pretty"); i.e. he acted on his own initiative outside the prescribed code. Graves, *GTAT*, 77–80 (quoted at 78). Mallory: Graves to Marsh, 29 December 1917, *Letters 1914–46*, 90; *GTAT*, 80; RPG (1), 85 (and letters by Graves quoted there).
33. Graves, *GTAT*, 91–7; RPG (1), 89, 90, 93, 103, 104; Seymour, *Graves*, 33–5.
34. For conflicts between English, British and Irish identities, see Robert Colls, 'Englishness and the Political Culture', in R. Colls and P. Dodd (eds), *Englishness: Politics and Culture 1880–1920* (Croom Helm, 1986), 39–43; D.G. Boyce, 'The Marginal Britons: The Irish', in ibid., 231, 234. These tensions were felt within the Graves family. During the Boer War there was tension between Alfred (whose political views were always orthodox') and his eldest son Philip, who was then Fenian and pro-Boer: Graves, *GTAT*, 53; cf. RPG (1), 45. When posted to Limerick in January 1919, where the battalion was helping deal with the growing unrest in Ireland, Graves declined to take part in a search for arms; 'I said I was an Irishman and did not wish to be mixed up in Irish politics'. *GTAT*, 344; RPG (1), 202–3.
35. Graves, *GTAT*, 44–51; RPG (1), 32, 45, 56–7.
36. The effort to stress his Irishness is apparent in his letter to Edward Carpenter, in which—having praised his *Iolaus: an Anthology of Friendship*—Graves asks him to remedy in later editions a deficiency, the lack of mention of the Cuchulain Saga ('There you have another Theban Band in the boy-troop of Ulster, who perish to a man against overwhelming odds with an account of blood-brotherhood'), and earnestly supplies scholarly reference. Graves to Carpenter, 30 May 1914, in *Fabian Economic and Social Thought Series One: The Papers of Edward Carpenter, 1844–1929, from Sheffield Archives, Sheffield Libraries and Information Services—Part 1: Correspondence and Manuscripts* (Marlborough: Adam Matthew, 1994), Reel 11, MSS 386–234.
37. Graves, *GTAT*, 50–1 (quoted), 64–5, 99–101, 258–60.
38. Graves, *GTAT*, 29–30, 39. Cf. above p.62.

39. The autobiographical account probably over-stated the earliness and depth both of his doubts about religion, and of his break with Rodakowski; the reality may have been more messy and conflicted. R.P. Graves suggests (RPG (2), 104) that in *GTAT* Graves treats religion 'with a certain cool cynicism', significantly backdating and oversimplifying his rejection of it. He convincingly argues (RPG (1), 70–1, 337 n.16) that the chronology Graves offers (*GTAT*, 75–6) for his threatened faith and resulting breach with Rodakowski is impossible. Cf. RPG (1), 75–6, 78–80, 84–5, 90–1, 91, 94, 96.
40. See above p.61.
41. Graves, *GTAT*, 40; RPG (1), 52; Seymour, *Graves*, 15–17. See below p.113.
42. Graves, *GTAT*, 41.
43. RPG (1), 63 nn.3–5, confirms Graves's account of the sexual atmosphere at Charterhouse.
44. Graves, *GTAT*, 40–1.
45. Graves, *GTAT*, 66. This is in fact close to his contemporary account: 'In houses where immorality is rife, for instance this house four years ago, fellows who had contracted dirty habits practised them not on the boy whom they loved but on some third person whom they didn't mind wronging.' Graves to Carpenter, 30 May 1914 (as n.36 above).
46. Graves, *GTAT*, 40; RPG (1), 87.
47. Graves, *GTAT*, 76–7 (quoted at 76). On the name 'Dick', for such a beloved, see Fussell, *Great War*, 275, cf. 208, 214, 272.
48. Graves, *GTAT*, 77.
49. Graves to Carpenter, 30 May 1914 (as n.36 above). For the widespread use of such Greek and other models for all-male friendships, see Weeks, *Coming Out*, 50–2; Jeffrey Richards, '"Passing the Love of Women": Manly Love and Victorian Society', in J.A. Mangan and J. Walvin (eds), *Manliness and Morality: Middle-Class Masculinity in Britain and America, 1800–1940* (Manchester: Manchester University Press, 1987), 101–2, 113; Robert Aldrich, *The Seduction of the Mediterranean: Writing, Art and Homosexual Fantasy* (Routledge, 1993), Introduction, ch.2; Linda Dowling, *Hellenism and Homosexuality in Victorian Oxford* (Ithaca, NY: Cornell University Press, 1994).
50. This is reinforced by Graves's (somewhat brash) urging of his own knowledge and speculations on Carpenter. As well as suggesting extra material for *Iolaus* (n.36 above) he also enquires: 'if you have ever noticed the same urning [homosexual] tendency in Richard Middleton the poet? He died without understanding the matter, ashamed of it: when he wants to confess his love for a boy in a poem he puts the words into the mouth of a childless woman or a girl: old evasions which I have often myself employed.' Graves to Carpenter, 30 May 1914 (as n.36 above).
51. Graves, *GTAT*, 87; RPG (1), 105–6. Graves's jealousy had already become apparent in a boxing match which he drove himself to knock out another boy who also loved Dick, who was a spectator at the fight: *GTAT*, 78–9.
52. The replacement for the sacked prep school headmaster himself died a fortnight later: Graves, *GTAT*, 41. The power of homoerotic jealousy has already been shown in the text through the incident which led to the closing-down of the Poetry Society: *GTAT*, 83–4; RPG (1), 84. In an ironic reversal, Graves notes

that during the war catching venereal disease (at a brothel which he sardonically calls the *Drapeau Blanc*) saved the lives of men whom it incapacitated for future trench service: *GTAT*, 294.

53. See below p.112.
54. Patrick J. Quinn, *The Great War and the Missing Muse: the Early Writings of Robert Graves and Siegfried Sassoon* (Selinsgrove, PA: Susquehanna University Press, 1993), 144–5.
55. Graves, *GTAT*, 84–5 (quoted at 85). They were mocking an official view that tennis was unsuitable for schools because insufficiently painful: Mangan, *Athleticism*, 187. Seymour, *Graves*, 35, suggests that the campaign was partly aimed at Alfred Graves, who had argued for compulsory games as part of the general school curriculum. Connell, *Masculinities*, 37, comments: 'School studies show patterns of hegemony vividly. In certain schools the masculinity exalted through competitive sport is hegemonic; this means that sporting prowess is a test of masculinity even for boys who detest the locker room. Those who reject the hegemonic pattern have to fight or negotiate their way out…"three friends"…scorned the school's cult of football. But they could not freely walk away from it; they had to establish some other claim to respect—which they made by taking over the school newspaper.'
56. Quinn, *Great War*, 144.
57. In September 1911, his father recorded that his diplomat uncle Robert had 'helped us to make him decide to go into his School Rifle Corps'. Graves, *GTAT*, 87–8; RPG (1), 75, 95–6, 99; RPG 1995, 336, 60/15, 60/19–23 (correcting chronology and Graves's precise role). Contemporary debate over compulsory service: Beckett, 'Nation in Arms', 2–4; Summers, 'Edwardian Militarism', 243–54.
58. Graves, *GTAT*, 99; RPG (1), 110.
59. RPG (1), 117. Cf. Sorley's response, and his comment on Rupert Brooke, below p.187.
60. Graves, *GTAT*, 102. A year into the war, his father could celebrate a letter from Robert appreciating what his parents had done for him with the words: 'Living so near to death is indeed a quickener of the Spirit.' RPG (1), 140. A few months later his uncle Charles published a comic poem celebrating his Robert's transformation: 'My gifted nephew… / Till just before the war / Was steeped in esoteric / And antinomian lore…frankly futuristic / And modern to the core…[Now]…purged of mental vanity / And erudite inanity / The clay of his humanity / Is turning fast to gold.' RPG (1), 110–11.
61. Caesar, *Taking It Like a Man*, 179–82. Carpenter: n.36 above. Cf. Seymour, *Graves*, 36, on the comradeship of climbing.
62. 'The nearest regimental depot was at Wrexham: the Royal Welch Fusiliers. The Harlech golf secretary suggested my taking a commission instead of enlisting. He rang up the adjutant and said that I was a public-school boy who had been in the Officers' Training Corps at Charterhouse. So the adjutant said: "Send him right along".' Graves, *GTAT*, 101–2.
63. '[W]e all agreed that regimental pride was the greatest moral force that kept a battalion going as an effective fighting unit, contrasting it particularly with patriotism and religion. Patriotism. There was no patriotism in the trenches.

It was too remote a sentiment, and rejected as fit only for civilians. A new arrival who talked patriotism would soon be told to cut it out...It was said that not one soldier in a hundred was inspired by religious feeling of even the crudest kind. It would have been difficult to remain religious in the trenches though one had survived the irreligion of the training battalion at home.' Graves, *GTAT*, 240–1.

64. The distinctive spelling 'Welch', to which the regiment clung fiercely, 'referred us somehow to the antique North Wales of Henry Tudor and Owen Glendower and Lord Herbert of Cherbury, the founder of the regiment; it dissociated us from the modern North Wales of chapels, liberalism, the dairy and drapery business, Lloyd George, and the tourist trade'. Graves, *GTAT*, 121.
65. Within the regiment, the contrast and rivalry between different battalions was a persistent theme. Graves greatly preferred the 1st Battalion, which had been stationed in England for many years before the war and so had felt the impact of the army reforms, to the 2nd Battalion which had been abroad since before the Boer War and maintained the full rigours of the Victorian mess code: *GTAT*, 164–72, 222–8, 254–60, 296–7. Despite the difficulties he encountered here, either Battalion was felt preferable to the Welsh Regiment, to which he had been posted on his first tour of duty: *GTAT*, 126–9; Graves to Marsh, 22 May 1915, *Letters 1914–46*, 33. Graves himself was drawn into this competitive evaluation. 'I used to congratulate myself on having chosen, quite blindly, this of all regiments. "Good God!" I used to think, "suppose that when the war broke out I had been living in Cheshire and had applied for a commission in the Cheshire Regiment." I thought how ashamed I should have been to find in the history of that regiment (which was the old Twenty-Second Foot, just senior in the line to the Royal Welch, which was the Twenty-Third) that it had been deprived of its old title "The Royal Cheshires" as a punishment for losing a battle.' Graves, *GTAT*, 117; cf. ch.11 *passim* on regimental history and traditions. Other regiments (regions of Britain, nationalities) were evaluated and ranked: Graves, *GTAT*, 175–6, 232–4, 238–40.
66. 'In the mess, [the newly joined subaltern] reverted to the lowest form of social life, something he had already experienced at preparatory school, public school': Simpson, 'Officers', 67–8 (quoted at 67). Cf. above p.58; Parker, *The Old Lie*, 35–7. Prejudice of regulars against temporaries: Simpson, 76–8; Sheffield, 'Officer-Man Relations', 417.
67. RPG (1), 140. Simpson, 'Officers', 68, on mess culture.
68. He initially offended his adjutant by his unsoldierly manner of dress. Early in 1915 he made a greater effort to enter into the life of the regiment, but his posting was still delayed, this time because he showed no interest in attending the Grand National in which the adjutant had a horse running. He was saved once again by boxing. He agreed to spar with sergeant in the regiment who was preparing for a championship fight; the adjutant, describing this as a 'great encouragement to the men', at last promised to draft him. Graves, *GTAT*, 108–9; RPG (1), 118, 121–2.
69. RPG (1), 130. For the continuation of these tensions once he had been to the front, with Graves himself feeling alienated because almost none of his fellow officers shared his literary interests, see Graves to Marsh, October 1915, 15

March 1916, *Letters 1914–46*, 34–5, 44; Graves to Sassoon, 27 May 1916, 23 June 1916, and to Nichols, 7 January 1917, ibid., 50, 51, 61; Graves, *GTAT*, 188. Contrast Graves to Marsh, October 1915, and to Sassoon, 31 July 1917, *Letters 1914–46*, 34, 80.

70. Graves, *GTAT*, 165–71 (quoted at 168). These difficulties intensified after Loos, according to Sassoon, because Graves began to question military decisions: Sassoon, *Memoirs of an Infantry Officer*, 80–1; RPG (1), 140. Graves reports these issues not only in regard to himself (Graves, *GTAT*, 180), but also to other officers (*GTAT*, 165–8, 207–8, 229–31, 315); cf. Wilson, *Sassoon (1886–1918)*, 329–30 (Sassoon treated this way in the 2nd Battalion as late as March 1917). His anger is expressed indirectly (displaced from officers to an 'Old Army' veteran in what the original version terms an 'allegory') in 'Sergeant-Major Money' (1917, first published 1924), in Robert Graves, *Poems about War*, ed. W. Graves (rev. edn, Mount Kisco, NY and London: Moyer Bell, 1990), 66, 98.
71. Graves, *GTAT*, 223. Although disliked by the older officers, he was better received by the younger ones, including Sassoon whom he met on this occasion for the first time. RPG (1), 141. For the changing profile of officers during the war, see Simpson, 'Officers', 81–4.
72. He hoped for a better reception since many of those who had given him a hostile one a year earlier were no longer there. However, one officer who remembered him restarted the rumour that he might be a spy. And, again, there was jealousy among line battalion officers at the faster promotion sometimes achieved by Special Reserve officers. Graves, *GTAT*, 258–60; RGP (1), 150.
73. Graves to Sassoon, 13 July 1916, *Letters 1914–46*, 55.
74. Graves, *GTAT*, 200–4 (damage caused by the right of the Governor-General of Jamaica to nominate a first lieutenant). The story 'Old Papa Johnson', in his *But It Still Goes On: an Accumulation* (Jonathan Cape, 1930; hereafter cited as *BISGO*), 57–70, imagines the devastating revenge taken by an experienced former junior officer on a snobbish former senior in the Indian Army who insists on his privileges.
75. His final invaliding home resulted from an all-night search for some highly-prized horses gone missing, since 'We had never lost a horse to any other battalion'. Graves, *GTAT*, 302–3.
76. Graves to Marsh, 9 February 1916, *Letters 1914–46*, 39; cf. to Sassoon, 23 June 1916, ibid., 53; Graves, *GTAT*, 117–26, 176–7, 179, 195–6, 222, 238–9.
77. Graves, *GTAT*, 239–40, 275–6.
78. Caesar, *Taking It Like a Man*, 189, 202–6; see n.133 below.
79. See 'A Renascence', in Graves, *Poems about War*, 15, which claims of the men in Flanders that 'of their travails and groans / Poetry is born again'. It was published in *Over the Brazier* in June 1916 after his effort to omit it came too late.
80. RPG (1), 130 n.66, points out that early in the war he went out patrolling in order to prove his courage, not (as he later cynically claimed: Graves, *GTAT*, 174) in the hope of getting a cushy wound. However, RPG (1), 140 and 345 n.99, contradicting *GTAT*, 218, is based on a misreading: it was the disgrace of being sent home for inefficiency that Graves wished to avoid, not the prospect of remaining in England as a training officer.

81. The sources for Graves's contemporary views are either his letters to family and friends, or their observations of him. The expression of his feelings in wartime letters is also tailored to some degree to particular recipients.
82. RPG (1), 137–8. Its impact on him is perhaps also registered in the addition—after the battle—of the final couplet of 'Big Words', which radically undermines its earlier claim of 'Winning a faith in the wisdom of God's ways / That once I lost', and being 'Ready, so soon as the need comes, to die'. Graves, *Poems about War*, 21, 93 note. For later reference by Graves himself to Loos as a major turning point, see below p.113; cf. Seymour, *Graves*, 47. Before Loos, he had already begun to write some poems which would earn him a reputation as one of the early realists among the war poets: e.g. 'A Dead Boche' (July 1915), *Poems about War*, 30.
83. Graves to Marsh, October 1915, *Letters 1914–46*, 34–5.
84. Direct impact: Graves, *GTAT*, 106–7, 327, 330; Graves to Sassoon, 9 July 1918, *Letters 1914–46*, 95. Atrocities: *GTAT*, 234–8; cf. Ferguson, *Pity of War*, 368–86; Bourke, *Intimate History of Killing*, 182–3, 189, 242; McCartney, *Citizen Soldiers*, 207.
85. Graves, *GTAT*, 76, 111, 159, 171, 205–6, 249–51, 283, 341–2.
86. 'Goliath and David', in Graves, *Poems about War*, 27–8. Quinn, *Great War*, 42, terms it a satire levelled 'not only at the traditional faith in God and country, but at those who write history in such a way as to suggest victory where none occurred'. It offers 'a bitter lament for the loss of innocence and the selfless sacrifice that young David made for his tribe'; his death 'is due as much to the deceptions and false tribal values' as to the enemy weapon.
87. Graves to Marsh, 15 March 1916, *Letters 1914–46*, 42–3, written three days before Thomas's death ('England's is a good cause enough'; but this letter has the air of whistling to keep his spirits up); Graves, *GTAT*, 249–52 (quoted at 252); RPG (1), 143–5. On the same night, two other officers were killed. For its impact, see below p.110–1.
88. Graves to Sassoon, 27 May 1916, *Letters 1914–46*, 50–1; cf. 23 June 1916 ('Roll on the trenches!...wish to hell I was with you—go on risking, and good luck. It's a man's game!'), ibid., 51–2.
89. Graves to Sassoon, 13 July 1916, *Letters 1914–46*, 55.
90. 'Letter to S.S., from Mametz Wood' (original title) and 'A Dead Boche', in Graves, *Poems about War*, 30, 40–2; RPG (1), 152–3.
91. Graves, *GTAT*, 272–80; RPG (1), 153–9.
92. Graves, *GTAT*, 141–2, 302.
93. RPG (2), 104 and n.127, 129–31; cf. RPG (1), 129; Graves, *GTAT*, 311–12. Graves, *BISGO*, 109–14, tells a black-farcical story (later incorporated into *GTAT* 1957, 165–7) of being morally blackmailed into accompanying his parents to church in 1916. For correction to the chronology, see RPG (1), 163, 346 n.127.
94. Graves, *GTAT*, 299, 309; but also Graves to Sassoon, 25 January 1917, *Letters 1914–46*, 63.
95. Graves, *GTAT*, 241–3.
96. Graves, *GTAT*, 160, 247–51; cf. 158–9, 189. Leed, *No Man's Land*, 127–8.
97. Graves, *GTAT*, 251–2; cf. 267.

98. The family had been holidaying there since 1897, when Amy decided to build a cottage; and in 1904, Graves had spent a convalescent term at a school there. From the summer of 1910, in particular, he had been drawn to it by its 'independence of formal nature' where he found 'a personal harmony independent of history or geography'. Graves, *GTAT*, 56–60 (quoted at 57, 58). This link to the area was strengthened when Mallory introduced him to rock-climbing in the Snowdon area immediately before the war (*GTAT*, 91–8). RPG (1), 34–6, 42–3, 52, 68–9, 151–2; Graves to Sassoon, 2 May 1916, *Letters 1914–46*, 45–6. It was to Harlech that Graves would go to recover his strength and nerves after demobilisation in 1919; and he was asked to make a speech about the glorious dead as the senior Man of Harlech who had served abroad (*GTAT*, 352).
99. Graves, *GTAT*, 253; RPG (1), 146–7; 'Over the Brazier', in Graves, *Poems about War*, 25.
100. Graves, *GTAT*, 57–8.
101. Graves, *GTAT*, 100, 187, 258–60.
102. The family trees in RPG (1), 10–15, show six members of the extended family killed on the German side, three on the British. Graves to Marsh, 7 August 1916, *Letters 1914–46*, 60; Graves, *GTAT*, 100–1, 175, 339. Richard Perceval Graves, *Robert Graves and the White Goddess, 1940–1985* (Weidenfeld &Nicolson, 1995; hereafter cited as RPG (3)), 500; Seymour, *Graves*, xvi, 432.
103. Graves to Marsh, 26 July 1916, *Letters 1914–46*, 56.
104. Typically, the trope of man becoming machine under the impact of war, which Ernst Jünger presents as desirable and other writers as regrettable (Bernard Bergonzi, *Heroes' Twilight: A Study of the Literature of the Great War* (3rd edn, Manchester: Carcanet, 1996), 145, 158–9), Graves presents as comic: the major with the transplanted gut ('Wonderful chaps these medicos. They can put in spare parts as if one was a motor-car'). Graves, GTAT, 292.
105. Graves himself notes twice, once with regard to a particular incident, once with regard to the war as a whole, that some situations defy comic treatment. Graves, *GTAT*, 155, 314; RPG (1), 125.
106. Graves, *GTAT*, 197–8.
107. Graves, *GTAT*, 205; cf. 211.
108. He notes the damaging effects on the men's morale of a temperance general who had forbidden the distribution of the daily rum ration through his division: Graves, *GTAT*, 296–7; and also gives other instances of officers needing drink to survive: 221, 299. He defends his handling of this question in *BISGO*, 17–18. This theme is also central to R.C. Sherriff's play *Journey's End* (1929).
109. The former had bred in Graves a prudishness which had made his time at Charterhouse miserable, and which continued to make him an object of banter among fellow officers during the war. Graves to Marsh, 3 February 1915, *Letters 1914–46*, 31; Graves, *GTAT*, 163–4, 231. His continuing discomfort comes through in his uneasy recounting of others' sexual exploits: *GTAT*, 105, 110, 127, 154, 163–4, 294, 311–12; Quinn, *Great War*, 32. Only by mid-1917 had he developed the confidence to retaliate in kind: *GTAT*, 313.
110. Caesar, *Taking It Like a Man*, 182–6, 190; Graves, *GTAT* 1957, 151.
111. Graves, *GTAT*, 163; cf. '1915' (winter 1915), Graves, *Poems about War*, 24 ('Dear, you've been everything that I most lack / ... Beautiful comrade-looks'); Seymour,

Graves, 45–6. Cf. RPG (1), 117; Graves to Marsh, October 1915, 24 February 1916, to Sassoon, 2 May 1916, *Letters 1914–46*, 34–5, 41–2, 46. Here again, the text by juxtaposition contrasts the 'solid and clean' (cf. earlier, 'chaste and sentimental', above p.103) love Graves felt for Johnstone, with the 'sordidness' of life at the front, which is represented immediately after (*GTAT*, 163–4) by stories of the degrading sexual behaviour with French women of both officers and men.

112. RPG (1), 130–1; cf. 135–6 (letter to his family leaving Johnstone his books).
113. Graves, *GTAT*, 163–4 (quoted at 163); RPG (1), 127–9.
114. Graves to Sassoon, 27 May 1916, *Letters 1914–46*, 50–1 (quoted); RPG (1), 148. For earlier anxieties about Johnstone's mother, Graves to Marsh, October 1915, 24 February 1916, *Letters 1914–46*, 35–6, 41. In the first draft of his 'Familiar Letter to Siegfried Sassoon' (written 13 July 1916), looking ahead to a desired post-war world, Graves hoped that Johnstone could win some of the affection Sassoon had felt for the dead David Thomas; these lines were omitted from the published version: Egremont, *Sassoon*, 105–6.
115. Graves to Sassoon, 4 August 1916, to Marsh, 7 August 1916, *Letters 1914–46*, 57, 60; RPG (1), 159, 166–7, 351 n.252; Graves to Sassoon, 25 January 1917, *Letters 1914–46*, 63.
116. Graves to Marsh, 12 July 1917, *Letters 1914–46*, 77; Graves, *GTAT*, 220; RPG (1), 177–8, 351 n.252.
117. Fussell, *Great War*, 214.
118. Graves, *GTAT*, 361; cf. 353. This shift would also replace one intense emotional moment, Sassoon's protest, with another, Loos.
119. Graves, *GTAT*, 306–7. A bond of sympathy may have been that she was given a hard time by other nurses for having a naturalised German father. On finding that she was engaged to a subaltern in Flanders, he stopped writing to her, even though she still seemed fond of him.
120. Graves, *GTAT* 1957, 204, makes a dramatic link between Marjorie and Johnstone: 'My heart had remained whole, if numbed, since Dick's disappearance from it, yet I felt difficulty in adjusting myself to the experience of woman love.' However, *GTAT*, 307, makes no such explicit connection, commenting simply: 'This was the first time that I had fallen in love with a woman, and I had difficulty in adjusting myself to the experience.' Instead, it connects Marjorie with his first date with Nancy, thereby reinforcing the caesura between the two forms of love: 332. Cf. RPG (1), 173–4, who reads this episode as representing the end of 'a prolonged adolescence of a kind not uncommon in the Graves family'.
121. Graves, *GTAT*, 39–40; cf. n.52 above. The plot of his melodramatic black farce of sexual confusion 'But It Still Goes On: a Play', in *BISGO*, 211–315, culminates in a murder and suicide. Cf. ch.9 n.28 below.
122. Graves, *GTAT*, 220. Johnstone had been bound over, and placed under medical care, treated and pronounced sufficiently cured to enlist. *GTAT*, 326; RPG 1995, 361, 234/4e. Cf. R.P. Graves's comment, RPG (1), 178: 'in doing so he played the part of a stern Victorian moralist not only with [Johnstone], but with himself'. In fact, Graves was still attached to and hurt by Johnstone years later. He underplays an occasion when, in 1920, he met him again: *GTAT*, 368. But

RPG (1), 225–6, cites a poem from this time partly about his loss; and Graves to Marsh, summer 1923, *Letters 1914–46*, 150, shows him still feeling it deeply (cf. RPG (1), 359 n.77). Graves later refused a legacy of books from Johnstone in 1949: Graves, *Letters 1914–46*, 78.

123. Carpenter: n.49 above; Sorley: Graves to Sassoon, [early May 1916], *Letters 1914–46*, 48.
124. Wilson, *Sassoon (1886–1918)*, 213–17, compares and contrasts the two men's personalities and backgrounds when they first met.
125. Graves to Marsh, 10 December 1915, *Letters 1914–46*, 37, describes Sassoon as 'a very nice chap but his verses, except occasionally, don't please me very much'. Sassoon, *Diaries 1915–1918*, 21 (2 December 1915), records reading Graves's poems in manuscript: 'some very bad, violent and repulsive'.
126. Graves, *GTAT*, 224, 261–2; RPG (1), 141. Cf. n.79 above.
127. It seems clear that the two men 'confided in each other and made reference to their own sexuality' (Wilson, *Sassoon (1886–1918)*, 307), since Graves's enquiry about Sorley's sexuality came in a letter to Sassoon, [May 1916], *Letters 1914–46*, 48. Sassoon later acknowledged, though he subsequently denied, the sexual element in his friendship with Graves: Wilson, 214–15.
128. Sassoon, *Diaries 1915–1918*, 98 (21 July 1916; quoted); Graves to Marsh, 10 December 1915, 15 March, 26 July 1916, *Letters 1914–46*, 37, 44, 56; to Sassoon, 2 May, [May], 27 May, 23 June, 13 July 1916, ibid., 45–55; Graves, *GTAT*, 263; RPG (1), 147–8, 150–2, 347 n.152; Wilson, *Sassoon (1886–1918)*, 273–6, 282–3. Thomas: 'Not Dead', in Graves, *Poems about War*, 32; RPG (1), 142–4. See also above p.109–10.
129. They were together for two weeks in Harlech, a week at Sassoon's family home, and seven weeks at Litherland.
130. Graves to Sassoon, 4 August 1916, *Letters 1914–46*, 57; *GTAT*, 263, 283, 288–9; RPG (1), 159, 161–2, 348 n.176; Wilson, *Sassoon (1886–1918)*, 283, 293–4. At this stage they planned a joint work like *Lyrical Ballads*: Wilson, 217, 283, 294, 297–8.
131. Graves, *GTAT*, 288. In *GTAT* 1957, 201–2, this discussion is moved to Graves's home posting in spring 1917: RPG 1995, 357, 218/10. RPG (1), 161–2.
132. For details, including a corrected timing of this joint visit (in mid-September 1916; *contra* RPG (1), 162 and 349 n.188), see Wilson, *Sassoon (1886–1918)*, 287–9, 294–6.
133. Graves, *GTAT*, 290–1 (quoted at 290); RPG (1), 163–4, 167–8, 349 n.195 (revising the timing of this sequence of events); Wilson, *Sassoon (1886–1918)*, 311–13, 318. Graves's less hostile attitude towards the war at this period is represented in two poems which praise the determination and constancy of the soldiers ('The Legion', 'To Lucasta on Going to the Wars—for the Fourth Time'), and a third which in celebrating his friendship with Sassoon seems to hark back to his view at the start of the war—'we faced him, and we found / Beauty in Death, / In dead men, breath' ('Two Fusiliers'). See Graves, *Poems about War*, 33–5. For Sassoon's evolving attitudes over this period, Wilson, 281–319.
134. Graves to Sassoon, 26 March, 21 April 1917, *Letters 1914–46*, 66–9; RPG (1), 171–2.

135. Graves, *GTAT*, 316–18 (quoted at 317–18); Graves to Sassoon, [30 June 1917], *Letters 1914–46*, 72.
136. Graves, *GTAT*, 318–19; RPG (1), 176–7.
137. Wilson, *Sassoon (1886–1918)*, 377; Egremont, *Sassoon*, 148–50; Graves to Marsh, 12 July 1917, *Letters 1914–46*, 77 (quoted).
138. He was helped by Robbie Ross and others with government contacts; and encouraged Sassoon's close friend Hanmer to urge him to withdraw: Wilson, *Sassoon (1886–1918)*, 380–1.
139. Graves, *GTAT*, 322–5; RPG (1), 177–81. For corrections to the misleading chronology in *GTAT*, see RPG (1), 351 n.250, 352–3 note to ch.14, 353 nn.255–6.
140. Graves, who believed that the pacifists had exploited Sassoon, was himself able to exploit the decision of the Board. He wrote to Russell informing him of the outcome, and to Marsh that 'I've written to the pacifists who were to support him telling them that the evidence as to his mental condition given at his Medical Board is quite enough to make them look damned silly if they go on with the game and ask questions in the House about his defiance.' Graves to Marsh, 19 July 1917 (quoted), to Russell [July 1917], *Letters 1914–46*, 79, 355 n.85.
141. Graves, *GTAT*, 325–6, 338.
142. Graves, *GTAT*, 338–9; RPG (1), 185–6. Graves had written to Sassoon: 'Everybody here who's been to France agrees with your point of view, but those that don't know you think it was not quite a gentlemanly course to take: the "quixotic-English-sportsman" class especially': 31 July 1917, *Letters 1914–46*, 80; Wilson, *Sassoon (1886–1918)*, 382.
143. The dilemma which both Graves and Sassoon were wrestling with here has been explored by Barham, *Forgotten Lunatics*, 60–2. Drawing on the work of Zizek and Lacan, he suggests that: 'what may have been at stake for some of the servicemen who took part in the Great War may be gleaned from the account of the subject whose life is bound to a traditional authority, and to a symbolic order (what Lacan terms the "big Other")'. For 'even if the subject may willingly have embraced the signifier which represents him for the other, as by volunteering for the cause, still it becomes apparent quite soon that there has been a misunderstanding, and that the subject's idea of who he is, and of what he has let himself in for, is quite at odds with the mandate that has been foisted upon him by the authorities.' Both Graves and Sassoon recognised that the contract or mandate was not what they had signed up for; for Graves it was essential to continue carrying it out nonetheless, for Sassoon to reject it.
144. Graves to Sassoon, 27 October 1917, *Letters 1914–46*, 85–6.
145. Quinn, *Great War*, 22: Graves 'seldom faced up to ugliness of battle…he looks but he does not want "to see".' After Sassoon's protest, Graves replaced him as dedicatee of his 1917 volume *Fairies and Fusiliers* with the RWF: Caesar, *Taking It Like a Man*, 201–2. Seymour, *Graves*, 70–1, quotes a letter from Graves to Gosse (24 October 1917) claiming to share Sassoon's feelings, but believing his role was 'keeping up my brother soldiers' morale'; nevertheless, a sense of hopelessness about both the war and the possibility of preventing another is evident in 'The Next War' (1917): Graves, *Poems about War*, 43–4.

146. Graves to Sassoon, [November 1917], *Letters 1914–46*, 87. Sassoon wrote to Ottoline Morrell: 'I don't think [Graves] feels things as deeply as some': RPG (1), 187. Seymour, *Graves*, 84–5, however, quotes poems of 1918 showing Graves haunted in much the same way as Sassoon: 'Dead, long dead, I'm ashamed to greet / Dead men down the morning street' ('Haunted'; Graves, *Poems about War*, 54).
147. Graves to Sassoon, 9 July 1918 (quoted), *Letters 1914–46*, 95; cf. 6 February 1918, Wilson, *Sassoon (1886–1918)*, 437; 26 August 1918 (quoted below p.119), 11 September 1918, *Letters 1914–46*, 95, 101–2.
148. Graves, *GTAT*, 339–41; RPG (1), 198–9.
149. Graves to Sassoon, 21 April 1917, *Letters 1914–46*, 68 ('I'm cured of the desire to go back to France (I know I'm more use here and would only crock [*sic*] up if I tried a fourth time)'); to Nichols, [Nov. 1917], ibid., 89 ('I'd go [lecturing in America] like a shot only I am still able to fight again and I feel I must.'). Graves, *GTAT*, 330–3; RPG (1), 183, 186.
150. Graves, *GTAT*, 289, 331–2 (quoted at 332); RPG (1), 168, 182–4; Seymour, *Graves*, 59.
151. Graves, *GTAT*, 332, 335; RPG (1), 188–9.
152. Graves to Sassoon, [November 1917]; to Nichols, [November 1917]; to Marsh, 29 December 1917; to Sassoon, 23 May 1918: Graves, *Letters 1914–46*, 88, 89, 90, 94; RPG (1), 186; cf. 188–9, 354 n.292. The language which Graves uses in these letters indicates a degree of defensiveness, and anticipation of surprise on the part of his friends. Sassoon's response, and subsequent distancing from Graves, suggests that he was both surprised and disappointed: Wilson, *Sassoon (1886–1918)*, 431–2.
153. Quinn, *Great War*, 52–4.
154. Graves, *GTAT*, 335–6; RPG (1), 191–4.
155. Graves to Sassoon, 11 January 1918, *Letters 1914–46*, 91; *GTAT*, 335; RPG (1), 190.
156. Graves, *GTAT*, 342. Cf. RPG (1), 193; Graves to Sassoon, 9 July 1918, *Letters 1914–46*, 95 ('if I only had myself to think about I'd change places with you at once despite my hellish fear of the La Bassée country and my waking terror of poison gas').
157. Graves to Sassoon, 26 August 1918, *Letters 1914–46*, 101.
158. Graves to Marsh, January 1919, *Letters 1914–46*, 107–8; RPG (1), 201, 356 n.364.
159. 'A Dead Boche', in Graves, *Poems about War*, 30.

5 Scott Macfie

1. The main biographical source for Macfie is the memorial volume published after his death, comprising Frederick George Ackerley, 'Friend of all the world: a memoir of Robert Andrew Scott Macfie', *Journal of the Gypsy Lore Society* (3rd Series) 14 [Special number] (1935), 5–43 (hereafter cited as Ackerley), and 'Memories of R.A. Scott Macfie', by his friends, ibid., 47–110 (cited as 'Memories'). His letters and related papers as Secretary of the Gypsy Lore Society are preserved in the GLS Archive, and the Scott Macfie Gypsy

Collection, Special Collections and Archives, Sydney Jones Library, University of Liverpool. Citations of his letters of 1913–14 from the GLS Letter Books include the volume and page number(s) (e.g. GLS A34 129). His letters to his family during the First World War are preserved in the Scott Macfie Papers, Department of Documents, Imperial War Museum, London. Citations include the volume number (e.g. IWM/1); the addressees are referred to by the familiar form of address which Macfie used. Grandfather: Ackerley, 7–8; Christine MacLeod, 'Macfie, Robert Andrew (1811–1893)', *Oxford Dictionary of National Biography* (Oxford: Oxford University Press, 2004; http://www.oxforddnb.com/view/article/17499, accessed 2.11.06). Macfie's father John William Macfie (1844–1924) and mother Helen, née Wahab, (1844–96) had ten children, of whom he was the eldest; eight survived into adult life. See Marilyn Ainslie Family Trees <http://www.ainslie.org.uk/genealogy/barbour/dat19.htm#4> (accessed 3.11.06).

2. Ackerley, 16; A.A. Cumming, in 'Memories', 65–6.
3. In one of his few direct references to his religious upbringing, he commented: 'I have a superstitious dislike of beginning anything and leaving it—the result of a Presbyterian upbringing and the text about setting one's hands to the plough!' Macfie to A. Russell, 30 July 1914, GLS A35 769.
4. G. H. Goldsmith, in 'Memories', 75. He later ran a weekend camp for young lads near Liverpool: E. Holden, ibid., 67. Cf. above p.75.
5. Ackerley, 15. Dwight L. Moody (1837–99) visited Britain in both 1891 and 1892.
6. The firm had taken over in 1894 a sugar-beet refining factory in Rawcliffe, East Yorkshire; and Macfie was sent there to run it. While there is nothing to suggest that its failure in the following year was in any way his responsibility, he may perhaps have reacted to this failure as a personal setback. Ackerley, 6–7, 16; J.A. Angus, in 'Memories', 64. There is some suggestion that his own conditions there were not very comfortable, though Macfie himself denied this was behind his action: 'Nearly everyone seems to have jumped to the conclusion that I was so ill treated at Rawcliffe, that I gave up and enlisted! Even the clerk…wrote to condole with me!': Ackerley, 17.
7. There was clearly an embarrassed reaction in his family. He wrote that a friend had said: 'the Pater [his father] wants my enlistment kept quiet. Please take no notice but mention it to everyone you can. If people try and hush it up and make a mystery of it, it will seem as if I have done something of which I am ashamed.' Ackerley, 17. The sources do not indicate whether he left of his own choice or under pressure from his family.
8. Ackerley, 18; cf. 15.
9. Ackerley, 18. Macfie wrote (quoted ibid.): 'While in London, I did a lot of reading in the British Museum and went to most of the places of entertainment (gallery as a rule) but as I had only working men's clothes with me I did no visiting except going twice to lunch with Uncle Ned. On the whole I had an interesting time but got eaten up by vermin.'
10. Ackerley, 18–19 (quoted at 19).
11. Koven, *Slumming*, 1–87; Peter Keating (ed.), *Into Unknown England 1866–1913: Selections from the Social Explorers* (Fontana, 1976), 11–31. Charles Booth, in his

investigation of London poverty in the 1880s, took lodgings in poor districts, but never disguised himself: T.S. Simey and M.B. Simey, *Charles Booth: Social Scientist* (Oxford University Press, 1960), 65, 103–6.

12. A striking parallel is T.E. Lawrence's re-enlistment as an airman in the mid–1920s. William Armstrong, in 'Memories', 69, compares Macfie with Lawrence: both men had 'a unique sympathy for the failures of this world and "the might-have-beens"'. Cf. H.C. Dowdall, ibid., 72–3.
13. Koven, *Slumming*, 4–5, 253–4. Such settlers 'refused to emulate the bourgeois paterfamilias's devotion either to traditional family life or to the single-minded pursuit of individual self-interest in the market place. By settling in the slums, these men carved out for themselves a social space where, with the approval of society, they could place fraternity before domesticity.' (281). Cf. Tosh, *A Man's Place*, ch.8.
14. Ackerley, 22. His concern for the workmen had been shared by his paternal grandfather, to whom he was close: 7–8; cf. 16–17.
15. Macfie to F. Shaw, 26 November 1913, A34 645–6; to Russell, 28 November 1913, A34 662–3; to F. G. Ackerley, 2 December, 16 December 1913, A34 681, 732–4; to F. S. Atkinson, 17 December 1913, A34 736–7; to H. Ehrenborg, 13 January 1914, A34 864–5.
16. Ackerley wrote (22): 'he had now, at the age of just over thirty, at last found his real vocation—a double vocation—the fostering of Gypsy studies on the one hand, and the building up into efficiency of the newly formed battalion of the Liverpool Scottish on the other. Until now he had been without any clear aim in life. The business of the firm never really engaged his full energies, though he did his work for the refinery thoroughly.'
17. Formally, the 8th (Scottish) Volunteer Battalion, The King's (Liverpool) Regiment; it was redesignated in 1908, on the replacement of the Volunteers by the new Territorial Force, as the 10th (Scottish) Battalion, The King's (Liverpool) Regiment; cf. above p.72. Continuity between Volunteers and Territorials: McCartney, *Citizen Soldiers*, 19.
18. McCartney, *Citizen Soldiers*, 30, 48, suggests that, although entry requirements included a non-manual occupation and an annual 10 shilling membership fee, recruitment was not in practice so exclusive, and reached down into the skilled artisan working class. Its Scottish social identity: 15, 20 (quoted), 30. A number of its recruits were drawn from the large Presbyterian congregations in the city, including Macfie's friend Sgt J.G.C. Moffat, who was a church elder. (52)
19. On his way to his brother's wedding in Canada in 1904, he wrote: 'I was rather glad to escape for a month from my double slavery of sugar and volunteering…I have been devoting absolutely the whole of my leisure and part of my sleep to volunteering with, at last, most gratifying results.' Ackerley, 22–4 (quoted at 24). His involvement may have been impelled in part by family influences. His paternal grandfather was described as 'in favour of economy in every public department without stinting the volunteer force': Michael Stenton (ed.), *Who's Who of British Members of Parliament, vol.1: 1832–1885* (Hassocks: Harvester, 1976), 251. His maternal grandfather, Charles Wahab, also Scottish, from whom he inherited 'marked traits', had been a Major-General in the Queen's Indian Service: Ackerley, 8.

20. The Club was founded in 1896; Macfie, one of those first elected, remained a member till 1903. This informal discussion circle brought him into contact with the group of leading scholars who were at that time building up the University College (which became an independent university in 1903). They included John Sampson, a self-educated scholar who became the first Librarian at the University of Liverpool and pioneer of Gypsy studies. Macfie seems to have begun to interest himself in Gypsies in the late 1890s. Before Christmas 1899 he lived in a tent with them outside Liverpool for a fortnight, and wrote: 'I am very much interested in the Gypsies and they seem to have taken to me in a way they seldom do to "foreigners" or *gorgios* as they call them. I am very proud of the title "Romano Rai", and enjoy cooking my own tea, supper and breakfast.' Ackerley, 20–1, 23–4; Anthony Sampson, *The Scholar Gypsy: the Quest for a Family Secret* (John Murray, 1997), 76–7. He later had Gypsies to stay in his house: Myers, in 'Memories', 56. On Gypsies camping near Liverpool in the early twentieth century, see Sampson, 18, 29, 60–2, 75, 107–9.
21. Dora E. Yates, *My Gypsy Days: Recollections of a Romani Rawnie* (Phoenix House, 1953), 163–7. He had to give up editing the journal when he enlisted in 1914; but arranged for three colleagues to take it over, and made determined efforts, including significant financial support, to keeping it alive during the war years; he later resumed the editorship in 1932–5: Yates, 171–7. For a positive evaluation of his role, see Angus Fraser, 'A Rum Lot', in Matt T. Salo, *100 Years of Gypsy Studies: Papers from the 10th Annual Meeting of the Gypsy Lore Society* (Gypsy Lore Society no.5: Cheverly, MD: The Society, 1990), 9–10; David Mayall, *Gypsy Identities 1500–2000: from Egipcyans and Moon-Men to the Ethnic Romany* (Routledge, 2004), 164. To avoid confusion in discussing the works of Macfie and his contemporaries, I use their terminology in referring to Gypsies and Mohammedan, although the preferred terms today would be Roma/Sinti and Muslim/Islamic; cf. Deborah E. Nord, *Gypsies and the British Imagination, 1807–1930* (New York: Columbia University Press, 2006), 18–19.
22. Yates, *My Gypsy Days*, 106.
23. There are some hints which may point towards a personal identification with Gypsies: Ackerley, 17, prefaces his account of Macfie's running away in 1895 by noting that there is a Scottish proverb: 'Every Macfie is a gypsy'. For similar claims by other Gypsiologists, see Sampson, *Scholar Gypsy*, 26.
24. Nord, *Gypsies*, chs 1–2.
25. Fraser, 'A Rum Lot'; Ken Lee, 'Orientalism and Gypsylorism', *Social Analysis: Journal of Cultural and Social Practice* [Adelaide] 44.2 (2000), 129–56; Mayall, *Gypsy Identities*, 162–4, 166. Nord, *Gypsies*, 126–7, 129–31, emphasises their status between amateur and semi-professional scholars, outside universities.
26. Lee, 'Orientalism and Gypsylorism', 135–6, comments: 'Romanies could be seen as exotic and anachronistic outsiders in a modern setting—the exotics/primitives within…Gypsies also provided an important symbolic construct as a rhetorically idealised source of Romantic principles of freedom and Nature.' Sampson, *Scholar Gypsy*, 21: 'the Romanophiles liked to see them as belonging to the youth of the world, to the golden age of innocence'; cf. 65, 69, 75, 99, 115, 143. On Borrow, see Nord, *Gypsies*, ch.3; and on his reinterpretation by late nineteenth-century Gypsiologists, 74–5, 126–30, 134, 136,

143. Cf. Mayall, *Gypsy Identities*, 156–61, who comments (161): 'The stimulus from Borrow was probably more to their [Gypsylorists'] (romantic) imagination than to their scholarly efforts.'

27. Fraser, 'A Rum Lot', 7–8; Sampson, *Scholar Gypsy*, 19, 27; Nord, Gypsies, 137–9; Macfie to J. Harris Stone, 5 May 1914, GLS A35 361–2 (evoking this romantic vision). Alan Sinfield, *The Wilde Century: Effeminacy, Oscar Wilde and the Queer Moment* (New York: Columbia University Press, 1994), 114–15, quotes John Addington Symonds's invocation, in 'Paths of Life' (1882), of comradeship which 'spreads / Tents on the open road, field, ocean, camp, / Where'er in brotherhood men lay their heads. / Soldier with soldier, tramp with casual tramp, / Cross and recross, meet, part, share boards and beds. / Where wayside Love still lights his beaconing lamp'; and C.K. Jackson's celebration, in 'The new chivalry' (1894), of the male companionship 'of the river, of the hunt and the moor, the evening tent-pitching of campers out, and the exhilaration of the early morning swim'. It is this aspect of the Gypsy way of life which seems to have strongly attracted Augustus John: Michael Holroyd, *Augustus John: a Biography* (rev. edn, Harmondsworth: Penguin, 1976), 356–60, 394–402.
28. Mayall, *Gypsy Identities*, 169.
29. Mayall, *Gypsy Identities*, 179. Although Macfie himself was a businessman, he seems to have been more content with the life of an independent scholar; and it was such a marginal role which he took up in retirement.
30. Alan Sinfield, *Out on Stage: Lesbian and Gay Theatre in the Twentieth Century* (New Haven, CT: Yale University Press, 1999), 48–9, writes: 'bohemia constituted a fairly sustained alternative [to the authority of Society], affording principled justification for what would otherwise have been merely disreputable behaviour'; and suggests that cities provided suitable spaces for Raymond Williams's dissident avant-garde class fractions. Cf. Nord, *Gypsies*, 131–2.
31. Nord, *Gypsies*, 137, suggests that: 'It is no accident that the Gypsy Lore Society grew up around Liverpool, with its urban intensity and its proximity to sparsely settled countryside.' Apart from Macfie himself, the Liverpool members included Sampson: Sampson, *Scholar Gypsy*, 47–8, 60, 65, 75; and (in 1901–2) Augustus John: Holroyd, *Augustus John*, 141–54, 156–66. Sampson, John and other Gypsiologists (and some of their artist friends) took the opportunity for short-lived encounters with Gypsy women: Sampson, 78–9, 91–6, 101–3, 106–9. Such behaviour had to be kept separate from daily professional life; Anthony Sampson, 68, writes of his grandfather's life after 1900: 'These young academics could openly pursue their romance with the gypsies beyond the confines of the city. But there were strict limits to the defiance of academic respectability. And [Sampson] was becoming increasingly divided between the two sides of his life, his respectable family ménage soon being threatened by his obsession with the gypsies and the lure of Bohemia.'
32. For the achievements of the GLS, see Mayall, *Gypsy Identities*, 41, 178; Nord, *Gypsies*, 126–7, 129–30, 140–3, 152–3.
33. Stereotyping: Nord, *Gypsies*, ch.5; Mayall, *Gypsy Identities*, ch.5. Patronage: Mayall, 174–9.
34. Herbert Heuss, 'Anti-Gypsyism Research: the Creation of a New Field of Study', in T. Acton (ed.), *Scholarship and the Gypsy Struggle: Commitment in Romani*

Studies (Hatfield: University of Hertfordshire Press, 2000), 52–3, links these two stances as opposite sides of the same coin in contemporary society.

35. Lee, 'Orientalism and Gypsylorism', offers a detailed analysis of what he terms 'Gypsylorism' as a parallel knowledge/power relationship to Said's *Orientalism*. 'Whilst Orientalism is the discursive construction of the exotic Other *outside* Europe, Gypsylorism is the construction of the exotic Other *within* Europe—Romanies are the Orientals within' (132). Cf. Fraser, 'A Rum Lot', 7; Nord, *Gypsies*, 2–5.
36. Macfie to J. Casey, 20 May 1914, GLS A35 466–9 (quoted at 467); cf. to Gilliat-Smith, 9 October 1913, A34 429–33. He was capable, at times, of more realistic, if regretful, perceptions, about the realities of contemporary Gypsy life on the margins of British cities, and about his own desire to see them as more exotic than perhaps they were: to Mrs C.M. Berry, 30 May 1914, A35 526–8; to E.O. Winstedt, 4 June 1914, A35 543–5.
37. Macfie to Mrs Duff, 15 April 1913, GLS A34 55.
38. Mayall, *Gypsy Identities*, 129, cites T.W. Thompson writing in 1910: 'They are untruthful, but their untruthfulness is simple the unfettered imagination of children.' Cf. E.O. Winstedt, 'Gypsy "Civilisation"', *Journal of the Gypsy Lore Society* New Series 1.4 (1907–8), 346.
39. E. Holden, in 'Memories', 67; cf. his assisting the army deserter: above p.124.
40. Macfie to Mrs Berry, 2 October 1913, GLS A34 406–7.
41. Macfie spent a total of six weeks in the Balkans, first visiting Gypsy communities in Athens and then Salonika, before arriving in Varna. He stayed there for just over three weeks, visiting various Gypsy groups, sometimes in the company of Gilliat-Smith. R.A.S. Macfie, 'Balkan notes. By Andreas', *Journal of the Gypsy Lore Society* New Series 7.1 (1914), 41–59.
42. Macfie to H.L. Williams, 15 April 1913, GLS A34 51; to Dr Hugh K. Anderson, 15 April 1913, A34 54; to Mrs Duff, 15 April 1913, A34 55; to Shaw, 6 August 1913, A34 100–2. He clearly looked forward to it, writing to Gilliat-Smith (15 April 1913, A34 53): 'The rest of my trousseau must be got today. I feel as if I were on the threshold of a great adventure.'
43. Robert Andrew Scott Macfie, *With Gypsies in Bulgaria*, by Andreas ('Mui Shuko') (Liverpool: Henry Young and Sons, 1916; hereafter cited as WGB), 3. 'Balkan Notes' briefly outlines his visits to Athens, Salonika, Varna and Galatz; while *WGB* gives a much fuller account of his journey from Varna to Rustshuk.
44. Ackerley, 19–20.
45. He referred to Bulgaria as: 'a country…peopled by representatives of several jealous races, with none of whom I could exchange a single word of conversation, but who all, except the Turks, are barbarian at heart in spite of an ancient Christianity and a new cheap plaster civilization which is rather apt to peel.' *WGB*, 35 (quoted), 38. Cf. Macfie to H.H. Malleson, 9 August 1913, GLS A34 122–3: 'I don't like the cloddish lout, the Bulgarian: and I do like the clean dignified and goodhumoured Turk.' He does here go on to admit: 'It would need a long residence there to understand the people.' In similar vein, his earlier praise of the Turks had been accompanied by the remark: 'My impression of the Armenian question is that the Armenians are a pack of ungrateful idiots.' Ackerley, 19–20.

46. Macfie, *WGB*, 35, 38, 78, 86.
47. Macfie, *WGB*, 46. Macfie's Turkophilia was within the dominant nineteenth century tradition of writing about the Balkans by the British elite, arising from a class-based aristocratic empathy with Ottoman notables, reinforced by the political imperative to support the Ottoman Empire against the growth of Russian power. He was not influenced by the emergent 'pro-Christian bias among the liberal middle class' which culminated in Gladstone's denunciation of the Bulgarian massacres after 1876. Maria Todorova, *Imagining the Balkans* (New York: Oxford University Press, 1997), 90–110 (quoted at 96); cf. Andrew Hammond, 'The Uses of Balkanism: Representation and Power in British Travel Writing, 1850–1914', *Slavonic and East European Review* 82.3 (2004), 605–14. Hammond argues, 603–5, that most British travellers to the Balkans in this period, whatever particular causes they supported, were agreed that the region needed to be governed by an external source (Ottoman or Austrian).
48. Macfie, *WGB*, 35, 37.
49. Macfie, *WGB*, 30, 37–8.
50. Macfie, *WGB*, 35–6, 45–6; cf. Macfie to Malleson, 19 December 1913, GLS A34 755–7, 27 June 1914, A35 643–5, 6 July 1914, A35 683–5; to Miss E. Durham, 24 July 1914, A35 755.
51. Ackerley, 15, notes that he was impatient of dogma and looked for religion to be practical.
52. Macfie, *WGB*, 50–1 (quoted at 50), 85–6 (quoted); cf. 78. His imagined comparison of it with 'a huge Byzantine cathedral' (85) reinforces the almost religious value he places on this practical building.
53. His association of Islam with a cleanliness which Christianity easily dispensed with may support this suggestion.
54. Macfie to the Rev. Kwaja Kiamil-ud-Din, 30 January 1914, GLS A34 941; 3 February 1914, A34 949. Already, shortly after his return, he had written: 'I always wished in Bulgaria that I was a Mohammedan—someday I must see if the change is practical politics.' Macfie to Russell, 25 September 1913, A34 379–80; cf. to Gilliat-Smith, 12 March 1914, A35 138–9.
55. J. G. Coltart Moffat, in 'Memories', 89. Ackerley, 14–15, himself an Anglican cleric, reported that Macfie used to tease him by asserting that he proposed to convert.
56. 'Of course, if one grants that our commercial civilization is the best possible civilization, there's nothing to be said for the Turk; but having so much to do with a factory I'm not sure that my men would not be better meditating and spoiling their livers with black coffee in some dignified little khan.' Macfie to Malleson, 9 July 1914, GLS A35 705–7.
57. Macfie, *WGB*, 96.
58. Macfie, *WGB*, 8–9.
59. Macfie's extended comparison with children here replicates tropes common throughout the writing of the Gypsiologists; cf. Mayall, *Gypsy Identities*, 129; Sampson, *Scholar Gypsy*, 21.
60. Macfie, *WBG*, 19–20.
61. Macfie, *WGB*, 22–6, 29–30 (quoted at 29); cf. 75–6.
62. Macfie, *WGB*, 27–8. He later came to suspect that all the group he travelled

with were also mixed up in coining: Macfie to Winstedt, 12 September 1913, A34 306; 16 September 1913, A34 317.

63. Macfie, *WGB*, 27; 77–8, 82–3, cf. 106, 125, 134; 108–9; 113–16, 125.
64. Macfie, *WGB*, 21, 56, 72, 74.
65. Macfie, *WGB*, 88–9. For a fuller discussion of this scene, see my 'Dis/Connecting Whiteness', 79–81.
66. Macfie, *WGB*, 20, 25, 72. He notes that Petrika's and Totana's temperaments 'seemed almost incompatible. He may have had a wild youth, but little wildness had survived'; and then gives a long account of an incident when—'[w]eary of respectability, bored to death, yearning for adventure'—she ran away from Petrika (25–6). This narrative seems to represent both the tension within Macfie himself, and perhaps between him and his father.
67. Macfie, *WGB*, 80.
68. Cf. his earlier escapade with the Army deserter.
69. Macfie remarked that 'filial piety came before brotherly love': *WGB*, 121, 126–7, 130 (quoted).
70. Macfie, *WGB*, 56, 116–17, 120–3, 131–3.
71. 'In the sight of God, he said, we were brothers.' Macfie, *WGB*, 126–7, 130 (quoted).
72. As they parted on the Danube steamer, Turi warned him in similar terms against the Romanians: Macfie, *WGB*, 141.
73. As well as the slightly earlier Symonds, they include Edward Carpenter and E.M. Forster; see Weeks, *Coming Out*, 47–56, 68–83; Sinfield, *Wilde Century*, 149–50. Weeks's description (79) of Carpenter's relationship with George Merrill, the working-class man with whom he lived for the second half of his life, touches on some elements of Macfie's attraction to Turi, and to Gypsies more generally. Carpenter 'found in Merrill that spontaneity, closeness to the earth and devotion that, while struggling against his bourgeois upbringing, he had always craved. He would excuse some of Merrill's excesses in later life by referring to his "childlike spontaneity"...The relationship did not entirely transcend the class or intellectual differences, and there was a strong romanticism on each side.'
74. Aldrich, *Seduction of the Mediterranean*, chs 2, 6.
75. Ackerley, 18–19, and E. Holden, in 'Memories', 67 (celebrating his return from the South African War in 1900).
76. Tosh, 'Masculinities', 333, underlines the Victorian valuing of the home as a haven from the materially and morally alienating features of urban, industrial, market-driven society. In that context, homosexuality was seen as 'a rejection of bourgeois masculinity, in seeming to place personal gratification above the demands of work and in undermining the authority of the domestic ideal' (338). Macfie's homosocial life-style, as both Volunteer and Gypsiologist, can be seen as offering a parallel haven, which yet rejects the domestic.
77. This is apparent in the closing scene of *WGB*, when Macfie and Turi, about to part, are joined by Dr Marko Markoff, a local lawyer who has campaigned on behalf of Roma. Macfie comments: 'It was strange to sit there in Turkish disguise, and burned brown as a Gypsy by the sun, enjoying intellectual intercourse after a week with semi-savages, and hearing again my own language.

But it was difficult to relapse suddenly into civilization, and perhaps the effort to present myself alternatively to Dr Marko as an educated man, and to the Gypsies as a comrade, intensified the pain of those last minutes.' *WGB*, 135, 139–41 (quoted at 139).

78. Macfie to Mrs Gilliat-Smith, 22 December 1913, A34 768–70; to Gilliat-Smith, 12 March 1914, GLS A35 138–9, 8–9 June 1914, A35 561–2, 14 July 1914, A35 723–5; to J. Casey, 28 April 1914, A35 337–8; to Miss Durham, 24 July 1914, A35 755. For a fuller exploration of the meanings of Macfie's journey, and his textual representations of it, see my 'Flirting and Translating: Concealing/Revealing Same-Sex Desire in the Writings of Scott Macfie' (in preparation).
79. Macfie, *WGB*, 96–7. Café: above p.130.
80. Through his paternal grandfather, Macfie had a Liberal political inheritance, which may well have influenced some of his attitudes and values. But he seems to have developed a pointed rejection of conventional politics and politicians that at times verged on a contempt for democracy. Macfie to Ehrenborg, 26 September 1913, GLS A34 388; Macfie to Shiela (he consistently spells her name thus), 12 July 1915, IWM/3. His irritated response to an approach to stand for Liverpool City Council in the Conservative and Protestant interests ('if I took to politics, I should become a rabid socialist or a "Free Fooder" or something extreme, and having distinct leanings, the result of my Balkan trip, towards Mohammedanism, I refused': to W. MacLeod, 19 August 1913, GLS A34 175; cf. to Gilliat-Smith, 14 August 1913, A34 157) suggests a rather inchoate, somewhat anarchic, stance, hostile to the political and religious establishment. During the war his anti-political position seems to have hardened: Macfie to Charlie, 10 November 1917, IWM/5; to Shiela, 29 September 1918, IWM/6.
81. Ackerley, 30; Macfie to D. MacRitchie, 4 August 1914, GLS A35 773; to Ackerley, 4 August 1914, A35 774; to Winstedt, 5 August 1914, A35 777.
82. Macfie to Jack (quoted), 9 August 1914; to Jenny, 14 August 1914; to father, 22 August, 30 August 1914; to Charlie, 9 September 1914; to Ailie, 2 January 1915 (all IWM/1). The upper age limit for volunteers, initially thirty, was raised to thirty-five at the end of August, and forty-five for former soldiers by late October 1914: Bourne, *Britain and the Great War*, ix; Beckett, 'Nation in Arms', 8–9.
83. Beckett, 'Territorial Force', 128–33. By September 1913, only 7% of officers and men had taken the Imperial Service obligation, committing themselves in advance to overseas service in the event of war. For details of the changing volunteering requirements for a unit to be sent abroad during August 1914, see Ian Beckett, 'The Territorial Force in the Great War', in Peter H. Liddle (ed.), *Home Fires and Foreign Fields: British Social and Military Experience in the First World War* (Brassey's Defence Publishers, 1985), 22–4.
84. Macfie to father, 25 August 1914; cf. to Shiela, 1 September 1914 (both IWM/1).
85. Macfie to Shiela, 12 July 1915, IWM/3; cf. to Jenny, 13 March 1917, IWM/5, re newly-arrived conscripts: 'I hope to have the pleasure of making the lives of some of these unpatriotic jelly-fish a misery to them!' Cf. n.91 below.

86. Macfie to Charlie, 31 March 1915, IWM/2; cf. 11 April 1915, IWM/2; 22 May 1915, IWM/3; 5 April 1916, IWM/4.
87. Macfie to father, 2 December 1914, 23 December 1914, IWM/1.
88. Macfie to father, 19 June 1915 (original emphasis), cf. to Shiela, 28 June 1915; to Jack, 3 July 1915 (all IWM/3). On Hooge, see McCartney, *Citizen Soldiers*, 203–9; ch.3 n.90 above. Cf. his earlier report of heavy losses: to father, 23 December 1914, IWM/1; and an account a year later to his father (15 August 1916, IWM/4) of an assault on a village which had often been attacked before, without success. The Liverpool Scottish effort was no exception: 'of my company 177 went up—twenty were killed, forty-two wounded, and about eight are missing (i.e. in all probability, dead). The want of preparation, the vague orders, the ignorance of the objective and geography, the absurd haste, and in general the horrid bungling were scandalous. After two years of war it seems that our higher commanders are still without common sense. In any well regulated organisation a divisional commander would be shot for incompetence—here another regiment is ordered to attempt the same task in the same muddling way. It was worse than Hooge, much worse—and it is still going on!'
89. Macfie to father, 13 December 1914; cf. to his brother Jack (a doctor), 3 January 1915 (both IWM/1): 'The doctor's duty is mostly to compell [*sic*] sick men to go on fighting until they actually collapse'.
90. On the death of Ackerley's nephew, Macfie wrote to him (7 July 1915): 'the sacrifice of these young and hopeful lives is one of the things—to me the most horrible—that make this War so utterly loathsome.' Quoted in Ackerley, 32–3; cf. 40. W. Armstrong, in 'Memories', 69, cites him as saying: 'It is the most terrible form of madness, gruesome and horrible in every aspect'.
91. Macfie to father, 21 December 1918; cf. to Shiela, 3 February 1919 (both IWM/6).
92. Moffat, in 'Memories', 92: 'his age manifestly unfitted him for service in the trenches'; S. E. Lyttle, in 'Memories', 94: 'He had no need to be at the Front. Promotion or Total Exemption were his for the asking.' Only in the desperate circumstances of April 1918 did the age of conscription catch up with Macfie: Beckett, 'Nation in Arms', 14.
93. No commission: Macfie to father, 30 August 1914; cf. to Jenny, 16 September 1914 (both IWM/1). No service back at base: see below p.137.
94. Macfie to father, 9 November 1914, 2 December 1914 (both IWM/1).
95. Not in front line: Macfie to Ailie, 2 January 1915, IWM/1; to father, 9 January 1915, IWM/2; to Jack, 3 July 1915, IWM/3. Moffat, in 'Memories', 92: 'when I joined him [in the trenches] in 1916, I found him close behind the line in a "forward dump". For he had no patience with the comparative safety of the other Quartermaster-Serjeants, who remained in their proper places with the...stores some miles to the rear. He distributed from his dump to the fatigue parties from the trenches during each night, got his sleep through the forenoon, and perambulated the whole Battalion sector of trenches in the afternoon, to see how things went and what could be done by him.' Cf. Ackerley, 34.
96. Ackerley, 34.
97. Back-pay: Ackerley, 41; Lt-Col A.M. Gilchrist, in 'Memories', 82; Macfie

Papers, vol.7, RSM 2/3 14, IWM, 17 November 1916 (letters to and from Capt G.B.L. Rae). Company roll: Macfie to Charlie, 11 April 1915, IWM/2; 22 May 1915, IWM/3; 6 August 1916, IWM/4; 25 July, 13 August, 15 August 1917, IWM/5; to Shiela, 28 June 1915, IWM/3; Moffat, in 'Memories', 90. Writing to relations: to Jenny, 30 June 1915, IWM/3.

98. Macfie to Charlie, 13 August, 15 August 1917; to Jenny, 16–18 September 1917; to Shiela, 1 March 1918 (all IWM/5).

99. Already in January 1915 he was writing to his brother Jack (3 January 1915, IWM/1) of the physical costs of the first months of front-line service. He wrote to Charlie (1 March 1916) that he was working from 7 am till 2 am: 'I can scarcely even eat, and regard sleeping as a waste of valuable time'; cf. to father, 19 March 1916, 23 June 1916; to Charlie, 5 April 1916 (all IWM/4); to Shiela, 23 July 1917 (IWM/5).

100. See Macfie letters from 13–16 September 1916 to 18 February 1917 *passim* (IWM/4–5).

101. Ackerley, 36, 38; H. Ehrenborg, in 'Memories', 53; H.C. Dowdall, ibid., 73; Moffat, ibid., 92.

102. Ackerley, 23; Major A.C. Jack, in 'Memories', 87.

103. Macfie to father, 25 August 1914, IWM/1, cited above p.135–6. While the correspondence does not record his father's (or the wider family's) response in detail, the implication of other letters is that investigations were made and at least some help offered. Macfie to father, 22 August, 27 August, 30 August, 20 September, 4 October 1914 (all IWM/1).

104. Cf. above p.76. Macfie never expressed himself in heightened terms in his wartime letters; but this is not surprising, since they were all written to members of his family. *WGB* is far more charged and emotionally revealing than the uniformly neutral or jocular tones which he habitually employed (partly no doubt for reassurance) during the war.

105. This might echo his position within the family, as the eldest child with nine younger siblings.

106. Moffat, in 'Memories', 91. His testimony may be coloured by his own situation as a sergeant; he reported that he shared Macfie's view. Macfie fitted very closely the profile of the typical Liverpool Scottish officer given by McCartney, *Citizen Soldiers*, 42–4.

107. Macfie to father, 15 August 1916, IWM/4, quoted above n.88. Fussell, *Great War*, 82–6. McCartney, *Citizen Soldiers*, 48, notes that his social status afforded him privileges not normally accorded to sergeants: 'Breaches of military convention were often overlooked, as was his virulent criticism directed against some officers.'

108. Macfie to father, 30 August 1914, IWM/1: 'In spite of what you say I think I shall be more use as a competent colour-sergeant than as an incompetent subaltern. The whole efficiency and comfort of a company depend on the colour-sergeant: a Lieutenant commands nothing, and has no work to do: simply runs about like a puppy after his captain. The captain himself is more of a figure head than anything else, and it is the colour-sergeant who does the work. I have enlisted for work, and I don't feel anxious to lounge about an officers' mess with a lot of idle and rather incompetent people.' Cf. to father, 22

August 1914, IWM/1; 1 November 1915, IWM/3; to Charlie, 27 October 1914, IWM/1; to Shiela, 1 March 1918, IWM/5; to Jack, 26 February 1919, to Jenny, 15 March 1919 (both IWM/6). Moffat, in 'Memories', 91.

109. See above pp.135–6.

110. The letters are addressed to 'My dear father', and close 'Your affectionate son'; when writing to his siblings he refers to him as 'the Pater'.

111. On the outbreak of war, he wrote to Jack (9 August 1914, IWM/1): 'The Ancient One seems to have been a little disagreeable—talking of *duty*: which means the duty of his daughters, six servants, grooms and gardeners, to see that he has his lunch comfortably in bed.' Cf. to Jack, 19 February 1915, IWM/2; to father, 30 August 1914, IWM/1; to Charlie, 9 August 1915, IWM/3. After the war, he was open about the difficulties he had with his father within the firm: 'Macfie and Sons is in a most unattractive state of discord—it never was a very satisfactory firm; the differences in age made any cordiality of co-operation impossible': to Jenny, 15 March 1919, IWM/6; cf. to Charlie, 8 July 1917; to Shiela, 5 January 1918 (both IWM/5); to Jenny, 13 April 1919, IWM/6.

112. R.A. Scott Macfie, *A Mother of France* (Liverpool, 1920; Macfie Papers, vol.7, K84/1371, IWM), 5.

113. Macfie to father, 29 May, 23 June, 13–14 July 1916; to Helen, 17 October 1916; to Jenny, 16 December 1916 (all IWM/4); to John, 2 May 1917, IWM/5. Already during the war, he had expressed the wish to write about her; and the booklet reproduced, in slightly more formal language, stories already recounted in his letters: to father, 29 May, 23 June, 1–2 July 1916 (all IWM/4); as well as her letter to him: 10 December 1916 (Macfie Papers, vol.7, RSM 2/3 Miscellaneous Papers, January 1915–April 1919).

114. Macfie, *Mother of France*, 9. He describes her as approaching seventy; his mother would then have been seventy-one. She herself adopted a quasi-maternal role, near to tears when Macfie and his assistants left the billet ('saying that we were now part of the family'), worrying about his health and safety, and writing to him when he was in the line elsewhere: 'Accept the friendship of an old mother who often thinks of you when she thinks of her son': ibid., 11–12; cf. Macfie to father, 13–14 July 1916, IWM/4. His own mother was 'a complete invalid and felt much distress when her eldest son set up an establishment on his own. The days of his weekly visit to her became the red-letter days of her life.' Ackerley, 15.

115. Macfie, *Mother of France*, 10–12, 15, 18–20; Macfie to father, 1–2 July 1916, IWM/4.

116. Macfie, *Mother of France*, 20.

117. Macfie, *Mother of France*, 16–17.

118. Note his distress at the death of his own mother (above p.124), and his preference for Totana over Petrika (n.66 above). Cf. Brenan's mother, above p.51.

119. Macfie to Jenny, 16–18 September 1917, IWM/5. On Chavasse, see above pp.84–5.

120. Earlier in the same letter, he had self-mockingly commented on his own new role as Regimental QMS that: 'in my present rank I don't go up to the trenches but stay with the transport waggons, the parson, and other slackers.'

121. Macfie to Shiela, 7–8 June 1918; cf. 30 October 1917 (both IWM/5).
122. 'Gypsies should know something about tents, and I am confirmed in my belief in the wisdom of the Egyptians by seeing that my bedroom, an English-Gypsy tent, is the only residence in the camp which has withstood rain and wind absolutely, and is perfectly comfortable and pretty warm.' Macfie to Jenny, 29 September 1915; cf. to Helen, 5 November 1915 (both IWM/3); to father, 29 July–1 August, 15 August 1916 (both IWM/4); to Charlie, 31 May 1917, IWM/5.
123. Macfie, *WGB*, iii–iv.
124. I am referring here to relationships involving some significant emotional mutuality. Exploitative relationships, whether prostitution or the securing of sexual favours from those in subordinate social positions, were of course common. For two later nineteenth-century examples of cross-class sexual relationships where the commitment to a lasting partnership provoked intense social anxiety, see Stanley (ed.), *Diaries of Hannah Cullwick*, on Arthur Munby and Hannah Cullwick; and Rubinstein, *Before the Suffragettes*, 58–63, on Edith Lanchester and James Sullivan.
125. Moffat, in 'Memories', 92–3: 'Macfie enjoyed it while it hurt him. The man around him living and dying, all had their goodness on top and dominant. Who could doubt the priceless value that [he] found in their friendship? It was well worth what it cost him.' Cf. Lyttle, in 'Memories', 94.

6 Alick West

1. West, *One Man in His Time*, 7–8.
2. West, *One Man in His Time*, 7.
3. After his return from internment, his father 'asked me if I remembered my mother, and I told him my few memories, and he said that he was glad that I had them': West, *One Man in His Time*, 50. Her loss may be reflected in his fear, aged nine, of losing his father: 9–10.
4. Dominic Hibberd, 'Introduction', to West, *Diary of a Dead Officer*, viii. His father once told West that after his wife's death 'the heavens were as brass above me', and he had almost lost his faith: West, *One Man in His Time*, 15.
5. West, *One Man in His Time*, 8.
6. West, *One Man in His Time*, 13.
7. West, *One Man in His Time*, 152–3; cf. 50, 54, 69.
8. West, *One Man in His Time*, 16, 51–2; cf. 69.
9. West, *One Man in His Time*, 9. This theme of fear of his father recurs repeatedly in West's text: 68, 128; cf. 107 (Crusoe's fear of having done wrong in disobeying his father).
10. West, *One Man in His Time*, 12–13. According to Davidoff, 'Class and Gender', 96 and n.38, the contrast with the open door of the servants' homes is a recurring image in middle-class memoirs of the period.
11. West, *One Man in His Time*, 11.
12. West, *One Man in His Time*, 12.
13. West, *One Man in His Time*, 10.
14. West, *One Man in His Time*, 47. Hibberd, 'Introduction', viii–ix, comments: 'The

eldest child became guide and protector to the rest, perhaps losing his own childhood as he stood between them and their father's loving sternness.'

15. West, *One Man in His Time*, 17.
16. West, *One Man in His Time*, 15–18, 20. He was also a member of the OTC: 24.
17. West, *One Man in His Time*, 7–8.
18. West, *One Man in His Time*, 10.
19. West, *One Man in His Time*, 13–16.
20. West, *One Man in His Time*, 17–19; cf. 21.
21. West, *One Man in His Time*, 20.
22. West, *One Man in His Time*, 24–5. Sorley was also arrested after Germany had entered the war, but before Britain had declared war on her. Hence he was released and able to make his way home via Belgium. Wilson, *Sorley*, 151–6; Sorley, *Letters*, 179, 263–8.
23. Two valuable sources of information on Ruhleben are Douglas Sladen (ed.), *In Ruhleben: Letters from a Prisoner to His Mother…* (Hurst and Blackett, 1917), and J. Davidson Ketchum, *Ruhleben: a Prison Camp Society* (Toronto: University of Toronto Press, 1965). Ketchum was a 22-year-old Canadian, studying music in Germany when the war broke out. After the war he trained as a social psychologist and sociologist, and he spent many years researching and writing an account and analysis of life at *Ruhleben*. This was based on his own memories, on published accounts and contemporary documents from fellow-internees, on questionnaires which he circulated in the 1930s, and on later correspondence and interviews. Ketchum, *Ruhleben*, xix–x, 44 n.4. (He refers to himself in the text as 'Denton': ix.) His book provides a useful contextual framework into which to place West's account of these years. See also the internees' own publications *In Ruhleben Camp*, nos 1–9 (June-December 1915); *Ruhleben Camp Magazine*, nos 1–6 (March 1916–June 1917); and, for the early days, A.D.M. Hughes, 'Ruhleben', *Cornhill Magazine*, NS 233 (November 1915), 662–72.
24. Ketchum, *Ruhleben*, 6–7; West, *One Man in His Time*, 24–6.
25. West was originally one of four in a box: *One Man in His Time*, 26–7. Numbers of internees: Ketchum, *Ruhleben*, 155. Lack of space, cold, and food supplies: Sladen, *In Ruhleben*, 25, 31–2, 199–201; Ketchum, 12–20, 155–63. Paid work in the camp: Sladen, 277–81; Ketchum, 205–6. From February 1915, the British government provided a weekly relief payment of four (later five) marks to those otherwise destitute (almost half the camp): Ketchum, 19, 92, 101, 177.
26. Sladen, *In Ruhleben*, 184–5; Ketchum, *Ruhleben*, 25–30, 86, 100–1, 190, 273–92, 298.
27. Ketchum, *Ruhleben*, 25–6, 32, 58–64, 79, 85–6, 178–9, 181; from early in 1915, the internees themselves encouraged an informal ban on rumours: 212.
28. Ketchum, *Ruhleben*, 5, 23, gives the following proportions: merchant seamen 35%, businessmen 24%, professionals 18%, and workers 17%. Types of British internees imprisoned at the start of the war, Sladen, *In Ruhleben*, 15; layout and structure of the camp: Sladen, 173–82; Ketchum, 13–18.
29. Ketchum *Ruhleben*, 45–56, argues that though both the intense mass solidarity, and the significant modification of values, of the early days were inevitably modified in turn as the camp settled down, nevertheless an unchanging

substratum remained, in which the supreme values were comradeship and patriotism.

30. On the ubiquity of this slogan, Ketchum, *Ruhleben*, 39; cf. 64, 70, 81, 349; West, *One Man in His Time*, 28. Ketchum, 38, describes this initial bonding in terms very similar to Poole on national identity: 'Belonging, however, is a reciprocal matter. The individual escapes from isolation and fear not merely by identifying himself with his fellows, but by the knowledge that the identification is mutual.'
31. Improvements after the American ambassador's first visit in March 1915: Ketchum, *Ruhleben*, 28, 91–3, 101.
32. Ketchum, *Ruhleben*, 20, 35–47, 93, 188–9 ('an experience of comradeship so stirring that they wanted to remember it always'), 253. There is an obvious comparison here with accounts of the bonds formed in front-line service.
33. Ketchum, *Ruhleben*, 35–44. This sense of community was linked to patriotism, in a way which echoes Anderson's imagined community: the final criticism of any bad practice, as the camp evolved, was that it was not British—which, says Ketchum (95), referred not to their actual class-divided homeland, but to the equality, fraternity and even liberty of the early weeks.
34. Turner, *Ritual Process*, 95.
35. Turner, *Ritual Process*, 167.
36. Ketchum, *Ruhleben*, 49–55, notes the gradual and partial, though never complete, restoration of traditional elements of hierarchy and social distinction. Those whose families could not provide financial support were those who undertook paid work within the camp: 205–6; West, *One Man in His Time*, 40.
37. 'The liminal group is a community or comity of comrades and not a structure of hierarchically arranged positions. This comradeship transcends distinctions of rank, age...Much of the behaviour recorded...in seclusion situations falls under the principle: "Each for all, and all for each".' Turner, 'Betwixt and Between', 100–1.
38. Ketchum, *Ruhleben*, 136 (values), 258 (careers).
39. Ketchum, *Ruhleben*, 22, gives his full periodisation of the camp's history.
40. On 4 March 1915, the camp captain announced that all exchange negotiations were at an end: Ketchum, *Ruhleben*, 93, 95.
41. Ketchum, *Ruhleben*, chs 10, 12, 13.
42. Ketchum, *Ruhleben*, 81, 86–7, 92, 195–9; Sladen, *In Ruhleben*, 219–28 (ASU). Interestingly, Sladen invokes comparisons with public school to suggest to his readers the spirit of the prisoners, inviting them to picture 4000 men 'keeping up a good heart and going about their business of study and sport as cheerily as boys who merely exchanged the sybarisms of home for the spartanisms of a public school': 11; cf. 9. Revealingly, Mangan, *Athleticism*, 112–13, uses the role of sport as release from boredom and stress in Ruhleben as an example of 'striving for a meaningful existence based on common values within a "total institution", which mirrors the straitjacket public school system'.
43. Sladen, *In Ruhleben*, 204–6, 210–18; Ketchum, *Ruhleben*, 198–201, 232–9 (quoted at 198).
44. Ketchum, *Ruhleben*, 196, 198–9; cf. 230–1.
45. Ketchum, *Ruhleben*, 92 (quoted), 201.

46. Ketchum, *Ruhleben*, 201, 239–43.
47. Thompson's translation of Ibsen's *The Master Builder*, bluntly rejected by the Ruhleben Dramatic Society as not fit for Ruhleben in June 1915, was produced by the ASU in November. Ketchum, *Ruhleben*, 239–40; West, *One Man in His Time*, 35.
48. 'That so few men could cause so much controversy is a tribute to their convictions and courage. Most of them were of a type taken for granted at universities today—uninterested in games, excited by contemporary art and literature, rebellious against bourgeois standards. In Ruhleben, however, they stood out sharply, for their *avant garde* views were publicly expressed in lectures, reflected on the stage, and ridiculed in the magazines and elsewhere.' Ketchum, *Ruhleben*, 259–61 (quoted at 259). He also describes them as 'tough-minded intellectuals' with 'modernist tastes' (261).
49. Ketchum, *Ruhleben*, 33–4. He notes that there were significant modifications to a wide range of customs and conventions (in clothing, speech, eating habits, expectations of decency); 'in the convergence upon common standards, it was the upper and middle classes that did most of the shifting; the new norms were closest to those of seamen and working men' (47–8, quoted at 48). As the camp settled down there was some (but by no means complete) movement back towards conventional standards and customs: 50–1, 55.
50. Leed, *No Man's Land*, 3, talks of those who had entered the war before they were twenty, and 'regarded their experience as a special form of higher education'.
51. Ketchum, *Ruhleben*, 56; cf. 249. 'This comradeship, with its familiarity, ease and...mutual outspokenness, is once more the product of interstructural liminality, with its scarcity of jurally sanctioned relationships and its emphasis on axiomatic values expressive of the common weal.' Turner, 'Betwixt and Between', 101.
52. West, *One Man in His Time*, 24, 27–9. The resonances of the slogan are indicated by its becoming a subject of caricature: 33; cf. *Ruhleben Camp Magazine* no.3 (May 1916), 6 (short story on this theme); no.5 (Christmas 1916), 4. It is last line of John Milton's 'On His Blindness', where the poet reflects that he has a place in God's world despite his disability.
53. Ketchum, *Ruhleben*, 36–7 (quoted at 37; original emphasis).
54. Ketchum, *Ruhleben*, 69–70, 74–5, 94–5 (quoted at 70); he notes (69) that some groups, especially the seamen, took this tough stance from the start, and that others converged on it.
55. Ketchum, *Ruhleben*, 66–7 (quoted at 66).
56. Ketchum, *Ruhleben*, 70.
57. Sladen, *In Ruhleben*, 22–5, reprints the case for an exchange made by Sir Timothy Eden (lately released from the camp) in a letter to *The Times* (22 November 1916). Eventually, those over 45, or in ill-health, were exchanged, under an agreement made in 1916 but not implemented till January 1918. For details of negotiations, see Ketchum, *Ruhleben*, 52 n.9, 61 (quoted); R.B. McLeod, 'Postscript', in Ketchum, 356–8.
58. The internee of military age 'was spending the war in a far safer and more comfortable place than the trenches, and he could not contemplate the fact without a disturbing sense of guilt...As time went on...the sense of inferiority

grew heavier': Ketchum, *Ruhleben*, 176; cf. 172–4, 265. While many internees privately advised their families through letters to discount the more lurid accounts of conditions from those repatriated, '[c]ollectively, however, such realism was taboo. No public reference to the camp dared depict its inhabitants except as forgotten heroes, keeping a stiff upper lip in spite of unending hardships' (173–4). In July 1915 the Ruhleben British Association had proposed a badge, possession of which 'would be proof of their having been detained as civil prisoners in German at the time of this war'. It would have been, suggests Ketchum, an alibi for guilt feelings about the question: 'what did you do in the war?' He gives an account (82, 184–8) of the controversy which led to the plan being dropped.

59. For the role of boxes in fostering strong (and sometimes lasting) bonds between their inmates: Ketchum, *Ruhleben*, 113, 130–8, 144–8.
60. Ketchum, *Ruhleben*, 30. This could be compared to the close bonds formed between soldiers in the same small unit such as a platoon.
61. Ketchum, *Ruhleben*, 130, 147–8.
62. West, *One Man in His Time*, 26–8, 33–5. Comparison of this account with Ketchum's self-depiction as 'Denton' (*Ruhleben*, 50, 74, 112, 123, 247, 257, 317, 325), and two passing references there to 'Alick' (112, 324), raise the possibility that West's 'David More' is Ketchum.
63. Ketchum, *Ruhleben*, 29, 74. Himself an ardent Anglican and active participant in the religious life of the camp, he notes (74, 246–8) that in the later, more relaxed stage of the camp's history from spring 1915 religious organisations did not share in the flourishing of educational and other activities; they became the concern only of those who kept them going. Ardent philosophical discussion was taking place, but not of religious topics: 'The old...had lost much of its relevance.' (247).
64. West, *One Man in His Time*, 34.
65. West, *One Man in His Time*, 34–5.
66. West, *One Man in His Time*, 29.
67. Ketchum, *Ruhleben*, 196, 259 (quoted), 262; cf. 91, 266–7, 307; compare the playbill for G. B. Shaw, *Androcles and the Lion*, in 'Ruhleben concentration camp: programmes of entertainment' [1915, 1916] (British Library) with West's statement (*One Man in His Time*, 31–2) that Thompson played the emperor. His obituary: Anon., 'Dr. H. S. Hatfield', *The Times* (14 December 1966, 12 col.f). In the text, I shall continue to refer to him as Thompson.
68. West, *One Man in His Time*, 29–30. Thompson was elected chairman of the ASU late in 1915: *In Ruhleben Camp* (Christmas 1915), 35.
69. West, *One Man in His Time*, 31–2. In the set of playbills preserved as 'Ruhleben concentration camp: programmes of entertainment' [1915, 1916], West appeared in at least fourteen productions between March 1915 and July 1916; all but one of the parts he played were women. For notices of his acting, see *In Ruhleben Camp* (Christmas 1915), 6; *Ruhleben Camp Magazine*, no.2 (April 1916), 8. After Thompson's departure, he rarely acted: *One Man in His Time*, 38.
70. West, *One Man in His Time*, 31–2, 35–6.
71. West, *One Man in His Time*, 35. For tensions between the Camp School and the ASU, see Sladen, *In Ruhleben*, 168, 209; for attacks on the ASU's high-brow

plays, 238–9, and *In Ruhleben Camp* (Christmas 1915), 8.

72. West, *One Man in His Time*, 36.
73. West, *One Man in His Time*, 36. Graeme was on active service in France, while Cecil served as a medical officer: 37.
74. West, *One Man in His Time*, 36. This break with More and religious attendance fitted two wider patterns noted by Ketchum. The development of associations and the new relationships they brought weakened some of the earlier friendships based on the practicalities of box-sharing (*Ruhleben*, 148–9). Once the camp was fully organised, more painful emotions subsided, the need for reassurance decreased, and religious activities became the concern only of those who kept them going (74, 205, 246–8).
75. West, *One Man in His Time*, 36–7.
76. West, *One Man in His Time*, 183–4.
77. West, *One Man in His Time*, 38. According to Sladen, *In Ruhleben*, 7, 'Richard Roe' had refused a release order procured by influential friends, because he felt he could be of more use in the camp. Sladen, 291, quotes a report by Hughes, 'Ruhleben', 670, that late in 1914 about 1500 prisoners had applied for release as militarily unfit; but one of them had assured a visiting journalist that they were not willing to be released if the British government did not wish them to. (It must be borne in mind that the article in which Hughes recounted this incident had been passed by the British censor.) Thompson and West, by being willing to work in industry in Germany, were emphatically rejecting this patriotic stance.
78. West, *One Man in His Time*, 32.
79. West, *One Man in His Time*, 38–9 (quoted at 38).
80. In the camp, Farleigh said about West's poems '"They're not quite it"': West, *One Man in His Time*, 38. Of his travel writing: '"But what", he asked, "are you trying to say?"' (72). He implied that West's literary stamina and creativity would not last to middle age (81).
81. Even his father's skills as a craftsman and engineer are paralleled by Arch's (failed) carpentry and Thompson's science. In his psychoanalytical self-appraisal, West, *One Man in His Time*, 90, wrote: 'I had never overcome my fear of my father, nor of his substitute images, Thompson and Paul.'
82. West, *One Man in His Time*, 41.
83. The diary and letter extracts, and selected poems, were published as West, *Diary of a Dead Officer*. There is a discussion of these literary remains by Dennis Welland, 'Arthur Graeme West: a Messenger to Job', in G.R. Hibbard (ed.), *Renaissance and Modern Essays; presented to Vivian de Sola Pinto*...(Routledge, 1966), 169–80; and Samuel Hynes, 'An Introduction to Graeme West', in M. Roucoux (ed.), *English Literature of the Great War Revisited: Proceedings of the Symposium on the British Literature of the First World War* ([Amiens]: Presses de l'U.F.R. Clerc Université Picardie, 1986), 74–83.
84. Joad states that the text includes all the diary except 'names and a few details that were too painful or too private for publication' ('Introduction', in West, *Diary*, xiv). Hibberd, 'Introduction', to the 1991 reprint by the Imperial War Museum, vii–viii, discusses Joad's editing. The extracts were selected and juxtaposed 'to show the dead officer as "C.J." wishes him to be seen. What matters

is not West's personality, but the development of his ideas and the destruction of an individual by war and the Army. The title is carefully chosen: this officer died in the spirit when he took his commission, seven months before his "irrelevant" death in the body.' He acknowledges that Graeme West might have approved of the editing, which articulated a protest he himself had failed to make (viii).

85. West, *One Man in His Time*, 44, 46. Cyril Joad (1891–1953) was an exact contemporary of Graeme West both as pupil at Blundell's School (from 1905) and as student of classics at Balliol College, Oxford (from 1910): Welland, 'Arthur Graeme West', 170. He had often stayed with the West family during holidays; while Alick had been fascinated by him, his father and stepmother had disapproved: West, *One Man in His Time*, 44. During the war, Joad took up a pacifist stance, arguing that a German invasion met with civil resistance would be a lesser evil than the war: Geoffrey Thomas, *Cyril Joad* (Birkbeck College, 1992), 18–21.
86. West, *Diary*, ix–x; Hibberd, 'Introduction', ix.
87. Hibberd, 'Introduction', x.
88. West, *Diary*, xi–xii.
89. Welland, 'Arthur Graeme West', 170, stresses the importance of the fact that the diary was written with no view to future publication.
90. The extracts from letters addressed to 'Dear Lad', are taken by Welland, 'Arthur Graeme West', 171, 176, to be to Joad himself.
91. West, *Diary*, 12–13 (letter, 12 February 1916).
92. West, *Diary*, xii, 2.
93. At this point, Graeme had served less than four months at the front, as a private. His general comments on the army during his period of training may also reflect the impact of this prior experience (as they certainly do with regard to the technical value of the training), but this is nowhere explicitly indicated. He was now undergoing training during what was for many others the shattering and demoralising experience of the Somme, from July 1916; see above p.79. Hibberd, 'Introduction', xi, notes that in structuring the book Joad sought to give weight to this period 'because he wants to demonstrate that the death of the "dead officer" began not under shellfire but as a result of military cruelty and incompetence at home.' He accepts that it is nevertheless a damning record.
94. See West, *Diary*, xii–xiii. *The Times Literary Supplement* review ('A Hamlet of the War', 30 January 1919), 49–50, stresses this individuality. Graeme's account of training: *Diary*, 17–42 *passim*, esp. 22–3 (12 May 1916) on the role of hate and fear in army training. Graves, *GTAT*, 227–30, 304–6, and Sassoon, *Memoirs of an Infantry Officer*, 8–15, also comment on the useless character of training at this period.
95. Hibberd, 'Introduction', xii, comments: 'His family's conventional views were exasperating. Even [his sister] Constance seemed farther from him than usual.' Later Graeme told her he was much happier in Surrey, where no-one expected him to believe in Christianity or the war. For these tensions, *Diary*, 47–8, 50.
96. According to Joad, this shift in values was unsuspected by those who spent this time with him. 'Introduction', in West, *Diary*, xiii.

97. Such as those to battalion, regiment or county: for which see n.115 below.
98. Any sensible man who 'goes to the British Museum and sees the meaningless lost-looking...Sphinxes and mummies...must feel that they are now nothing; when he thinks of the wars whose voice has come ever so faintly down to us from those ages, and of all the men and women of those times, he must understand that all existence [is] of no absolute or continuous importance.' West, *Diary*, 33–6 (quoted at 34–5). This entry is undated but clearly belongs to the period of army training; Joad places it between entries for 27 and 28 May 1916.
99. West, *Diary*, 35–6; cf. 58 (24 September 1916).
100. West, *Diary*, 49.
101. West, *Diary*, 47 (8 August 1916). Welland, 'Arthur Graeme West', 174, notes the difference from Sassoon (and Owen), who rejected the Old Testament God, but not the historical figure of Christ.
102. West, *Diary*, 49 (19 August 1916).
103. West, *Diary*, 50 (19 August 1916). Cf. 12 (12 February 1916), 56 (last year 'I had not thought out the position of the pacifist and the conscientious objector, I was always sympathetic to these people, but never considered whether my place ought not to have been rather among them than where I actually was': 24 September 1916).
104. West, *Diary*, 49, 52 (quoted; 19 August 1916); cf. 58–9 (24 August 1916). A key text that weekend was H.G. Wells's 'The Last Trump', a parable of the blindness of human beings that allows war to be fought: 49, 51 (19 August 1916); Hynes, 'Introduction to Graeme West', 77–8.
105. The weekend of 19–21 August 1916.
106. West, *Diary*, 50 (19 August 1916).
107. He tried to send a telegram to his Commanding Officer, but again failed to make himself do so. He then read some of Russell's essay to his sister Constance, shocking her with what he revealed of his own views. West, *Diary*, 51–2; West, *One Man in His Time*, 47–8. This 'undoing' (as Freud described it) could be regarded as forming a similar compromise to that of war neurosis.
108. West, *Diary*, 50–3 (19 August 1916); West, *One Man in His Time*, 48 (also reprinting, 45, key elements of Graeme's account of this episode). For the possible impact of Russell's essay on him, see Welland, 'Arthur Graeme West', 175.
109. West, *Diary*, 54–5 (letter, 21 August 1916). (He appears to have believed that he might face the death penalty for desertion.) He there quoted Hamlet ('Now is the native hue of resolution sicklied o'er w the pale cast of thought!'), giving the *TLS* review its title. Welland, 'Arthur Graeme West', 176, commented that he rejoined his unit 'not in the spirit of altruistic responsibility to his comrades that took Owen and Sassoon back, but because of an understandable reluctance to give pain and distress to his family'. This is perhaps not surprising, since he had not yet served as an *officer* at the front. By his last diary entry (76, 10 February 1917), he was writing of his men: 'But how I love them all.'
110. Samuel Hynes, *A War Imagined: the First World War and English Culture* (Bodley Head, 1991), 150–1.
111. West, *Diary*, 79–81; Hibberd, 'Introduction', xiii–xiv, xxi nn.9–10. The realistic style of the poem matches that of some of the late prose in the diary after his return to the front, e.g. West, *Diary*, 66–9 (20 September 1916). On West's

writing, see Hynes, *War Imagined*, 114–16, 157–8.

112. West, *Diary*, xii, xiv.
113. West, *Diary*, 57, 66–9. Welland, 'Arthur Graeme West', 175, 177, notes the similarity between Graeme's own honestly-recorded defensive response to these sights, and what Russell in 'Justice in War Time' had denounced as the destructive effects of the war on humane feelings.
114. 'So deep have the changes in me been recently through Christianity, Theism, Paganism, to Atheism and Pessimism, and so rapidly have they consummated themselves, that I seemed till only a few weeks ago an entirely new being.' West, *Diary*, 53 (24 August 1916).
115. At a training school early in 1917, he recorded that the other men were nice, but did not understand him. 'They thought I was a pro-German, a Socialist, and a Poet. Anyone who isn't at once intelligible is put down at any rate as the first of these. They are full of petty loyalties to regiment or county.' West, *Diary*, 75 (10 February 1917—for the dating of this entry to 1917, rather than 1916 as printed, see Welland, 'Arthur Graeme West', 176 n.12); cf. 71 (30 September 1916), 72 (1 October 1916), 74 (5 October 1916). For Sassoon, see below p.171.
116. 'What *good*, what *happiness* can be produced by some of the scenes I have had to witness in the last few days?' West, *Diary*, 57 (24 September 1916; original emphasis).
117. West, *Diary*, 73 (5 October 1916), 58 (24 September 1916; original emphasis); cf. 56 ('How is it that so much blood and money cannot be poured out when it is a question of saving and helping mankind rather than of slaying them?': 11 September 1916).
118. '[N]o one is willing to revise his ideas or make clear to himself his motives in joining the war; even if anybody feels regret for having enlisted, he does not like to admit it to himself. Why should he? Every man, woman, and child is taught to regard him as a hero; if he has become convinced of wrong action it lands him in an awkward position which he had much better not face. So everything tends to discourage him from active thinking on this important and, in the most literal sense, vital question.' West, *Diary*, 55 (11 September 1916).
119. West, *Diary*, 72 (1 October 1916).
120. Bertrand Russell, *The Autobiography of Bertrand Russell: vol.2: 1914–1944* (Allen and Unwin, 1968), 71–2 (3 September 1916). Russell replied with a statement of what the War Office had been doing to him recently: West, *Diary*, 72 (1 October 1916).
121. Russell, *Autobiography 2: 1914–1944*, 76 (27 December 1916). After Graeme's death, Russell published these letters in the *Cambridge Magazine* (19 May 1917, 627 col. 1; Hibberd, 'Appendix' to the 1991 reprint, xxiii–xv). Its columns were open to views critical of the war; for its reputation, see below p.175. Graeme's fiancée Dorothy Mackenzie also met and corresponded with Russell after his death: Russell, *Autobiography 2: 1914–1944*, 71, 77; Hibberd, 'Introduction', xx n.8.
122. In this context, his sympathy with the views Russell had expressed a decade earlier on religion and spirituality—he had been drawn to the mystical-sceptical essay 'A Free Man's Worship'—undoubtedly strengthened Russell's attractiveness for him: West, *Diary*, 50, 53–4.

123. At first Alick criticised Graeme for failing to recognise the 'unreality' of the war from the point of view of the artist: West, *One Man in His Time*, 49. But later, Graeme became a political model to look to: 59, 117–18, 161.
124. Cf. Brenan, above p.68.
125. West, *One Man in His Time*, 50–1 (quoted at 50).
126. West, *One Man in His Time*, 51–2.
127. West, *One Man in His Time*, 52.
128. West, *One Man in His Time*, 53; cf. 68.
129. West, *One Man in His Time*, 53–4.
130. See above p.146. Cf. his reflections on his book about Bernard Shaw: West, *One Man in His Time*, 187–8.

7 The Encounter of Siegfried Sassoon and W.H.R. Rivers

1. See above pp.78–80.
2. Leed, *No Man's Land*, 169, notes that the breadth and ambiguity of the category 'shell-shock' made it effective, 'isolating the aberrant, and treating him on an individual basis in a medical rather than a judicial setting'.
3. For silent protest, see above p.81. Graeme West similarly suppressed his protest against the war; see above p.161.
4. Slobodin, *Rivers*, 55, 59, 66.
5. Leed, *No Man's Land*, 176–7.
6. Stone, 'Shellshock', 258–9, 264–5.
7. Report by Rivers on Sassoon at admission to Craiglockhart, reproduced in Sassoon, *Sassoon's Long Journey*, 134–5 (quoted at 135). For further discussion, see Wilson, *Sassoon (1886–1918)*, 394–5.
8. Sassoon to Morrell, 30 July 1917, *Diaries 1915–1918*, 183–4; cf. Egremont, *Sassoon*, 163–4 (to Graves, 10 August 1917: 'My opinions remain four-square').
9. Sassoon, *Sherston's Progress*, 12.
10. Sassoon to Graves, 19 October 1917, Sassoon, *Diaries 1915–1918*, 191–2. For this, and Graves's reassurance, see above p.118. For a parallel 'joke' against Rivers, below p.178.
11. Sassoon, *War Poems*, 94 (October 1917; first published under the title 'Death's Brotherhood').
12. Sassoon, *Sherston's Progress*, 12, 17–18, 50–1 (quoted at 51, 17).
13. Sassoon to Morrell, 11 October 1917: Egremont, *Sassoon*, 171.
14. Sassoon to Morrell, 28 October 1917, *Diaries 1915–1918*, 192–3 (original emphasis).
15. Sassoon to Morrell, [17 October 1917], *Diaries 1915–1918*, 190–1; cf. to Graves, 19 October 1917, 191–2; to Morrell, 28 October 1917, 192–3; to Graves, 7 December [1917], 196.
16. Sassoon, *Sherston's Progress*, 45, attributes his choosing to miss the board, after he had been kept waiting for his hearing, to irritable impatience at being 'mucked about by the War'. Showalter, *Female Malady*, 186, not unreasonably interprets this as a 'final act of unwitting protest'. However, her wider interpretation here seems overstated if not inaccurate. She claims that after Sassoon offered to return to the front Rivers 'urged him to recant fully', which seems

at best a strained reading of the letters to Morrell which she cites (the only relevant passage seems to be 'I have told Rivers that I will not withdraw anything that I have said or written' [Sassoon, *Diaries 1915–1918*, 190], which need not imply that Rivers had asked him to do so). She adds that after Sassoon 'agreed to recant his views' (which he clearly did not do), 'he began, for the first time, to have recurring nightmares about the war'; no evidence is cited for this, but it may be based on *Sherston's Progress*, 48–50, which in fact refers to recurring dreams *after* the war. (Egremont, *Sassoon*, 174, cites a letter to Morrell [13 November 1917] in which Sassoon said his nightmares about the war made him feel even more certain he should go back; cf. Wilson, *Sassoon (1886–1918)*, 427.) This may be partly due to Showalter's reading the events of 1917 through the prism of Sassoon's autobiography, on which see below p.172.

17. Sassoon, *Sherston's Progress*, 31–5, 43, 48–50 (quoted at 43, 50); Egremont, Sassoon, 176–8.
18. Sassoon, *Diaries 1915–1918*, 197–8 (19 December 1917); cf. 203 (12 January 1918). Wilson, *Sassoon (1886–1918)*, 430. Cf. Graves's comment on his being too sane as the meaning of an anti-war complex: above p.118. Sassoon, *Sherston's Progress*, 47, notes that he fell into this detached and unconcerned state of mind immediately after he had apologised to Rivers for missing the medical board; cf. Showalter, *Female Malady*, 186.
19. Wilson, *Sassoon (1886–1918)*, 436–7.
20. Sassoon, *Diaries 1915–1918*, 255 (21 May 1918); cf. 251, 257 (19, 24 May 1918).
21. Sassoon, *Diaries 1915–1918*, 261 (4 June 1918: 'After all, I am nothing but what the Brigadier calls "a potential killer of Germans (Huns)". O God, why must I do it? *I'm not.* I am only here to *look after* some men'; original emphasis); 269 (14 June 1918: '"I want to go and fight!" Thus had I boasted in a moment of folly, catching my mood from the lads who look to me as their leader.') Cf. ch.3 n.43 above.
22. Sassoon, *Diaries 1915–1918*, 132 (15 February 1917), 242 (4 May 1918); cf. 142 (4 March 1917), 238 (23 April 1918), 240 (27 April 1918). Roper, 'Between Manliness and Masculinity', 350, suggests that Edwardian manliness 'encouraged...an attitude of forgetfulness of self in favour of action in the world'.
23. Showalter, *Female Malady*, 179–89 (quoted at 185), citing Sassoon, *Sherston's Progress*, 17.
24. Slobodin, *Rivers*, 62–3 (quoted at 63); cf. Caesar, *Taking It Like a Man*, 91.
25. In May 1918, Sassoon noted in his diary: 'I must never forget Rivers. He is the only man who can save me if I break down again. If I am able to keep going it will be through him.' *Diaries 1915–1918*, 246 (9 May 1918). In his powerful 'Letter to Robert Graves', composed while recuperating in hospital, he wrote: 'O Rivers please take me. And make me / Go back to the war till it break me'—lines which combine erotic desire with masochistic self-sacrifice. *War Poems*, 132; cf. Egremont, *Sassoon*, 209. In August he wrote to Marsh that he 'loved [Rivers] at first sight': Wilson, *Sassoon (1886–1918)*, 393–4 (quoted at 393).
26. Sassoon, *Sherston's Progress*, 15–16, 27–9, 35–6, 58; Siegfried Sassoon, *Diaries 1920–1922*, ed. R. Hart-Davis (Faber, 1981), 162–70; Showalter, *Female Malady*, 184–5; Jean Moorcroft Wilson, *Siegfried Sassoon: the Journey from the Trenches: a Biography (1918–1967)* (Duckworth, 2003), 12, 29 (Sassoon describing Rivers

as his 'father confessor'), 136–7 (as his 'fathering friend' [1930]).

27. Sassoon, *Memoirs of an Infantry Officer*, 172, 176–7, 195–9, 206, 211, 232, 235. For an analysis of the narrative positioning in Sassoon's autobiographical trilogy, see Caesar, *Taking It Like a Man*, 104–7. Such interrogation of his own motives was already under way in 1918: Egremont, *Sassoon*, 211.
28. Sassoon, *Sherston's Progress*, 22–7, 136.
29. Showalter, *Female Malady*, 185–6. If Macamble is a fictional device to represent retrospectively the pacifist 'temptation' which Sassoon had now repudiated, he nevertheless encodes part of Sassoon's contemporary dilemma. Macamble, planning Sassoon's 'liberation from the machinations of the uniformed pathologist', proposes that he abscond to London where he will be examined by an 'eminent alienist' who will certify that he is completely normal and responsible for his actions. To this, Sassoon responds: 'Good Lord, he's trying to persuade me to do the dirty on Rivers!' *Sherston's Progress*, 26–7. However, that very plan was one which, as has been seen, Sassoon himself briefly considered as his only alternative. In other words, an ambivalence which in the autobiography is split between Sassoon and his tempter is his own in his letters at the time: n.10, n.14 above.
30. Leed, *No Man's Land*, 169.
31. Leed, *No Man's Land*, 170–6 (moralists), 176–86 (analysts).
32. Leed, *No Man's Land*, 175.
33. Leed, *No Man's Land*, 180.
34. Laurinda Stryker, 'Mental Cases: British Shellshock and the Politics of Interpretation', in G. Braybon (ed.), *Evidence, History and the Great War: Historians and the Impact of 1914–18* (Oxford: Berghahn, 2003), 160. She critiques (155–60) inaccuracies in Showalter's original formulation of this context.
35. Stryker, 'Mental Cases', 160–3 (quoted at 163).
36. Stryker, 'Mental Cases', 165.
37. After the publication of *Counter-Attack* in summer 1918, Rivers wrote to Sassoon that he could not 'imagine any instrument more potent against the war': Egremont, *Sassoon*, 205.
38. Showalter, *Female Malady*, 178–89; Hynes, *War Imagined*, 176–86; cf. Wilson, *Sassoon (1886–1918)*, 387, 391–5, 426–8, 425.
39. 'I prefer...to regard the dream as the expression of a conflict, and as an attempt to solve the conflict by such means as are available during sleep.' W.H.R. Rivers, *Conflict and Dream* (Kegan Paul, Trench, Trubner, 1923), 17–18, 31 (quoted at 17). He understands the unconscious, on a parallel with the then dominant model of the nervous system, to be organised in a hierarchy of levels of both experience and mental functioning. Hence 'the level recording the forgotten experience of youth would, when it found expression, reveal any special modes of mentality which belong to youth.' W.H.R. Rivers, *Instinct and the Unconscious: a Contribution to a Biological Theory of the Psycho-Neuroses* (2nd edn, Cambridge: Cambridge University Press, 1922), 229–30 (quoted at 230).
40. Hynes, *War Imagined*, 177.
41. Rivers, *Conflict and Dream*, 118–26.
42. Rivers, *Conflict and Dream*, 120. The *Cambridge Magazine* would later publish many of Sassoon's bitterest anti-war satires: Wilson, *Sassoon (1886–1918)*, 243,

253–4, 262, 286, 303, 305, 375, 379, 404, 411, 417, 431, 440. Cf. ch.6 n.121 above.

43. Rivers, *Conflict and Dream*, 120–2.
44. Rivers, *Conflict and Dream*, 123.
45. Rivers, *Conflict and Dream*, 123–4.
46. Rivers, *Conflict and Dream*, 124; cf. n.39 above.
47. Rivers, *Conflict and Dream*, 126.
48. The conflict Rivers was experiencing in 1917 also fed into his more general theorising. Three years later, in his critique and revision of Freud's theory of the unconscious, one of the elements Rivers rejected was the concept of censorship: Rivers, *Instinct and the Unconscious*, App.V (first published in 1920). He argued (229): 'There are many, however, prepared to go far with Freud in their adherence to his scheme of psychology, who yet find it difficult to accept a concept which involves the working within the unconscious of an agency so wholly in the pattern of the conscious as is the case with Freud's censorship. The concept is based on an analogy with a highly complex and specialised social institution, the endopsychic censorship being supposed to act in the same way as the official whose business it is to control the press and allow nothing to reach the community which will, in his opinion, disturb the harmony of its existence.' Unhappy with this attribution of a quasi-intentionality to the ego, Rivers preferred this unconscious agency to be conceived differently. 'It is to physiology rather than to sociology that we should look for the clue to the nature of the process by which a person is guarded from such elements of his unconscious experience as might disturb the harmony of his existence.' (229). He then explained it in terms of his favoured neurological parallel: the fantastic nature of dreams was not due to distortion produced by any 'agency partaking of a demonic character', but was rather the natural outcome of the removal during sleep of the more advanced levels of mental activity, so that 'the lower levels with their infantile modes of expression come to the surface and are allowed to manifest themselves in their natural guise.' (230–1) A year later, his re-analysis of his 'Reproachful Letter' dream led Rivers to acknowledge that he himself in 1917 had contemplated playing the role of an 'official whose business it is to control the press and allow nothing to reach the community which will, in his opinion, disturb the harmony of its existence.' It is perhaps not surprising that in his theorising he preferred to disavow the existence of such a (motivated) agency, referring its putative functions instead to the (motiveless) effect of a physiological regression of mental functioning.
49. What he had read in the *Cambridge Magazine* were reports by certain French journalists suggesting that Germany was so economically crippled it would be unable to pay any post-war indemnity if defeated. He linked this to a newspaper report of the new French cabinet which did not include Briand, and 'wondered how far it indicated a diminution in the strength of the *jusqu'au boutiste* element in France, and proceeded to think about the possible influence of the change on the conduct of the war.' Rivers, *Conflict and Dream*, 119–20 (quoted at 119).
50. Rivers, *Conflict and Dream*, 165–77; cf. Hynes, *War Imagined*, 178–9.
51. Rivers, *Conflict and Dream*, 168.

52. This connected with the earlier speculations about Germany's financial situation.
53. Rivers, *Conflict and Dream*, 168–9.
54. Rivers, *Conflict and Dream*, 169–70, 172–3.
55. Slobodin, *Rivers*, 68, interprets the dream as indicating a shift towards desire for a negotiated finish; but this seems to convert a potential into an actual change of stance.
56. Rivers, *Conflict and Dream*, 168. Reference to 'the humorous side of the imagined situation' (Sassoon, *Sherston's Progress*, 35, also mentions this counterpart of the 'anti-war complex' jest) exemplifies a classic English elite way of downplaying what might be in danger of being taken too seriously. Cf. Russell, *Autobiography 2: 1914–1944*, 72–3, which reprints a memo he wrote after an interview concerning his anti-war lectures in 1916 with General Cockerill of the War Office, a masterly exponent of understated upper-class mores. Cockerill commented: '"You and I probably regard conscience differently. I regard it as a still small voice, but when it becomes blatant and strident I suspect it of no longer being a conscience…Do you not think there is a lack of a sense of humour in going on reiterating the same thing?"'
57. Rivers, *Conflict and Dream*, 169.
58. Rivers, *Conflict and Dream*, 171. 'B' is Sassoon: cf. 166–7.
59. Rivers, *Conflict and Dream*, 171; see above p. 000.
60. The emotional effect on Rivers of the distressed soldiers he was dealing with is noted by Sassoon, who had a night-time apparition of a dead fellow officer to whom he had been very close. When he related this incident to Rivers 'the strong emotion underlying my narrative must have been apparent' and 'I saw that my story had affected him strongly'. *Sherston's Progress*, 21–2, 36 (quoted). But (emotion-provoking) Barbusse does not reappear in Rivers's discussion of the 'Pacifist' dream after the first mention, whereas the (policy-oriented) *English Review* article recurs several times.
61. Rivers, *Conflict and Dream*, 22–39; the captain had been his patient at Craiglockhart, and now saw him in London: 35.
62. Rivers, *Conflict and Dream*, 22.
63. The alter ego had blue eyes and 'luminous gold' hair; in boyhood the patient had wished to have fair hair and blue eyes. Rivers, *Conflict and Dream*, 23, 25.
64. Rivers, *Conflict and Dream*, 23, 25. The patient's in-laws were Canadian, and this steward carried a form of caduceus, the symbol of medicine.
65. Rivers, *Conflict and Dream*, 23.
66. Rivers, *Conflict and Dream*, 23–4 (quoted at 24). The Canadian threatened to put the *alter ego* into a 'lady's corset' as a 'straight-waistcoat'; i.e. to render him silenced/pathologised/feminised. The Canadian's role is unclear; since he represents the forces wanting the patient to remain a doctor, it is surprising that he attacks the *alter ego* when he supports the patient's pro-war declamations. This may be because of an ambiguity in the patient's words. What appears to be a speech in favour of the war ('"Better let us die than lose our manhood…"') can also be read against the grain as his proclamation of defiance against his wife's family. Rivers does not comment on this. See further below p.183.
67. Rivers, *Conflict and Dream*, 24.

68. Rivers, *Conflict and Dream*, 25.
69. Rivers, *Conflict and Dream*, 25–6.
70. Rivers, *Conflict and Dream*, 26. This sentence is curiously ambiguous; the contrast which it apparently sets up seems to require the phrase 'deeper feelings' to be followed by some such words as 'of revulsion'.
71. Rivers, *Conflict and Dream*, 24.
72. Rivers, *Conflict and Dream*, 26–7.
73. Only in his re-analysis of the 'Reproachful Letter' dream did Rivers allow the political conflict to assume greater importance than the professional.
74. Showalter, *Female Malady*, 188, quoting Rivers, *Instinct and the Unconscious*, 210. Max Plowman, a socialist writer, who was shell-shocked and treated at Craiglockhart in 1917, resigned from his regiment in similar fashion to Sassoon in January 1918, saying he was opposed to all war. He was court-martialled and dismissed from the army in April. He had sent a copy of his resignation statement to Sassoon, who passed it on to Rivers; but when Rivers attempted to steer him along Sassoon's course, Plowman refused to be persuaded by what he saw as Rivers's insistence on the individual accommodating himself to society. Hynes, *War Imagined*, 183–5.
75. Slobodin, *Rivers*, 68–9 (quoted at 69).
76. Slobodin, *Rivers*, 68–72.
77. See also his lecture at a working-men's club in spring 1922, and subsequent invitation to one of its members, a Nelson cotton weaver who had written an essay drawing on some of his ideas, to come to Cambridge as his secretary and study with him. Slobodin, *Rivers*, 68, 79, 81–2.
78. Slobodin, *Rivers*, 79–81.
79. Showalter, *Female Malady*, 188: 'his postwar writing reveals no moral ambivalence, no second thoughts about the immediate effects of his successful therapies, no painful reconsideration of his own service to the state'.
80. José Brunner, *Freud and the Politics of Psychoanalysis* (rev. edn, New Brunswick, NJ: Transaction, 2001), 106–16. For a comparison of the different responses of the British and German psychiatric professions to the pressures of the war, see Barham, *Forgotten Lunatics*, ch.7; Shephard, *War of Nerves*, 97–102.
81. Brunner, *Freud and the Politics of Psychoanalysis*, 113–14, 116.
82. Stryker is here restating an ethical consensus of the time. A more radical critique might question why individuals should be required to sacrifice themselves for the good of the nation.
83. Stryker, 'Mental Cases', 164–5.
84. M.D. Eder, 'The Psycho-pathology of the War Neuroses', *The Lancet*, no.4850 (12 August 1916), 266. The trope of eviscerated horses howling in pain is also found in Erich Maria Remarque, *All Quiet on the Western Front* (1929; Vintage, 1996), 44–5; Graves, *GTAT*, 261, comments on dead horses and mules: 'it seemed wrong for animals to be dragged into war like this'.
85. Stryker, 'Mental Cases', 165.
86. Carl E. Schorske, 'Politics and Patricide in Freud's *Interpretation of Dreams*', in his *Fin-de-Siècle Vienna: Politics and Culture* (New York: Vintage Books, 1981), 181–207. See my 'Freud, the Politics of the 1890s, and the Origins of Psychoanalysis' (in preparation).

87. See Laplanche and Pontalis, *Language of Psychoanalysis*, 82–3.
88. For the 'snags' which this reading in isolation encounters, see above pp.179–80.
89. This would explain the ambivalence in the behaviour both of the Canadian steward, who threatens the *alter ego* when he cheers the speech, and of the *alter ego*, when he shifts from cheering to depression. These ambivalences represent transition points between the two meanings of the dream, the gestalt shift between hearing 'manhood and independence' as referring to Britain or the Captain: see n.66 above.
90. As noted above p.180, Rivers recognises this dual meaning, before again marginalising the anti-war perspective to concentrate on the career conflict.

8 Fractured Loyalties: the Nation and the War

1. Nor does the general model set out in Chapter 1 apply only to upper-middle-class men. I am preparing a study of George Hewins (1879–1977), a labourer, which explores the class and gender dimensions of his service in, and mutilation by, the First World War.
2. Bergonzi, *Heroes' Twilight*; Simon Featherstone, *War Poetry: an Introductory Reader* (Routledge, 1995), ch.1; Elizabeth A. Marsland, *The Nation's Cause: French, English and German Poetry of the First World War* (Routledge, 1991), 14–15; Bond, *Unquiet Western Front*. See also Ferguson, *Pity of War*, ch.12; McCartney, *Citizen Soldiers*, chs 6–8.
3. Robin Prior and Trevor Wilson, 'Paul Fussell at War', *War in History* 1.1 (1994), 63–80; Fussell, *Great War*.
4. Prior and Wilson, 'Paul Fussell at War', 66–72.
5. Paul Fussell, *Wartime* (New York: Oxford University Press, 1989); Prior and Wilson, 'Paul Fussell at War', 74–9, include among the corollaries of Fussell's approach that 'wars are never warranted and never produce results less harmful than the failure to take up arms': 79.
6. Prior and Wilson, 'Paul Fussell at War', 72–3, 79.
7. One reason which Prior and Wilson give is that most British soldiers felt they had to see it through for the defence of parliamentary democracy. 'Paul Fussell at War', 73; cf. 80. By the same logic, presumably most Germans who continued fighting did so in order to promote Germany's militaristic expansion. In one unguardedly oversimplified formulation (68), they endorse F. E. Manning's *Her Privates We* (1930), a novel Fussell does not discuss, since 'it is about the fact that war and its continuation comes from within the combatants themselves and is not imposed upon them'.
8. Bergonzi, *Heroes' Twilight*, 135. Cf. Joad, ch.6 n.85 above.
9. Bergonzi, *Heroes' Twilight*, 45–52; see further below pp.201–2.
10. Sorley to A.E. Hutchinson, 10[?] August 1914, *Letters*, 184. There is an edge of late-adolescent provocation in the tone both of this remark, and of his expressions of pro-German sentiment.
11. When, in the early weeks, he finds: 'I am almost convinced that war is right and the tales told of German barbarism are true', this leads to the paradoxical conclusion 'I have become non-individual and British': Sorley to Hutchinson, August 1914, *Letters*, 187.

12. 'I am giving my body (by a refinement of cowardice) to fight against the most enterprising nation in the world.' Sorley to Hutchinson, 14 November 1914, *Letters*, 200. His much-quoted criticism of the claims to self-sacrifice in Rupert Brooke's sonnets turns a similarly sceptical and deflating eye on motivation: 'it is merely the conduct demanded of him (and others) by the turn of circumstances, where non-compliance with this demand would have made life intolerable. It was not that "they" gave up anything of that list he gives in one sonnet: but that the essence of those things had been endangered by circumstances over which he had no control, and he must fight to recapture them.' Sorley to Mrs Sorley, 28 April 1915, ibid., 218–19.
13. Sorley to Arthur Watts, 26 August 1915, *Letters*, 254; cf. 245.
14. In his autobiography, Brenan, *Life of One's Own*, 207, stressed his divided and ambivalent attitude towards the war and its continuance. He was shocked in retrospect to find that, in a letter to his father immediately after the Somme, he had broken out into 'a eulogy of battle'. In charge of an observation post on the first day of the Somme, his view of the chaos of the British attack, and his task ten days after the battle of burying hundreds of bodies, led to the point where 'I found that my morale had completely vanished' (185–92, 194–7, 201–4, quoted at 204). He was torn between pacifist resistance to the horrors of war, a personal desire simply to escape, and a sense of responsibility to keep fighting till the German army was completely defeated, the necessary condition for lasting peace. (213; cf. 218–19, 223) War also represented for Brenan reality, both the harsh reality he had earlier desired in contrast with his sheltered childhood, and an objective reality which it would be escapism to evade. (218, 223) He came increasingly to feel the desire to lead in battle: 'I longed to lose myself in the little group, bound together by their duties and their mutual obligations and by their ever-present awareness of danger, and slough off my sick and feeble individuality in a sense of responsibility for others.' (214) In May 1918 he was finally given command of a company, and began a policy of frequent, risky patrolling. (219, 224–33) Evaluating his own performance, he concluded that he 'lacked that capacity for headstrong aggressive action' which belonged to every good soldier. Despite this, he had got closer to his men, who he felt liked and trusted him. 'And so a new ideal opened out before me—that of the good company officer who puts the welfare of his men before everything else.' (233–4; cf. 235).
15. Bergonzi, *Heroes' Twilight*, 14, 23–7, 93, 223; Robert Ferguson, *The Short Sharp Life of T.E. Hulme* (Allen Lane, 2002), 230–42.
16. J.P. Stern, 'The Embattled Style: Ernst Jünger, *In Stahlgewittern*', in H. Klein, (ed.), *The First War in Fiction: a Collection of Critical Essays* (Macmillan, 1976), 112–25. Leed, discussing Jünger, comments that he was one of a few participants in the war who 'could not resign themselves to the status of common men, passive sufferers of the will of material. They sought to recover their lost potency through an identification with the autonomous mechanism of "the War" that so victimized the "masses".' *No Man's Land*, 152–62 (quoted at 152). Cf. the case cited in E.E. Southard, *Shell-shock and Other Neuropsychiatric Problems Presented in Five Hundred and Eighty-nine Case Histories* (Boston: W.M. Leonard, 1919), 259–60, of the artillery officer who eroticised his machinery; and Eric

Leed, 'Fateful Memories: Industrialized War and Traumatic Neuroses', *Journal of Contemporary History*, 35.1 (2000), 96–7.

17. Bergonzi, *Heroes' Twilight*, 145, 158–9. Cf. Joe Lunn, 'Male Identity and Martial Codes of Honor: a Comparison of the War Memoirs of Robert Graves, Ernst Jünger, and Kande Kamara', *Journal of Military History* 69.3 (2005), 722–7.
18. Mosley, *Grenfell*, 344, 348–9, 358, 361. MacKenzie, *Children of the Souls*, 148: 'he had never resolved the conflict between the values of his upper-class upbringing and his search for more congenial expressions of his rebellious temperament'.
19. Mosley, *Grenfell*, 362–4; cf. 157–8.
20. Mosley, *Grenfell*, 379–80 (original emphasis); cf. above p.67.
21. Note too that this linear summary omits the many oscillations of stance—at a given moment, and from moment to moment—discussed above pp.88, 117.
22. Bond, *Unquiet Western Front*, 75.
23. Bond, *Unquiet Western Front*, vii–viii; cf. 40.
24. Bond, *Unquiet Western Front*, 28–30, 33–4, 63–8.
25. Bond, *Unquiet Western Front*, 79–80, 86–7.
26. Bond, *Unquiet Western Front*, 1.
27. Bond, *Unquiet Western Front*, 28, 81.
28. Bond, *Unquiet Western Front*, 2 ('In the post-war settlement Britain achieved most of its objectives with regard to Europe, and its empire expanded to its greatest extent'), 6 ('Britain…fought the war first and foremost to preserve its independence and status as a great imperial power by resisting the domination of Europe by the Central Powers. But a second purpose, less evident until the late stages of the war, was to gain a peace settlement which would also enhance Britain's and its Empire's security *vis-à-vis* its allies and co-belligerents'), 22–3.
29. Bond, *Unquiet Western Front*, 2 ('It was not the fault of those who won the war on the battlefields that the anticipated rewards soon appeared to be disappointing.'), 23.
30. Wilson, *Myriad Faces of War*, 850–2, argues this case.
31. A subordinate theme in Bond, *Unquiet Western Front*, is his wish to repudiate the common caricature of British generals and staff officers as callous and bungling incompetents. Instead, he insists (20–2, 97–9), professional military historians over the last two decades and more have studied the 'learning curve' which allowed the general staff to come to terms with the unprecedented problems posed by industrial warfare, and to develop command-and-control systems, and integrated methods of attack, which enabled them in 1918 to dislodge and defeat the entrenched German enemy.
32. It is in addressing this perspective that Bond's efforts to be even-handed show signs of strain. He quotes Correlli Barnett on Sassoon as a 'brave but whingeing poet': *Unquiet Western Front*, 81; and himself borrows the adjective to refer to Pat Barker's *Regeneration* trilogy as expressing the 'authentic whingeing note of the 1990s transposed unconvincingly to 1918': 77; cf. 15–17, where he judges Sassoon's protest 'politically unacceptable and impractical' (quoted at 17). Again quoting Barnett, he suggests that junior officers were not only in no position to question the politics and strategy of the war, but also excessively

'sensitive and imaginative': 27.

33. Cf. the assessment of David Stevenson, *1914–1918: The History of the First World War* (Penguin, 2005), 594–601.
34. 'Despite this grim evidence [casualty lists in newspapers] a spirit of stoic endurance persisted. The idea of sacrifice in a just cause did not collapse into cynicism for the war generation. But this was not true of the generation which followed for whom "The war lit a slow fuse under the values which had done most to sustain it".' Bond, *Unquiet Western Front*, 24–6 (quoted at 24, quoting J.M. Bourne, *Britain and the Great War, 1914–1918* [Edward Arnold, 1989], 231).
35. Bond, *Unquiet Western Front*, 33–5 (quoted at 35), also citing Graves as similarly surprised by the reception of *GTAT*. This powerful impact of the play was very evident at the 2004–5 revival directed by David Grindley (Comedy Theatre, then Duke of York's Theatre, London). Bond's own response accords with this, in his interpretation that all the main characters die by the play's end. See also Roper, 'Between Manliness and Masculinity', 353–7.
36. Bond, *Unquiet Western Front*, 68–70 (quoted at 70).
37. Bond, *Unquiet Western Front*, 26, 100. Cf. the argument of Prior and Wilson, 'Paul Fussell at War'. In a sense, this replicates the reason/emotion split which I suggested Rivers operated.
38. Leed, *No Man's Land*, 34–6 (quoted at 35).
39. Poole, *Morality and Modernity*, 104, argues that the willingness of the individual to act, suffer and die on behalf of the nation signals that he has 'identified his existence with that of the nation'.
40. Bryan S. Turner, 'Preface to the Second Edition', in Emile Durkheim, *Professional Ethics and Civic Morals* (2nd edn, Routledge, 1992), xxii, xxxiv–v; Durkheim, *Professional Ethics and Civic Morals*, 69–70. Marsland, *Nation's Cause*, argues that the patriotic-heroic verse of the later nineteenth century was not part of a longer tradition of war poetry (which in fact earlier had evoked loyalty also to leader, clan or communal group, and was often ambivalent about the nature and costs of war). She sees it rather as an invented tradition of the era of increasing national rivalry: 'the intense and apparently spontaneous homogeneity of the patriotic verse of 1914, and especially its similarity across national boundaries, suggests a vigorous poetic form perfectly suited to its historical role; and an analysis of its widely-shared characteristics confirms that this poetry is indeed a modern phenomenon, the voice *par excellence* of the new sense of nationhood that came to fruition with the onset of war.' 21–2 (quoted at 22), 70–1, 80, 106–7. Consequently, she reads much of what has conventionally been understood as anti-war poetry as expressing primarily a protest against those poetic conventions that lent support to war: 107–9, 113–14, 118–19, 134, 137, 141–2, 145–55.
41. Durkheim, born into a Jewish family in Lorraine, had good reason to have a high regard for the post-revolutionary French state for its role in the emancipation of the Jews. Turner, 'Preface', xxxiv.
42. 'Nothing works better to sharpen a boundary than for someone to be killed in its name. The line becomes more distinct for the people who do the killing, since it gives them—whether before or after the fact—a justification for the blood on their hands.' Kai Erikson, 'On Pseudospeciation and Social Speciation', in

C.B. Strozier and M. Flynn (eds), *Genocide, War and Human Survival* (Lanham, MD: Rowman and Littlefield, 1996), 57.

43. Anderson, *Imagined Communities*, ch.8, 'Patriotism and Racism', strives to assert that love and sacrifice are primary nationalist motivations, rather than hate and killing. Poole, *Nation and Identity*, 1, 9, 74, is more direct and realistic in confronting this aspect of the nation. But it is acknowledged, rather than fully integrated into his analysis. This becomes apparent when he introduces the term 'illusory community': *Morality and Modernity*, 108. While emphasising the importance of the *creative, imaginative* elements in nation-building which Anderson was concerned to foreground, Poole still wants to assert that the nation is an *illusory* community. But this leads him into difficulties when he also wants to be able to distinguish true from false national identities (his implicit purpose here being to exclude the Nazi project as a true form of nationalism). His grounds for doing so are that the Nazis invoked a false mythological/racial notion of Aryan identity (and presumably also that they denied 'certain relations of interdependence on each other' between Gentiles and Jews). Both these points are correct; but it is not clear that they are different in kind, rather than degree, from the separations (based on language, religion, history, ethnicity, etc.) enforced by many other nationalist projects.
44. Anderson, *Imagined Communities*, talks of the nation 'inspiring' (141), 'asking for' and 'persuading' (144). Poole, *Nation and Identity*, 12, agrees with Anderson that: 'if we are to understand the moral presence of the nation in our lives, we must come to terms with its capacity to demand and be freely given these sacrifices.' But he does not explore the tension between 'demand' and 'freely given'. It recurs (69) between the nation 'requiring' and 'asking' sacrifices.
45. Poole, *Morality and Modernity*, 105; Durkheim, *Professional Ethics and Civic Morals*, 70.
46. Grenfell: above p.67; Brenan: above p.68; contrast the unavoidable circumstances which drove the working-class Hewins into the army, n.1 above.
47. This was recognised by many doctors treating shell-shocked patients. John MacCurdy, an American psychiatrist who visited British military hospitals in 1917, wrote that most cases of war neuroses were people who were 'well adapted to civil life but capable to only a limited degree of enduring the strains of modern warfare', since they display 'independence of judgment, and a strong feeling of sympathy for those in pain' whereas 'the ideal soldier must be more or less of a natural butcher, a man who can easily submit to the domination of intellectual inferiors': *War Neuroses* (Cambridge: Cambridge University Press, 1918), 129.
48. 'When once the patient sees that his disinclination to return to the front is essentially a selfish desire to avoid his responsibilities as a citizen, he is in a position to decide quite consciously whether he wishes to be a slacker or to assume his share of his country's burden.' MacCurdy, *War Neuroses*, 85. Dr H.W. Kaye reported from the front that 'every moral stimulus must be applied to keep as many as possible up to the collar in fairness to all those who "stick it out" with such splendid endurance': Shephard, *War of Nerves*, 38. Contrast the fate of Lt Geoffrey Kirkwood, Regimental Medical Officer, who allowed men whose unit had suffered terribly during the first days of the Somme to report ill with shell

shock; ibid., 42–3; Barham, *Forgotten Lunatics*, 115–16.

49. Poole, *Morality and Modernity*, 104.
50. To play on the Cold War trope of 'Better dead than Red'. Cf. Grenfell, quoted in ch.3 n.40 above. By contrast, Leed, *No Man's Land*, 172, cites the case of a French soldier who surrendered to the Germans crying out 'Comrades, what difference does it make to me whether I am German or French?'
51. McCartney, *Citizen Soldiers*, 51, argues that the Liverpool Territorials were fighting for the honour of their city, and also to safeguard the power and authority of the middle class in Liverpool from both external and internal threats. So both provision and recognition were operative motives.
52. These contradictions form one of the central themes of Leed, *No Man's Land*.
53. Jünger resolved the contradiction by embracing it utterly, wanting to turn himself into a killing machine; in this way he anticipated, perhaps contributed to, a trope of fascism.
54. Cf. above p.56. Parker, *The Old Lie*, explores some of the literary and historical traditions contributing to this celebration of early, self-sacrificial death: doomed youth (91–5), Classical tradition (95–9), chivalry (99–105, 226–41). For an extreme example of this muscular Christian fusion, by the well-known padre G.A. Studdert Kennedy ('Woodbine Willie'), see Bourke, *Intimate History of Killing*, 272–3.
55. Allen J. Frantzen, *Bloody Good: Chivalry, Sacrifice and the Great War* (Chicago: University of Chicago Press, 2004), 39.
56. Frantzen, *Bloody Good*, 44–6.
57. Frantzen, *Bloody Good*, 32.
58. Frantzen, *Bloody Good*, 24; cf. Bourke, *Intimate History of Killing*, 270.
59. Frantzen, *Bloody Good*, 31.
60. Frantzen, *Bloody Good*, 24.
61. Frantzen, *Bloody Good*, 27. He highlights (178–81) the tension between this view and Jesus's original teaching in the opposing messages of two different contemporary postcards commemorating the Saarburger Kreuz, a surviving crucified Christ from a Calvary destroyed in 1914.
62. Expressed most perversely by the 'influential clergyman' who apparently urged soldiers, as they plunged their bayonets into the enemy, to murmur 'This is my body broken for you'. Bourke, *Intimate History of Killing*, 275.
63. As Chavasse did, above p.84. Anne Summers comments: 'Edwardian Christianity…espoused militarism with a seemingly uncritical enthusiasm': 'Edwardian Militarism', 249–53 (quoted at 252).
64. Bourke, *Intimate History of Killing*, ch.9; Alan Wilkinson, *The Church of England and the First World War* (SPCK, 1978). After an evening in which Ross read out extracts from a sermon by the Bishop of London, A.F. Winnington-Ingram, Sassoon wrote '"They"': 'The Bishop tells us: "When the boys come back / They will not be the same; for they'll have fought / In a just cause: they lead the last attack / on Anti-Christ"': *War Poems*, 56. See also 'Joy-Bells' (125), which sarcastically calls for church bells 'Whose tones are tuned for peace' to be melted down for armaments, and 'Vicarious Christ' (141). Cf. Egremont, *Sassoon*, 116–17; Wilkinson, 35–6, 47–8, 180–2, 217–18, 251–5; Kerr, *Wilfred Owen's Voices*, 174–6 (on Winnington-Ingram's preaching).

65. Alan Wilkinson, *Dissent or Conform?: War, Peace, and the English Churches, 1900–1945* (SCM Press, 1986), ch.2; Barry M. Doyle, 'Religion, Politics and Remembrance: a Free Church Community and its Great War Dead', in M. Evans and K. Lunn (eds), *War and Memory in the Twentieth Century* (Oxford: Berg, 1997), 223–38.
66. Bourke, *Intimate History of Killing*, 270–1; cf. n.131 below. The journalist C.E. Montague had the clarity to recognise that his continuing commitment to fighting meant that he no longer accepted all of Christ's teaching: 303.
67. Summers, 'Edwardian Militarism', 252. This continued even during the war: Parker, *The Old Lie*, 67–8. Marsland, *Nation's Cause*, 79–83, 149–51, shows that this attitude also prevailed in wartime poetry: 'the heroes of the mass army are eulogised...because they are innocent, and above all because they have died as victims' (81). (Some Christian teachers, however, managed to divine that were Christ alive in the twentieth century his weapon of choice would be the bayonet. Bourke, *Intimate History of Killing*, 272–3, 275.)
68. Frantzen, *Bloody Good*, 253–4 (quoted at 253).
69. Cf. Marsland, *Nation's Cause*, 145–7.
70. Frantzen, *Bloody Good*, 254–5.
71. Frantzen, *Bloody Good*, 20. He ascribes the impulse to continue violence to fellow soldiers who wished to revenge their fallen comrades; but the imperative was felt perhaps more strongly at the national level ('We owe it to the fallen.').
72. Leed, *No Man's Land*, 105; cf. Bourke, *Intimate History of Killing*, ch.3, esp. 71–3, 77–8, 89–92.
73. For responses to having killed, see Bourke, *Intimate History of Killing*, ch.7, esp. 219–20, 222, 227, 229–31, 235–6, 238–9. Marsland, *Nation's Cause*, 149–51, comments that, since the patriotic writers did not confront this, 'the guilt for performing the act of killing rests on the "heroes" alone, not on the people who incited them to go to war' (151). Sassoon addressed this theme in 'Remorse' ('there's things in war one dare not tell / Poor father sitting safe at home'), and in the satirical squib 'Decorated' (about a soldier receiving a VC for killing five men): *War Poems*, 58, 118. Cf. below p.200. Though dealing with a very different context, Alessandro Portelli's lucid and scrupulous analyses of the ways in which Italian Resistance fighters strove to make ethical sense of their killing of Nazi soldiers brings out powerfully the inner conflicts which even actions felt to be fully 'justified' may provoke: see 'The Battle of Poggio Bustone: Violence, Memory and Imagination in the Partisan War', in his *The Battle of Valle Giulia: Oral History and the Art of Dialogue* (Madison, WI: University of Wisconsin Press, 1997), 126–39; and his *The Order Has Been Carried Out: History, Memory and Meaning of a Nazi Massacre in Rome* (New York and Basingstoke: Palgrave Macmillan, 2003), 107–15.
74. Sassoon, *War Poems*, 29 (1916). For a fuller account of his reaction to the bayonet training, *Diaries*, 59–60 (25 April 1916), 249 (15 May 1918); Wilson, *Sassoon (1886–1918)*, 252–3; Egremont, *Sassoon*, 90–1. Bourke, *Intimate History of Killing*, 89–92, 272–3 (the Rev. Kennedy's enthusiasm for 'the spirit of the bayonet').
75. Leed, *No Man's Land*, 107; cf. Bourke, *Intimate History of Killing*, 248–51.
76. Leed, 'Fateful Memories', 92–3.
77. Turner, 'Betwixt and Between', 105. Leed, *No Man's Land*, 28–9, applies Turner to the Western Front.

78. Leed, *No Man's Land*, 75. Cf. ch.9 n.8 below.
79. Bernard [Bill] Adams, *Nothing of Importance: a Record of Eight Months at the Front with a Welsh Battalion*, October, 1915 to June, 1916 (1917; Naval and Military Press, 2001), 299–308.
80. Brenda Giblin, 'Perceptions of the Great War: a Polemical Perspective' (MA Dissertation, Liverpool John Moores University, 2002), v–vii, 9, 17, 50; her unpublished research also cites the following diary entry: '15 August 1916: During the last few weeks I have seen sights enough to send a man crazy. To see one's pals die, to bleed to death, has provoked an earnest desire to understand it all. A belief, a support in some way is what I have craved for, prayed for. I am convinced I have at last found this support. It is an ardent belief in Christ and sacrifice. No other support will apply in the same way. My prayers have been answered.' Cf. McCartney, *Citizen Soldiers*, 214, 216.
81. Frantzen, *Bloody Good*, 243–7. Frantzen, 244, describes him as 'a literary man of the sort studied by Fussell, steeped in the verities of Victorian culture.'
82. Graves, *GTAT*, 242; Kerr, *Wilfred Owen's Voices*, 176–7. Cf. below p.204.
83. Sassoon, *Diaries*, 166, asks of Lady Brassey's invocation of the dead who help us: 'What was this "other world" that she spoke of? It was a dream he had forgotten years ago—the simplicity of his childish prayers, the torment of his mocking youth that denied the God of priests, and triumphed in the God of skies and waters.' Cf. above p.91–2. See also Wilson, *Sassoon (1886–1918)*, 365, 470; 'In the Church of St Ouen' ('lost to God, I seek him everywhere'; March 1917): Sassoon, *War Poems*, 72. Cf. Graves to Sassoon, 25 January 1917, *Letters 1914–46*, 63 ('I spent today going round the Rouen churches and the Cathedral—by God, they are wonderful, almost persuade one to be a Christian.')
84. See, for example, 'Absolution': *War Poems*, 15.
85. Sassoon, *War Poems*, 16–17; the poem was revised in March 1916. Wilson, noting that the poem was begun on the very day he met Graves, comments: 'If the comparison between the soldier...with his heavy burden and Christ carrying His cross smacks somewhat of the heroic tradition, this is undercut by the irreverent colloquialism...of the last two lines, with their snatch of convincing blasphemy': *Sassoon (1886–1918)*, 219 (quoted), 246. My view is that, even after the 1916 revisions, the balance of the poem is still towards affirming rather than undermining the identification, with the final couplet acting rather to point up the 'homeliness' of the Tommy.
86. Sassoon, *War Poems*, 19.
87. Sassoon, *War Poems*, 28; Wilson, *Sassoon (1886–1918)*, 249–50, sees this poem as a pivotal moment in the emergence of Sassoon's satirical voice.
88. Sassoon, *War Poems*, 45–6. Sassoon did not publish this poem, nor even show it to anyone, regarding it as an ambitious failure. He later wrote: 'I intended it to be a commentary on the mental condition of most front-line soldiers for whom a roadside Calvary was merely a reminder of the inability of religion to co-operate with the carnage and catastrophe they experienced.' (46–7).
89. Cf. above p.66.
90. Above p.109. But for their continuing attachment to the idea of self-sacrifice, see above pp.88, 108.

91. Wilfred Owen, 'The Parable of the Old Man and the Young', in *The Collected Poems of Wilfred Owen*, ed. C. Day Lewis (Chatto & Windus, 1963), 42. Graves had added a marginal note to 'Goliath and David', imagining a world in which 'War should be a sport for men above forty-five only', and their sons would praise their sacrifice while regretting that they themselves could not serve: *GTAT*, 288–9.
92. See Henry Newbolt's comments on Wilfred Owen, cited in Bergonzi, *Heroes' Twilight*, 117–18.
93. Mosley, *Grenfell*, 198–9, 345–7. After her two sons were killed in 1915, Sydney Herbert wrote to Ettie: 'I feel as if all of us were dead, and only they were alive' (345); and she wrote in 1918 to her close friend Mary Elcho, who had herself lost two sons: 'As these agonising days go on one can feel *almost* glad that Ego and Ivo and Julian and Billy are safe in the dream of peace' (347; original emphasis). Cf. MacKenzie, *Children of the Souls*, 186. Or again the views of Lady Brassey: 'a slow / Spiritual brightness stole across her face.../ "But they are safe and happy now," she said. / I thought "The world's a silly sort of place / When people think it's pleasant to be dead."' Sassoon, 'Supreme Sacrifice', in *War Poems*, 81; cf. above pp.91–2. Marsland, *Nation's Cause*, 83, comments: 'The English patriotic poets celebrate heroic death...but with an emphasis on immortality rather than martyrdom. Since the heroes are eternally young, they have escaped the burden of living'.
94. Frantzen, *Bloody Good*, 207–8 and plate 15.
95. Caesar, *Taking It Like a Man*, 96, 189, suggests that what attracted Sassoon (and Graves) to their working-class soldiers, ennobling them in their officers' eyes, was the men's capacity for serving and suffering. He argues, 228–9, that this valorisation of suffering and self-sacrifice had already been instilled in both Sassoon and Graves before the war; it was a resource with which they responded to war, rather than simply a coping mechanism developed during it. Seymour, *Graves*, xiv–xvi, 101–2, 174, 185–6, 194, 259, suggests that this masochistic pattern can be traced through Graves's relationships with both Nicholson and Riding in the 1920s and 30s, and (in a variant of late Romanticism) was central to his theory of the White Goddess as source of poetic inspiration.
96. This was Sorley's first period away from family and public school, and so had something of the character of a moratorium. He began to test his independence, and met an English Assistant at the university, the slightly older Arthur Watts, who briefly became a mentor. Wilson, *Sorley*, 134–5, 139, 193, 201; Sorley, *Letters*, 22–6.
97. Sorley, *Letters*, 193, 210. He expresses his admiration through a joking identification with Germany: it is his Vaterland, and the landlady whose anti-heroic attitude to the war—when told 'she ought to be proud and glad to give her sons to fight'—he approves of is dubbed a sensible German hausfrau. Sorley to Hutchinson, 10[?] August, 14 November 1914, ibid., 183, 185, 200; to A. J. Hopkinson, October [?] 1914, ibid., 194; to Mrs Sorley, March 1915, ibid., 217 (quoted).
98. Sorley to Hopkinson, October[?] 1914, *Letters*, 192–4 (quoted at 193); to Hutchinson, 14 November 1914, ibid., 200.

99. Sorley to Hopkinson, October[?] 1914, *Letters*, 192–3; to the Master of Marlborough, 27[?] December 1914, ibid., 210–11.
100. Sorley to Hopkinson, October[?] 1914, *Letters*, 193.
101. He had no illusions about war as just or glorious, remarking bluntly: 'There is no such thing as a just war. What we are doing is casting out Satan by Satan.' Sorley to Mrs Sorley, March 1915, *Letters*, 217–18; cf. n.97 above.
102. Barham, *Forgotten Lunatics*, 6–8, 369–70.
103. Barham, *Forgotten Lunatics*, 5–6, 8–9, 17–19, 32–5, 39–43, 76–9, 82–3, 99–133, 145–64.
104. Barham, *Forgotten Lunatics*, 78: 'these "failures" also exemplify an alternative stance or vantage point within life, a competing sensibility one might say'; they 'do seem to have a point'.
105. Barham, *Forgotten Lunatics*, 68–9; 71–2 (William Bellamy: fantasy of attending a funeral which might have been his own; heard voices telling him he was going to be shot by someone); 73 (Charles Abberley: had asked an orderly to cut his throat, because 'he felt "funny and shaking with trying to take on—to make a soldier of myself"; he had heard voices saying "You daft bugger, cut your throat!" He did not especially wish to die, he said, but had come round to the view that it was perhaps the best course when he "can't make a good soldier".'). Barham comments (114): 'A failing as a soldier did not necessarily indicate a want of patriotic resolve, for those who remained perplexed, anguished citizens were often their own harshest critics in lambasting themselves for their ineffectual performance in the national cause.' They may be compared with the suicidal wishes of Graeme West—as an escape from his dilemma about whether to return to the front (above p.161), and the RAMC doctor—from his dilemma about returning to his profession (above p.179).
106. This 'mirrored his own sense of himself as the source of his own problems, but rather sidestepped surely pertinent questions as to how exaggerated expectations of manliness, together with repressive attitudes towards sexuality, might bring men to consider themselves as worthless human beings.' Barham, *Forgotten Lunatics*, 72.
107. 'This was, after all, a culture in which an authoritative strand of opinion held that men who could not make efficient and brave soldiers deserved to be shot, and though some military authorities were more lenient than others, such attitudes formed part of the atmosphere which ordinary soldiers breathed.' Barham, *Forgotten Lunatics*, 73. Shephard, *War of Nerves*, 71, quotes Dr H.W. Hills, an Army neurologist, who recorded a colleague saying: 'If a man lets his comrades down he ought to be shot. If he's a loony, so much the better.' Barham cites (74–5) four examples of soldiers who were executed, contrasting them (58–60) with a similar case who, supported by his Commanding Officer, was evacuated to Napsbury. 'In some instances it is difficult to avoid the conclusion that the line which separated the soldier who was shot at dawn from the serviceman who was evacuated to a war mental hospital—was largely adventitious, reflecting local circumstances in the field, luck, and the sympathies of medical officers.' (75). On malingering, see also Joanna Bourke, *Dismembering the Male: Men's Bodies, Britain and the Great War* (Reaktion Books, 1996), ch.2.
108. Barham, *Forgotten Lunatics*, 72, refers to 'the miserable feeling that Bellamy has

about himself that stimulates a punitive voice into being'; this is certainly part of the truth, but should not obscure the degree to which Bellamy also carries with him his experience at the front, where he may well be going to be shot by someone. Cf. Southard, *Shell-shock*, 60, 419–20.

109. Barham, *Forgotten Lunatics*, 73.
110. Barham, *Forgotten Lunatics*, 79 (Read's emphasis); cf. the French soldier quoted in n.50 above. Read was among the more liberal medical officers: 45–7, 159, 236. Two pioneering military psychiatrists, Elliot Smith and Pear, suggested in 1919 that shell-shocked men had not lost their reason, but rather their senses were 'functioning with painful efficiency': quoted in Joanna Bourke, 'Effeminacy, Ethnicity and the End of Trauma: the Sufferings of "Shell-shocked" Men in Great Britain and Ireland, 1914–39', *Journal of Contemporary History* 35.1 (2000), 58. For other examples of such 'unwelcome' truths, see Southard, *Shell-shock*, 245, 249.
111. Stone, 'Shellshock', 261–2, citing Ivor Gurney, *War Letters: a Selection*, ed. R.K.R. Thornton (Manchester: Carcanet, 1983), 233–4. Barham, *Forgotten Lunatics*, 387 n.13 cites Stanford Read, *Military Psychiatry in Peace and War* (H.K. Lewis, 1920), 5: 'This individualism in the normal newly joined recruit soon gives way as he becomes more and more a machine, and the goal idea of all to work hard, obey, and become efficient soldiers at an early date fills the mind.' Shephard, *War of Nerves*, 56, cites a field ambulance doctor writing after Passchendaele in late 1917 about the change he had observed over the previous two years: 'No keen curiosity now, no careless enthusiasm, not even hate to carry them on: but instead a sense of duty, and a bowing down to the inevitable—the inevitable power which drives them on from behind. The troops have settled down to the war as slaves to their task'.
112. Sassoon: above p.172. On identification with the aggressor, see Laplanche and Pontalis, *Language of Psychoanalysis*, 208–9.
113. Several historians have suggested that the hold of such nationalist ideologies was less strong among the subaltern classes: ch.3 n.1 above.
114. Stone, 'Shellshock', 262; he uses it to refer to Kitchener's 'Pals' system, used to recruit together groups of men from existing communities; I am extending it here to refer to the bonds within groups formed at the front.
115. Owen, *Collected Poems*, 82.
116. Hynes, 'Introduction to Graeme West', 80: the 'story of a sensitive man's failure of nerve, under the pressure of family and society'.
117. 'In so far as our identities are formed through specific conceptions of social life, we find ourselves subject to the commitments and constraints, standards of behaviour and criteria of success provided by these conceptions. We do not choose these; nevertheless, we find them difficult, and sometimes impossible, to eschew.' Poole, *Nation and Identity*, 45–6.
118. Bertrand Russell was one of those prosecuted, fined, banned from speaking in certain parts of Britain and from travelling abroad, and ultimately imprisoned for campaigning against the war. *Autobiography 2: 1914–1944*, 24, 32–7, 79–81.
119. Brock Millman, *Managing Domestic Dissent in First World War Britain* (Frank Cass, 2000).
120. By 1917, general public concern about the direction of the war had grown,

making it easier for Sassoon than for Graeme West to carry through a public protest: Stevenson, *1914–1918*, 347–50, 356–9.

121. He draws a contrast between pre-bourgeois, dynastic ruling-classes, and the emergent bourgeoisie. Pre-bourgeois ruling elites, he argues, generated cohesions outside (print) language; their solidarities were 'the products of kinship, clientship, and personal loyalties'. 'The relatively small size of traditional aristocracies, their fixed political bases, and the personalization of political relations implied by sexual intercourse and inheritance, meant that their cohesion as classes were as much concrete as imagined.' By contrast, the emergent bourgeoisie could only visualise the thousands of separated others who were like themselves through the new medium of print-language. 'Thus in world-historical terms bourgeoisies were the first classes to achieve solidarities on an essentially imagined basis.' Anderson, *Imagined Communities*, 76–7. He may somewhat overstate his case here: pre-bourgeois elites undoubtedly used language (though not necessarily print-language) in many culturally-elaborated forms to define their identity, while even emergent bourgeoisies certainly did construct networks of intermarriage and inheritance (if only on a local basis at first). Nevertheless, the broad contrast does hold. This parallel between nation and bourgeoisie as imagined communities is no mere empty homology for Anderson. Emergent bourgeoisies are seen as crucial driving forces in some forms of nationalism; the secular 'pilgrimages' of peripatetic proto-bourgeois absolutist functionaries, or indigenous imperial civil servants, are deemed crucial to defining the boundaries of postcolonial states (53–9, 114–31); and in one rich passage he traces ways in which new forms of writing (novels and newspapers) usually associated with the rise of the bourgeoisie construct the nation as existing within a new mode of time—secular, empty, homogeneous (22–36).

122. At which point, Anderson's factory-owners from Lille and Lyon could indeed 'marry each other's daughters or inherit each other's property': *Imagined Communities*, 77.

123. Anderson, *Imagined Communities*, 10, pointedly remarks that the meaning of cenotaphs and tombs of Unknown Soldiers 'becomes even clearer if one tries to imagine, say, a Tomb of the Unknown Marxist or a cenotaph for fallen Liberals. Is a sense of absurdity avoidable? The reason is that neither Marxism nor Liberalism are much concerned with death and immortality…The great weakness of all evolutionary/progressive styles of thought, not excluding Marxism, is that such questions [concerning human suffering] are answered with impatient silence.' While there is much truth in this, it seems to underestimate the degree to which socialist activists have seen themselves as part of an enduring movement with the right to demand sacrifice (cf. below p.211). Anderson himself allows (144) that 'Dying for the revolution also draws its grandeur from the degree to which it is felt to be something fundamentally pure…it may be that to the extent that Marxist interpretations of history are felt (rather than intellected) as representations of ineluctable necessity, they also acquire an aura of purity and disinterestedness.' Furthermore, his comment neglects the extent to which what comes to seem generally appropriate/absurd is shaped by state policy (the Soviet post-revolutionary regime introduced their

own ceremonials in which class-heroes, foreign and native, were commemorated). For the role of war commemoration in establishing and sustaining national identity, see also Poole, 'Structures of Identity', 78–9.

124. The term 'actually-existing' is borrowed from Rudolph Bahro's concept of 'actually-existing socialism', in his *The Alternative in Eastern Europe* (1977; New Left Books, 1978); but I am using it here in a quite different sense.

125. The repeated invocation in British political discourse to 'put the "Great" back into "Great Britain"' is precisely a rhetorical attempt to bridge the gap between actually-existing and imagined reality (the latter here projected both back into the past and forward into the future).

126. See Anderson, *Imagined Communities*, chs 4, 5, 7. Gellner, *Nations and Nationalism*, 58–70, 88–109, develops a valuable economic-cultural model of the circumstances in which significant populations found it in their interest to embark on such nation-building endeavours. Not all such efforts, of course, were successful.

127. Sorley's detachment about the possibility of a German victory and the direction in which Germany might then develop, and Graeme West's comparison of the British Empire with the rule of the Pharaohs (ch.6 n.98 above), represent refusals to accept that projection of imagined nationhood.

128. Hobsbawm, *Nations and Nationalism*, 11. His point can be supported from the British experience of initial volunteering on the outbreak of war in 1914, discussed by John Stevenson, *British Society 1914–45* (Harmondsworth: Penguin, 1984), 46–54. He comments (50): 'the call for recruits tapped the powerful group loyalties of Edwardian society, seen most dramatically in the "Pals" battalions formed in the autumn of 1914—men who enlisted with their "pals" from the same occupations, factories, offices and clubs.' For a detailed case-study of Bury, see Geoffrey Moorhouse, *Hell's Foundations: A Town, Its Myths and Gallipoli* (1992; Sphere, 1993).

129. Again, Freud may be taken as an example. Recent research (including that cited in the Introduction n.13 above) has shown him in the 1890s both politically and emotionally torn between his Jewish identity (which then had no nation, though Herzl in Vienna was just formulating the theory of Zionism), his political liberalism, and a strong identification with German nationalism.

130. David Fitzpatrick, 'Ireland since 1870', in R.F. Foster (ed.), *The Oxford History of Ireland* (1992; Oxford: Oxford University Press, 2001), 193–211; Charles Townshend, *Ireland: the 20th Century* (Arnold, 1999), ch.5.

131. Martin Ceadel, *Pacifism in Britain 1914–45: the Defining of a Faith* (Oxford: Clarendon Press, 1980), ch.4; Wilkinson, *Church of England*, 46–56; Wilkinson, *Dissent or Conform?*, ch.2.

132. Durkheim had direct experience of the expansionist potential of the German Empire, which had annexed Alsace-Lorraine in 1870–1. He argued against the pan-Germanism of his contemporary von Treitschke. Bryan S. Turner, 'Preface', xxvii, xxxv.

133. Durkheim, *Professional Ethics and Civic Morals*, 70. It was this perspective which motivated T. E. Hulme to insist on the need to oppose Germany: n.15 above.

134. Russell threw himself into campaigning against the war: Russell, *Autobiography 2: 1914–1944*; Jo Vellacott, *Bertrand Russell and the Pacifists in the First World War* (Brighton: Harvester, 1980).

135. F. L. Carsten, *War Against War: British and German Radical Movements in the First World War* (Batsford, 1982); Paul Ward, *Red Flag and Union Jack: Englishness, Patriotism, and the British Left, 1881–1924* (Woodbridge: Boydell Press, 1998), chs 6–7; Stargardt, *German Idea of Militarism.*
136. Cyril Pearce, *Comrades in Conscience: the Story of an English Community's Opposition to the Great War* (Francis Boutle, 2001).
137. James Hinton, *The First Shop Stewards' Movement* (Allen and Unwin, 1973); Iain McLean, *The Legend of Red Clydeside* (Edinburgh: Donald, 1983); Alan McKinlay and R.J. Morris (eds), *The ILP on Clydeside, 1893–1932: From Foundation to Disintegration* (Manchester: Manchester University Press, 1991), chs 1, 4, 5; and, for a historiographical/theoretical overview, Terry Brotherstone, 'Does Red Clydeside Really Matter Any More?', in Robert Duncan and Arthur McIvor (eds), *Militant Workers: Labour and Class Conflict on the Clyde, 1900–1950* (Edinburgh: Donald, 1993), 52–80.
138. Hinton, *First Shop Stewards' Movement*; Millman, *Managing Domestic Dissent.*
139. The reference here is to countries where the Communist Party was not in power, and so party membership did not bring material or status benefits from the state. See, for examples of such commitment, James K. Hopkins, *Into the Heart of the Fire: the British in the Spanish Civil War* (Stanford, CA: Stanford University Press, 1998), chs 4–6.
140. Schorske, *German Social Democracy*. In Britain, the Communist Party established a powerful community-wide presence only in a handful of particular industrial localities: Stuart Macintyre, *Little Moscows: Communism and Working-Class Militancy in Inter-war Britain* (Croom Helm, 1980).
141. Anderson, *Imagined Communities*, 7, defines the nation as 'sovereign' ('nations dream of being free, and, if under God, directly so') but 'limited' ('No nation imagines itself coterminous with mankind'); the socialist project imagined itself becoming sovereign but unlimited. Anderson's work had its origins as a response to the implications of wars between Communist states for Marxist theory: xi, 1–4.

9 New Attachments: Confronting the Post-war World

1. Ackerley, 36. For his tenants, see Edward Frankland, in 'Memories', 96; Edward Ashton, ibid., 99.
2. Ashton, in 'Memories', 98; Richard M. Chapman, ibid., 99; Ella Pontefract and Marie Hartley, ibid., 104. One memoirist said that: 'in his comparatively short residence among them, [he] identified himself with all their interests', and described him as 'imbued with an insatiable desire to help, by every legitimate and honourable means, his neighbours far as well as near.' Robt S. Seton, ibid., 107.
3. Frankland, in 'Memories', 96–7; Edward F. Grainger, ibid., 101–2; Wilson Scarr, ibid., 106; Robt S. Seton, ibid., 107–8.
4. Ashton, in 'Memories', 98; J. Howard Preston, ibid., 104–5; Ackerley, 40–1.
5. Quoted in O. Elton, in 'Memories', 74. Macfie himself wrote: 'Here the people have never had a resident parson nor a squire, and "wouldn't call the Queen their Aunt". They don't consider me, nor do I pretend to be, their equal. I know

a lot of useless things, of course, but I can't tell one sheep from another; so they are rather sorry for me and try to put me at their ease—which, after all, is just good manners.' Quoted in Ackerley, 37.

6. This emphasis on democracy, and lack of a mediating priesthood, may owe something to Macfie's Scottish Presbyterian upbringing, which emphasised democratic rule by elders of the kirk, an unmediated relationship to God, and a (Calvinist) demonstration of one's redemption by the performing of good works.
7. Chapman, in 'Memories', 100; cf. Pontefract and Hartley, ibid., 103–4.
8. Graves, *GTAT*, 437. For a rich discussion of the impact of war trauma on identity, see Leed, 'Fateful Memories', 85–100. He suggests (89): 'This sequence of forgettings required of citizen-soldiers equips the survivors of war with a double past—a pre-war past and a wartime past—linked but incommensurate…With this double past all postwar judgments are made in the consciousness that what was once presumed true was made false and became an illusion, then that disillusioning reality of war itself became a superseded past, a discrete duration full of things no longer true or remembered.' For the wider context of *GTAT*, among literary responses to the war, see Roper, 'Between Manliness and Masculinity', 346, 352–6.
9. Graves, *Poems about War*, 72–6; RPG (1), 306–7, 372 n.183.
10. Ll. 23, 35. This refers to the incident on 5 July 1916 when Sassoon single-handedly cleared a trench of Germans: Wilson, *Sassoon (1886–1918)*, 268–70; cf. above p.89.
11. Ll. 54–5, 60–2. For 'unless [he] had really died / Could he have so recovered from his wounds / As to go climbing less than two months later?' (Ll. 75–7).
12. Ll. 70, 86.
13. Ll. 156–7. Graves was seriously ill with Spanish flu in February 1919, immediately after his demobilisation: Graves, *GTAT*, 347–51; RPG (1), 202–3, 207. For this theme of death in life, see above p.198.
14. Graves was one of 200,000 soldiers given post-war pensions for war-related nervous disorders: Young, 'Rivers', 359. (120,000 were still in receipt of such pensions in 1939: Shephard, *War of Nerves*, 144.) He was initially awarded a pension of £60 p.a., which was later made permanent at £42: Graves, *GTAT* 353, 391. This seems to equate to a 50% disability rating for war neurosis: Leese, *Shell Shock*, 148–9.
15. Graves to Marsh, 7 October 1920, *Letters 1914–46*, 119–20; to Blunden, 10 March 1921, ibid., 123; to Marsh, [July 1922], [December 1924], ibid., 142, 156; to Sassoon, [1926], ibid., 171; Graves, *GTAT*, 351–4, 360–1 (quoted at 361); RPG (1), 230–1 (1920), 242–3 (1921), 274, 278, 285 (1923). To this must be added the fear that this war had only prepared the way for another, which Graves was already expressing in 1917–18; see 'The Next War' and 'Peace', in *Poems about War*, 43–4, 67.
16. See below p.217.
17. 'How furiously against your will / You kill and kill again, and kill / …Each cries for God to understand, / "I could not help it, it was my hand".' Robert Graves, 'Country at War', in his *Country Sentiment* (Martin Secker, 1920), 72–3. Cf. RPG (1), 231–2; Quinn, *Great War*, 64, 80–4.

18. Graves, *GTAT*, 87–90, 249–51, 342.
19. Graves to Sassoon, 16 July, 12 October 1918, *Letters 1914–46*, 97, 103; Graves, *GTAT*, 341.
20. Graves to Sassoon, [July 1922], *Letters 1914–46*, 143; Graves, *GTAT*, 325–6, 400–1, 404–5; RPG (1), 273, 296.
21. Graves, *GTAT*, 404–5.
22. Graves, *GTAT*, 343, 367–8, 386–9.
23. Child-rearing: Graves, *GTAT*, 387–9. Nicholson's career: *GTAT*, 353, 372, 388; RPG (1), 184. Servants: *GTAT*, 353, 356, 372, 380, 387, 391–3; RPG (1), 213, 221, 223, 230, 234, 241–3, 271, 305, 310.
24. RPG (1), 291; Graves, *GTAT*, 405–6; Graves, *GTAT* 1957, 236.
25. Graves, *GTAT*, 336, 356, 373; Graves, *GTAT* 1957, 237; RPG (1), 192, 212–13, 217, 227, 241–2, 252–3, 358 n.44; Seymour, *Graves*, 91, 97, 119, 124.
26. Graves, *GTAT*, 353, acknowledges that in 1919 he and Nancy were living well above their income. Apart from his writing, Graves's only regular sources of income in these years were his army pension (£60 in 1919, later £42 [*GTAT*, 353, 391]), his government student grant and Oxford Exhibition (£200 plus £60, 1919–21; *GTAT*, 345–6, 358, 393; RPG (1), 217–18, 222), and rental from his Harlech cottage (*GTAT*, 393). From October 1920 to April 1921, they tried to secure a regular income by running a general store on Boar's Hill where they were living; but after initial success it failed, leaving them with a substantial loss (*GTAT*, 377–83; RPG (1), 234–5, 238–40, 243–4). For their own reasons, both Graves and Nicholson were reluctant for him to take up the teaching posts which his family tried to secure for him: RPG (1), 219, 239, 242, 281 (though by early 1924 Nicholson felt he needed to take up full-time paid work: 291). Consequently, he was reliant on gifts and loans from his and Nicholson's family and friends: Graves, *GTAT*, 383, 384, 386, 396, 405; RPG (1), 219, 221, 227 with 359 n.85, 239–40, 242, 244), 246, 247, 261, 278, 289 with 368 n.110, 290, 302 with 371 n.167, 311, 317 with 374 n.230, 319, 320. These included Sassoon: Graves to Sassoon, 16 July, 27 July 1918, 19 February 1924, [autumn 1925], *Letters 1914–46*, 97–9, 153, 159; RPG (1), 198, 292; Lawrence: RPG (1), 243; and Marsh: RPG (1), 229, 277, 287, 308. Cf. Seymour, *Graves*, 121, 124.
27. 'I don't know what the financial solution is for us, Edmund. It's all the fault of the Romantic reaction to the Patronage system.' Graves to Blunden, [1926], *Letters 1914–46*, 172. Jonathan Gathorne-Hardy, *Gerald Brenan—the Interior Castle: a Biography* (1992; Sinclair-Stevenson, 1994), 321, comments that Brenan, by the 1930s, 'never seems to have met, didn't even realise there existed, writers without private incomes'. Nicholson pointed out that they were substantially better off than the local farm labourers: Graves, *GTAT*, 395.
28. RPG (1), 294–5; Seymour, *Graves*, 77–8, 91–2. This resentment is finally expressed rawly in Graves, 'But It Still Goes On: a Play', 217, 260–1; cf. RPG (2), 142–3. A similar unease also contributed to the difficulty of his relationship with Sassoon in this period: Graves to Sassoon [February 1924], 19 February 1924, 20 February 1930, *Letters 1914–46*, 152, 153, 203.
29. When convalescing in 1918, Sassoon had asked Carpenter about the possibility of getting a job as an ordinary worker in Sheffield; the men in his company

had made him think about 'labour', how 'the whole world depends on it': to Carpenter, August 1918, Egremont, *Sassoon*, 215; cf. 225. Quinn, *Great War*, 23: 'They realised that the sacrifices of their comrades required some tangible results, and for a brief period both Graves and Sassoon flirted with socialism in hopes that it would assist the working man to achieve a greater share of the national wealth.'

30. Graves, *GTAT*, 351; Wilson, *Sassoon (1918–1967)*, 30–1; Egremont, *Sassoon*, 228–9. Sassoon had himself been approached to be Labour candidate for Hampstead: Egremont, 218.
31. Graves to Sassoon, 13 January 1918, *Letters 1914–46*, 106–7; RPG (1), 209, 215; Seymour, *Graves*, 90. But he read the *Daily Herald*, which 'spoilt our breakfast for us every morning. We read in it of unemployment all over the country, due to the closing of munitions factories, of ex-servicemen refused re-instatement ...of market-rigging, lockouts, and abortive strikes...Nancy and I took all this to heart; we now called ourselves socialists.' Graves, *GTAT*, 351, 354 (quoted). Nicholson was a strong feminist; her socialism focussed especially on the struggle for equality of the sexes: *GTAT*, 332, 355–6.
32. Graves, *GTAT*, 354–5 (quoted at 355); cf. 53; RPG (1), 213, 215.
33. He remained a strong pacifist until the late 1930s, joining the Peace Pledge Union on its foundation in 1935. Sassoon, *Diaries 1920–1922*, 30, 56–62 (1921); Wilson, *Sassoon (1918–1967)*, 35–8, 41–2, 47, 71–2, 98, 102, 136–7, 274–5, 291, 311; Egremont, *Sassoon*, 231, 233–5, 266, 291–2. Caesar, *Taking It Like a Man*, 99, comments there is little to suggest his politics went beyond a patrician sympathy for the working class.
34. RPG (1), 242, 274; Graves, *GTAT*, 397–8; cf. 364, 391.
35. Graves, *GTAT*, 396–9; RPG (1), 274, 310.
36. Graves, *GTAT*, 51, 402–3.
37. Graves, *GTAT*, 381–2; RPG (1), 231; but the 1921 episode was so serious it drove him to consult Rivers, who referred him to a London nerve specialist (RPG (1), 243). A further recurrence in 1923 drove him to resume psychoanalysis, though it is unclear whether this involved professional help or an attempt at self-analysis (RPG (1), 278, 285, 367 n.78). He also obscured in his autobiography the precise nature and duration of his involvement with psychotherapy, presenting it as largely a matter of self-cure: Graves, *GTAT*, 381; RPG (1), 363 n.154, 367 nn.69, 78. In 1924, he wrote that he no longer believed in the New Psychology of Jung and Freud (RPG (1), 231); but it had clearly influenced his thought (RPG (1), 266), and in 1928 he was discussing the Oedipus Complex with Phibbs: RPG (2), 74. Cf. Seymour, *Graves*, 100, 104, 106.
38. He used it, tactlessly, to point out to Blunden the supposed familial roots of his identification with the poet John Clare, paralleling it with his own identification with Skelton; in his own case, this arose from an 'inferiority complex' deriving from his mother's shortcomings. Graves to Blunden, June 1922, *Letters 1914–46*, 139–40. He and Sassoon sparred with each other about the use of psychoanalysis: to Sassoon, 31 May 1922, 135.
39. Graves, *GTAT*, 400–1; Graves to Blunden, 10 March 1921, to Sassoon, 29 May 1921: *Letters 1914–46*, 123, 126; cf. 122; Seymour, *Graves*, 105–8; Quinn, *Great War*, 89–90.

40. R. P. Graves comments, RPG (2), 37: 'Robert, dominated throughout his childhood by the moral force of his virtuous and living mother, could only find happiness when he could love and obey someone else as he had loved and obeyed her.' When he was still at Charterhouse, Mallory's wife had noted that Graves liked to attach himself to a stronger figure and follow them. RPG (1), 173; cf. 278 (Mallik).
41. In emphasising to Sassoon the centrality of his marriage, he wrote: 'When I married I identified myself and do identify myself more and more with Nancy...You identify me in your mind with a certain Robert Graves now dead...Don't. I am using his name, rank and initials...but I am no more than his son and heir': Graves to Sassoon, 31 May 1922, *Letters 1914–46*, 134. His father, annoyed at her thwarting one of his efforts to find Graves a job, referred to him as wax in her hands: RPG (1), 281. RPG (2), 13, writes of Graves's departure for Egypt in January 1926: 'he was in serious need of a strong and self-reliant person upon whose judgment he could rely, and in whose affection he could feel secure.'
42. RPG (1), 197, 216, 231–2, 241, 361 n.128. Guilt: Quinn, *Great War*, 80–4. Eventually, under the influence of Mallik's relativist ethics, he moved towards belief in a divinity which could not and should not be defined in terms of any particular cult: 280; Quinn, 109.
43. Graves, *GTAT*, 51, 332; RPG (1), 184.
44. Seymour, *Graves*, 114–15, 118.
45. RPG (2), 50, 59. In May 1918, Graves wrote to Sassoon: 'I didn't know a great deal about her when we got married except what I saw at once by instinct': 23 May 1918, *Letters 1914–46*, 94.
46. Quinn, *Great War*, 44–5, 75, 83–4; RPG (3), 23, 38, 40, 318, 378; Seymour, *Graves*, 80–1, 139, 143. Graves's sexual anxieties are represented in a raw form in 'But It Still Goes On: a Play'. The plot elements include a heterosexual man and woman each in love with someone they do not recognise as homosexual; failed attempts to resolve resulting emotional *mésalliances* through marriage, leading to the murder by his wife of a closet homosexual; and an intense oedipal rivalry between a father and son, both writers, in which the (lecherous) father gains a young bride but is 'punished' in the plot resolution by their double suicide. RPG (2), 142–3; Caesar, *Taking It Like a Man*, 218–19.
47. Graves, *GTAT*, 343; Quinn, *Great War*, 56, 75.
48. Graves to Sassoon, 9 July 1918, *Letters 1914–46*, 96; Graves, *GTAT*, 335, 368; RPG (1), 189, 191–2, 208, 357 n.9; Seymour, *Graves*, 68.
49. In their first year living in Harlech: 'she held that all the wrong in the world was caused by male domination and narrowness. She refused to see my experiences in the war as in any way comparable with the sufferings that millions of married women of the working-class went through...Male stupidity and callousness became an obsession with her and she found it difficult not to include me in her universal condemnation of men.' Graves, *GTAT*, 355; cf. 395–6; Seymour, *Graves*, 81, 94–5.
50. RPG (1), 195, 278, 291, 306; Seymour, *Graves*, 78–9, 101. Cf. Quinn, *Great War*, 56, 73, 86, 88, 117–18.
51. RPG (1), 299–300, 303–4, 314, 321–5.

52. Graves to Sassoon, [October 1925], *Letters 1914–46*, 159; Graves, *GTAT*, 406; RPG (1), 302–3, 318–20.
53. In addition, his half-sister Mollie was married to a judge. Graves, *GTAT*, 409–10, 418; Graves, *GTAT* 1957, 270–2; RPG (2), 17–18; Seymour, Graves, 136–7.
54. Graves to T.S. Eliot, Sassoon and Blunden, 1926, *Letters 1914–46*, 163–7, 172; Graves, *GTAT*, 411–14, 418–19, 428, 435 (quoted); RPG (2), 20–2, 25–7, 32, 49. Graves's text expresses a disingenuous surprise by the extent of British control. 'I had been told that Egypt was an independent kingdom, but it seemed that my principal allegiance was not to the King, who had given me my appointment and paid me my salary, but to the British High Commissioner. Infantry, cavalry, and air squadrons were a reminder of his power.' (Graves, *GTAT*, 418) He was ironically aware of the British contempt for Egyptian nationalist aspirations, but during his brief time there had no involvement in politics.
55. RPG (2), 23–4, 27, 33, 41–2.
56. RPG (2), 38. R. P. Graves suggests that, intellectually, Nicholson was not a companion for Graves: RPG (1), 208, 264–5; RPG (2), 13–15, 37–8; cf. Seymour, *Graves*, 114.
57. RPG (2), 33–42, 46–50, 57–67.
58. RPG (2), 77.
59. Graves, *GTAT*, 444–5; RPG (2), 79–83.
60. Clarissa attempted to offer this perspective, describing it as an interesting social experiment: RPG (2), 50, 64; contrast 39.
61. RPG (2), 84–5.
62. In 1932, Clarissa set up a Family Tea Club, which met monthly to discuss family matters: RPG (2), 168, 178, 352 n.176.
63. Graves's sister, Rosaleen, had used her connections as a doctor to ensure the best possible treatment for Riding; and so was horrified by the latter's selfish behaviour as a patient and its effect on her own reputation. RPG (2), 87, 96–7, 107, 110. Riding's suicide attempt was also potentially a criminal matter: RPG (2), 111–12. The publication of *GTAT* caused his parents considerable anxiety, both for themselves and the possible effect of indiscretions, such as the remarks about Egypt on Richard's career. RPG (2), 118–19, 131, 134, 149. They were also hurt by the less measured follow-up, *BISGO*: RPG (2), 142, 153–5.
64. RPG (2), 38–41, 48–50, 57–9, 61–6.
65. RPG (2), 46, 47, 48, 87, 99. Already in early 1927, William Nicholson had withdrawn Nancy's allowance for as long as Riding was any part of the household. In June 1929, Amy gave Robert notice to quit the Islip house because Nancy was living with Phibbs. When he moved to Spain that autumn, she cut him out of her Will in favour of his children. RPG (2), 46, 108–9, 119. Such struggles conducted via money continued once he had settled permanently in Spain, centred round his mother's refusal to pay for the education of his children if they were allowed to visit him in Majorca. RPG (2), 152–4, 159.
66. Writing to Robert in July 1930 to prepare him for the publication of his own autobiography, Alfred concluded his letter: '[I] can only pray as I do daily that your future life may be directed from above so that you may lead an unselfish, honourable and useful life.' RPG (2), 150; cf. 154–5. During a family dispute

over the education of his son David in 1932, Graves wrote to his brother John: 'About Mother again. There's a strong bond between us but it is only a human one: and she doesn't want it human. She won't risk her chances of Heaven by behaving towards me as she would humanly like to': RPG (2), 179–81 (quoted at 181). For her continuing influence on him: RPG (3), 50–1, 72, 152–3, 183–4.

67. RPG (1), 103–4, 106; RPG (2), 103 (quoted). Butler: Graves to Marsh, 15 March 1916, Graves to Sassoon, [May 1916], 27 May 1916, *Letters 1914–46*, 43, 48–9, 50.
68. See above p.101.
69. Graves, *GTAT*, 59–60. Elspeth Graham, discussing Milton's *Paradise Regained*, notes that: 'The Son's attainment of absolute masculine poise is...further symbolised in his balancing on the pinnacle, in the course of the final temptation, while Satan falls from it.' 'Feminist Teaching and Masculine Modes: *Paradise Regained* as an Instance', in A. Thompson and H. Wilcox (eds), *Teaching Women: Feminism and English Studies* (Manchester: Manchester University Press, 1989), 137.
70. Graves to Sassoon, 4 August 1916, *Letters 1914–46*, 57; Graves, *GTAT*, 277, 281–2. 'Escape' (1916) celebrates him as an Orpheus who returns successfully from the Underworld: *Poems about War*, 31; Seymour, *Graves*, 55. Graves also took the episode as meaning 'You'll never make a man of me', since God had 'let me always stay a child': 'Died of Wounds' (October 1916), *Poems about War*, 51.
71. Graves had earlier made a similar link between a—hoped for but disappointed—moment of recovery and 1916. When Phibbs's wife rejected the group's attempt to maintain the four-life by drawing her into a five-life, Riding had an hysterical outburst, 'where you seemed to die' (in Graves's words), in a Rouen hotel which he had chosen as auspicious for the meeting because it was on the site of the hospital where he had lain near to death. RPG (2), 81–2.
72. Graves, *GTAT*, 443 (quoted); RPG (2), 78, 110 (quoted).
73. Connell, *Masculinities*, ch.2. Graves refers to 'winning confidence in those quiet days / Of peace, poised sickly on the precipice side / On Lliwedd crag by Snowdon', 'Big Words' (1915), in his *Poems about War*, 21.
74. Cf. above p.78; Bourke, *Intimate History of Killing*, 248–50.
75. Graves's mastery of movement also embodied a mastery of anxiety. After confronting the master who has supposedly kissed Johnstone (above p.105), to 'work off steam' he had rushed to the swimming-pool and leaped into the water from the full height of the spring board: RPG (1), 106. His worst pre-war climb had been when a raven had circled round his party. 'This was curiously unsettling, because one only climbs up and down, or left and right, and the raven was suggesting all the diverse possibilities of movement, tempting us to let go of our hold and join him.' Graves, *GTAT*, 98. RPG (1), 104, reads this as the 'shadow of a suicidal thought'. It might also represent the impulses (and temptations) which were *not* incorporated into this late adolescent consolidation of his masculinity, the absolute poise, that Mallory was assisting, where nevertheless once again one had to move only in certain (orthogonal) directions.
76. West, *One Man in His Time*, 38–9, 78, 92. He turned this perspective even against Graeme's wish to refuse to serve (49): 'This, I thought, was the herd-instinct disguised; it was not for the artist either to serve or defy a system to which only

the herd accorded reality.'

77. West, *One Man in His Time*, 51, 54, 55, 69.
78. West, *One Man in His Time*, 58, 62, 64–6.
79. West, *One Man in His Time*, 59–66.
80. West, *One Man in His Time*, 60, 62, 64 (quoted).
81. West, *One Man in His Time*, 62–3.
82. West, *One Man in His Time*, 65–6.
83. West, *One Man in His Time*, 75, 87, 95, 100.
84. The father who is the source of Nonconformist values and practical skills is contrasted with the Victorian patriarch who threatens to cut his son out of his Will: see West, *One Man in His Time*, 50–3 (quoted above p.165), 68–9. Cf. his father's reaction to the currency crisis in 1931: 'But it was not so much any fall in the value of his investments that troubled him as the collapse of the pound itself—it was his loyal faith in it that had made me handle with awe the first gold sovereign he had given me.' (139) For another example, see the Swiss man of culture who was also the public prosecutor: 102–3, 134–5; cf. 145.
85. West, *One Man in His Time*, 134.
86. West, *One Man in His Time*, 129–30 (visit to Strasbourg Cathedral in 1930); cf. Sassoon's and Graves's responses to Rouen churches, ch.8 n.83 above. Despite his rejection of Christianity, his self-interrogation continued to be marked by both the practice and some of the language of a Nonconformist examination of conscience, as well as by the touchstone of Nietzsche's aphorisms: West, 41, 67, 78–80, 89, 92; cf. 17–18.
87. West, *One Man in His Time*, 83–4. For Farleigh's theory of the Three Realities, see 100–1, 107, 113, 134, 140, 152, 158, 159–60. During their time in the camp, West felt he had sensed in Farleigh a religious fear, repressed behind the conscious atheism: 38–9. This might also be a way of representing his own fears.
88. West, *One Man in His Time*, 117, 120, 130, 160.
89. West, *One Man in His Time*, 96–9, 101–2, 109; cf. 118 (individuals rebelling against the state).
90. West, *One Man in His Time*, 77 (surprised to be described as a socialist in 1923), 94, 97 (when he also first came into contact with Soviet film and Communist papers), 113, 118–19, 122–3, 124 (quoted). Cf. above p.147.
91. West, *One Man in His Time*, 124–7, 129 (quoted at 124, 125).
92. She had mental health problems, and had previously attempted suicide. West, *One Man in His Time*, 103, 112.
93. West, *One Man in His Time*, 103.
94. For West's views of his own family as bearer of bourgeois values, needing to be resisted, see *One Man in His Time*, 43, 124–5, 128–9. Offers of marriage: 125–6, 130, 133, 142–3, 144. Conflicts over marriage: 120–1, 127, 131–2, 138, 142, 144–5.
95. West, *One Man in His Time*, 109.
96. West, *One Man in His Time*, 125.
97. West, *One Man in His Time*, 146–7.
98. Via study of his free associations (in Dublin in 1919–20), of dreams (in the sanatorium in 1925–6), and—in a rather obsessional way—of chains of associations

(soon after leaving the sanatorium). West, *One Man in His Time*, 58, 90–2, 98.

99. West, *One Man in His Time*, 116–18, 138, 146.
100. On this, see my article '"To Kill the Priest and the King"' (in preparation). The deployment of a combination of Nietzsche and Freud in the struggle to free oneself from the ideological and emotional bonds of family and nation at this time was not unique to Alick West. Ofer Nordheimer Nur has explored a similar worldview and its evolution in the collective diary of a group of young Zionists who came to Palestine from Eastern Galicia and Vienna in 1920 to establish the kibbutz way of life. This group, for a short period of about one year, submitted enthusiastically to a combination of Freudian and Nietzschean principles which were adopted to allow for the construction of a model of a "new man" and a new manliness. See his 'Hashomer Hatzair Youth Movement, 1918–1924 From Eastern Galicia and Vienna to Palestine: A Cultural History' (PhD Dissertation, Dept of History, UCLA, 2004), forthcoming as *Eros, Community, Kibbutz: Jewish Male Fantasies 1913–1924* (University of California Press, 2008).
101. West, *One Man in His Time*, 135–6.
102. West, *One Man in His Time*, 138–40 (quoted at 140). He rejected Farleigh's suggestion that they get in touch with Oswald Mosley's recently-formed New Party.
103. For further criticism of the National Government, see West, *One Man in His Time*, 139–40, 142.
104. West, *One Man in His Time*, 152–3.
105. West, *One Man in His Time*, 152–3, 161–2 (quoted).
106. See above p.32.
107. See my '"To Kill the Priest and the King"' (in preparation).
108. West, *One Man in His Time*, 146–7, 149, 153, 155–7.
109. West, *One Man in His Time*, 163–4.
110. West, *One Man in His Time*, 163–5.
111. West, *One Man in His Time*, 122–3.
112. West, *One Man in His Time*, 163.
113. Raphael Samuel wrote, of his Communist upbringing: 'Notwithstanding our commitment to equality, and in many spheres a real attempt to practise it, we had an almost Tory craving for authority figures and a "thread of devotion" to leaders. Though rejecting those on offer to us, in army, church and state, we constructed a whole pantheon of our own: heroic individuals who exemplified Communist virtue like Dimitrov at the Leipzig trial.' 'Staying Power: the Lost World of British Communism, Part Two', *New Left Review* 156 (March/April 1986), 97.
114. West, *One Man in His Time*, 161.
115. When debating inside himself against Dr Schmid's view of society as man's self-murder, West had similarly drawn on his brother for support: 'If I acquiesce in such ideas, I disown Graeme.' (117–18) Cf. above p.164.
116. West, *One Man in His Time*, 152–3; cf. 68–9.
117. Barham, *Forgotten Lunatics*, 161–4 (quoted at 163). He cites (162) Alison Light, *Forever England: Femininity, Literature and Conservatism Between the Wars* (Routledge, 1991), 73, identifying a 'quest for a bearable masculinity which could make

what had previously seemed even effeminate preferable to the bulldog virtues of 1914'. Jay Winter, 'Shell-shock and the Cultural History of the Great War', *Journal of Contemporary History* 35.1 (2000), 7–11, explores the ways in which the term 'shell shock' 'in some places became a metaphor for the nature of industrialized warfare, a term which suggests the corrosive force of the 1914–18 conflict *tout court*' (quoted at 8). Roper, 'Between Manliness and Masculinity', explores the impact of psychological modes of thought within post-war questionings and renegotiations of received masculinity.

Bibliography

Place of publication is London unless otherwise stated.

1 Diaries, Letters, Plays, Poetry, Stories, Travel Writing by Key Figures

Fabian Economic and Social Thought Series One: The Papers of Edward Carpenter, 1844–1929, from Sheffield Archives, Sheffield Libraries and Information Services—Part 1: Correspondence and Manuscripts (Marlborough: Adam Matthew, 1994)

Graves, Robert, *But It Still Goes On: an Accumulation* (Jonathan Cape, 1930)

Graves, Robert, *Country Sentiment* (MartinSecker, 1920)

Graves, Robert, *In Broken Images: Selected Letters of Robert Graves, 1914–46*, ed. Paul O'Prey (Hutchinson, 1982)

Graves, Robert, *Poems about War*, ed. W. Graves (rev. edn, Mount Kisco, NY and London: Moyer Bell, 1990)

[Grenfell, Ethel, Lady Desborough (ed.)], *Pages from a Family Journal, 1888–1915* (Eton College, 1916)

Macfie, Scott, Letters and Papers, Gypsy Lore Society Archive, and Scott Macfie Gypsy Collection, Special Collections and Archives, Sydney Jones Library, University of Liverpool

Macfie, Scott, Macfie Papers, Department of Documents, Imperial War Museum, London

Osborn, E.B., (ed.), *The Muse in Arms: a Collection of War Poems* (John Murray, 1917)

Owen, Wilfred, *The Collected Poems of Wilfred Owen*, ed. C. Day Lewis (Chatto & Windus, 1963

Sassoon, Siegfried, *Diaries 1915–1918*, ed. R. Hart-Davis (Faber, 1983)

Sassoon, Siegfried, *Diaries 1920–1922*, ed. R. Hart-Davis (Faber, 1981)

Sassoon, Siegfried, *The War Poems of Siegfried Sassoon*, ed. R. Hart-Davis (Faber, 1983)

Sorley, Charles Hamilton, *The Collected Letters of Charles Hamilton Sorley*, ed. J. M.

Wilson (Cecil Woolf, 1990)
[West, Arthur Graeme], *The Diary of a Dead Officer, being the Posthumous Papers of Arthur Graeme West* (Allen and Unwin, [1918])

2 Biographies and Autobiographies of Key Figures

Ackerley, Frederick George, 'Friend of all the world: a memoir of Robert Andrew Scott Macfie', *Journal of the Gypsy Lore Society* (3rd series) 14 [Special number] (1935), 5–43
Brenan, Gerald, *A Life of One's Own: Childhood and Youth* (1962; Cambridge: Cambridge University Press, 1979)
Brenan, Gerald, *Personal Record 1920–1972* (1974; Cambridge: Cambridge University Press, 1979)
Clayton, Ann, *Chavasse: Double VC* (Leo Cooper, 1992)
Clayton, Ann, 'Chavasse, Noel Godfrey (1884–1917)', *Oxford Dictionary of National Biography* (Oxford University Press, 2004; http://www.oxforddnb.com/view/article/55355)
Egremont, Max, *Siegfried Sassoon* (Picador, 2005)
Gathorne-Hardy, Jonathan, *Gerald Brenan—the Interior Castle: a Biography* (1992; Sinclair-Stevenson, 1994)
Graves, Richard Perceval, *Robert Graves: the Assault Heroic, 1895–1926* (Weidenfeld & Nicolson, 1986)
Graves, Richard Perceval, *Robert Graves: the Years with Laura, 1926–40* (Weidenfeld & Nicolson, 1990)
Graves, Richard Perceval, *Robert Graves and the White Goddess, 1940–1985* (Weidenfeld & Nicolson, 1995)
Graves, Robert, *Goodbye to All That: an Autobiography* (Jonathan Cape, 1929)
Graves, Robert, *Goodbye to All That: an Autobiography* (rev. edn, 1957; Harmondsworth: Penguin, 1960)
Graves, Robert, *Goodbye to All That: an Autobiography*, ed. R.P. Graves (Oxford: Berghahn, 1995)
MacLeod, Christine, 'Macfie, Robert Andrew (1811–1893)', *Oxford Dictionary of National Biography* (Oxford: Oxford University Press, 2004; http://www.oxforddnb.com/view/article/17499)
Marilyn Ainslie Family Trees <http://www.ainslie.org.uk/genealogy/barbour/dat19.htm#4> (acc. 3.11.06)
'Memories of R.A. Scott Macfie', by his friends, *Journal of the Gypsy Lore Society* (3rd series) 14 [Special number] (1935), 47–110
Mosley, Nicholas, *Julian Grenfell: His Life and the Times of his Death 1888–1915* (1976; Persephone Books, 1999)
Sassoon, Siegfried, *Memoirs of an Infantry Officer* (1930; Faber, 1965)
Sassoon, Siegfried, *Sassoon's Long Journey: an Illustrated Selection from Siegfried Sassoon's 'The Complete Memoirs of George Sherston'*,ed. P. Fussell (Faber,1983)

Sassoon, Siegfried, *Sherston's Progress* (1936; Faber, 1983)
Russell, Bertrand, *The Autobiography of Bertrand Russell: vol. 2: 1914–1944* (Allen and Unwin, 1968)
Seymour, Miranda, *Robert Graves: Life on the Edge* (1995; Doubleday, 1996)
Slobodin, Richard, *W.H.R. Rivers* (New York: Columbia University Press, 1978)
West, Alick, *One Man in His Time: an Autobiography* (Allen and Unwin, 1969)
Wilson, Jean Moorcroft, *Siegfried Sassoon: the Making of a War Poet: a Biography (1886–1918)* (Duckworth, 1998)
Wilson, Jean Moorcroft, *Siegfried Sassoon: the Journey from the Trenches: a Biography (1918–1967)* (Duckworth, 2003)
Wilson, Jean Moorcroft, *Charles Hamilton Sorley: a Biography* (Cecil Woolf, 1985)
Woolf, Leonard, *An Autobiography 1: 1880–1911* (Oxford: Oxford University Press, 1980)

3 Theoretical and Methodological Perspectives: Identity, Masculinity, Nation, Class, Liminality, Life Stories

Alexander, Sally, and Barbara Taylor, 'In Defence of "Patriarchy"', in Raphael Samuel (ed.), *People's History and Socialist Theory* (Routledge, 1981), 370–2
Althusser, Louis, 'Ideology and Ideological State Apparatuses', in his *Lenin and Philosophy and Other Essays* (New Left Books, 1971), 127–86
Anderson, Benedict, *Imagined Communities: Reflections on the Origin and Spread of Nationalism* (1983; rev. edn, Verso, 1991)
Ashplant, T. G., 'Psychoanalysis in Historical Writing', *History Workshop Journal* 26 (1988), 102–19
Bahro, Rudolph, *The Alternative in Eastern Europe* (1977; New Left Books, 1978)
Barnett, Anthony, 'After Nationalism', in Samuel (ed.), *Patriotism*, 140–55
Beauvoir, Simone de, *The Second Sex* (1949; Harmondsworth: Penguin, 1972)
Bellaby, Paul, 'Histories of Sickness: Making Use of Multiple Accounts of the Same Process', in S. Dex (ed.), *Life and Work History Analyses: Qualitative and Quantitative Developments* (Routledge, 1991), 20–42
Benjamin, Jessica, *The Bonds of Love: Psychoanalysis, Feminism and the Problems of Domination* (Virago, 1990)
Bettelheim, Bruno, *The Uses of Enchantment: the Meaning and Importance of Fairy Tales* (1976; Harmondsworth: Penguin, 1978)
Bhabha, Homi K., 'Introduction: Narrating the Nation', in H.K. Bhabha (ed.), *Nation and Narration* (Routledge, 1990), 1–8
Bowlby, John, *Attachment and Loss* (3 vols, 1969, 1973, 1980; Harmondsworth: Penguin, 1981)
Breen, Dana, 'General Introduction', in Breen (ed.), *Gender Conundrum*, 1–48
Breen, Dana (ed.), *The Gender Conundrum: Contemporary Psychoanalytic Perspectives on Femininity and Masculinity* (Routledge, 1993)

Carrigan, T., B. Connell and J. Lee, 'Hard and Heavy: Toward a New Sociology of Masculinity', in Kaufman (ed.), *Beyond Patriarchy*, 139–92

Chodorow, Nancy, *The Reproduction of Mothering: Psychoanalysis and the Sociology of Gender* (Berkeley: University of California Press, 1978)

Connell, R.W., 'Class, Gender and Sartre's Theory of Practice', in his *Which Way is Up?*, 63–79

Connell, R.W., 'Men's Bodies', in his *Which Way is Up?*, 17–32

Connell, R.W., *Gender and Power: Society, the Person and Sexual Politics* (Cambridge: Polity Press, 1987)

Connell, R.W., *Masculinities* (Cambridge: Polity Press, 1995)

Connell, R.W., *Which Way is Up?: Essays on Sex, Class and Culture* (Sydney: Allen and Unwin, 1983)

Dinnerstein, Dorothy, *The Rocking of the Cradle and the Ruling of the World* (1976; Souvenir Press, 1978)

Durkheim, Emile, *Professional Ethics and Civic Morals* (2nd edn, Routledge, 1992)

Elder, Glen H., 'Family History and the Life Course', in T.K. Hareven (ed.), *Transitions: the Family and the Life Course in Historical Perspective* (New York: Academic Press, 1978), 17–64

Elder, Glen, 'History and the Life Course', in D. Bertaux (ed.), *Biography and Society: The Life History Approach in the Social Sciences* (Beverly Hills, CA: Sage, 1981), 77–115

Erikson, Erik H., *Childhood and Society* (rev. edn, Paladin, 1977)

Erikson, Erik H., *Identity: Youth and Crisis* (1968; Faber, 1971)

Erikson, Erik H., *Life History and the Historical Moment* (New York: W.W. Norton, 1975)

Erikson, Erik H., *Young Man Luther: a Study in Pschoanalysis and History* (1958; Faber, 1972)

Erikson, Kai, 'On Pseudospeciation and Social Speciation', in C.B. Strozier and M. Flynn (eds), *Genocide, War and Human Survival* (Lanham, MD: Rowman and Littlefield, 1996), 51–7

Fish, Stanley, 'Withholding the Missing Portion: Psychoanalysis and Rhetoric', in his *Doing What Comes Naturally: Change, Rhetoric, and the Practice of Theory in Literary and Legal Studies* (Oxford: Clarendon Press, 1989), 525–54

Franz, C.E., and K.M. White, 'Individuation and Attachment in Personality Development: Extending Erikson's Theory', *Journal of Personality* 53.2 (1985), 225–56

Freud, Sigmund, 'Group Psychology and the Analysis of the Ego' (1921), in his *Civilization, Society and Religion*, Pelican Freud Library vol.12 (Harmondsworth: Penguin, 1985), 95–178

Freud, Sigmund, 'Mourning and Melancholia' (1917), in his *On Metapsychology: the Theory of Psychoanalysis*, Pelican Freud Library vol. 11 (Harmondsworth: Penguin, 1984), 251–68

Freud, Sigmund, 'Three Essays on the Theory of Sexuality' (1905), in his *On*

Sexuality, Pelican Freud Library vol.7 (Harmondsworth: Penguin, 1977), 39–169

Frosh, Stephen, *The Politics of Psychoanalysis: an Introduction to Freudian and Post-Freudian Theory* (2nd edn, Basingstoke: Macmillan 1999)

Gay, Peter, *Freud for Historians* (New York: Oxford University Press, 1985)

Gellner, Ernest, *Nations and Nationalism* (Oxford: Blackwell, 1983)

Gilmore, David, *Manhood in the Making: Cultural Concepts of Masculinity* (New Haven, CT: Yale University Press, 1990)

Graham, Elspeth, 'Feminist Teaching and Masculine Modes: *Paradise Regained* as an Instance', in A. Thompson and H. Wilcox (eds), *Teaching Women: Feminism and English Studies* (Manchester: Manchester University Press, 1989), 132–44

Harris, Chris, 'The Individual and Society: a Processual Approach', in A. Bryman et al. (eds), *Rethinking the Life Cycle* (Macmillan, 1987), 17–29

Herman, Nini, *My Kleinian Home: a Journey through Four Psychotherapies—Into a New Millennium* (Karnac, 2001)

Hobsbawm, Eric, *Nations and Nationalism since 1780: Programme, Myth, Reality* (2nd edn, Cambridge: Cambridge University Press, 1992)

Holmes, Jeremy, *John Bowlby and Attachment Theory* (Routledge, 1993)

Jackson, David, *Unmasking Masculinity* (Unwin Hyman, 1990)

Kaufman, Michael, 'The Construction of Masculinity and the Triad of Men's Violence', in Kaufman (ed.), *Beyond Patriarchy*, 1–29

Kaufman, Michael (ed.), *Beyond Patriarchy: Essays by Men on Pleasure, Power and Change* (Toronto: Oxford University Press, 1987)

Laplanche, Jean, and J. B. Pontalis, *The Language of Psychoanalysis* (1967; Karnac Books, 1988)

Nairn, Tom, *The Break-Up of Britain: Crisis and Neo-Nationalism* (New Left Books, 1977)

Nandy, Ashis, *The Intimate Enemy: Loss and Recovery of Self under Colonialism* (Delhi: Oxford University Press, 1983)

Plummer, Ken, *Documents of Life 2: an Invitation to a Critical Humanism* (Sage, 2001)

Poole, Ross, *Morality and Modernity* (Routledge, 1991)

Poole, Ross, *Nation and Identity* (Routledge, 1999)

Poole, Ross, 'Structures of Identity: Gender and Nationalism', in P. Patton and R. Poole (eds), *War/Masculinity* (Sydney: Intervention Publications, 1985), 71–9

Portelli, Alessandro, 'The Battle of Poggio Bustone: Violence, Memory and Imagination in the Partisan War', in his *The Battle of Valle Giulia: Oral History and the Art of Dialogue* (Madison, WI: University of Wisconsin Press, 1997), 126–39

Portelli, Alessandro, *The Order Has Been Carried Out: History, Memory and Meaning of a Nazi Massacre in Rome* (New York and Basingstoke: Palgrave

Macmillan, 2003)

Richards, Barry, 'Masculinity, Identification and Political Culture', in J. Hearn and D. Morgan (eds), *Men, Masculinities and Social Theory* (Unwin Hyman, 1990)

Roazen, Paul, *Erik H. Erikson: the Power and Limits of a Vision* (New York: Free Press, 1976)

Rosaldo, Michelle Zimbalist, 'Women, Culture and Society: Theoretical Overview', in M.Z. Rosaldo and L. Lamphere (eds), *Woman, Culture and Society* (Stanford, CA: Stanford University Press, 1974), 17–42

Rosenwald, George C., 'A Theory of Multiple-Case Research', in D. P. McAdams and R.L. Ochberg (eds), *Psychobiography and Life Narratives* (Durham, NC: Duke University Press, 1988), 239–264

Sharpe, Jim, 'History from Below', in P. Burke, (ed.), *New Perspectives on Historical Writing* (Cambridge: Polity Press, 1991), 24–41

Sieder, R., 'A Hitler Youth from a Respectable Family: the Narrative Composition and Deconstruction of a Life Story', in D. Bertaux and P. Thompson (eds), *Between Generations: Family Models, Myths and Memories: International Yearbook of Oral History and Life Stories vol.II* (Oxford: Oxford University Press, 1993), 99–119

Stallybrass, Peter, and Allon White, *The Politics and Poetics of Transgression* (Methuen, 1986)

Stanley, Liz, *The Auto/Biographical I: the Theory and Practice of Feminist Auto/biography* (Manchester: Manchester University Press, 1992)

Steedman, Carolyn, *Landscape for a Good Woman* (Virago, 1986)

Thompson, E.P., *The Making of the English Working Class* (rev. edn, Harmondsworth: Pelican, 1968)

Tolson, Andrew, *The Limits of Masculinity* (Tavistock, 1977)

Tosh, John, 'Hegemonic Masculinity and the History of Gender', in Dudink et al. (eds), *Masculinities in Politics and War*, 41–58

Turner, Bryan S., 'Preface to the Second Edition', in Emile Durkheim, *Professional Ethics and Civic Morals* (2nd edn., Routledge, 1992), xiii–xlii

Turner, Victor W., 'Betwixt and Between: the Liminal Period in *Rites de Passage*', in his *The Forest of Symbols: Aspects of Ndembu Ritual* (Ithaca, NY: Cornell University Press, 1967), 93–111

Turner, Victor W., *Dramas, Fields, and Metaphors: Symbolic Action in Human Society* (Ithaca, NY and London: Cornell University Press, 1974)

Turner, Victor W., *The Ritual Process: Structure and Anti-Structure* (Routledge and Kegan Paul, 1969)

Wolfenstein, Eugene Victor, *Victims of Democracy: Malcolm X and the Black Revolution* (1981; Free Association Books, 1993)

4 First World War

Adams, Bernard [Bill], *Nothing of Importance: a Record of Eight Months at the Front with a Welsh Battalion, October, 1915, to June, 1916* (1917; Naval and Military Press, 2001)

Anon., 'A Hamlet of the War', *The Times Literary Supplement* (30 January 1919), 49–50

Anon., 'Dr. H.S. Hatfield', *The Times* (14 December 1966, 12 col.f)

Barham, Peter, *Forgotten Lunatics of the Great War* (New Haven, CT: Yale University Press, 2004)

Barker, Pat, *The Regeneration Trilogy* (Viking, 1991–5)

Beckett, Ian, 'The Nation in Arms, 1914–18', in Beckett and Simpson (eds), *A Nation in Arms*, 1–35

Beckett, Ian, 'The Territorial Force', in Beckett and Simpson (eds), *A Nation in Arms*, 127–63

Beckett, Ian, 'The Territorial Force in the Great War', in Peter H. Liddle (ed.), *Home Fires and Foreign Fields: British Social and Military Experience in the First World War* (Brassey's Defence Publishers, 1985), 21–37

Beckett, Ian F.W. and Keith Simpson (eds), *A Nation in Arms: A Social Study of the British Army in the First World War* (1985; Tom Donovan, 1990)

Bergonzi, Bernard, *Heroes' Twilight: A Study of the Literature of the Great War* (3rd edn, Manchester: Carcanet, 1996)

Bogacz, Ted, 'War Neurosis and Cultural Change in England, 1914–22: the Work of the War Office Committee of Enquiry into "Shell-Shock"', *Journal of Contemporary History* 24.2 (1989), 227–56

Bond, Brian, *The Unquiet Western Front: Britain's Role in Literature and History* (Cambridge: Cambridge University Press, 2002)

Bourke, Joanna, *Dismembering the Male: Men's Bodies, Britain and the Great War* (Reaktion Books, 1996)

Bourke, Joanna, 'Effeminacy, Ethnicity and the End of Trauma: the Sufferings of "Shell-shocked" Men in Great Britain and Ireland, 1914–39', *Journal of Contemporary History* 35.1 (2000), 57–69

Bourke, Joanna, *An Intimate History of Killing: Face-to-face Killing in Twentieth-century Warfare* (Granta Books, 2000)

Bourne, J.M., *Britain and the Great War, 1914–1918* (Edward Arnold, 1989)

Brittain, Vera, *Testament of Youth: an Autobiographical Study of the Years 1900–1925* (1933; rp. Virago, 1978)

Caesar, Adrian, *Taking It Like a Man: Suffering, Sexuality, and the War Poets: Brooke, Sassoon, Owen, Graves* (Manchester: Manchester University Press, 1993)

Campbell, James, '"For You May Touch Them Not": Misogyny, Homosexuality, and the Ethics of Passivity in First World War Poetry', *English Literary History* 64 (1997), 823–42

Carsten, F.L., *War Against War: British and German Radical Movements in the First*

World War (Batsford, 1982)

DeGroot, Gerard J., *Blighty: British Society in the Era of the Great War* (Harlow: Longman, 1996)

Doyle, Barry M., 'Religion, Politics and Remembrance: a Free Church Community and its Great War Dead', in M. Evans and K. Lunn (eds), *War and Memory in the Twentieth Century* (Oxford: Berg, 1997), 223–38

Eder, M.D., 'The Psycho-pathology of the War Neuroses', *The Lancet* no.4850 (12 August 1916), 264–8

Featherstone, Simon, *War Poetry: an Introductory Reader* (Routledge, 1995)

Ferguson, Niall, *The Pity of War* (1998; Harmondsworth: Penguin, 1999)

Ferguson, Robert, *The Short Sharp Life of T.E. Hulme* (Allen Lane, 2002)

Frantzen, Allen J., *Bloody Good: Chivalry, Sacrifice and the Great War* (Chicago: University of Chicago Press, 2004)

Fussell, Paul, *The Great War and Modern Memory* (New York: Oxford University Press, 1975)

Giblin, Brenda, 'Perceptions of the Great War: a Polemical Perspective' (MA Dissertation, Liverpool John Moores University, 2002)

Hibberd, Dominic, 'Introduction', in [West, Arthur Graeme], *The Diary of a Dead Officer, being the Posthumous Papers of Arthur Graeme West* (rp. Imperial War Museum, 1991)

Hughes, A.D.M., 'Ruhleben', *Cornhill Magazine* New Series 233 (November 1915), 662–72

Hynes, Samuel, 'An Introduction to Graeme West', in M. Roucoux (ed.), *English Literature of the Great War Revisited: Proceedings of the Symposium on the British Literature of the First World War* ([Amiens] : Presses de l'U.F.R. Clerc Université Picardie, 1986), 74–83

Hynes, Samuel, *A War Imagined: the First World War and English Culture* (Bodley Head, 1991)

Hynes, Samuel, *The Soldier's Tale: Bearing Witness to Modern War* (Allen Lane, 1997)

In Ruhleben Camp 1–9 (June-December 1915)

Joad, Cyril, 'Introduction', in [West, Arthur Graeme], *The Diary of a Dead Officer, being the Posthumous Papers of Arthur Graeme West* (Allen and Unwin, [1918]), ix–xiv

Kerr, Douglas, *Wilfred Owen's Voices: Language and Community* (Oxford: Clarendon Press, 1993)

Ketchum, J. Davidson, *Ruhleben: a Prison Camp Society* (Toronto: University of Toronto Press, 1965)

Leed, Eric, 'Fateful Memories: Industrialized War and Traumatic Neuroses', *Journal of Contemporary History* 35.1 (2000), 85–100

Leed, Eric, *No Man's Land: Combat and Identity in World War I* (Cambridge: Cambridge University Press, 1979)

Leese, Peter, *Shell Shock: Traumatic Neurosis and the British Soldiers of the First World*

War (Basingstoke: Palgrave Macmillan, 2002)
Lunn, Joe, 'Male Identity and Martial Codes of Honor: a Comparison of the War Memoirs of Robert Graves, Ernst Jünger, and Kande Kamara', *Journal of Military History* 69.3 (2005), 713–35
McCartney, Helen B., *Citizen Soldiers: the Liverpool Territorials in the First World War* (Cambridge: Cambridge University Press, 2005)
MacCurdy, John T., *War Neuroses* (Cambridge: Cambridge University Press, 1918)
MacKenzie, Jeanne, *The Children of the Souls: a Tragedy of the First World War* (Chatto & Windus, 1986)
Marsland, Elizabeth A., *The Nation's Cause: French, English and German Poetry of the First World War* (Routledge, 1991)
McLeod, R. B., 'Postscript' in Ketchum, *Ruhleben*, 337–79
Millman, Brock, *Managing Domestic Dissent in First World War Britain* (Frank Cass, 2000)
Monteith, Sharon, et al. (eds), *Critical Perspectives on Pat Barker* (Columbia, SC: University of South Carolina Press, 2005)
Moorhouse, Geoffrey, *Hell's Foundations: A Town, Its Myths and Gallipoli* (1992; Sphere, 1993)
Parker, Peter, *The Old Lie: the Great War and the Public School Ethos* (Constable, 1987)
Pearce, Cyril, *Comrades in Conscience: the Story of an English Community's Opposition to the Great War* (Francis Boutle, 2001)
Prior, Robin, and Trevor Wilson, 'Paul Fussell at War', *War in History* 1.1 (1994), 63–80
Quinn, Patrick J., *The Great War and the Missing Muse: the Early Writings of Robert Graves and Siegfried Sassoon* (Selinsgrove, PA: Susquehanna University Press, 1993)
Remarque, Erich Maria, *All Quiet on the Western Front* (*Im Westen Nichts Neues*) (1929; Vintage, 1996)
Rivers, W. H. R., *Conflict and Dream* (Kegan Paul, Trench, Trubner, 1923)
Rivers, W. H. R., *Instinct and the Unconscious: a Contribution to a Biological Theory of the Psycho-Neuroses* (2nd edn, Cambridge: Cambridge University Press, 1922)
Rivers, W. H. R., 'War Neurosis and Military Training', *Mental Hygiene* 2.4 (1918), 513–33
Roper, Michael, 'Between Manliness and Masculinity: the "War Generation" and the Psychology of Fear, 1914–1950', *Journal of British Studies* 44.2 (2005), 343–62
Roper, Michael, 'Maternal Relations: Moral Manliness and Emotional Survival in Letters Home during the First World War', in Dudink et al. (eds), *Masculinities in Politics and War*, 295–315
Ruhleben Camp Magazine 1–6 (March 1916-June 1917)

'Ruhleben concentration camp: programmes of entertainment' [1915, 1916] (British Library)

Sheffield, Gary, 'Officer-Man Relations, Discipline and Morale in the British Army of the Great War', in Hugh Cecil and P. H. Liddle (eds), *Facing Armageddon: the First World War Experienced* (Leo Cooper, 1996), 413–24

Shephard, Ben, *A War of Nerves: Soldiers and Psychiatrists, 1914–1994* (2000; Pimlico, 2002)

Showalter, Elaine, *The Female Malady: Women, Madness and English Culture, 1830–1980* (Virago, 1987)

Simpson, Keith, 'The Officers', in Beckett and Simpson (eds), *A Nation in Arms*, 63–96

Sladen, Douglas, (ed.), *In Ruhleben: Letters from a Prisoner to His Mother...* (Hurst and Blackett, 1917)

Southard, E. E., *Shell-shock and Other Neuropsychiatric Problems Presented in Five Hundred and Eighty-nine Case Histories* (Boston: W. M. Leonard, 1919)

Spiers, Edward M., 'The Regular Army in 1914', in Beckett and Simpson (eds), *A Nation in Arms*, 37–60

Stallworthy, Jon, *Anthem for Doomed Youth: Twelve Soldier Poets of the First World War* (Constable / Imperial War Museum, 2002)

Stargardt, Nicholas, *The German Idea of Militarism: Radical and Socialist Critics 1866–1914* (Cambridge: Cambridge University Press, 1994)

Stern, J. P., 'The Embattled Style: Ernst Jünger, *In Stahlgewittern*', in H. Klein, (ed.), *The First War in Fiction: a Collection of Critical Essays* (Macmillan, 1976), 112–25

Stevenson, David, *1914–1918: The History of the First World War* (Penguin, 2005)

Stevenson, John, *British Society 1914–45* (Harmondsworth: Penguin, 1984)

Stone, Martin, 'Shellshock and the Psychologists', in W. F. Bynum, R. Porter and M. Shepherd (eds), *The Anatomy of Madness: Essays in the History of Psychiatry, vol. 2: Institutions and Society* (Tavistock, 1985), 242–71

Stryker, Laurinda, 'Mental Cases: British Shellshock and the Politics of Interpretation', in G. Braybon (ed.), *Evidence, History and the Great War: Historians and the Impact of 1914–18* (Oxford: Berghahn, 2003), 154–71

Thomas, Geoffrey, *Cyril Joad* (Birkbeck College, 1992)

Vellacott, Jo, *Bertrand Russell and the Pacifists in the First World War* (Brighton: Harvester, 1980)

Welland, Dennis, 'Arthur Graeme West: a Messenger to Job', in G. R. Hibbard (ed.), *Renaissance and Modern Essays; presented to Vivian de Sola Pinto…* (Routledge, 1966), 169–80

Wilkinson, Alan, *Dissent or Conform?: War, Peace, and the English Churches, 1900–1945* (SCM Press, 1986)

Wilkinson, Alan, *The Church of England and the First World War* (SPCK, 1978)

Wilson, Trevor, *The Myriad Faces of War: Britain and the Great War, 1914–1918*

(Cambridge: Polity Press, 1986)
Winter, Jay, 'Army and Society: the Demographic Context', in Beckett and Simpson (eds), *A Nation in Arms*, 193–209
Winter, Jay, 'Shell-shock and the Cultural History of the Great War', *Journal of Contemporary History* 35.1 (2000), 7–11
Winter, Jay, and Blaine Baggett, *The Great War and the Shaping of the Twentieth Century* (New York: Penguin Studio, 1996)
Wohl, Robert, *The Generation of 1914* (Cambridge, MA: Harvard University Press, 1979)
Young, Allan, *The Harmony of Illusions: Inventing Post-Traumatic Stress Disorder* (Princeton, NJ: Princeton University Press, 1995)
Young, Allan, 'W.H.R. Rivers and the War Neuroses', *Journal of the History of the Behavioral Sciences* 34.4 (1999), 359–78

5 Social, Cultural and Literary History, 1850–1930

Aldrich, Robert, *The Seduction of the Mediterranean: Writing, Art and Homosexual Fantasy* (Routledge, 1993)
Ashplant, T. G., 'Dis/Connecting Whiteness: Biographical Perspectives on Race, Class, Masculinity and Sexuality in Britain *c.*1850–1930', *L'Homme: Zeitschrift für Feministische Geschichtswissenschaft* (Vienna) 16.2 (2005), 68–85
Ballhatchet, K., *Race, Sex and Class under the Raj: Imperial Attitudes and Policies and their Critics, 1793–1905* (Weidenfeld & Nicolson, 1980)
Beckett, Ian, 'Grenfell, William Henry, Baron Desborough (1855–1945)', *Oxford Dictionary of National Biography* (Oxford: Oxford University Press, September 2004; online edn, May 2006; http://www.oxforddnb.com/view/article/335660)
Bernheimer, Charles, and Claire Kahane (eds), *In Dora's Case: Freud, Hysteria, Feminism* (2nd, enlarged, edn, Virago, 1990)
Boyce, D.G., 'The Marginal Britons: The Irish', in Colls and Dodd (eds), *Englishness*, 230–53
Brunner, José, *Freud and the Politics of Psychoanalysis* (rev. edn, New Brunswick, NJ: Transaction, 2001)
Caine, Barbara, *Destined to be Wives: the Sisters of Beatrice Webb* (Oxford: Clarendon Press, 1987)
Cannadine, David, 'The Context, Performance and Meaning of Ritual: the British Monarchy and the "Invention of Tradition", *c.*1820–1977', in Hobsbawm and Ranger (eds), *Invention of Tradition*, 120–38
Chandos, John, *Boys Together: English Public Schools 1800–1864* (1984; Oxford: Oxford University Press, 1985)
Cohn, Bernard S., 'Representing Authority in Victorian India', in Hobsbawm and Ranger (eds), *Invention of Tradition*, 165–210
Colls, Robert, 'Englishness and the Political Culture', in Colls and Dodd (eds),

Englishness, 29–61

Colls, Robert, and Philip Dodd (eds), *Englishness: Politics and Culture 1880–1920* (Croom Helm, 1986)

Cunningham, Hugh, 'The Language of Patriotism', in Samuel (ed.), *Patriotism*, 57–89

Cunningham, Hugh, *The Volunteer Force: a Social and Political History 1859–1908* (Croom Helm, 1975)

D'Arch Smith, Timothy, *Love in Earnest: Some Notes on the Lives and Writings of English 'Uranian' Poets from 1889 to 1930* (Routledge and Kegan Paul, 1970)

Davenport-Hines, Richard, 'Gordon, Charles George (1833–1885)', *Oxford Dictionary of National Biography* (Oxford University Press, 2004; http://www.oxforddnb.com/view/article/11029)

Davidoff, Leonore, 'Class and Gender in Victorian England: the Diaries of Arthur J. Munby and Hannah Cullwick', *Feminist Studies* 5.1 (1979), 87–141

Davidoff, Leonore, 'Mastered for Life: Servant and Wife in Victorian and Edwardian England', *Journal of Social History* 7 (1974), 406–28

Dawson, Graham, 'The Blond Bedouin: Lawrence of Arabia, Imperial Adventure and the Imagining of English-British Masculinity', in Roper and Tosh (eds), *Manful Assertions*, 113–44

Dawson, Graham, *Soldier Heroes: British Adventure, Empire and the Imagining of Masculinities* (Routledge, 1994)

Decker, Hannah S., *Freud, Dora and Vienna 1900* (New York: Free Press, 1991)

Dowling, Linda, *Hellenism and Homosexuality in Victorian Oxford* (Ithaca, NY: Cornell University Press, 1994)

Dudink, Stefan, Karen Hagemann and John Tosh (eds), *Masculinities in Politics and War: Gendering Modern History* (Manchester: Manchester University Press, 2004)

Dyhouse, Carol, *Feminism and the Family in England 1880–1939* (Oxford: Blackwell, 1989)

Finney, Brian, *The Inner I: British Literary Autobiography of the Twentieth Century* (Faber, 1985)

Fitzpatrick, David, 'Ireland since 1870', in R.F. Foster (ed.), *The Oxford History of Ireland* (1992; Oxford: Oxford University Press, 2001), 175–229

Fraser, Angus, 'A Rum Lot', in Matt T. Salo, *100 Years of Gypsy Studies: Papers from the 10th Annual Meeting of the Gypsy Lore Society* (Gypsy Lore Society no. 5: Cheverly, MD: The Society, 1990), 1–14

Gathorne-Hardy, Jonathan, *The Public School Phenomenon, 597–1977* (Hodder and Stoughton, 1977)

Gillis, John R., *Youth and History: Tradition and Change in European Age Relations 1770–Present* (New York: Academic Press, 1974)

Gordon, Eleanor, and Gwyneth Nair (eds), *Public Lives: Women, Family and Society in Victorian Britain* (New Haven, CT: Yale University Press, 2003)

Gott, Richard, 'Little Englanders', in Samuel (ed.), *Patriotism*, 90–102

Green, E., and M. Taylor, 'Further Thoughts on Little Englandism', in Samuel (ed.), *Patriotism*, 103–9

Greene, Graham, (ed.), *The Old School: Essays by Divers Hands* (Cape, 1934)

Hammond, Andrew, 'The Uses of Balkanism: Representation and Power in British Travel Writing, 1850–1914', *Slavonic and East European Review* 82.3 (2004), 601–24

Heuss, Herbert, 'Anti-Gypsyism Research: the Creation of a New Field of Study', in T. Acton (ed.), *Scholarship and the Gypsy Struggle: Commitment in Romani Studies* (Hatfield: University of Hertfordshire Press, 2000), 52–67

Heward, Christine, *Making a Man of Him: Parents and Their Sons' Education at an English Public School 1929–50* (Routledge, 1988)

Hickson, Alisdare, *The Poisoned Bowl: Sex, Repression and the Public School System* (Constable, 1995)

Hobsbawm, Eric, 'Mass-Producing Traditions: Europe, 1870–1914', in Hobsbawm and Ranger (eds), *Invention of Tradition*, 263–307

Hobsbawm, Eric, and Terence Ranger (eds), *The Invention of Tradition* (Cambridge: Cambridge University Press, 1983)

Holroyd, Michael, *Augustus John: a Biography* (rev. edn., Harmondsworth: Penguin, 1976)

Honey, John de S., *Tom Brown's Universe: the Development of the Victorian Public School* (Millington, 1977)

Hopkins, James K., *Into the Heart of the Fire: the British in the Spanish Civil War* (Stanford, CA: Stanford University Press, 1998)

Horne, John, 'Masculinity in Politics and War in the Age of Nation-states and World Wars, 1850–1950', in Dudink et al. (eds), *Masculinities in Politics and War*, 22–40

Hyam, Ronald, *Empire and Sexuality: the British Experience* (Manchester: Manchester University Press, 1990)

Jalland, Pat, *Women, Marriage and Politics, 1860–1914* (Oxford: Clarendon Press, 1986)

Joyce, Patrick, *Work, Society and Politics: the Culture of the Factory in Later Victorian England* (Brighton: Harvester, 1980)

Keating, Peter (ed.), *Into Unknown England 1866–1913: Selections from the Social Explorers* (Fontana, 1976)

Koven, Seth, 'From Rough Lads to Hooligans: Boy Life, National Culture and Social Reform', in A. Parker et al. (eds), *Nationalisms and Sexualities* (New York and London: Routledge, 1992), 365–91

Koven, Seth, *Slumming: Sexual and Social Politics in Victorian London* (Princeton, NJ: Princeton University Press, 2004)

Krenis, Lee, 'Authority and Rebellion in Victorian Autobiography', *Journal of British Studies* 18.1 (1978), 107–30

Lambert, Royston, *The Hothouse Society: an Exploration of Boarding-school Life*

Through the Boys' and Girls' Own Writings (Weidenfeld & Nicolson, 1968)

Lee, Ken, 'Orientalism and Gypsylorism', *Social Analysis: Journal of Cultural and Social Practice* [Adelaide] 44.2 (2000), 129–56

Lewis, Peter M., 'Mummy, Matron and the Maids: Feminine Presence and Absence in Male Institutions, 1934–63', in Roper and Tosh (eds), *Manful Assertions*, 168–89

McBride, Theresa, '"As the Twig is Bent": the Victorian Nanny', in A. S. Wohl (ed.), *The Victorian Family: Structures and Stresses* (Croom Helm, 1978), 44–58

McGrath, William J., *Freud's Discovery of Psychoanalysis: the Politics of Hysteria* (Ithaca, NY: Cornell University Press, 1986)

MacKenzie, J. M., '"In Touch with the Infinite": the BBC and the Empire, 1923–53', in J. M. MacKenzie (ed.), *Imperialism and Popular Culture* (Manchester: Manchester University Press, 1986), 165–91

MacKenzie, J. M., *Propaganda and Empire: the Manipulation of British Public Opinion, 1880–1960* (Manchester: Manchester University Press, 1984)

McKinlay, Alan and R. J. Morris (eds), *The ILP on Clydeside, 1893–1932: from Foundation to Disintegration* (Manchester: Manchester University Press, 1991)

Mangan, J. A., *Athleticism in the Victorian and Edwardian Public School: the Emergence and Consolidation of an Educational Ideology* (Cambridge: Cambridge University Press, 1981)

Mangan, J. A., *The Games Ethic and Imperialism: Aspects of the Diffusion of an Ideal* (Harmondsworth: Viking, 1986)

Mangan, J. A., 'Social Darwinism and Upper-class Education in Late Victorian and Edwardian England', in Mangan and Walvin (eds), *Manliness and Morality*, 135–59

Mangan, J. A., and James Walvin (eds), *Manliness and Morality: Middle-Class Masculinity in Britain and America, 1800–1940* (Manchester: Manchester University Press, 1987)

Mayall, David, *Gypsy Identities 1500–2000: from Egipcyans and Moon-Men to the Ethnic Romany* (Routledge, 2004)

Miles, Andrew, *Social Mobility in Nineteenth- and Early Twentieth-Century England* (Basingstoke: Palgrave, 1999)

Mosse, George L., *Nationalism and Sexuality: Respectability and Abnormal Sexuality in Modern Europe* (New York: Howard Fertig, 1985)

Nicolson, Harold, 'Pity the Pedagogue', in Greene (ed.), *The Old School*, 103–20

Nord, Deborah E., *Gypsies and the British Imagination, 1807–1930* (New York: Columbia University Press, 2006)

Perkin, Harold, *The Rise of Professional Society: England since 1880* (Routledge, 1989)

Richards, Jeffrey, '"Passing the Love of Women": Manly Love and Victorian Society', in Mangan and Walvin (eds), *Manliness and Morality*, 92–122

Roper, Michael, and John Tosh, 'Introduction: Historians and the Politics of Masculinity', in Roper and Tosh (eds), *Manful Assertions*, 1–24

Roper, Michael, and John Tosh (eds), *Manful Assertions: Masculinities in Britain since 1800* (Routledge, 1991)
Rosenbaum, S.P., *Victorian Bloomsbury: the Early Literary History of the Bloomsbury Group, vol.1* (Macmillan, 1987)
Rowbotham, Sheila, and Jeffrey Weeks, *Socialism and the New Life: the Personal and Sexual Politics of Edward Carpenter and Havelock Ellis* (Pluto Press, 1977)
Rubinstein, David, *Before the Suffragettes: Women's Emancipation in the 1890s* (Brighton: Harvester, 1986)
Sampson, Anthony, *The Scholar Gypsy: the Quest for a Family Secret* (John Murray, 1997)
Samuel, Raphael, 'Staying Power: the Lost World of British Communism, Part Two', *New Left Review* 156 (March/April 1986), 63–113
Samuel, Raphael, (ed.), *Patriotism: the Making and Unmaking of British National Identity: vol. 1, History and Politics* (Routledge, 1989)
Schorske, Carl E., *German Social Democracy 1905–17: the Development of the Great Schism* (Cambridge, MA: Harvard University Press, 1955)
Schorske, Carl E., 'Politics and Patricide in Freud's *Interpretation of Dreams*', in his *Fin-de-Siècle Vienna: Politics and Culture* (New York: Vintage Books, 1981), 181–207
Scoble, Christopher, *Fisherman's Friend: a Life of Stephen Reynolds* (Tiverton: Halsgrove, 2000)
Simey, T.S., and M.B. Simey, *Charles Booth: Social Scientist* (Oxford University Press, 1960)
Sinfield, Alan, *Out on Stage: Lesbian and Gay Theatre in the Twentieth Century* (New Haven, CT: Yale University Press, 1999)
Sinfield, Alan, *The Wilde Century: Effeminacy, Oscar Wilde and the Queer Moment* (New York: Columbia University Press, 1994)
Stanley, Liz (ed.), *The Diaries of Hannah Cullwick, Victorian Maidservant* (Virago, 1984)
Stenton, Michael, (ed.), *Who's Who of British Members of Parliament, vol.1*: 1832–1885 (Hassocks: Harvester, 1976)
Summers, Anne, 'Edwardian Militarism', in Samuel (ed.), *Patriotism*, 236–56
Todorova, Maria, *Imagining the Balkans* (New York: Oxford University Press, 1997)
Tosh, John, 'Domesticity and Manliness in the Victorian Middle Class: the Family of Edward White Benson', in Roper and Tosh (eds), *Manful Assertions*, 44–73
Tosh, John, *A Man's Place: Masculinity and the Middle-Class Home in Victorian Britain* (New Haven and London: Yale University Press, 1999)
Tosh, John, 'Masculinities in an Industrializing Society: Britain, 1800–1914', *Journal of British Studies* 44.2 (2005), 330–342
Townshend, Charles, *Ireland: the 20th Century* (Arnold, 1999)
Trimberger, Ellen Kay, 'Feminism, Men and Modern Love: Greenwich

Village, 1900–25', in A. Snitow, C. Stansell and D. Thompson (eds), *Desire: the Politics of Sexuality* (1983; Virago, 1984), 169–89

Verschoyle, Derek, 'Indian Innocence, Ltd.', in Greene (ed.), *The Old School*, 199–214

Walker, Pamela J., '"I Live But Not Yet I For Christ Liveth in Me": Men and Masculinity in the Salvation Army', in Roper and Tosh (eds), *Manful Assertions*, 92–112

Weber, Eugen, *Peasants into Frenchmen: the Modernization of Rural France, 1870–1914* (1976; Chatto & Windus, 1977)

Weeks, Jeffrey, *Coming Out: Homosexual Politics in Britain from the Nineteenth Century to the Present* (Quartet, 1977)

Yates, Dora E., *My Gypsy Days: Recollections of a Romani Rawnie* (Phoenix House, 1953)

Yeo, Stephen, 'A New Life: The Religion of Socialism in Britain 1883–1896', *History Workshop Journal* 4 (1977), 5–56

Yeo, Stephen, *Religion and Voluntary Organisations in Crisis* (Croom Helm, 1976)

Index

The major conceptual themes of the book are indexed under the following headings: *attachment; career; class; family; gender; identity; individual; imagined community; killing; liminality; masculinity; mentor; moratorium; nation; religion; self-sacrifice; sexuality*

First World War is abbreviated as FWW.
Pseudonyms given to individuals are indicated by (pseud.).